LET'S TALK!

America's Favorite Talk Show Hosts

James Robert Parish

PIONEER CELEBRITY PRESTIGE SERIES

The Hollywood Death Book by James Robert Parish   ISBN #1-55698-307-7
WHOOPS! The 101 Worst Blunders by Warren Etheredge   ISBN #1-55698-371-9 (OCT)
The New Country Music Stars by James Robert Parish   ISBN #1-55698-374-3   (NOV)

—and much more to come!

Library of Congress Cataloging-in-Publication Data
James Robert Parish

Let's Talk!: America's Favorite Talk Show Hosts

1. Let's Talk!: America's Favorite Talk Show Hosts (television, popular culture)
I. Title

Published by Pioneer Books, Inc., 5715 N. Balsam Rd., Las Vegas, NV, 89130.

First Printing, 1993

ACKNOWLEDGEMENTS:

The author wishes to gratefully thank the following individuals and institutions for their generous assistance in the writing of this book.

Academy of Moton Picture Arts & Sciences:
        Center for Motion Picture Study
Beverly Hills Public Library
Larry Billman
John Cocchi
Collectors Bookstore
Brenda Casale
Ernest Cunningham
Eddie Brandt's Saturday Matinee
        (Donovan Brandt)
Steve Eberly
Don Eckhart
Jocelyn K. Faris
Film Favorites (Linda Rauh, Karen Martin)
Charlene George
Alex Gildzen
Kent State University Library
Jane Klain
Larry Edmunds Book Shoppe (Peter Bateman)
Alvin H. Marill
Doug McClelland
Ann V. McKee

Jim Meyer
Eric Monder
Movie World Book Store (Sandy Weinberg)
New York Public Library
        for the Performing Arts
Jeb Perry
Michael R. Pitts
Howard H. Prouty
Barry Rivadue
Jerry Roberts
Brenda Scott Royce
Eric Roberts
Margie Schultz
Arleen Schwartz
Kevin Sweeney
Vincent Terrace
Jerry Vermilye

Editorial Consultant: Allan Taylor

Publisher and Designer: Hal Schuster   **Editor: David Lessnick**

CONTENTS

DEDICATION

TO
MISS KATE SMITH
(1907-1986)
The First "First Lady of Television"

LET'S TALK !

AMERICA'S FAVORITE TALK SHOW HOSTS

Introduction

A BRIEF HISTORY OF TALK SHOWS

A phenomenon of recent years is the staggering volume of TV/cable programming hours devoted to talk shows. Equally amazing are the huge numbers of fascinated viewers who spend hundreds of minutes daily watching such programs. Currently, there are so many talk shows on the air that now E!TV Cable created a special program, "Talk Soup," devoted exclusively to a daily roundup of the highlights from the past day's genre offerings. Without a doubt, America has become addicted to talk show programming, as it has always been addicted to the daily soaps.

With so much air time devoted to talk shows, it is no wonder that the hosts of such high-rated programs have become the mega stars of today's television. These days, Oprah Winfrey, Phil Donahue, Arsenio Hall, Jay Leno, Joan Rivers, Geraldo Rivera, Jenny Jones, Maury Povich, Montel Williams, Sally Jessy Raphael, Regis Philbin et al are as well known to the general public as any of the celebrity guests they might interview. As such, these talk show emcees have become fodder for the supermarket tabloids who delve into the hosts' private lives with the same voraciousness once reserved for movie and music superstars.

Greg Kinnear, host of E! Entertainment Television's "Talk Soup," the cable program providing daily highlights of the past day's many TV talk shows.

All of the talk show superstar hosts have unique, colorful personalities, quite in contrast to each other. They shape their TV forums to reflect their own personal natures and their particular agenda of interests. Thus, nowadays, viewers will tune in to a particular talk show just as frequently to share time with a favored moderator as to satisfy an interest in a particular guest or theme show presentation. As a result, the more time we spend with a familiar "friend" (the talk show host), the more we want to know about their offcamera lives, their romances, their tragedies, their intriguing pasts.

TV talk shows come in two basic formats with many variations within each. On one hand, there is the concept of the host with the invited celebrity guests. The latter, after singing or telling jokes or displaying their latest cosmetic surgery, just might give us a peak into the lifestyles of the rich and famous. Then there are the rash of theme-type talk programs in which a panel of visitors discuss their experiences and/or expertise on a given subject with the host/moderator. Meanwhile, on such programs, studio viewers and home audiences (via telephone) add in their opinions to the discussion at hand.

A CLOSER LOOK

Focal topics on these interactive talk shows, cover a wide spectrum. Subject matter may seesaw from the mundane ("what was it like playing opposite Tom Cruise in your new picture?") to the exploitational ("husbands who sleep with their wives' sisters") to the educational ("AIDS education for teenagers"). Sometimes the TV forums ignite great emotional outbursts, occasionally leading to an onstage fracas in which the refereeing talk show host gets mixed up in the resultant melee. At times, studio and home viewers, let alone show guests, become so outspoken in their heated reaction to a topic that their words are bleeped from broadcasts.

Sometimes the program's theme provides a solid community service by alerting viewers to warning signs for a particular disease, to new methods for curing a health or mental problem, or even ways to cope with economic plight. Equally often, the tantalizing topic (e.g. male or female strippers) is merely a tease excuse for titillating displays of provocative human anatomy. On yet other occasions, a talk show program becomes an economical forum for political candidates to reach a huge mass of voters, a situation that was particularly true in the 1992 U.S. Presidential campaign.

Today's growing list of TV talk shows is a result of many factors. In our age of high tech, the home viewer has a wide selection of TV and cable channels, as well as TV sets on which several shows can be watched simultaneously. (Then too, the VCR allows us to record talk shows while we are busy elsewhere and to play them back at our leisure.) With the availability of so many channel outlets and options, there has arisen the specialized broadcasting marketplace, appealing to special audience types. This, in turn, has led to talk shows which cater, for example, to women, to young adults, or to particular ethnic groups. In today's broadcasting environment, if one prefers a talk show program with a hip tempo or a laid-back atmosphere, there are several such tailored-made offerings available.

Another consideration for the growth of TV talk shows is the bottom-line economics of producing such programming. Not only is such video fare relatively easy to assemble from the start-up, but the ongoing costs are inexpensive compared to the price of producing a weekly TV series like "Knots Landing" or "Cheers."

Another factor is the late 1980's explosion of "infotainment" TV shows which feed on the public's insatiable desire to learn and/or be nosy about an amazing number of topics. We are in a mode, so it seems, when we are happiest peeking into other people's lives, comparing our economical, sexual, political and religious habits with those of the famous or the average man/woman in the street. We are in a frame of mind of wanting to know more and more. And that process, once considered educational, has now become entertainment. We are a new breed of the TV generation.

WAY BACK WHEN

While TV talk shows (and their radio counterparts) may be crowding the airwaves today, the species is certainly not new. It has been around since the first years of commercial television in the early 1950s, when stations and sponsors sought a way to fill programming hours and amuse viewers.

The most famous TV talk show in U.S. history is "The Tonight Show." Its beginning dates back to early 1950, when Sylvester L. "Pat" Weaver, Jr., a NBC-TV network executive, dreamed up a new type of late night program. It was to be called "Broadway Open House" and it would feature a mix of vaudeville skits and sight gags, song and dance. Weaver chose Don "Creesh" Hornsby, a California-based comedian, to host the nightly hour-long series which was to start on May 16, 1950 at 11 PM.

Hornsby came to New York City in early May 1950. On the day he was to sign for the series, he contracted polio and died two weeks later. Weaver quickly signed Jerry Lester and Morey Amsterdam, both veteran comedians, to fill Hornsby's shoes. The plan was to have Lester host for three nights with Amsterdam in charge on the other two evenings. The supporting cast for the nightly program included Wayne Howell (announcer), Andy Roberts, Jane Harvey and David Street (singers), Milton DeLugg (accordionist), Ray Malone (tap dancer) and Dagmar (the shapely dumb blonde).

"Broadway Open House," a rather formless elephant of a show, struggled through fifteen months on the air. The cast of supporting characters changing frequently. By the spring of 1951 the program had been cut back to three nights a week and eventually both Lester and Amsterdam departed, to be followed by Jack Leonard as host. On August 24, 1951, NBC called it quits and "Broadway Open House" went off the air.

GRASS ROOTS

Although the TV show format had failed on a national level, the variety/talk show continued onward on a local level. One of the several personalities who was making a name for himself in this genre was Steve Allen. Having come from Los Angeles to Manhattan in 1950 to emcee quiz and game shows, he began hosting his own late night program, "The Steve Allen Show," over WNBC-TV in Manhattan on July 27, 1953. The show was so successful that NBC decided to turn it national. Thus on September 27, 1954, "Tonight!" was launched with 105 minutes of nightly entertainment. Network publicity boasted about the show:

> At a time of night when the "Great White Way" of Broadway is at its most glamorous, the camera of "Tonight" will bring the crossroads of the world to viewers across the country. Acting as Stagedoor Johnny for millions of viewers, "Tonight" will chat with the stars of Broadway's biggest hits shortly after the curtain drops. Stars and featured entertainers at New York's smartest night clubs will be frequent visitors to the "Tonight" set.

It was during Steve Allen's reign over the late night network program that the established format was forged and refined. The prime ingredients for "Tonight!" proved to be the host desk/chair and guest couch. With this setup, the amiable host, after an introductory monologue, could easily interview a parade of celebrity visitors who might or might not do a solo turn singing, telling jokes, etc. Soon, there were studio audience participation games ("Stump the Band") to fill in the gaps between the array of notables who came on air (at minimum scale pay) for the golden opportunity to promote their latest film, play, TV series, book, album, etc.

Not that the famous were the show's only guests. In Allen's regime, he introduced an assortment of offbeat common "salt of the earth" people, ranging from Ben Belefonte, "the rhyming inventor," to Joe Interleggi, "the human termite." To share some of his nightly duties, Allen relied on a sidekick-announcer (Gene Rayburn), employed resident singers (including Steve Lawrence, Eydie Gorme, Andy Williams and Pat Marshall), and used a house band (led by Skitch Henderson).

CALLING IT QUITS

After 2 years of the grind, the hard-working, creative Steve Allen, who was then also hosting a weekly variety TV show, had had enough of "Tonight!" His last episode was on January 25, 1957. There followed six months of chaos, or "Tonight: After Dark." This disaster was slapped together as a stopgap measure after Allen walked away from the highly-popular "Tonight!" The misguided brainstorm offered Jack Lescoulie (most famous from his stint on TV's "The Today Show") as a host of sorts, with correspondents based in different cities providing segments of news, chatter, on-location interviews, and entertainment.

The original cluster of correspondents included Bob Considine, Hy Gardner and Earl Wilson (New York); Irv Kupcinet (Chicago); and Paul Coates and Vernon Scott (Los Angeles). The Lou Stein Trio provided the music. By June 1957, as more network affiliate stations cancelled airing the show. Lescoulie was replaced by Al "Jazzbo" Collins, the Lou Stein Trio gave way to the Mort Lindsey Quartet who, in turn, departed in favor of the Johnny Guarnieri Quartet. On July 26, 1957, NBC threw in the towel on this unsuccessful follow-up to "Tonight!"

Determined to reestablish a profitable late night program, NBC turned to another game show alumnus, Jack Paar, to host "Tonight" which bowed on July 29, 1957. The very unpredictable Paar, noted for wearing his emotions on his shirt sleeve and his tart thoughts on his lips, proved very successful at his chores. He developed a tremendous following, with viewers addicted to his nightly forum on which he might harangue the network, a newspaper columnist, the U.S. Senate or Teamster leader, Jimmy Hoffa. With Paar, anything was possible and the unexpected always happened. He frequently put his foot in his mouth and spent the remainder of the program extricating it, stumbling through heart-felt apologies. If sufficiently annoyed, he might—on air—announce he was quitting the show, and walk off the stage.

Paar, like Steve Allen, had a resourceful talent as an adroit conversationalist. Besides the requisite procession of celebrity guests, Jack developed his own group of regulars, who appeared on the program almost as frequently as did Paar's jovial announcer-sidekick, Hugh Downs. In Paar's reign, the core group included such diverse visitors as French-born singer Genevieve, England's Hermione Gingold and Alexander King, Hungary's Zsa Zsa Gabor, and such American-bred personalities as society matron Elsa Maxwell, comedian Dody Goodman, actor Hans Conried and writer Jack Douglas.

HEEEERRRE'S JOHNNY

After many threats of leaving "Tonight," Paar made good his warning by quitting as of March 30, 1962. NBC was prepared for the walk-out. By then, the network had settled on TV game/quiz show host and comedian, Johnny Carson as Paar's replacement. However, Carson was committed to hosting TV's "Who Do You Trust?" until October 1962. In the interim, NBC turned to a series of guest hosts (ranging from Jerry Lewis to Merv Griffin to Arlene Francis) to guide "Tonight" through the transition. Through most of this interim period, Hugh Downs remained as announcer, with Skitch Henderson and his band providing the musical backup.

On October 1, 1962, a new era began with "The Tonight Show Starring Johnny Carson." To be his announcer-sidekick, Carson chose his pal, Ed McMahon, who had handled similar chores on "Who Do You Trust?" As Carson settled into his hosting duties, he developed an extremely loyal following. During the next thirty years, Carson remained his low-keyed midwestern self, most content when conversing with mainstream, establishment guests like Bill Cosby, Elizabeth Taylor, Tony Bennett or Bette Midler. The show's length shrunk from 105 minutes to 60 minutes, and by the end of his tenure, Johnny was only hosting the program three nights weekly. McMahon remained through to the end, but Skitch Henderson departed in 1966, to be replaced in 1967 by trumpeter Carl "Doc" Severinsen, who took over the house band. The series also moved its permanent base from New York to Los Angeles in 1972.

During the Carson Years, Johnny developed several ongoing characters, including an inept magician (Carnac the Magnificent), a gabby senior citizen (Aunt Blabby), a seedy afternoon movie TV host (Art Fern), and a mega patriot (Floyd R. Turbo). In the early years, there were also "first person adventures" in which Carson went on location to perform stunts (skydiving, flying with the Navy Thunderbirds, etc.) and later came The Mighty Carson Art Players to perform satirical skits. Continuing Steve Allen's gambit, Johnny employed such audience participation games as "Stump the Band."

Highlights of "Tonight" shows over the Carson years included visits by hatchet-wielding Ed Ames, a joint appearance by John Lennon and Paul McCartney, the on-the-air wedding of eccentric singer Tiny Tim to Miss Vicki, and author Alex Hailey presenting a bemused Johnny with his genealogical charts. To chart some of the more embarrassing moments and flubs on the nightly program, there were the annual anniversary programs.

ON TOP OF THE WORLD

While Johnny maintained fairly high ratings for most of his three decades on "The Tonight Show," his late night

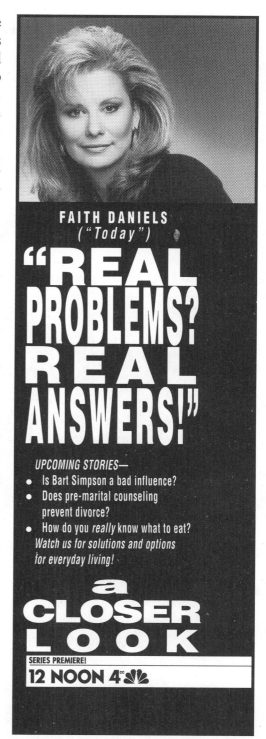

FAITH DANIELS
("Today")

"REAL PROBLEMS? REAL ANSWERS!"

UPCOMING STORIES—
- Is Bart Simpson a bad influence?
- Does pre-marital counseling prevent divorce?
- How do you *really* know what to eat?
Watch us for solutions and options for everyday living!

a CLOSER LOOK

SERIES PREMIERE!

12 NOON 4

Faith Daniels of the "Today" show.

competitors fell by the wayside. Among the many rivals who came and went during Carson's tenure were Les Crane, Joey Bishop, Dick Cavett, Merv Griffin (on CBS-TV), David Brenner, Alan Thicke, Garry Shandling, Pat Sajak and Dennis Miller. Perhaps Johnny's most famous opponent was Joan Rivers, who had been Johnny's permanent guest host on "The Tonight Show" from 1983 to 1986. Her own late night offering, on the new Fox Broadcasting network, lasted less than a year (1986-1987). However, it did spawn the eventual birth of "The Arsenio Hall Show" which, in turn, would become Johnny's greatest TV rival.

On May 22, 1992 the seemingly impossible happened. Johnny Carson bid farewell to his TV audience as the host of "The Tonight Show." He was replaced by fellow comedian Jay Leno, who began on May 25, 1992. Leno, previously a frequent guest host on "The Tonight Show," made his own crew changes. Among them was the replacing of the big band sound of Doc Severinsen with the jazzy "now" sound of Branford Marsalis and his musicians. Instead of a side-kick who was also the announcer, Leno's new announcer (Edd Hall) was, surprise, surprise, just an announcer. And so the new "Tonight Show" carries the tradition onward, complete with monologues, audience participation games, and that indispensable item, THE NEXT CELEBRITY GUEST.

Meanwhile, today's TV airwaves are crowded with an assortment of talk shows, each geared to particular audience needs. If the mainstream "The Tonight Show with Jay Leno" is too staid for one's tastes, there is the hipper "The Arsenio Hall Show" or the antic "Late Night with David Letterman" (soon to have his own earlier late evening talk program). If one finds

Radio host, best-selling author, and now TV talk show host, Rush Limbaugh.

Whoopi Goldberg too passive in her one-on-one conversations, there is the far more abrasive "The Howard Stern Show" or the rambunctious "Vicki!" hosted by the irrepressible Vicki Lawrence.

There are highly right-wing oriented genre shows ("The Rush Limbaugh Show," "The Wally George Show") and very liberal offerings ("The Phil Donahue Show," "Larry King Live!"). There are middle-of-the-road entrants such as those hosted by dignified Jane Whitney or by more flamboyant Jenny Jones (an ex-drummer turned comedian turned talk show host).

FULL SPECTRUM

Today's microphone holders range from thoughtful Jerry Springer and Montel Williams to pouty Regis Philbin and brash, "let's go for it" Geraldo Rivera. If Sally Jessy Raphael is a concerned moderator, then Joan Rivers is a flippant funster and Kathie Lee Gifford a non-stop gabber. Having celebrated over 25 years in the interactive talk show business, Phil Donahue is now considered the dean of TV talk shows, while Oprah Winfrey, earning over $42 million yearly, is regarded as the new genre maven.

And if that is not enough to choose from, waiting in the green room for upcoming chances at grabbing a TV audience share are comedians Chevy Chase and Dana Carvey, "Entertainment Tonight" co-anchors, Leeza Gibbons and John Tesh, and, geared for the younger crowd, actress Ricki Lake.

In selecting subjects for this book, *TV's Favorite Talk Show Hosts*, there were a wealth of individuals to choose from among past and current TV talk show hosts. The list of personalities who have hosted their own local, regional or national shows over the years range from Mary Martin to Gyspy Rose Lee, Pamela Mason and Marsha Warfield, from Joe Namath to Sammy Davis Jr, Jerry Lewis, John Davidson, Joe Franklin, and on to Rick Dees and Dennis Miller. The 23 personalities selected for this volume represent the full spectrum of the medium, from the early days (Steve Allen, Virginia Graham, Jack Paar, et al) to later entrants (Johnny Carson, David Frost, Dinah Shore, Dick Cavett, Mike Douglas, et al) and on to today's crop (Jay Leno, Oprah Winfrey, David Letterman, Larry King, Dr. Ruth Westheimer, Whoopi Goldberg, Arsenio Hall, Kathie Lee Gifford, et al).

Each subject chronicled in this book come from a diverse background, ranging from the Cleveland ghettos to World War II-torn Germany to surburban northern California. No matter what the subjects' pedigrees, or the contrasting and exciting paths that led them on to TV fame, they all share at least two things in common: an abiding fascination with the television medium and a desire to meet, converse with, and attempt to understand that most unpredictable of all beings, the human spirit.

PAST FAVORITES
THE FOUNDING FORCES

Chapter 1
STEVE ALLEN

If imitation is the sincerest form of flattery, then 6'3" Steve Allen's ego should be monumental (it is, but in a positive way). A great deal of the pranksterish concepts he developed during television's pioneer days of the 1950s have been borrowed, distilled or revived by many subsequent late night talk show hosts including Johnny Carson and David Letterman. As the star of NBC-TV's fledgling "Tonight!" (1954-1957), Allen was the molder of the "Tonight Show" formula, a format which has been entertaining television viewers for five decades.

Few avenues of the creative arts have escaped multi-talented, highly intellectual Steve Allen, who is a one-man show business factory. This "egghead" has authored thousands of songs (including "This Could Be the Start of Something Big") and written nearly forty books (ranging from autobiographies to philosophical studies, from verse to joke books and slick detective novels).

He has appeared in many motion pictures/TV movies (most notably as the star of THE BENNY GOODMAN STORY, most ignobly as a participant of COLLEGE CONFIDENTIAL) and starred in several TV series (ranging from the erudite "Meeting of Minds," to the silly "The Steve Allen Comedy Hour," to an assortment of quiz/game shows like "I've Got a Secret"). "Hi-Ho Steverino," as he is frequently called, plays the piano with the same ease and spontaneity with which he ad libs humorous responses. If one moment Steve Allen is deadly earnest and rapsodizing in a highly intellectual mode, the next he is most likely to be fracturing listeners with an unexpected piercing cry of the infamous jungle bird yelping "Schmock!-Schmock!"

In short, Steve Allen, of the horn-rimmed glasses and plaid sports jackets, captures all the qualities that once made television so unique and captivating: impromptu, daring, unpredictable, full of wild mood changes that range from the seriously intimate to wildly bizarre slapstick, and always...always entertaining.

IN THE BEGINNING

Stephen Valentine Patrick William Allen was born on December 26, 1921 in New York City's Harlem. His mother was Belle Donahue, whose grandfather had been a farmer in County Cork, Ireland. He had married a country girl and come to the U.S. before the turn of the century. Belle, one of their sixteen children, was born in Chicago and, by the age of nine, had gone on the road with circus aerialists. Later, she became a chorus girl, then a comedienne known as Belle Montrose. One of her partners was vaudevillian straight man Billy Allen whom she married. He died when Steve was only eighteen months old.

The widowed Belle continued her vaudeville touring. When baby Steve became very ill, he was left in a San Francisco hospital for many months. One of her several sisters, Rose, took care of Steve thereafter. When he was a year old, he was taken to Chicago to see his mother. One of his first responses at the meeting was to slap her hard; she returned the blow. Whenever Belle was on a long road trek, young Steve would be boarded with assorted relatives.

When Steve was still quite young, his mother remarried, but the union soon dissolved. By this point, the precocious youngster had formed very definite opinions about his old-fashioned but irrepressible parent and her unique clan. (He would say later, "Mother and all the members of her family were, I think, born in the wrong century.") It was growing up with the "sarcastic, volatile, sometimes disparaging, but very, very funny" relatives that taught Steve to develop quick retorts to any given statement. He would reflect later, "My whole family talked that way.... I never worked at it. I never trained myself for it. It's not like anything I strove for. It's like having brown eyes."

Money was never in great supply during Steve's childhood, even before the great Depression. He and Belle would move from cheap boarding house to house. For a time they lived in the area back of the Chicago stockyards. At one point, Steve was sent to live with an aunt in Los Angeles. For a brief period, when finances were better, he spent time at St. Joseph's Institute, a boarding school in La Grange, Illinois.

CLASS CLOWN

By the time he was thirteen, the "pampered bean pole," who was always the class clown, was attending St. Thomas the Apostle School in Chicago. It was but one of the thirteen different learning institutions he attended during childhood. While at the St. Thomas School, one of Steve's best friends was Richard Kiley, the future stage/film actor. Later, Steve spent his sophomore year at Loyola High School in Los Angeles, having run away from home, a trait which seemed a way of life with the Donahues.

By the time he returned home that June, his mother had moved to Chicago's near North Side. However, Steve got himself entered in Hyde Park High, a more swank South Side school. A fellow student there was future singer/musician Mel Torme, with whom Steve became friends. During the summer of 1939, Steve had a taste of the adult business world when he worked at the Washington Shirt Company, both as a stock boy and a salesperson.

After completing his junior year of high school, Steve suffered a severe asthma attack. He and Belle left Chicago for warmer climates, taking the train westward. When they reached Phoenix, Arizona, they decided suddenly that this was as good as any other dry spot. So they disembarked. Steve signed up for his senior year at Phoenix Union High School.

While a senior at Phoenix Union, Steve met a pert sophomore named Dorothy Goodman, who would soon play an important role in his life. Meanwhile, with his show business pedigree, sharp wit and well-modulated speaking voice, he found a job at a local radio station (KPHO). There he hosted a rather impromptu program called "Ted and Steve."

A TRUE SUN DEVIL

After a year in Phoenix, Steve and Belle returned to Chicago for the summer. Because there was an available journalism scholarship to Drake University in Des Moines, Iowa, Steve, who had been on his high school newspaper, accepted the funding. However, the tuition was for one year only, and he could not afford to continue on his own. Therefore, in the summer of 1942, he was back in Chicago, but had more asthma attacks. He and Belle returned once again to Phoenix. He entered Arizona State Teachers College (now Arizona State University) in Tempe, outside of Phoenix. On campus, he remet Dorothy Goodman and they began dating.

Meanwhile, after a few months of school he quit to take a part-time job at radio station KOY. His chores included announcing, writing, piano playing and acting. Always the antic clown, he incorporated all kinds of horseplay into his act. If it would generate a laugh he was not above re-writing commercials for the station's unsuspecting announcers who found themselves suddenly reading gibberish.

By mid-1943, Allen's asthma had cleared up and he knew he would be drafted into the Army of World War II, which happened. He did his basic training at Camp Roberts, California near Paso Robles. In August of that year he and Dorothy were married at the camp's chapel. Then, a few weeks later, his asthma returned. As a result, he was demobilized and the couple returned to Phoenix, where KOY rehired him.

At the radio station, to amuse himself, he began developing comedy character voices (such as Claude Horribly) that he employed on his morning disc jockey show. He and Wendell Noble, a fellow station announcer who had a penchant for funny voices and

Steve Allen and his bride-to-be, actress Jayne Meadows, in 1954.

singing, worked up a comedy act. However, the team broke up several months later when Wendell moved to Los Angeles to become an announcer with KHJ, a Mutual Broadcasting station. Still employed at KOY, Steve did several man-on-the-street spot interviews during the presidential campaign of 1944. Before long, these interchanges turned into pranksterish gag sessions.

TORN BETWEEN FAMILY AND CAREER

In 1944 Stephen, Jr. was born. By now, Allen wanted to move to Los Angeles, but Dorothy did not. Determined as ever, Steve went to California to job search, with $1,000 he had saved from working nights as a pianist/singer at a local steak house. He made the rounds of the Los Angeles radio stations with no luck. Then he thought he had a job with an ad agency. With this in mind, he urged Dorothy to come westward with Steve, Jr. By the time they arrived, Steve had learned he did not have a real position, just the right to use space in an agency office. The Allens moved from apartment to apartment as their finances dwindled.

Finally, Steve negotiated an announcer's job at KFAC and then, a few months later in 1945, he moved over to KMTR. He was now 23 years old. Having reactivated his act with Wendell Noble, Steve quit his KMTR job in 1946 to do "Smile Time," a daily fifteen minute radio show at KHJ with Wendell. They added June Foray to the cast as well as two musicians, including Skitch Henderson (who would work later with Steve on TV).

When they ran out of material for this morning program, they improvised with old joke books, bad radio scripts, the Sunday funnies, anything to keep themselves and audiences amused. They strung out "Smile Time" for over 500 episodes. Also during this period, Noble and Allen did a poorly-received club act on Vine Street in Hollywood. Meanwhile, in 1947, Steve and Dorothy's son Brian was born and the Allens purchased a two-bedroom cottage in nearby Venice, California.

After "Smile Time" was cancelled in 1948, Steve worked for radio station KNX, the local CBS outlet. His assignment was a disc jockey show. The late night program soon became known as "Breaking All Records" because on the show, antic Allen more often broke records than played them. One day the station's programming department sent him a memo: "We hired you to play records, not to do a comedy program." He read the warning on the air and listeners sent in letters supporting their anti-dj.

IN SEARCH OF COMEDY

Before long, he began embellishing his announcer/dj act with reading letters and piano playing. Soon an impromptu studio audience (of maybe 10 to 12 people) began appearing for his nightly 11 PM show. One evening, a new singing movie personality named Doris Day was set as the program guest. When she failed to appear, a restless Steve carried his microphone into the audience to chat with them. (Art Linkletter had done this gambit before on radio, but, according to Allen, while Linkletter was searching for fun, Steve was searching for comedy.)

From 1948-1950 Steve hosted his KNX program, being paid initially $100 per week. What with Steve's growing reputation for zaniness and his love of accepting outrageous dares, singer Frankie Laine bet him that he could not write fifty songs a day for seven consecutive days. The wager was for $1,000. Steve accepted the challenge. To prove that he was actually composing by the time-line rules, he did his song-writing in the window of a downtown Los Angeles music store.

He won the bet (and lots of publicity), with several of the tunes being published and two making it to the industry hit charts. As Steve's popularity grew, CBS gave him a large studio on Sunset Boulevard to use for his program. On Friday nights, he broadcast from the thousand-seat Studio A where he did two shows, one to air live and one for delayed broadcast on Monday. Often celebrities such as Al Jolson would come by to hear the broadcast. To keep himself busy, Steve also hosted a more traditional early evening radio program for CBS as well as a daytime radio comedy quiz show, "Earn Your Vacation." He also wrote a column for the magazine, *Song Hits.*

Steve remembers that the first time he ever saw television was in 1947 in Los Angeles, Two years later, in the fall, ABC-TV hired him to announce wrestling matches from Ocean Park Arena. In December 1949, the Allen's third son, David, was born. Soon thereafter, the family moved to Van Nuys in the San Fernando Valley. Also that year, Steve made his movie debut, writing the screenplay and narrating the commentary for DOWN MEMORY LANE a low-budget entry which strung together a host of old Mack Sennett silent and sound comedy shorts.

STEVE ARRIVES

The next year, he was featured as a disc jockey in a major motion picture, the musical I'LL GET BY, starring June Haver and Gloria DeHaven, For five weeks in 1950, he and Wendell Noble reunited and did a thirty-minute show called "Comedy Store" for CBS's west coast TV. In the summer of 1950, Steve replaced Eve Arden with his own network CBS radio show, signalling his arrival in show business circles.

In late 1950, CBS offered Steve a national network TV show on condition that he do the program from New York City. Although his marriage to Dorothy was already in trouble, he brought the family east. They rented a home in Westport, Connecticut. However, within a few weeks, due to constant squabbles, Dorothy and their three children returned to Los Angeles. Meanwhile, Steve's daily half-hour variety show had debuted on Christmas Day, 1950.

Variety reported: "Allen has a number of assets that make him excellent video-comic material. He's got a sharp sense of humor, a fine flair for ad-libbing, an easy, relaxed delivery and a pleasant appearance. He moves easily and appears at home before the cameras." The program reflected Steve's trademark brand of goofiness, mixed with wit and the unexpected.

One of the most unusual show openings was from the huge swimming pool at the St. George Hotel in Brooklyn Heights, a sequence that featured Allen with Olympic swimmer/movie star Buster Crabbe. Another time, when the studio audience seemed listless, energetic Steve initiated a conga line of the 300 guests, then locked them out on the street. He spent the remaining few minutes of the show playing poker with crew members.

ON THE REBOUND

Now a bachelor in New York City (he and Dorothy were divorced by 1952), Steve began reading voraciously. In the summer of 1951 he added to his TV chores by emceeing "Songs for Sale" for a season. When he left that TV musical show, he also wound up "The Steve Allen Show."

In the closing minutes of the final show, he bid farewell to the regulars (which included singer Peggy Lee and Llemuel the Llama) and dismantled the set. He put on his hat and coat, walked across the bare stage and out the back door and into the street. It was in this period that Steve first met actress Jayne Meadows at a dinner party. She, like him, was recuperating from a divorce.

With too much talent and time to sit still, Steve kept juggling a busy professional schedule. He had a late night CBS radio program, then, in quick succession in 1953, he hosted TV's "Talent Patrol" which showcased entertainment hopefuls, as well as a role on "What's My Line."

Through Jayne Meadow's friend, game show creator/producer Mark Goodson, Steve became a regular panelist on this latter show. (It was Allen who patented the phrase, "Is it bigger than a breadbox?") Also at Jayne's suggestion, he tried Broadway. Unfortunately, "The Pink Elephant" lasted a mere five performances. Ironically, despite the flop comedy, he was offered several more Broadway shows, but hardly any TV work.

To fill the void, on July 27, 1953, Steve began hosting a local late night talk show on WNBC-TV. It developed quite a following, particularly when he began his own on-the-air crusade against racketeering. On July 31, 1954 he and Jayne were married at her aunt's house in Waterford, Connecticut. (They would have one son, William Christopher.)

THE START OF SOMETHING BIG

NBC decided to take Steve's program national and paid him $3,000 a week for starters to handle the chores. "Tonight!" debuted on September 27, 1954, telecast from the old Hudson Theatre on West 44th Street. Gene Rayburn was the announcer, Skitch Henderson was soon the bandleader, and, at first, there were no official writers (sometimes Steve would write a sketch). When he ran out of chatter, Allen would climb a ladder into the theatre's balcony to do audience interviews. His constantly changing repertoire of spontaneous shenanigans became exceedingly popular with viewers.

As with any classic TV show, "Tonight!" developed its own array of gimmicks. Steve made celebrities out of audience regulars, such as Mrs. Sterling and Mrs. Miller. Then there was John Schafter, the farmer from upstate New York, Ben Belefonte, "the rhyming inventor," and Carmen Mastren who sang every song on one note, not to mention Joe Intellegi, the Italian immigrant who ate wood.

To stir up the mix, Steve would sometimes open the show with shots of him portraying a hot dog vendor or frying eggs in a skillet set up on the sidewalk outside the theatre. Or, if inspiration failed him, he would open the back door of the theatre and point a camera out into the night, or read angry letters from the Letters to the Editor column of New York newspapers or have audience members try to stump the band with obscure tune requests.

Sometimes he would go on location and create mayhem in his path. For example, in Miami, he staged a mock military invasion of Miami Beach. He encouraged staid guests to do the unexpected, as when he had Carl Sandburg singing "Home on the Range" with actor Charles Coburn. "Tonight!" often did single-subject shows, with themes focusing on drugs, prison reform, civil rights, jazz, etc.

Being a man for all seasons, Steve could not resist an offer to star as jazz great Benny Goodman in THE BENNY GOODMAN STORY (1955). While filming the feature in Los Angeles during the summer of 1955, he worked on the sound stages by day and did his "Tonight!" show chores nightly. (One of his most memorable gimmicks during this period was having a heavy concert grand hoisted to the roof of Hollywood's Capitol Records building, so he could play with a panorama of Los Angeles behind him.)

GETTING THEIR MONIES WORTH

Being an unquenchable performer and the network wanting to exploit him to the fullest, Steve agreed to add to his duties by starting "The Steve Allen Show." It was to be NBC's Sunday night competition to CBS's highly-rated "The Ed Sullivan Show." Allen's program debuted on June 24, 1956, and his second show boasted an appearance by Elvis Presley.

Before long, there was a race (sound familiar?) between Allen and Sullivan to grab the hottest talent and to keep the other program from showcasing the most-in-demand personalities. What made Steve's variety show far different from dour Sullivan's was the accent on humor. To accomplish this, Allen corralled a group of funny men, which, over the years, included Louis Nye, Don Knotts, Tom Poston, Gabe Dell, Pat Harrington, Jr, Bill Dana, et al. Allen brought back his man-on-the-street interviews and created a succession of manic humor sketches (which frequently showcasted the talents of Jayne Meadows).

Eventually, the pace was too much even for hyper active Steverino. He asked Ernie Kovacs to host the "Tonight!" show on Mondays and Tuesdays. Even this break did not provide enough relief for Steve. He advised NBC that he must abandon one or the other program. Since the Sunday night offering was kicking the stuffings out of Sullivan's ratings so well, it was agreed he would drop the late night entry.

As of January 25, 1957, Steve Allen and "Tonight!" were no more. (Later in the year, the mantle was picked up by Jack Paar.) Years thereafter, Steve reminisced, "My 'Tonight' show years were happy years. It was tremendous fun to sit there night after night reading questions from the audience and trying to think up funny answers to them....introducing the greats of comedy, jazz, Broadway, and Hollywood...[and] welcoming new comedians like Shelley Berman, Jonathan Winters, Mort Sahl, and Don Adams."

UPS AND DOWNS

In 1959 "The Steve Allen Show" won the Peabody Award, but, strangely, in the 1950s Allen never won an Emmy despite several nominations. When his variety show began slipping in the ratings due to competition from ABC's "Maverick," the show moved to Monday night in the fall of 1959.

When this move did not help, it transferred to Los Angeles later in the season, hoping to corral brighter guest performers. By June 1960, the latest "The Steve Allen Show" had faded. That same year, he and Jayne, who had established a permanent residence in the San Fernando Valley, could both be seen in the embarrassing movie, COLLEGE CONFIDENTIAL.

In 1960, Steve generated a good deal of publicity when he wanted to do an intellectual TV show called "Meeting of the Minds." (The premise was to have great historical figures come together for discussions.) However, NBC bawked at the last minute. When asked to estimate his standing in the industry, he modestly informed *TV Guide* mid-year, "I've been in show business 15 years and it's been a long, slow development. I don't feel any different now than I did when I started. I don't think of myself as a celebrity. That's something that exists only in other people's minds." To set the record straight, he wrote the first of several autobiographies, *Mark It and Strike It*, proving once again that he was a literate, perceptive man.

Like so many pioneering mavericks of TV, Steve appeared unable to generate the same career momentum in the more staid 1960s that he had in the rambunctious 1950s when most of TV was aired in black-and-white and nearly anything was possible and tried. ABC hired him for "The New Steve Allen Show," which actually had many cast members from his past medium successes. However, it also showcased such new faces as Jim Nabors, Tim Conway and the Smothers Brothers. Unfortunately, it failed after thirteen weeks, unable to compete with NBC's "Wagon Train."

NEVER SAY DIE

Always game, Steve went the syndication route with "The Steve Allen Show" (1962-1964), packaged by Westinghouse with comedian Allan ("Hello Mudda, Hello Fadda") Sherman as producer. When queried what type of show he would be presenting, Steve responded offhandedly that, having viewed several kinescope tapes of his old "Tonight!" program, he thought they were fairly amusing and that he now intended to do much the same type of programming.

·Although he was already in his forties, Allen's new showcase found him continuing to execute crazy stunts such as being strapped to the hood of a car, which was driven through a wooden fence set afire. On one program, the show's opening found Steve sitting in a bathtub high on a platform above Vine Street. The show boasted a lot of sidewalk camera work and bizarre audience guests (such as Gypsy Boots and Professor Voos). There were theme shows devoted to Israel and Italy, and others boasted the appearance of such new talent as Woody Allen, The Supremes, The Carpenters and Bob Dylan.

Allen expanded his old "Funny Fone Calls" gimmick (which led to a two-record LP album.) In many marketplaces, this zestfully chaotic ninety-minute talk show entry was in competition with "The Tonight Show," now just begun to be hosted by yet another Steve Allen successor, Johnny Carson. On the final "The Steve Allen Show" in 1964, Steve performed a song he had written for his failed Broadway musical, "Sophie," based on the life of Sophie Tucker. In retrospect, Allen says, "The syndicated show is better remembered by critics today as a milestone of experimental comedy entertainment."

In the 1950s Jayne Meadows had been a permanent panelist on the TV quiz show, "I've Got a Secret" and, in 1964 (the year Allen's mother died), Steve succeeded Garry Moore as moderator of this enduring CBS program. He remained there for three seasons, replaced thereafter by Bill Cullen. Next, lured back to the comedy/variety format, Steve starred in "The Steve Allen Comedy Hour," a summer 1967 hour-long color program. *Variety* observed: "Allen has little of the pleasant blandness that makes for the maximum tv variety show host. He has a busy, bright and charming tv personality, and when he goes off camera an attention vacuum is created that makes it nearly impossible for a singer or comic to pick up the tempo."

IF IT WORKED ONCE. . .

Joining him on this short-lived venture were Jayne Meadows and comedians Louis Nye, Ruth Buzzi and John Byner. Filmways teamed with Allen's own production company for Steve to host a "Tonight Show" clone which began syndication in April 1968 and lasted through 1971. One of the few format differences between his entry and that of Johnny Carson or Merv Griffin or Joey Bishop was that Steve did not use an announcer sidekick.

The program emanated from a Hollywood theatre half a block south of Sunset on Vine. There was a notable relaxation of his usual mayhem in this latest series, with the atmosphere far more conventional except for an occasional flare-up of Allen-inspired lunacy.

If there was any "lull" in Allen's TV career it was the early 1970s, but even then he was always doing something: writing songs or books (such as the novel *The Wake*, 1972, which also became a play) or articles, performing on record albums, lecturing, doing radio and TV guest appearances, etc. In 1976, "Steve Allen's Laughback" spotlighted Steve and Jayne, along with guests, reflecting back on kinescope clips from old Steve Allen TV shows of the 1950s. Finally, in January 1977, Steve was able to launch "Meeting of Minds" on PBS-TV as an ongoing series.

For the premiere episode, Cleopatra (Jayne Meadows) met with Thomas Aquinas, Thomas Paine and Theodore Roosevelt to discuss matters from the past, present and future. The unique talk show, which won a Peabody Award in 1977 as well as an Emmy, lasted until 1981 through 24 installments. To date, it remains one of the proudest periods of Steve's distinguished entertainment career.

UNWANTED COMPETITION

In 1980, when "The Tonight Show" considered cutting down from ninety to sixty minutes, NBC programming executive Fred Silverman wanted Steve to host the 12:30-1:30 AM time slot with his own entry. This concept was supposedly vetoed by forces at Johnny Carson's "The Tonight Show," but later revived in February 1982 for "Late Night with David Letterman."

Instead, Steve did a series of comedy specials for NBC, which featured the "Krelman Players," a contingent of recurring comedians (including Kaye Ballard, Joe Baker, Nancy Steen and Catherine O'Hara). Each program featured man-on-the-street interviews, a spoof of network news shows ("Eyewitless News"), and "Camera on the Street." The latter found Allen commenting in fine ad lib style on hidden camera footage taped outside the Hollywood studio. By January 1981, this sporadic hour-long show had vanished after only six episodes.

In 1982, Steve did several network comedy specials and, that October, brought his musical comedy revue ("Seymour Glick Is Alive But Sick") to the King Cole Room of Manhattan's St. Regis-Sheraton Hotel. He also authored *Beloved Son: A Story of the Jesus Cults* (1982), dealing with his son Brian's experience on joining a religious commune. Two years later, Steve was on The Disney (Cable) Channel with six comedy outings. Using a talk show format, the only subject of the show was, predictably, comedy.

When the Allens' Encino, California home caught fire in October 1984, TV cameras were soon on location to capture the $250,000 blaze. Steve rose above the tragedy by humorously telling a fledgling TV reporter that, despite the new high prices of prime real estate, "No, I don't think we'll be trying to sell our home this week."

ALWAYS CREATING

Steve packaged together several of the best sequences from various past specials, etc. to create "Life's Most Embarrassing Moments," an ABC-TV summer series in 1985. It was filled with celebrity outtakes much in the vein of "TV Bloopers and Practical Jokes." Also for Disney, he would later host "Steve Allen's Music Room," six specials featuring top musicians/singers having fun around a piano.

The syndicated "The Start of Something Big" (1985-1986) had Allen interviewing notables about their show business backgrounds and other segments dealing with the history of particular products. When William B. Williams, the host of radio's "The Make Believe Ballroom," died in 1986, Allen was hired at a six-figure annual salary to co-host the long-lasting show. He began those chores in 1987, via hookup from his Los Angeles home.

On TV, Steve continued his guest appearances on dramatic shows by playing (with Jayne Meadows) the parent of the eccentric Dr. Ehrlich (Ed Begley, Jr.) on several "St. Elsewhere" episodes. Meanwhile, when not writing magazine articles or taping audio books, he created his string of murder mystery novels, including *The Talk Show Murders* (1982), *Murder on the Glitter Box* (1989), *Murder in Manhattan* (1990) and *Murder in Las Vegas* (1991). He also wrote think-books such as *Steve Allen on the Bible, Religion and Morality* (1990). In 1992, he published his latest reminiscences, *Hi-Ho Steverino: My Adventures in the Wonderful Wacky World of TV.*

Forever an enthusiast of the radio medium, in November 1992, he began as correspondent for KABC Talk Radio's "Ken and Barkley Company," sharing stories and observations on current issues with listeners. These days, if one can catch up with the ever-energetic Allen, he is sure to be carrying a pocket tape recorder to take down ideas for his next creative projects.

He admits of his fertile imagination: "All of the work takes place on automatic pilot up in my skull and my volition has remarkably little to do with it." As to his enormous energy, he says, "there are, no doubt, psychological reasons...most mysterious." For Allen the humorist, his greatest joy is "a big, gutsy, meaty sketch where the audience gets its money's worth."

Louie Nye, Tom Poston and Bill Dana reunite with their comedy leader Steve Allen on "Hour Magazine" hosted by Gary Collins.

At a recent industry luncheon in Los Angeles, 600 guests participated in a tribute to veteran entertainer Steve Allen, who was named to the TV Hall of Fame in 1986. Long-time confrere Bill Dana, in describing his former boss, called Allen "The greatest underacknowledged talent in the history of show business." Without a doubt, that is who Steve Allen is.

TV AND CABLE SERIES

Wrestling Matches (ABC west coast, 1949)
Comedy Store (CBS west coast, 1950)
The Steve Allen Show (CBS, 1950-1952)
Songs for Sale (CBS, 1951-52)
Talent Patrol (ABC, 1953)
What's My Line (CBS, 1953-1954)
The Steve Allen Show (NBC, 1953-1954)
Tonight! (NBC, 1954-1957)
The Steve Allen Show (NBC 1956-1959)
The Steve Allen Plymouth Show
    (NBC, 1959-1960)
The New Steve Allen Show (ABC, 1961)
The Steve Allen Show
    (Syndicated 1962-1964)
I've Got a Secret (CBS, 1964-67)
The Steve Allen Comedy Hour (CBS, 1967)
The Steve Allen Show
    (Syndicated, 1968-1971)
Steve Allen's Laughback (Syndicated, 1976)
Meeting of Minds (PBS, 1977-1981)
The Steve Allen Comedy Hour
    (NBC, 1980-1981)
Life's Most Embarrassing Moments
    (ABC, 1985)
The Start of Something Big
    (Syndicated, 1985-1986)

FEATURE FILMS:

Down Memory Lane (1949)
Spin That Platter (1950) [short subject]
I'll Get By (1950)
The Benny Goodman Story (1955)
The Big Circus (1959)
College Confidential (1960)
Don't Worry, We'll Think of a Title (1966)
A Man Called Dagger (1967) [music only]
Warning Shot (1967)
Where Were You When the Lights Went Out?
    (1968)
Now You See It, Now You Don't
    (1968) [TV movie]
The Comic (1969)
The Sunshine Boys (1975)
Rich Man, Poor Man (1976) [TV miniseries]
Stone (1979) [TV movie]
The Gossip Columnist (1980) [TV movie]
Heart Beat (1980)
The Ratings Game (1984) [TV movie]
Amazon Women on the Moon (1987)
Great Balls of Fire! (1989)
The Player (1992)

Chapter 2
JOHNNY CARSON

By now, veteran TV personality Johnny Carson, the man we all THINK we know for better or worse, is entrenched as a living legend. But what makes a legend? Visibility is a key component, and he certainly had that professionally as the host of NBC-TV network's "The Tonight Show Starring Johnny Carson." Longevity is another ingredient for enduring fame. In Carson's case, generations of TV viewers made a daily habit of staying up and/or going to bed watching "The Tonight Show." During his thirty-year reign as THE

"The Tonight Show" troupe: Doc Severinsen, Johnny Carson and Ed McMahon.

talk show host, the U.S. went through seven Presidents and seven vice-presidents.

Equally important to becoming a legend, is the celebrity's personality, both on and off camera. Johnny Carson confessed once about his private self, "I'm Midwestern, but I'm not a yokel on any level." His second wife Joanne observed, "Johnny isn't complicated. Complicated implies difficult. Johnny isn't difficult really; he's multifaceted. The difference is everything." His one-time confrere turned rival, Joan Rivers insists, "Television lies. Don't give me this nonsense that television tells the truth. Excuse me. Look at Johnny. He's totally isolated but he has great charm, boyishness, on the air."

Carson has a well-earned reputation for being shy in public. (He never travels with an entourage, has no driver; in short, nothing to make himself stick out as famous but himself.) Once away from work, he prefers and demands to be out of the limelight. As he admitted once, "The word that's always applied to me is 'aloof,' or 'private,' or any combination of those two. That's me. I didn't invent it. I was that way in high school, although then the word was 'conceited.' It's easy to be popular, but you also become a carrot in the meantime."

This excessively private man is perpetually the little boy. One rare night, for example, when forced to mingle socially at a Hollywood party, he spent the whole evening away from the cocktail chatter playing drums while Dudley Moore was at the piano. Does he feel guilty about not wanting to share himself with admirers away from the TV studio? No! As he has long maintained, "Look, I don't owe the public anything except a good performance!"

GOLDEN SILENCE

In categorizing this media veteran, *TV Guide* printed years ago, "although he hosts the country's most successful 'talk' show, Carson in fact, is the least talkative host around.... Carson's job is primarily that of a catalyst." Comedian Jackie Mason, no great fan of Carson, explained, "He has a great idea of taste and balance, and he's a master at keeping the show in a light vein. Carson is perfect at what he does."

Former co-worker and genre rival, Dick Cavett observed, "he seems to have an uncanny instinct for knowing when you're going for a laugh." Joan Rivers noted, "Carson is...one of the great straight men of the century. He is a brilliant reactor who becomes the audience, asking its questions, having its reaction...." Rick DuBrow (*Los Angeles Times*) summed up Carson's professional success with, "Carson...captured the pulse and vibes of America as perhaps no other performer of our lifetime has done."

Confirming that he has always known his show business side well, Carson is his own best analyst. Decades ago, he said, "I believe in a slow build when it comes to a career. Acceptance is everything." Years later, he would "jest": "If I had given as much to marriage as I gave to 'The Tonight Show,' I'd probably have a hell of marriage."

When asked once what drove him to a show business career, he responded, "I suppose it's the manipulation. I suppose it's the sense of power, the center of attention and the me-ism." Of achieving and maintaining his professional goals, he has conceded of his "Tonight Show" stint: "I think you can tell I'm having fun out there. I love the applause, the cheers, and sometimes when an audiences rises to their feet...that's a hell of a thrill! It's great to go home in the evening and know you've entertained thousands of people. I wanted to be an entertainer and to be myself and I've made it."

MEET THE CARSON FAMILY

John William Carson was born in Corning, Iowa on October 23, 1925, the second of three children of Homer Lloyd and Ruth (Hook) Carson. (There was older Catherine and there would be younger brother, Richard.) His father, "Kit," worked for the Iowa-Nebraska Electric Light & Power Company, first as a linesman, then later as a manager. During Johnny's first five years, the family moved a great deal.

By 1930, the Carsons were living in Avoca, Iowa, a town of 1,500 people. Although the Depression was gaining momentum, Kit, unlike most of the farmers in the area, had a full-time job and he always provided for his family. As parents, the Carsons were definitely not outgoing, many townfolk regarded them as rigid and coldish. Ruth was the real force of family. As for quiet Kit, he would reflect his own creed by advising his younger son constantly, "Keep your nose clean. Be a good boy."

As a youngster, Johnny was shy; some say distant. There was always a barrier which prevented him from establishing a closeness with others. His first girlfriend (as TV audiences would come to know from "Tonight Show" anecdotes) occurred in the third grade. He asked hometown pal Peggy Leach to the movies. When friends saw them at the theatre, he ran home. Even then, he wanted to avoid sticking out in the crowd.

It was also while Carson was in the third grade that his household was relocated to Norfolk, Nebraska (population 10,000+). In 1937, when Johnny was almost twelve, he made his first visit to California, as part of a family vacation. In school, Johnny participated in class plays, such as "A Christmas Carol."

By the fifth or sixth grade, there was a growing dichotomy between the Johnny who wanted to be anonymous and the Johnny who sought attention. He later recalled that it was during this period that he first realized he could "get attention by being different, by getting up in front of an audience or even a group of kids and calling the attention to myself by what I did, or said or how I acted. And I said, 'Hey, I like the feeling.'"

HOCUS POCUS

Carson was about thirteen when he read *Hoffman's Book of Magic* and, shortly thereafter, sent to Chicago for a magic act kit. He worked hard at honing his skills as a solo magic "act." By age fourteen, the skinny kid with the black cape, top hat and magic table was performing at the local Rotary Club, billed as "The Great Carsoni." He earned $3 a gig. Soon, he began entertaining throughout the state with other teen talent for the Chamber of Commerce.

Carson reflected later that magic always helped him with girls "but not with marriage. There were not too many magic moments in marriage." In high school, Johnny was an intricate mix of cockiness and shyness. He had his own newspaper column, "Carson's Corn," and he was the class clown. He employed ventriloquism to destroy a classroom. His biggest prank was placing hydrogen sulfide into the school's ventilating system, leading to the students being given the rest of the day off.

In 1943, Johnny graduated high school, receiving an "A" for humor in the yearbook. With America involved in World War II, he enlisted in the Navy's V-12 program as an air cadet. Before reporting to boot camp the summer after high school graduation, Johnny went to California again. His most memorable experience on that trip was attending a radio broadcast of his favorite comedian, Jack Benny.

Once in the service, Carson attended Millsaps College in Jackson, Mississippi for his academic preparation. However, when there were no openings in the air cadet program, he was dispatched to midshipmen's school. By the summer of 1945, he was an Ensign and sent to the South Pacific to join the *U.S.S. Pennsylvania*. Two days before he arrived, the ship was torpedoed near Okinawa. Once aboard, he joined the crippled vessel as it went into drydock in Guam. Later, the ship headed to Seattle. After brief state-side duty, he returned to Guam where he spent much of his time entertaining the troops as the Great Carsoni.

SCHOOL YEARS

By the fall of 1946, Carson was demobilized and was attending the University of Nebraska at Lincoln. At first, he thought of becoming a psychiatrist, but then choose a journalism major. He later switched to radio and speech. By now, the Carsons had moved to Lincoln and Johnny could live at home part of the time. Although he pledged Phi Gamma Delta fraternity in the fall of 1947, he was still, at heart, a loner.

Nevertheless, he participated that year in the frat revue, playing Cleopatra. To gain media experience, he had a job at local radio station KFAB on a morning serial, "Eddie Sosby and the Radio Rangers." He also did magic shows at $25 per outing. As his assistant, he used Jody Wolcott, a local girl from North Platte, whom he also dated.

He graduated from the University in 1949 and moved to Omaha where he found employment at a local radio station. On the morning "Johnny Carson Show" he would play records, read news, weather, sports, and do patter. All this for $47.50 a week. For no extra charge he threw in his impish humor, telling hammy jokes, adopting outrageous accents on the air, etc.

On October 1, 1949, he and Jody, were married at North Platte's Episcopalian Church. Johnny made his television debut in 1950 as the star of WOW-TV's afternoon program, "The Squirrel's Nest." He performed as host and quick skit artist. One of his favorite routines was the role of Professor Carson, the wacky instructor on "the Homework School of the Air." To supplement his income, he continued performing magic as The Great Carsoni. One day, when he could not make a Lions Club engagement in Lincoln, Nebraska, his replacement was young Dick Cavett.

The Carsons first child, Chris, was born on November 7, 1950. At the time Johnny was earning $57.50 a week at the TV station. To better support his family, he was determined to accelerate his career. He made an audition tape which he took with him, when he, Jody and their baby went to California in the summer of 1951. He almost got a job in San Francisco, but when he asked for too much salary, he was rejected.

GETTING STARTED

In Los Angeles, Bill Brennan, a fellow Iowan (also from Avoca), was working at program manager for KNXT-TV, the CBS affiliate. He said he would keep on the lookout for a job for Carson. Meanwhile, no one would sign Johnny to do a new version of "The Squirrel's Nest," and the dejected Carsons were forced to return to Omaha.

In the fall of 1951, Bill Brennan called Johnny with a station job offer at $100 weekly. However, Carson would have to start the very next week. An enthusiastic Carson rushed to the coast, while his pregnant wife and son joined him later in Los Angeles. Johnny became a staff announcer at KNXT-TV, and also had a five-minute radio show, "Carson's Corner." Next, he was asked to translate his radio program into a half-hour variety show for this local TV station.

Already making $135 weekly, he was given $50 additional for doing the TV outing, and $25 weekly to cover the costs of props. "Carson's Cellar" debuted in October 1952. Its aim was to be hip and savvy. The offbeat program began drawing a faithful audience, including several celebrity viewers. Sometimes the latter, such as Fred Allen, Groucho Marx or Red Skelton, would drop by the studio and make an appearance. Next came "The Johnny Carson Show," also for KNXT-TV, but the station attempted to make the fractious show both conventional and bland, and it went off the air in June 1953.

Carson's son Richard (Rick) had been born on June 16, 1952 and son Cory was born on November 2, 1953. However, the ever restless Johnny was anything but a typical family man. As part of the freewheeling braodcaster's life, he was caught up in drinking heavily and playing around. He frequented the party circuit, and gravitated to several beautiful women. Once, when his wife Jody asked to go out with him socially, he reportedly snubbed her by saying, "Why take a ham sandwich to a banquet?" Ironically, at home (a ranch house in suburban Encino), Carson was very strict with his spouse and sons.

TAKING OFF

In TV's early days, it was possible for a talent to be involved on many levels. Johnny had his own twice-weekly five minute TV show "Carson's Coffee Break," was host of the CBS network TV quiz show "Earn Your Vacation" (summer, 1954) and wrote sketches for Red Skelton's TV comedy hour. One day (August 18, 1954) when Red got knocked unconscious during a skit rehearsal, Carson replaced him on the air. He was a hit.

As a token of faith, CBS offered Johnny his own evening "The Johnny Carson Show," a half-hour venture which debuted on June 30, 1955. Instead of letting the pleasant, tall, thin, snub-nosed young comic (who by now had had his teeth fixed) be himself, the network suffocated Carson with production numbers.

They pressed him to be more like Jackie Gleason, Red Skelton, or George Gobel. While his TV wife on the show was Virginia Gibson, and off camera he was becoming a true swinger, network publicity had him featured on the cover of *TV Guide* with wife Jody and had him introduce his family on the airwaves. Although *Daily Variety* rated Johnny "a disarming character, a wit with a fresh approach and delivery," the network's tinkering with his image caused the show to die after 39 weeks. This crash course in failure toughened Johnny.

CBS gave him another opportunity, this time hosting the daytime, daily "The Johnny Carson Show," which bowed on May 28, 1956. *TV Guide* was unimpressed, labeling it "a take-it-or-leave it fiddle-de-dee with occasional moments of witless banter....Johnny is a junior Steve Allen. His humor is casual, he spoofs commercials." The program was cancelled as of September 28, 1956. To the press, Carson insisted, "I'd rather be out of work in TV than out of work in insurance or some other field."

But the successive failures had taken their toll on his personal life. He reputedly was getting out of control more frequently and, on one occasion allegedly beat his wife in public at an all-night party. With too much free time, he tried out his standup comedy in distant Bakersfield, California, but his act bombed.

SMART MOVE

Switching agents, Johnny landed a $500 weekly job, as the new emcee of "Do You Trust Your Wife?" which had been hosted the previous season by Edgar Bergen. Because the ABC network show required Carson to operate from New York City, the family resettled in suburban Harrison, New York. With Johnny at the helm, the daily show began televising from the Little Theatre on Manhattan's West 44th Street.

In the new genre, Carson proved pleasant and popular. In this successful mode, he could rationalize, "I once looked down on quiz giveaways, as I'm sure a lot of comedians do, but it hasn't been a bad life. At least it's not a maudlin-type show." In the summer of 1958, the program was retitled "Who Do You Trust?" More importantly, in the fall of 1958, the show's announcer, Bill Nimmo, decided to leave.

There were seven candidates. After a seven-minute chat with one of them, Carson selected Edward Leo Peter McMahon, Jr., the son of a carnival pitchman as his sidekick. It was the start of a 34-year professional relationship. Ed, himself a healthy drinker, would be the one to show Johnny the ropes of swinging New York City. For a time, they were a familiar duo, starting their nightly rounds at Sardi's Restaurant, which was next door to their TV studio.

Using his quiz show as a wedge, Johnny branched out in show business. In mid-January 1958, Carson took over for Tom Ewell in the Broadway comedy "Tunnel of Love," staying with the play until it closed in late February that year. (His performance led to Carson being offered the lead in the musical, "Bye, Bye Birdie," but TV commitments prevented him from accepting.) Carson also was the substitute host for Jack Paar for two weeks on his late night talk show, and proved adept at that format as well.

SOCIAL BOMB/ENTERTAINMENT HIT

Socially, Johnny was often seen with Jill Corey, a TV singer who had been a cast member on the nighttime "Johnny Carson Show." As for the neglected Jody, she was reportedly drinking heavily and visiting a therapist, while finding an emotional outlet in painting. By September 30, 1959, the couple had separated legally, and he had moved to a one-bedroom apartment on East 53rd Street.

Meanwhile, "Who Do You Trust?" continued to climb in the popularity ratings and Johnny was fully credited for its success because of his unique abilities to ad lib on air. In 1960 Carson met blonde, 5'2" Joanne Copeland, a 28-year old cast member on the TV quiz show, "Video Village." (In 1952, she had been briefly under contract to Howard Hughes at RKO Pictures. When she had been a flight attendant in the 1950s she had been married to a Pan Am engineer, a union that was later annulled.) Early in 1961, Johnny moved into the York Avenue apartment building on the upper east side where Joanne lived. She resided on the eighth floor; he was on the sixth.

Carson continued his quiz show stint, but was seeking greater professional challenges elsewhere. The problem was he was not sure what would be best. He did a TV sitcom pilot, "Oh Johnny," which did not sell, and then rejected Carl Reiner's offer to star in another TV comedy, which became the classic "The Dick Van Dyke Show." ABC-TV offered him, tentatively, a talk show, opposite NBC's Jack Paar, but the offer remained just talk.

Meanwhile, Paar was threatening to quit his own vehicle. Both Johnny and Merv Griffin, each of whom had subbed successfully for Jack, were high contenders to replace Paar when and if he left the long-running "The Tonight Show." When Paar finally did leave at the end of March 1962, the network attempted a new format, retitling the show "Tonight: America After Dark."

Governor Ronald Reagan and his wife Nancy on "The Tonight Show" with Johnny Carson

However, it was such a rating disaster that by late summer of 1962, they decided to return to the tried-and-true, and chose Johnny over Merv to host "The Tonight Show." Nevertheless, Carson had to finish his quiz show contract, with his last appearance on "Who Do You Trust?" being on September 7, 1962.

GOOD OL' ED

Initially, Hank Simms, who had been announcer for Johnny's CBS-TV daytime show, was to have been Carson's sidekick on the late night talk program. But he became ill, so Carson turned to Ed McMahon. On Monday, October 1, 1962, "The Tonight Show" debuted, featuring Skitch Henderson and his band (a holdover from the Paar days), Johnny's brother Dick as director, and Ed as the benevolent, ho-ho-ho announcer and compatriot.

Groucho Marx was persuaded to introduce Johnny to the viewing audience, with the slightly bemused Carson telling TV watchers, "Jack Paar was king of late-night television. Why don't you just consider me the prince?" Guests on the debut outing were Joan Crawford, Rudy Vallee, Mel Brooks and Tony Bennett. During the premiere edition, he made the first of his Richard Nixon jokes. According to Bennett, at the end of the program, Carson sighed off camera: "Well, that's the first one. I hope this works." According to Jack Gould (*New York Times*) it did: "Mr. Carson's style is his own. He has the proverbial engaging smile and the quick mind essential to sustaining and seasoning a marathon of banter."

In the early years of "The Tonight Show," youngish Johnny was far more willing to take a dare, to try something new, to improvise. He did a great many physical gags, dancing a hula with Miss U.S.A., fencing with a champ, performing a snake dance with Margo, exercising with fitness maven Debbie Drake, wrestling with a pro, and flying with the U.S. Air Force Thunderbirds. Almost from the start, an undertext of his monologues waqs to poke fun at the studio/home audience, but never going too far. With his air of boyish innocence, he could make "blue" jokes seem clean.

By January 14, 1963, a new pattern evolved on "The Tonight Show," with singer Jimmy Dean the first of more than a 124 guest hosts who substituted for a vacationing Johnny. Carson did not have Jack Paar's family of (semi-) regular entertainers to make the show click. Therefore, he introduced recurring routines such as Johnny and Ed arguing over the relative intelligence of pigs and horses.

POPULAR CHARACTERS

He began his bewigged "Aunt Blabby" routine, making the feisty senior citizen a show favorite. Other characters that Carson would add to his repertory over the years included failed magician El Moldo, borderline mystic, Carnak the Magnificent, TV Tea-Time Movie pitchman Art Fern, Carswell the psychic, and super patriot Floyd R. Turbo.

Meanwhile, he made his feature film debut in LOOKING FOR LOVE (1964), a mediocre Connie Francis musical. This one-shot cured him of the medium, for he appreciated that on TV he was playing "himself" and that he was uncomfortable playing other characters. (He would later reject roles in THE THOMAS CROWN AFFAIR, BLAZING SADDLES and THE KING OF COMEDY. However, as a favor to pal Bob Hope he did a cameo walk-on in CANCEL MY RESERVATION, 1972.)

Although Carson was achieving professional success and financial largess, he has called this period of divorcing Jody "the lowest I've ever felt, the worst personal experience of my life." He began drinking extremely heavily and would occasionally get into nasty snide sessions at parties. All of this behavior climaxed in Nevada, when he was beaten up for being rude to a Las Vegas showgirl.

Later, he stated on "60 Minutes": "I just found out that I did not drink well. That's one reason I found that it was probably best for me not to tangle with it." Having obtained a Mexican divorce from Jody at a bargain settlement rate, Johnny and Joanne wed on August 17, 1963 at Marble Collegiate Church on Fifth Avenue. The newlyweds set up house at 450 East 63rd Street. In 1967 they moved to the swank United Nations Plaza on the 39th floor, while the three Carson sons attended boarding school.

MEETING THE DEMANDS

By mid-1964, Johnny was headlining as a comedian in Las Vegas and Lake Tahoe. Two changes occurred in "The Tonight Show" format as of 1965. Carson refused to do the 11:15-11:30 PM segment of the 105 minutes program, because so many affiliate stations were preempting that fifteen minute time period. Ed and Skitch were used to fill in till Johnny arrived at 11:30. (In 1967, the show would be cut to ninety minutes).

To reduce his TV performing/exposure, Carson no longer appeared on the Monday night show; a substitute host filled in. Because the profitable program had a viewing audience of ten million, the network had no choice but to give in to Carson's demands. He was now earning $200,000 yearly, and soon his salary would escalate to $390,000. It was also in 1965 that the most famous skit occurred on "The Tonight Show."

Singer Ed Ames, then performing on "Daniel Boone," demonstrated his hatchet prowess on the Carson showcase. He threw the weapon at a cowboy drawn on a wooden board. The hatchet sank into the crotch of the cutout figure. As Ames retrieved the hatchet, Johnny stopped him. After milking the laughter, Johnny snapped, "I didn't even know you were Jewish.... Welcome to Frontier Bris!"

In 1966 Carson introduced The Mighty Carson Art Players (to do skits). That same year, Skitch Henderson left "The Tonight Show." Milton DeLugg took over, and, then, in 1967, was followed by Carl "Doc" Severinsen (who had been a show trumpeter since 1962) and his big band. The latter soon included Tommy Newson as assistant music director.

Just as Johnny's marriage to Jody had soured, so did his relationship with Joanne. Author Truman Capote, a UN Plaza neighbor to the Carsons, would recall of this period, "He was mean as hell to her. And they lived right next door. He would holler and get drunk and start beating her and she would take refuge in my apartment." At the time, Carson was linked with Mamie Van Doren and also Israeli starlet, Alicia Bond.

PLAYING HIS CARDS

After nearly five years as America's favorite talk show host, Johnny well understood his bargaining powers with the network. In April 1967, Carson charged NBC with breaching his contract by rerunning unauthorized shows which he felt revealed him in a bad light, since the topical jokes on the old programs seemed inappropriate when re-aired.

Johnny staged one of his famous walk-offs and while he was gone singer Jimmy Dean filled in. But ratings dropped, and, above all, there was real competition from ABC-TV's new late night talk show entry, featuring comedian Joey Bishop. With Carson's faithful public following each step of the negotiations, he forged a lucrative new contract with NBC. It was said to be worth over $4 million during the next three years.

Returning to the airwaves, Johnny instituted changes behind the cameras, including the later leaving of brother Dick, who then moved over to the "Merv Griffin Show". (Insiders

Bill Cosby, Muhammad Ali on "The Tonight Show" with Johnny Carson.

insisted that at one point in the 1960s, Carson even threatened to fire Ed McMahon for getting too many laughs on the show.) To one and all, there was no doubt that Johnny, of the greying temples, was in full charge. In the industry, he was being characterized as uptight, nervous and short tempered; all attributes he wisely hid from TV audiences.

By 1969, as his marriage further disintegrated, Johnny was faced with the heavy competition of three other New-York based talk shows: Merv Griffin, Dick Cavett and David Frost. NBC spent $2 million renovating Johnny's TV studio. Coming aboard thereafter was executive producer Fred De Cordova, a film/TV veteran who had worked for two of Johnny's favorite comedians, Jack Benny and George Burns.

HERE COMES THE BRIDE

The biggest audience-grabber of the "Tonight Show" season, and one of the all-time great TV outings was the December 17, 1969 wedding ON AIR of oddball singer Tiny Tim to Miss Vicki. Forty-five millions viewers watched as the high-pitched vocalist wed Victoria May Budigner, while a formally-clad Johnny Carson benignly looked on. (For the record, the couple divorced in 1977.)

In June 1970, Johnny told Joanne he wanted a divorce. Two days later he changed the locks on their apartment's front door. The pending divorce was kept quiet till the end of the year, with Joanne recouping at Shirlee and Henry Fonda's Manhattan town house. In January 1971 she filed for divorce asking $7,000 a week alimony. More than a year later, in June 1972, the actual divorce occurred, in which she received approximately $200,000 in cash and up to $100,000 yearly.

Carson began joking about his marital woes on air, until Joanne threatened to sue him. The day of the divorce hearing, Joanne visited a jeweler and had her wedding ring melted down, silver-plated and converted into a silver tear drop. She would say of her ex-spouse, "he was my first and only love...Johnny is a genius. I'm still his number one fan...." Meanwhile, in

September of 1971, Johnny met brunette Joanna Holland, originally from Queens. She had been twice married (one spouse had committed suicide; the other had divorced her). There was a son, Tim Jr. by one union, and, since then, she had been involved romantically with several distinguished elder businessmen.

To gain access to a better mix of show business guests, "The Tonight Show" moved to Los Angeles in May 1972. It also allowed Johnny to pursue Joanna, who was now California-based. In the interim, Joanne had relocated to Los Angeles where, for a time she had a local TV show, "Joanne Carson's VIPs" a celebrity interview show. NBC built a $1.5 million annex to their Burbank studio headquarters to accommodate "The Tonight Show."

THE PRICE OF FAME

When Johnny emerged on the West Coast-based TV talk show, he looked refreshed and younger (thanks to cosmetic surgery on his eyes). Johnny had hardly settled into his expansive Bel Air home than a hand grenade was found on the premises. It proved to be fake, but not so a threatening extortion note from a potential kidnapper. Shortly thereafter, the would-be abductor was arrested by the police. The day before his tenth anniversary "Tonight Show" celebration at the Beverly Hilton Hotel, Johnny, age 46, wed Joanna, nearly twenty years his junior.

With Carson, matrimonial patterns died hard. In 1974, Johnny and Joanna secretly split for three months. However, he later returned home. Son Chris, who hoped to be a golf pro, had moved to Ft. Lauderdale. Rick, who a few years earlier had much publicized bouts of possessing drugs, was now an "associate" director of NBC's "Tomorrow Show." As for Cory, he had wanted to become a classical guitarist, but now had a part-time job on "The Tonight Show," running errands and assisting the band.

Much in demand, Johnny signed a contract with Caesars Palace in Las Vegas for a reported $200,000 fee to do one show a night for a week. By now, he was taking off at least one week a month from "The Tonight Show." Although there were signs that the program was becoming formula-ridden and a bit tired, NBC renewed his pact in 1976 at $3 million yearly. That May Johnny returned to Norfolk, Nebraska to deliver his old high school's commencement address. He confided to his audience: "Hindsight is wonderful, but I've been relatively happy and think if I had it to do over I'd stumble along as I did."

In the late 1970s, Carson, who once had his own restaurant franchise and, more successfully, a line of men's clothing, became involved in several new business enterprises. These ventures included a California bank, a Nevada TV station, and a complex deal to purchased the Aladdin Hotel in Las Vegas. Like Jack Paar before him, Johnny was crying wolf repeatedly about quitting the TV rat race, especially after tussles with NBC programming chief Fred Silverman (who left the network in 1981).

However, so loyal was Carson's TV following, that the end result was always to appease Johnny and to reward him handsomely for his rebellion. Continuing his pattern of voicing domestic and business problems on air, he told his cheering fans in the spring of 1980, "Applaud all you want. I'm stuck for three more years." The new pact called for the program to be trimmed to one hour nightly, Carson to do only four shows a week (he wanted to do only three) and he to be paid over $5 million yearly. Additionally, Carson would be producer/owner of the show and NBC agreed to purchase assorted projects from Johnny's production company. (This would soon include "Late Night with David Letterman," a protegee of sorts of Carson, who, at one time, would be in the running to succeed him on "The Tonight Show.")

TESTY TABLOIDS

In March 1981, a supermarket tabloid insisted that Johnny's marriage #3 was in trouble. He ranted on air that this was untrue. However, in actuality the paper was correct. That September Johnny spent time at his Malibu home and pursued other romantic attachments. He again returned to Norfolk, Nebraska, ostensibly to attend a Class of 1943 reunion, but more importantly to shoot a ninety-minute documentary, "Johnny Goes Home" (aired in February, 1982).

In later February 1982, while going out to dine with his wife in Hollywood, he was stopped by the police for driving with an expired license plate sticker. When asked to walk the line, he swayed. He joked about the event the next night on TV, and that April pleaded "no contest" to a misdemeanor count. In March 1982, the month he again was host for TV's airing of the Oscars, he and Joanna publicly acknowledged their separation. He moved into their weekend house on Carbon Beach in Malibu.

He played this for all it was worth on his TV show, posturing as the poor sap kicked out of his own house. After Joanna was awarded temporarily support of $44,600 a month (she had wanted $220,000 monthly), Carson kidded about it on TV, especially after she sought an increase of $6,000 monthly. Less publicly, Carson began dating several Hollywood figures, including Sally Field, Angie Dickinson, Dyan Cannon and Morgan Fairchild.

As Carson approached age sixty, he lost his parents; his father dying in 1983 and his mother in 1985. In the summer of 1983, Johnny was sunning himself on the deck of his Malibu home one afternoon, when he spotted Alexis Mass, a tall, 33-year-old blonde walking across the sand. Born in a suburb of Pittsburgh, this stunning college graduate had worked on the staff of Governor Michael Dukakis and her social life had included dating ballet star Mikhail Baryshnikov.

She was now a stockbroker's secretary in Los Angeles. At the same time, on TV, Carson was heard to quip that he now had a new hero, England's Henry VIII, who had beheaded a few of his wives. His comment was a reaction to the ongoing, complex divorce agreement with Joanna. It was finally settled in August 1985 with she receiving a reported $7.7 million, plus $12 million in other assets, including their Bel Air house, as well as $35,000 monthly alimony for the next five years and four months. As a consolation prize, Johnny, now worth an estimated $42-$100 million, bought himself a new cliffside residence in Malibu for $8.9 million. Friends joked that the living room resembled a glorified set from "The Tonight Show." (It did!)

FRIENDSHIP GONE SOUR

From 1983 onward, comedian Joan Rivers had been Johnny's regular guest host on "The Tonight Show" and it was assumed she was in contention when and if he ever retired permanently from the program. Their professional relationship ended acrimoniously when Rivers claimed to have learned that she was not one of the finalists in the "list" of permanent successors to Carson.

She rebounded by deserting to Fox Broadcasting, a new TV network which offered Joan her own late night show. By May 1987 she was off that show and Johnny had the "last laugh." But at NBC, now part of the General Electric conglomerate, there was a lot of belt-tightening and Carson was not so pleased with the new regime. By now, comic Jay Leno was Johnny's regular guest host. Personally, the celebrity had to cope with the publicity generated by son Chris, then a "golf pro" in Florida.

Chris was living on and off with a black woman, Tanena Love Green, by whom he had a love child, Crystal Love. Carson also had to contend with the California arrivals and departures of Jody, who had grown increasingly more desperate with years of emotional mishaps.

Having resolved a new NBC deal in the spring of 1987 (for more than $7 million yearly, plus fifteen weeks of vacation and only three nights of weekly performing), Johnny and Alexis were married. The wedding occurred on June 20, 1987 at his Malibu home, with Carson's brother Dick present and Alexis being given away by her father, who did his chore via speaker phone.

That October, on the day of the latest California earthquake, Johnny taped his 25th anniversary show. On that airing, he admitted he had been thinking of quitting the grind, but he had decided "to stick around for a while." Many viewers noticed that, of late, in order to keep up with the competition (especially Arsenio Hall), Carson had grown far more biting and sex-oriented in his show humor, although his guest roster remained more traditional than hip. If much of the public had remained blinded to Carson's human frailties over the years, they were paraded forth in detail in a 1989 biography, the steamy *King of the Night*. This book led *USA Today* to headline, "Johnny, We hardly knew you."

TRAGIC ACCIDENT

Tragedy struck on June 21, 1991. Son Rick, 39, died as his four wheel-drive vehicle plunged off a cliff in Cayucos, California. He was then a free-lance photographer and it was deduced that he had taken his eyes off the road while photographing the landscape. Ironically, Carson had recently visited his son at his North Hollywood condo and had vowed that after he retired from "The Tonight Show" in 1992 he hoped to rebuild his relationship with his sons.

The grieving Carson (whose good friend Michael Landon had died on July 1, 1991) returned to the "Tonight Show" forum on July 17, 1991. He uncharacteristically revealed his private self by showing a series of Rick's photos. Just before doing so at show's end, he paid tribute to his late son with "He was an exuberant young man, fun to be around.... He tried so darn hard to please."

Years back, Johnny Carson had been shocked deeply when his idol and good friend Jack Benny had been dumped unceremoniously from network TV by the changing times and regimes. Carson always vowed that this would never happen to him. Undoubtedly this memory was part of his reasoning for resigning finally from "The Tonight Show" especially with ratings declining and more competition from other TV shows and the flourishing cable networks.

For his farewell week, May 18-22, 1992, Johnny boasted a parade of big name celebrities (including Elizabeth Taylor, Robin Williams, Bette Midler, Steve Martin, and Mel Brooks who had been on his very first "The Tonight Show") who dropped by to pay homage to the chairman of talk shows. For the final outing, May 22, 1992, there were no tickets available to the public. They were all reserved for the family and friends of both cast and crew. (Attending that night were Alexis Carson, Johnny's sons Chris and Cory, as well as Carson's brother Dick.)

GOOD NIGHT

Carson showed clips from past shows, acknowledging that the program's first ten year of tapes no longer existed. After exchanging sentimental quips with Ed McMahon and Doc Severinsen, a teary-eyed Carson bid his fans farewell. ("I'm one of the lucky people in the world. I found something I've always wanted to do and I have enjoyed every...single...minute of it.... I bid you a very...heartfelt... good night.") His thirty-year reign, which had seen over 22,000 guests sit on the famous couch, was over.

The following Monday, Jay Leno was ensconced as the new host of "The Tonight Show," complete with a new band and NO sidekick. An American tradition had passed. The TV week didn't seem the same anymore. However, as Ted Koppel (of TV's "Nightline" fame) assessed,

"It's like missing a family member or a popular person around the office. There's a dull ache for a while, but you don't quite know what's missing. Is American going to come to a grinding halt? No. Is it sad that's he leaving? Sure it is."

With new-found freedom, it was anticipated Johnny would learn to enjoy domesticity more and focus increasingly on his hobbies: tennis, drumming and astronomy. However, he could not stay out of the professional limelight for long. Industry gossip had it that Johnny felt annoyed when Leno did not acknowledge his predecessor at his debut as the new full-time star of "The Tonight Show," although Carson had not referred to Leno when he left TV. (This matter was remedied on December 11, 1992 when, at the end of his "The Tonight Show" monologue, Jay belatedly paid tribute to "the man who made this program what it is" and then showed tape clips of Carson being given, earlier that day, the Medal of Freedom from President Bush.)

Soon Johnny was back at work, albeit briefly, taping a voice-over for a character in a segment of TV's animated sitcom "The Simpsons." He appeared as the opening presenter at the American Teacher Awards (December 6, 1992) on the Disney Channel, with his successor, Jay Leno, positioned as the final presenter of the evening's festivities. Meanwhile, Carson and NBC signed a pact for future unspecified projects. Like any seasoned pro, Johnny was keeping his options open for a show business return. Only a few years earlier, he had stated, "Creative people are spooked when they're not working. And that scares me.... Still, I'll know when to walk away. I hope."

TV & CABLE SERIES:

The Squirrel's Nest (Nebraska local, 1950-1951)
Carson's Cellar (Los Angeles local, 1952-1953)
The Johnny Carson Show (Los Angeles local, 1953)
Earn Your Vacation (CBS, 1954)
Carson's Coffee Break (Los Angeles local, 1954-1955)
The Johnny Carson Show (CBS, 1955-1956)
The Johnny Carson (Daytime) Show (CBS, 1956)
Do You Trust Your Wife? [Who Do You Trust?] (ABC, 1957-1962)
The Tonight Show Starring Johnny Carson (NBC, 1962-1992)

FEATURE FILMS:

Looking for Love (1964)
Cancel My Reservation (1972)

Guest Bette Davis with Johnny Carson on the TV special "Sun City Scandals" (1972).

Top: Mike Douglas, with co-host of the week, Burt Reynolds on "The Mike Douglas Show."
Bottom: Hamming it up with Robert Goulet and the cast of GREASE (1978).

Chapter 3
MIKE DOUGLAS

Mike Douglas once called himself "a Henry Kissinger of the talk shows," while George Gent (*New York Times*) described him as "A midwestern leprechaun who discovered the pot o'gold buried in the heart of the American kitchen."

In retrospect, it is difficult to pinpoint what ingredients made wholesome Mike Douglas (not to be confused with Kirk Douglas's actor son Michael) such a sensation as a TV gab show moderator. Talk show maven Larry King observed once of the 5'10", blue-eyed, brown-haired dimpled performer: "Mike Douglas is an affable former band singer who in all the years he's been on the air has never developed a personality as an interviewer. One senses his questions come right off the TelePrompter." Impressionist Rich Little analyzed Douglas: "If you listen to him on a tape, nothing really comes at you." Even Mike, at the height of his TV success (which did not come until his mid-thirties), admitted modestly, "Dick Cavett had his clipboard, [Johnny] Carson uses cards, but 90 percent of our show is off the seat of our pants. The key is to listen. If someone says something provocative, pick it up and you're off and running...."

On the other hand, Irish crooner Douglas had a very long run (1963-1982) in the on-going marathon of TV talk shows. This self-acknowledged square who never smoked, drank or gambled, had the knack for attracting a large viewership to his daily daytime entry. At one point in his professional heyday during the early 1970s, he was outdrawing the leading nighttime competition by two to one and grossing over $10 million yearly in sponsors' advertising. He was the first syndicated talk show host to win an Emmy Award (1966-1967 season). Obviously, the highly-religious Mr. Sentimentality knew exactly how to please the TV masses.

Perhaps at the heart of Douglas's success was his ability to remain Mr. Nice Guy. His former boss, renown bandleader Kay Kyser noted, "Mike hasn't changed one iota. Success hasn't lifted his feet off the ground and his head into the clouds. He's the same sincere, honest, intelligent, talented family man he was from the time I met him...." Mike was also Mr. Average Guy, the perennial star-struck fan.

MODEST MIKE
He conceded readily, "You never lose your awe of big picture stars. They're larger-than-life people." When labeled by the press as modest, he quipped, "I really don't believe I'm anything." In coming to grips with the essence of his hosting job, Douglas explained on one occasion to show guest Nelson Rockefeller, "Mr. Vice President, what you do—meaning politics—seems to me to be a lot like show business. You have to please the people or find another line of work."

He was born Michael Delaney Dowd, Jr. on August 11, 1920 in the bedroom of a first floor, six-room apartment in the Maywood section of Chicago's west side. He was the third child (Robert was born five years earlier, followed by Helen three years later) of Michael Delaney Dowd and Gertrude Elizabeth (Smith) Dowd. Michael Sr., whose parents had come from Ireland, was born in Nashville, Tennessee, while his wife-to-be, Gertrude, was Chicago-bred. Mr. Dowd had spent ten years with the Northwestern Railroad as chief rate clerk. Then, two years before Mike, Jr.'s birth, he joined the Canadian Pacific Railroad in a similar capacity and would remain with that utility for over forty years.

Because Michael, Sr.'s job required him to be away a great deal, young Mike looked up to his older brother even more than normal. Douglas would recall, "My brother Bob was a star in everything that he did and he was my hero. He was my special champion and protector." While Gertrude Dowd had a passion for singing, the rest of the Dowd household was sports-mad. Michael, Sr. instructed his younger son at an early age in the art of self-defense. Mike remembered later, "I was fast. I was lithe. I was strong. And as a result of all *this*, I was cocky."

Young Mike attended a parochial grammar school, but was never a good student "(I don't have an academic bone in my body. As a kid I got passing grades, but I never opened a book"). When the Great Depression came, the Dowds were better off than most because Michael, Sr. had a steady job. However, the family had to move from place to place in Chicago and watch their pennies carefully. Mike held part-time jobs after school and during vacations, fluctuating between delivering papers, toting groceries and helping in a paint store. Being a very physical child, he sometimes caddied at the golf links. (Not until later in life could he afford to play; then the game became a passion with him.)

THE SINGING BUG

Mike first performed publicly at the age of ten when he sang in a school show, adopting a Irish tenor lilt like that of John McCormack. Before long, the enterprising youth was making the rounds of Irish saloons in the neighborhood, singing a few Irish ballads. He coached his pals to toss coins into the cap he set at his feet, and soon other patrons did the same. On one occasion he earned $9 or so singing at Rafferty's bar. His mother ordered him not to do that again, but acknowledged, "You must have been pretty good." Mike would say later, "These words and the wonder of the heavy money that could be made just by singing, I think unlocked the door to my decision to enter show business."

The family never had money for Mike to have a formal musical education, but he listened to the radio constantly, mimicking his favorite crooners. It became a weekly tradition for he and his mother to attend the Chicago Theatre which offered live stage shows between the movie presentations. At church, he was in the choir.

At age eleven, over his father's objections, Mike auditioned for radio station WLS's "National Barn Dance" and was offered a contract. However, under the Child Labor Law, he was too young to perform. The next year, he and an enterprising pal formed an act, hoping to circumvent the bothersome Child Labor Law. However, nobody would hire them. At fifteen, Dowd won a talent contest and was booked to perform for a week at a local Chicago theatre on the same bill with professionals who were earning as much as $500 a week. Audience response to the novice singer was hardly enthusiastic. "It was a shock to my entire system. It was a tough, almost traumatic experience. I couldn't understand it."

By the time he was in Proviso Township (Public) High School young Dowd, who played on the football team until he broke an ankle and a wrist in a game, had been performing for some time on radio's amateur "The Irish Hour." However, he soon tired of being a professional Irishman and wanted to croon. He was impressed particularly with Bob Eberle who sang with

Jimmy Dorsey's orchestra. Also, by this juncture, he had a new motivating force to become a crooning vocalist: "Sing and make the girls scream."

TURNING PRO

In 1936, at the age of sixteen, Mike turned professional over his dad's continued disapproval. He served as master of ceremonies at the American Legion Hall in Forest Park for $5. His stint was successful and he was on his way, soon singing in clubs and with bands around Chicago. He found it no hardship to miss school a good deal of the time. He joined Bill Carlsen's Band of a Million Thrills and traveled with the group when they played the Texas Hotel in Fort Worth. One summer he sang on the C & B Great Lakes cruisers, receiving $35 a week plus room and board. Ever restless, Mike took a singing job in Iowa, but his dad came after him to bring him home to finish high school, which he did in 1938.

After a spell of assorted singing jobs, Mike auditioned for a NBC station in Chicago. The successful test led to his being given a $60 a week job as staff singer at radio station WKY in Oklahoma City. In between working shifts, he took real estate courses at Oklahoma City University, deciding he needed a back-up profession to his precarious show business career.

For Thanksgiving 1941, fellow WKY employee, continuity writer Charles Purnell, invited Mike to join his family for holiday dinner. Mike was attracted immediately to Purnell's high school sophomore sister, Genevieve. However, she was only fifteen years old, too young at the time for a serious romance with such a "sophisticated" older man. Nevertheless, soon she and Mike began dating secretly. Two years later, on the night of her seventeenth birthday, Genevieve was at the radio station visiting Mike and he proposed to her. By now her parents approved of their relationship, but had no idea the couple had matrimony in mind.

Meanwhile, Mike had finally received his draft notice in Oklahoma City from the Chicago draft board. Before reporting for his physical, Mike, then a cocky amateur boxer, tried to separate two guys fighting in front of a neighborhood candy store. For his efforts, he ended with what he thought was a sprained ankle. He went to the draft exam and stood in line on crutches. Later that day the doctors told him he had a broken leg, and he was given a ninety-day reprieve.

ARMED AND MARRIED

With his temporary freedom, Mike and Genevieve decided to marry, which they did on April 6, 1943 in Norman, Oklahoma in front of a justice of the peace. To avoid the need for parental approval, she stated she was nineteen, although she was actually seventeen. (Ten years later, the couple would remarry in a Catholic ceremony at St. Luke's in River Forest, Illinois.)

In mid-April 1943, Mike began his World War II naval duty. He was sent to the University of Wisconsin as a student in the Navy's V-12 program, which was intended to lead to a commission in the Naval Reserve. In typical Mike Dowd fashion, he avoided his academic training whenever possible, spending much time away from the base with his wife, and singing at the commanding officer's Happy Hour in the Officer's Mess.

After failing the ninety-day course twice, he was taken out of the program and sent to radio school in California where he eventually reached the rank of radioman, 3rd class. Genevieve had followed Mike to his training at Treasure Island, California, but when he was ordered aboard the Liberty ship, S.S. *Carole Lombard*, she returned home to finish her senior year of high school.

One night on leave while the ship was loading in Long Beach, California, Mike and his friends went to Earl Carroll's Theatre Restaurant in Hollywood. A pal talked the emcee into allowing Mike to sing in front of the audience. Carroll was impressed and told Dowd that, once he was free of the service, he would have a job for him.

The mission for the crew of the *S.S. Carole Lombard* was to cart 4,000 tons of explosives to Australia. En route and thereafter, Mike got to see a great deal of the world, including Australia, Ceylon, and Hong Kong. On one occasion, while the ship was passing through the Indian Ocean, they picked up sixty survivors of a vessel sunk by a Japanese submarine.

MOVING FAST

In 1944, Dowd received a medical discharge, because of a curvature of the spine which had led to a chronic aching back. He was demobilized finally in Baltimore. Some months after he and Genevieve were reunited, she fell victim to pregnancy-induced toxemia. She recovered and their twin daughters, Christine and Michele, were born on March 26, 1945.

The year 1945 found Mike and his wife moving to Los Angeles. He bullied his way into meeting agent Everett Crosby (brother of Bing), hoping that he would negotiate the promised deal with Earl Carroll. But unknown to Mike, Everett and Carroll had a long-standing feud, which prevented Mike from working at Carroll's club. In turn, Mike fired Crosby. Later, thanks to re-meeting an old friend from his band years in Chicago, Dowd got radio work at KNX in Los Angeles singing on "Hollywood Barn Dance." But neither this assignment nor spotty singing jobs at small local clubs brought in much income. The Dowds had to live in an assortment of small rented rooms.

In due time, Dowd got his break when vocalist Ginny Simms heard Mike perform and invited him to appear on her radio show "Johnny Presents," making him the first ex-serviceman to sing on the program. Simms's former boss, big bandleader Kay Kyser, always listened to her show and heard Dowd's performance. It so happened that Kyser's featured singer, Harry Babbitt, who had just completed his own Navy hitch, had decided to go out professionally on his own. Kyser was impressed with Dowd and wanted to hire him. Almost simultaneously, Republic Pictures offered Mike a seven-year contract, but Mike chose to go with Kyser instead.

Kyser proved to have a tremendous impact on Mike's career. Initially, he altered his employee's surname. (Kyser would recall "I changed his name from 'Dowd' to 'Douglas' because it had a softer sound and more rhythm.") Kay also had a "thing" about Irish tenors, so converted Mike (or Michael Douglas as he was now known) into a baritone by pitching his bandstand arrangements two octaves too low. Mike soon became a fixture on Kyser's very popular NBC radio show, "Kay Kyser's Kollege of Musical Knowledge." Not only would he sing, but he participated in comedy exchanges with co-performer Mervyn Bogue (better known to listeners as Ish Kabibble, the daffy guy with the wild haircut). Douglas quickly exhibited a flair for doing imitations, bolstered by his zany laugh and his wacky sense of humor. By now, the Douglas clan had moved into a $7,500 G.I.-loan bungalow they had built in nearby Burbank.

FROM TOP TO BOTTOM

In 1946, two very popular recordings ("The Old Lamplighter" and "Ole Buttermilk Sky") Mike made with Kyser's band reached to the (near) top of the music industry charts. Everything seemed to be going well professionally. However, the next year, Harry Babbitt decided to return to Kay Kyser and there was no question that the very loyal bandleader would take back the vocalist. Christmas 1947 was Mike's last day on the show. The next two years were very rough for Douglas, and he was reduced to taking any sort of singing job, even at $75 a week. In 1949, he spent nine days (at $100 a day) doing vocal work for Walt Disney's feature-length animated cartoon CINDERELLA.

Fortunately, Kyser again came to Mike's professional rescue. The NBC network had decided to bring the "Kollege of Musical Knowledge" to television and Kay felt that Harry Babbitt looked too old for TV. Mike grabbed the assignment which began December 1, 1949. Jack Gould (*New York Times*) reported that the show consisted "of about equal parts of questionable quiz and corny charade" and said of Douglas that he "delivers a number with becoming straight forwardedness and assurance." The program was telecast from New York City, but in these infancy days of the medium, it was aired to only six NBC stations, most of which broadcast blurry kinescope (tape) versions of the show.

Mike was paid $200 a week for being on the outing. At first the Douglases lived in Long Island and he commuted by train to the city, but then he and the family moved into a Manhattan hotel so he could be near the TV studio in Columbus Circle. During the summer of 1950, Kyser took a vacation while Mike and Ish Kabibble went on tour as a comedy team. Ironically, Kay's summer replacement ("Ford Star Revue" with Jack Haley) proved so successful that the network/sponsor cancelled the bandleader's airtime in November 1950.

Ever the optimist, Mike and his family returned to Los Angeles. Impractically, they sold their Burbank bungalow and bought a more pretentious home in Encino. Their lifestyle and the lack of lucrative singing assignments made it rough going. When not singing at the Bar of Music club on Beverly Boulevard, he and Ish Kabibble toured in minor playdates as a road company Martin and Lewis or Abbott and Costello. Advertised as "Kay Kyser's Graduates of Song and Comedy" their success was minimal. After a year of driving around the countryside (Mike and Ish each in separate cars with their families), they broke up the act. Ish went into real estate (eventually getting wealthy as a broker in Hawaii), while Mike decided to try Oklahoma City again.

FAMILY AND FRIENDS

Until they became solvent, Mike and his family lived with his wife's parents. Before long, he went to work at local WKY-TV and got his own show at $250 a week. However, this job proved to be short-lived, and soon he was traveling wherever there was jobs, playing a lot of low class piano bars, where he would sing a little, do a bit of emceeing, tell a story, make faces, etc.

Thanks to one of Kay Kyser's long-time friend, who was now general manager of WGN-TV in Chicago, Mike was hired to be sidekick to Ernie Simon on his daily variety show, "Luncheon Party." The star had a drinking problem and frequently Douglas would sub for him. Later in the year, also for WGN-TV, he did "Hi Ladies" (1953-1955). Meanwhile, Douglas also could

Mike Douglas with his wife Genevieve and his parents, Gertrude and Michael Delaney Dowd, Sr.

be heard on local radio shows. His Chicago chores soon included appearing on Dumont TV network's nighttime "Music Show" (1953-1954) as well as NBC-TV's daytime "Club 60" (1957-1958).

By 1958, Mike had an urge to try Hollywood again. Soon after the birth of daughter Kelly Anne (April 23, 1958) the family sold their home in River Forest and returned to Los Angeles. In another impractical move, they purchased a big home with a swimming pool, intent, as he said, to "go Hollywood in a big way." However, luck was against him, and he was reduced again to singing in clubs such as Whittinghills in Sherman Oaks for $125 a week plus tips. He tried for roles in upcoming Broadway musicals, but nothing gelled.

Desperate to support his family, by 1961 Mike was ready to abandon show business and go into real estate full time. (Genevieve had already enrolled in real estate school). Then Douglas's former agent, Jack Russell, got Mike together with budding TV producer Woody Fraser and Chet Collier (program manager of Cleveland's KYW-TV). Their plan was to package a TV talk show interlaced with a variety format, in which the rule was that guests had to perform, not just talk. They did several test shows co-hosted with different personalities, searching for the right formula. He was the ninth entertainer to audition for the role of emcee, before he was selected. (Ironically, Douglas would admit later, "This was definitely the last fling. If it hadn't gone over, I don't know what I would have done.")

CHANGED FOREVER

Finally on December 11, 1961, "The Mike Douglas Show" bowed modestly on Cleveland TV. (The only other "big" talk program at the time was Jack Paar's network "Tonight Show.") The *Cleveland Press* reported: "His geniality, ready wit, personable appearance and pleasant singing voice all conspired to show him off as a nimble pro." At the start Mike received $400 weekly. The family moved into the Marine Towers on Edgewater Drive in Lakewood. The twin girls initially remained in a California boarding school, but soon joined their parents and sister in Ohio.

Mike's ninety-minute daytime show became a low-profile hit, attracting an interesting array of young co-hosts (eager for exposure) and seasoned co-hosts (who happened to be passing through town). One of the new talent who appeared as Mike's co-host one week was Barbra Streisand. For Douglas, no stunt was too outlandish, no risk too great, if it would draw viewers to the program. One misguided event on the show was having an 8', 600-pound bear who, in front of the cameras, grew weary of his trainer and tossed him twenty feet.

The trainer blacked out, but, to everyone's relief, revived in time to drag the bear off. After one year of airing locally, "The Mike Douglas Show" turned to national syndication. Then with twenty stations aboard, the program embarked on its first remote broadcasts. One of the initial ones was a trek to Irish Boston with Pat O'Brien as co-host. By 1964, Douglas was able to attract bigger name stars. For example, Bette Davis was in Cleveland promoting her new film and he lured her onto the program. She thought she was being honored with a special award, but instead (as a practical joke) it went to actress Gloria DeHaven. Davis roared, "Who's the son-of-a-bitch who thought that up?" She loved it!

By early 1965, the syndicated "The Mike Douglas Show" had risen from 47 stations to 60. However, by mid year the Federal Communications Commission and the Department of Justice decreed that Westinghouse Broadcasting (which owned the station where Mike produced his program and also distributed the show) and the NBC network-owned TV station in Philadelphia should switch locations. As a result, it evolved that Douglas's program would relocate to Philadelphia to station KYW-TV. The transition occurred in August 1965, with the first live Pennsylvania airing on August 30th. (The night before there had been a half-hour prime-time local TV special, "Here's Mike.")

GROWING MATURITY

Effusive vocalist Vic Damone was the co-host the first Philadelphia week. With the program's new proximity to Manhattan, Douglas was able to draw on a lot more New York City and Washington, D.C. talent/celebrities. Meanwhile, having learned their lessons about overextending themselves financially, the Douglases purchased a modest $10,000 suburban home in Radnor, Pennsylvania.

By now "The Mike Douglas Show" had given up airing live even in its home base city. This decision was the result of having Zsa Zsa Gabor on his program one day. She got furious with comedian Morey Amsterdam for his re-telling a joke she had botched a few minutes earlier. She called Amsterdam a "son of a bitch" and added other profanities. Mike warned Gabor that if she uttered one more foul word he would remove her. She said he would not dare. He retorted, "Try me!" She behaved. But that was the end of live sessions.

It was said frequently that, while Douglas was relaxed and boyish on camera, he, backed by the strong influence of Genevieve, could be extremely demanding of staff workers off camera. In January 1967, the program went to color and, a few months later, Mike won an Emmy for "outstanding individual achievement in daytime programming." (He would be renominated in 1973 and 1974.)

Newsweek magazine endorsed that Mike's show was "for the housewife who's interested in serious things." (While Mike could be credited with having Ralph Nader on his show in Nader's first TV forum for his battle with General Motors, Douglas was just as prone to showcase comedians like fussy Billy De Wolfe, the latter with his trademark mincing words, "messy desk, means messy underwear." Another funster given a big build-up on Mike's series was comedian Totie Fields.

DING DING

About this time, a national news wire service reported, "Philadelphia is famous for two things, the Liberty Bell and Mike Douglas...they're both cracked. You can see it clearly on the bell and you can figure it out about Douglas when you learn that after winning an Emmy and very wide viewer acceptance with his afternoon show, he chose to remain in Philadelphia instead of heading for Hollywood where the wells-spring of stars is constantly a-bubbling." Obviously, by now Douglas was feeling very secure in off-the-track Philadelphia where he was the big/only media attraction in town (in contrast to his TV genre competition in New York City which included such major players as Johnny Carson, Merv Griffin, and soon Dick Cavett and David Frost)

In 1967 the Douglases moved into a 31-room Tudor-style stone mansion originally built in 1930 at a cost of $1 million. The fourteen-acre estate was situated atop a hill in suburban Gladwyne, twenty minutes from downtown Philadelphia. As part of the extensive renovations to the manse, Mike and Genevieve had a swimming pool imported from Italy. Clearly, the Douglases were in Philadelphia to stay. A few years later, they would acquire a Society Hill apartment in a high-rise near Philadelphia's KYW-TV; this in addition to a golf place near Lost Tree, Florida and a condo at Jupiter Beach, Florida, and a later elaborate home built as part of Florida's mammoth Bonaventure development in Broward County.

In February 1968, Douglas was supposed to go to Rome to play a priest, the founder of Boys Towns in Italy, but the movie project fell through. In June 1969, as part of Mike's 1,500th show, his old boss, Kay Kyser, taped a surprise message for the program. In September of that

Maurice Chevalier crosses swords with Mike Douglsa on the latter's TV talk show.

year, Mike's brother Bob was suffering from terminal cancer in Berwyn, Illinois. Rushing to the hospital to visit their dying son, Mr. and Mrs. Dowd were injured in a car accident. When Mike arrived to see his older brother, Mrs. Dowd herself was a patient on another floor of the same hospital. (Mrs. Dowd would die of cancer in the mid-1970s; Mr. Dowd would pass away in 1979.)

By the early 1970s, "The Mike Douglas Show" was reaching the zenith of its popularity, still drawing viewers with its wide variety of co-hosts ranging from Buddy Hackett to Ono and John Lennon. (A favorite gimmick theme on the program was "Stars and Their Moms.") When Douglas hosted his show on location from Miami he got Jackie Gleason to end a three-year TV sabbatical by co-hosting for a week. "The Fat One" had so much fun, he stayed for an unprecedented second week of co-hosting.

ANYTHING GOES

Mike was expert at inspiring co-hosts and guests to do the unexpected: e.g., Julie Nixon Eisenhower as part of a bicycle act, Chubby "Lets Do the Twist" Checker making his debut as a dramatic actor, Arlene Francis introduced as a trombone player, etc. Expanding on his celebrity status, Mike performed a club act at Las Vegas and Lake Tahoe casinos for six-figure salaries, repeating many of the songs he had sung on the air and in his four LP albums, including his biggest hit "The Men in My Little Girl's Life." In 1972, he was named the "Television Father of the Year."

Commenting on Douglas's persona as comfortable and bland, at the May 1972 Emmy Awards, Johnny Carson said of his rival, "He's as indigenous to Philadelphia as cream cheese—and about as funny." Carson added, "We had to get Mike on early tonight, because 10:30 is his beddytime." But Douglas could afford to laugh at such jibes; audiences had to wait fourteen weeks for tickets to his show.

At the peak of his success, Mike signed a new five-year contract with Westinghouse in March 1973. The lucrative deal provided him with a $2 million yearly salary, plus $6 million for Mike Douglas Enterprises projects. (This led Johnny Carson to quip on air, "The price of Philadelphia cream cheese has gone up.") Despite his affluent status, Douglas still loved low-brow sight gags on his program. In January 1974 on his annual Florida excursion, co-host Burt Reynolds was asked to be a human chopping block.

A blindfolded kung fu expert chopped watermelon over Reynolds' stomach. Later in the year, to boost ratings further, Mike and his talk show traveled around the continental U.S. and to Hawaii, and ended that October by going to the Soviet Union. While on one segment he might have the husband-and-wife team of Masters and Johnson discussing sex research, Douglas was just as likely on camera to play polo on Philadelphia's Walnut Street with Zsa Zsa Gabor, get into a boxing ring with Muhammad Ali, do tag team wrestling with Jerry Lewis, allow an elephant to put its foot on Mike's dome, take part in an ostrich race, go scuba diving with frogmen in Puerto Rico or venture into a bullring with a bull. On a more "serious" note, Douglas was prone to randomly calling up strangers, during the course of a show, to say "I love you."

STARTING TO SLIP

The watershed mark for "The Mike Douglas Show" was 1975. By now the portly entertainer was in a larger, refurbished studio at the Philadelphia headquarters, and acknowledged as one of the city's major tourist attractions. Having survived an appendectomy early in the year, he was now feeling the brunt of the TV talk show wars. His base of 180 station outlets in 1969 had fallen to 130 and was still dropping, due to the popularity of such new syndicated daytime shows as Dinah Shore's "Dinah!" Douglas tried to be more substantial on some programs, as when, in September 1975, he had co-host Eddie Fisher (a Philadelphian back in town) talking candidly about his problems with drugs, gambling and three wives. Another somber occasion was the time Tony Orlando discussed his manic depression on air.

There was also a serious note in Douglas's private life. The seesawing friction with daughter Chris (which had begun when she had married over her parents' objections) had been alleviated over the years as she gave birth to four children. However, the prolonged singleness of daughter Michele, who was living in Florida and teaching grade school, greatly upset her parents. Mike's business activities now included real estate deals in Florida, while Genevieve continued to participate heavily (sometimes to the TV show staff's distraction) with his contracts, wardrobe, show themes, etc.

In 1975, as a favor to pal Burt Reynolds, Mike had played a cameo as a southern governor in GATOR, an action feature starring and directed by Reynolds. The next year, Mike did a guest appearance as himself interviewing a character on his show for NASTY HABITS, a movie satire starring Sandy Dennis and Melina Mercouri. It was also in 1976 that Legionnaire's disease struck at the city's Bellevue Stratford Hotel killing 29 guests. Douglas recalls "We had co-hosts cancelling left and right. I mean nobody wanted to come to Philadelphia."

In 1978, Mike authored his autobiography, *My Story*, aided by Carroll Carroll. By mid-year, with ratings slipping further, Mike Douglas acceded to the inevitable. The last Philadelphia taping was on July 27, 1978. Following belatedly in the path of Johnny Carson, Merv Griffin, et al, he moved the show to Los Angeles. At least now, he said, when a scheduled guest cancelled at the last minute, he could walk into such places as the Polo Lounge, and find a celebrity replacement. Due to its relocation, the program seemed rejuvenated and ratings once again soared, which led Westinghouse to propose a new lucrative five-year contract.

NOTHING LASTS FOREVER

However, the honeymoon was short-lived. By 1980, Westinghouse had decided that Douglas was drawing a much-too elderly viewing audience. They summarily dropped Douglas in favor of far younger singer/actor John Davidson and began syndicating "The John Davidson Show" (which itself lasted less than two years).

Unbowed, at least publicly, Mike transferred his daily talk show to Syndicast for distribution. With ragged ratings, in the fall of 1981, the program was revamped into "The Mike Douglas Entertainment Hour." The new premise was only to have guests who were comedians, singers or dancers. When this did not boost ratings, Douglas left the expensive Hollywood TV studios and took the show on the road to Las Vegas, Cleveland, etc. Nevertheless, after 26 weeks "The Mike Douglas Entertainment Hour" faded and Douglas and Syndicast Services part-ed ways.

Thereafter, Mike negotiated with Ted Turner of superstation WTBS in Atlanta for a new lease on talk show life. Under the next new format Mike was only to host 25% of the shows, others to be emceeded by Bill Cosby, Steve Kalaley (of TV's "Dallas") et al. However, the two strong-willed men could not come to terms and negotiations ended. With a great deal of free time, Mike decided to his return to his career of old, singing, and cut an album of "oldie" songs.

After so many years in the limelight, Mike Douglas disappeared from the show business scene, retreating into his private life. In May 1992 he made a brief flurry in the industry when he emerged to sue Westinghouse Broadcasting, Co., Inc. and its Group W Prods. Inc. in Los Angeles Superior Court. He alleged the defendants failed to properly promote the old "The Mike Douglas Show" in the resyndication market, as well as citing the defendants for reputedly losing or damaging tapes to his series.

THE NATURAL LOOK

Even though Mike Douglas and his long-running talk show is now nostalgia, future talk show hosts could learn a lot about his rules of the game. He once said, "I don't watch myself on tele-vision-and for a reason. I don't want to become what I call a studied performer. I might not like my walk, or some gesture, or something. Since I've been successful as I am, I want to keep it that way."

On another occasion, he observed about the art of being a talk show host: "The trick is making it look easy—and it isn't an easy job. The hard thing is you can never expect it be the same any two days in a row. We do research; we sit down and decide what to say to the guests, but that seldom happens—you have to use your own built-in whatever-you-call-it.... I can sense—this may sound egocentric—but I have an antenna for the type of audiences. I think the audience changes, not the performance...."

TV & CABLE SERIES:

Kay Kyser's Kollege of Musical Knowledge (NBC, 1949-1950)
The Mike Douglas Show (Oklahoma City local, 1952)
Luncheon Party (Chicago local, 1953)
Hi Ladies (Chicago local, 1953-1955)
The Music Show (Dumont, 1953-1954)
Club 60 (NBC, 1957-1958)
The Mike Douglas Show (Cleveland local, 1961-1963)
The Mike Douglas Show (Syndicated, 1963-1981)
The Mike Douglas Entertainment Hour (Syndicated, 1981-1982)

FEATURE FILMS:

Cinderella (1950) [voice only]
Gator (1975)
Nasty Habits (1976)

Chapter 4
VIRGINIA GRAHAM

The evolution of American television would not have been the same without zesty, one-of-a-kind Virginia Graham. She is the first person to admit, "I'm a very strong personality. When I walk into a room, there's no question that I've walked in. I don't have to open my mouth. I'm there."

Caftan-loving Virginia Graham rose from the 1950s media trenches to host the network teleseries, "Girl Talk" (1962-1969), a forerunner of the intimate TV talk show. This self-assertive Jewish housewife turned a knack for gabbiness and story-telling into a national institution. She demonstrated, with the aid of her program guests, that the "fair sex" were intellectually and emotionally far more complex and sophisticated than pre-women's lib society had ever admitted or permitted. (It was the same anti-chauvinist thesis that Phil Donahue would promote on his TV talk show in the later 1960s and continue right up to today.)

Full-figured, perky Virginia had tremendous appeal for viewers attracted by her ability to chat on the air about the serious

The Virginia Graham of today.

and the trivial (some said drivel!). At a moment's notice this nothing-is-sacred individual would sound off on any subject. En route, she displayed a wonderful sense of humor and a deep knowledge of human nature. On her show, she was a mix of catalyst, referee and censor, but always a congenial, vigorous hostess. Depending whether one was pro or anti-Virginia, she was outspoken or opinionated, boisterous or obnoxious, sincere or calculating, unabashed or naive. However, everyone agreed that this vivacious personality loved people, understood all types of women very well, and never, never was at a loss for words.

One of the greatest attributes of a talk show host is the ability to put any type of guest at ease; to make the subject relaxed enough to confide to viewers intimate thoughts on a wide range of

Virginia Graham with her daughter Lynn and her grandchild.

topics. Virginia had been doing this all her life. Even after her second TV talk show ("The Virginia Graham Show") faded in 1973, she continued in the limelight as a multi-media celebrity personality (motion pictures, summer stock, TV soap opera star, author, lecturer, talk show circuit favorite, etc.) Full of self-confidence, boundless energy and the courage to rise above personal tragedies, Virginia Graham has long been a role model for many Americans. When asked once about her dynamic personality, she replied, "I was absolutely not born with cool. I developed it."

THE ROOTS

She was born Virginia Komiss in Chicago on July 4, 1913. Her father, David Stanley Komiss, was Prussian-born and came to the U.S. at the age of thirteen with $13 sewed into the lining of his jacket. He later migrated on foot to Kansas City, Kansas selling needles, thread and buttons. Eventually, he rose to become a Chicago businessman who owned a chain of women's clothing stores.

Her mother, Bessie Jane (Feiges) Komiss was a native of Chicago and, like David, was the youngest of eleven children. At birth, Virginia weighed ten to twelve pounds, an indication that in adulthood she would be tall (5'8") and big-boned ("zaftig"). She was preceded in birth by brother Justin, who was 21 months older than she. Graham would recall later of her father: "He was a deeply religious man and used to read me Bible stories when I was a little girl. He was interested in music and art, and we used to go to concerts and museums together." (One of Virginia's grandparents was Rabbi Joseph Ben Benjamin, who presided over Temple Sinai in Chicago.)

Pampered by her upper middle-class family, Virginia was breast-fed till the age of five. At ten, the budding talent wrote a one-act play, "Shadows," which won the youngster a lot of publicity, including a spread in the Chicago *Tribune*. It was also in this year that she contracted typhoid fever. Although she recovered quickly, her illness would lead to delayed medical repercussions later in life. She attended the private Francis Parker School in Chicago, where, because of her size, she twice skipped grades.

She once recalled, "As a matter of fact, I've often felt like a female impersonator because in school I took all the male leads." At school dances, she was always the lead partner because of her height, causing her to refer to her short escorts as her "navel" cadets. During the summers, the Komiss family frequently took extended trips and, in 1928, they made a grand tour of continental North America, including stop-overs in Los Angeles and Banff.

A TIMELY MURDER

In 1929, her last year of high school, Virginia won a temporary cub reportership on the *Chicago Tribune* by describing in 25 words or less why she loved Abraham Lincoln. On Valentine's Day that year, she was in the classroom when she heard gunshots nearby. She and several classmates rushed outside to investigate. At a nearby garage they came across the results of the St. Valentine's Day massacre. Graham rushed to a pay phone and was the first to call in the story to the *Tribune*. As a reward, she was given a byline to her news story.

Because at 16 she was still too young for college, she was sent to National Park Seminary, a finishing school in Forest Glen, Maryland. One of her classmates was the future screen star, Margaret Lindsay, while another was Doris Warner, whose father, Jack, was head of Warner Bros. Pictures. At National Park, Virginia edited the school's newspaper, and thrived on a curriculum which included not only proper etiquette, but such practical items as secretarial courses. In this period, the already-rebellious Virginia bleached her dark brown hair to blonde, and trimmed down her full figure.

After the seminary, Virginia studied briefly at the University of Chicago, taking accelerated courses, majoring in anthropology and being elected to Phi Beta Kappa. In 1931, her father, like a multitude of others, was wiped out financially by the Depression. To help support the household, Virginia took a job selling cleansing cream and cosmetics door-to-door. In the midst of this, she had an operation to remove an ovarian cyst which had developed years before as a result of her bout of typhoid fever. In the course of the surgery, she had a partial hysterectomy and the physicians said the likelihood of her ever having children was extremely remote. She was eighteen at the time.

By 1934, gregarious, resourceful Virginia was helping a friend gather votes for an alderman on the Democratic ticket. This effort led to her first office job, in the Illinois branch of the Federal Home Loan Administration where she read quit-claim deeds all day. By the age of 21, she was earning a then-impressive $125 weekly. She had also embarked on a modeling career, posing for fashion and advertising photos, which, in turn, led to a brief foray as a fashion reporter on Chicago radio station WBBM. Meanwhile she enrolled at Northwestern University to study journalism and speech.

WHEN HARRY MET VIRGINIA

In the fall of 1935, Virginia traveled East to visit a National Park classmate, who had married and lived on Long Island. While there, she met 34-year-old Harry William Guttenberg, whose grandfather had started the theatrical costume firm of Louis Guttenberg & Sons in 1869. After a two-week courtship, Harry proposed. (Years later, Virginia recounted, "When we fell in love, I told him we could never have children, and he said, 'Isn't that amazing, you've never asked me if I could father a child. How do you know I can?' I thought that was the most marvelous thing I ever heard and it showed me what a special person he was.") The next May, the couple married in New York City and went on a honeymoon cruise to Central America. Almost immediately, Virginia became pregnant and, on February 7, 1937 gave birth to Lynn Karen. Now a mother, Virginia abandoned her budding writing career, reasoning "My writing was great as a child. But then I grew up and my writing didn't.... It lacked realism."

After a year of professional inactivity, through family friends, Virginia was hired by Manhattan radio station WMCA to write commercials (reportedly she developed the first dramatized commercials ever utilized in the medium). She was paid $75 weekly for her work which she accomplished at home. Then she was promoted to ghost writing for ex-silent movie star Mae Murray who was doing an advice-to-the-lovelorn radio show.

When that assignment concluded, Graham turned to writing a local radio cooking show, performing as "Betty Baker." Not expert about the culinary arts, she once provided an on-the-air recipe for muffins filled with baked beans, forgetting to warn listeners to pour off the bean juice first. As a result, countless ovens were wrecked. By 1939, when her WMCA tenure ended, the Guttenbergs were renting a home in Great Neck, Long Island.

When a fire broke out at the Guttenbergs' home, it had been Red Cross volunteers who came to the rescue. In gratitude, civic-minded Virginia joined the Red Cross Motor Corps in the pre-Pearl Harbor days. She helped to replace male drivers who were going off to military duty. When the U.S. entered World War II in late 1941, Harry was exempt from the draft because of his age and bad back.

CIVIC DUTY

Virginia felt obligated to work twice as hard as a Red Cross worker, and never once turned down an assignment. She rose to the rank of master sergeant in the motor corps, additionally serving as a first aid instructor. Known as "Sunshine," she later received a citation for her wartime duties from the commander of the Army Air Forces at Mitchell Field, on Long Island, where she was based.

In 1947, while visiting her ailing father in Phoenix, Arizona, she had her own medical checkup and hospital doctors advised her she should have a hysterectomy or she would surely develop cancer. While back in New York City having a Paps smear (which indicated that surgery was not necessary), she learned that her dad had died at age 74. It was about this time that she began working for United Cerebral Palsy, spurred on by two friends in Great Neck who had Cerebral Palsy children. (As one of the founding forces of this charity, Graham would be a tireless organizer for the cause and appeared at countless charity benefits and telethons around the country. Later she also became an active fundraiser for Muscular Dystrophy.)

About this time, Virginia's life took a new direction through one of her sister-in-laws who was married to an eastern sales representative for the Bonat Company (which manufactured beauty products/hair dryers, etc.) Vivacious, gregarious Graham was asked to speak at the International Beauty Show, an annual trade fest in New York City. The day before her emceeing chore, she lunched at Billy Reed's Little Club in Manhattan. There a fortune teller predicted that Virginia would be "a great woman in the world of entertainment."

The crystal ball gazer suggested that she change her surname. Ever-practical Virginia chose "Graham" since her towels at home were monogrammed "V.G." As a footnote, the fortune teller mentioned that Virginia would suffer from a fatal disease, but survive. (It was the same prognosis a predictor had made when Virginia was nine.)

ONE THING LEADS TO ANOTHER

So successful was her Beauty Show hosting, that she repeated the chore for four years in succession. In 1950, the trade show's public relations man contacted Dave Garroway of NBC's "Today Show" and said he had a bright woman who could speak of the new look in women's beauty. Virginia went on the network TV show for ten minutes instructing viewers on how a woman must look to hold a man. Her patter set Garroway and studio technicians to laughing. Two months later, when Garroway was on vacation, she was asked to host the show for a week. Only later did she realize, "I pushed too hard, irritated everyone, and when the week was over, I'm sure everyone connected with the program was enchanted to see me go."

Never long out of the limelight, Virginia next hosted a millinery fashion show for Cerebral Palsy on Ed Herlihy's local TV program. An NBC executive saw her devastate the fashion parade with her witticism on hats and asked her to make a pilot for a cooking show. However, no advertisers were willing to sponsor this TV show concept.

On June 13, 1951, Virginia had a "d and c" to abort a problematic pregnancy. When she awoke after the surgery, doctors told her they had found cancer and that she had better "get her house in order." When her doting husband Harry heard the bad news, he fainted. It was the start of Guttenberg's long, deep depression. The day before her scheduled new surgery, Graham was of two minds. She contemplated suicide; then on a more optimistic note, she went A.W.O.L. from Presbyterian Hospital.

Escorted by a nurse, she taxied to Larry Matthews fashionable hair salon to have her coiffure re-dyed and styled. On June 21st (her mother's birthday) she awakened from her latest operation. The prognosis was good, although she had to endure 35 deep chemotherapy treatments as a preventative follow-up. (It was not until five years later that her doctors officially gave Virginia a clean bill of health. It was a stressful period: "The only way to live under a suspended sentence of death is to live from day to day. I had to vow to myself I would live through 24 hours without thinking about the cancer, and at the end of one 24 hour cycle renew my vow for the next.")

TOO MUCH TO TAKE

In September 1951, Harry's costume shop was gutted when another firm in the building had the structure arsoned. The loss devastated the emotionally fragile Harry and he had to be institutionalized for two months. While he was undergoing shock treatment, Virginia rented new premises on West 45th for Harry's costume business and got his operation running again. During this time, Graham also had to be the sole parent to her daughter. "For her sake I had to be a cheerful and reassuring mother; she needed the security of positive thinking on my part."

At a party, during the late fall of 1951, Graham re-met Zeke Manners, who had had a WMCA radio program back in 1937 when she worked for the same station. He now had a daily chatter/variety show ("Zeke Manners & His Beverly Hillbillies") on WJZ (later WABC)-TV. He invited Virginia to be a guest on the program, then soon hired her as a regular at $100 weekly. The assignment lasted six months, until the AFTRA union demanded that she be paid $800 a week. The outcome of this was her being fired from the program. She rebounded by being hired by the Dumont TV network to host the daytime show, "Food for Thought" (1952-1957).

Additionally, she could be heard over late night radio on WABC doing an interview/variety program in 1953-1954. Never idle, she also was a regular on the TV quiz show "Where Was I?" (1953). In mid-1954, she emceed Dumont's "Summer in the Park," an hour variety show which was an extended plug for Palisades Amusement Park in New Jersey.

As a result of being the lively subject of a February 1956 episode of TV's "This Is Your Life," NBC network executives hired Virginia to replace Margaret Truman on the national radio show, "Weekday." Her co-host, Mike Wallace, resented his female co-worker and played all sorts of pranks on her on the air. One day, during a broadcast, Virginia retaliated by launching into a tirade against his non-stop jibing at her. In mid-stream, she broke into hysterical laughter. This was her tit-for-tat prank. It was the last time he played jokes on her and they quickly became pals. She remained with the program from February to July 1956.

SPEAKING OUT

Virginia made her feature film debut in A FACE IN THE CROWD (1957), starring Andy Griffith. She was in a Sardi's Restaurant scene, seated with Faye Emerson. She was not supposed to have any dialogue, but on the spot, irrepressible Graham blurted out, "Water on the rocks, please." For her impromptu dialogue, the producer sent her a dozen American Beauty roses, with the thorns still attached. The Guttenbergs now owned a cooperative apartment in Manhattan across the street from the Metropolitan Museum of Art.

One day as a hostess of a fashion show, when a model became indisposed, Graham regaled the audience with jokes. Cafe society voyeur Elsa Maxwell was there and, when next on Jack Paar's TV talk show, Maxwell reported on the amusing Virginia. This led Paar to inviting Graham on the "Tonight Show" where she became a frequent, favorite guest, and she even hosted the program briefly two years later.

The year 1961 was a turning point for Virginia. She was host of a radio show, "At Home with Virginia Graham." In June, the Guttenbergs' daughter was married. That summer, to celebrate their 25th anniversary, Virginia and Harry took a European tour. When they returned, Graham talked her way into a post with Clairol beauty products as a spokesperson. Whenever she traveled, the always-possessive Harry traveled with her, handling the business/travel arrangements. (In later years, he would handle her fan mail, responding to all correspondence in her name, and always including high praise for her "beloved, wonderful husband.") The ultra closeness of the Guttenbergs led one of Graham's sister-in-laws to observe, "Virginia. You haven't changed at all [over the years], but Harry has become Virginia Graham!"

Carol Channing, Virginia Graham, and her husband, Harry Guttenberg, in 1963.

In the fall of 1961, ABC-TV asked Virginia to do a pilot for a TV show similar to David Susskind's long-running syndicated talk show "Open End." The test entry was done with entertainer Abbe Lane and novelist Rona Jaffe discussing with host Virginia the topic "Can a Younger Woman Fall in Love with an Older Man?" A year later, the network half-hour program went on the air. The segments were taped in Manhattan before live audiences and always in the evening, because Graham insisted women talk better at night.

WILD AND WACKY

Never using cue cards, facile conversationalist Virginia thrived on bizarre combinations of female guests, such as Margaret Truman with Jolie Gabor. Although her show often emerged as fluff punctuated with confrontations between conflicting guests, Graham frequently invited meaningful women from the political and journalistic arenas to appear on the program. *Variety* would report, "Ringleader Virginia Graham, an ample, jolly femme with blonde hair teased into a mountain, seems to have a strong instinct for the gossip that will give the sunshine viewers their kicks, and under the joviality, she firmly steers the conversation into areas of her choosing."

Among the notable celebrity guests on "Girl Talk" (1962-1969) were Joan Crawford, Barbara Walters, Phyllis Diller, Merle Oberon, Jessica Tandy, Rosemary Clooney, Ann Landers and Joan Rivers. Occasionally, Virginia would travel on location for a program, as when she flew to Rome to interview the granddaughter of Mahatma Gandhi. On one program, Virginia had Madame Nehru of India as a guest, along with columnist Cindy Adams. Adams kept answering every question, even those directed to Mrs. Nehru about her homeland. At the end of the gab fest, tart-tongued Virginia said on air, "Thank you, Madame Nehru. You must come back again with Cindy, so she can tell you more about your country."

Never one to be idle, even while hosting a major daily talk show, Virginia played a columnist in the feature film, THE CARPETBAGGERS (1964), toured in summer stock with "Late Love" and "Butterflies Are Free" and wrote her first autobiography, *There Goes What's Her Name* (1965). Now a grandmother, she also contributed a column, "Under the Dryer" for a trade magazine distributed to 100,000 beauty shops. These columns led to a beauty tips book, *Don't Blame the Mirror* (1967).

In 1968, her brother Justin died of a heart attack in Houston, Texas (where their 84-year-old mother was residing in a nursing home). Graham toured with stock productions of "Dear Me, the Sky Is Falling" and "The Crocodile and the Cockeyed Moose." In her "spare" time, she was a volunteer fundraiser for the American Cancer Society. In early 1969, when it was decreed to add male panelists on some "Girl Talk" shows, Virginia objected and dropped out of the series, replaced by Betsy Palmer and Gloria DeHaven. (One of the lasting results of Virginia's innovative "Girl Talk," was to give a new and positive connotation to the TV industry's term "women's programming.")

NOTHING SACRED

Although temporarily without her own TV show forum, Virginia continued to be one of America's most outspoken persons. Her trademarked frankness even caused experienced talk show host Merv Griffin to gasp on air one day in early 1970 when she was a guest on his TV talk program. The occasion occurred shortly after she had undergone cosmetic surgery to remove the bags from under her eyes, etc.

Merv: "Virginia, you look simply wonderful."

Virginia: "I should. I just had my face done."

Merv: "You what!.... I can't believe you're saying this. Here you are in front of 25 million people...."

Virginia: "Is that your rating, Merv? That's wonderful!"

Merv: "How can you admit it?"

Virginia: "I'll tell you the truth, Merv. If a few of you men would look in the mirror, you'd get the name of my doctor."

Graham's rejuvenated look was in preparation for launching her new syndicated TV talk show, "The Virginia Graham Show [Virginia Graham Talks]." The 90-minute (60-minutes in some markets) program which debuted in the summer of 1970, had politically radical Jane Fonda as one of her first guests. This led *Variety* to observe of "the former 'Girl Talk' gabber': "The Graham show is apparently going to reach out for controversial people, with queries from the studio inserted practically all of the time.... Miss Graham let the proceedings turn into a circus, which raised all kind of questions—and answered none." The series was taped in Los Angeles and lasted for three years, often shown in prime time around the country. However, it never gained the momentum of the earlier "Girl Talk."

The mid-1970s really tested Virginia's resiliency. Hardly had the Guttenbergs moved back to Manhattan and redone their cooperative apartment, then it was destroyed in a fire. In September 1974, the Gutterbergs' son-in-law, Sy, a stock market executive, developed cancer of the jaw. He was operated on, but 22 months later the disease reactivated and he died in 1977, leaving his widow and two children. To keep active, and to help replenish the family finances, Virginia continued her theatre touring ("Irene," "Any Wednesday," "Catch Me If You Can"), did the PBS-TV movie "A Secret Place" (1973) and wrote her second autobiography, *If I Made It, So Can You* (1978). From July 1978 to January 1979 she was a regular contributor on the NBC-TV daytime magazine show, "America Alive!", providing gossip and interview segments.

ON HER OWN

All through the 1970s, Virginia's husband had been in declining physical health. For the last two years of his life, he was confined to the Actors' Home in Englewood, New Jersey. Whenever she was not on the road, she visited him there twice weekly and phoned him twice daily. She admitted later there was "a lot of guilt" over hospitalizing him, but acknowledged that it was the best and only thing to do, especially since he seemed happy to be surrounded at the facility by fellow show business people.

In October 1980, Graham was performing in "My Daughter, Your Son" in Maryland when she received word that Harry was dying. He had been on dialysis for some weeks. She had to take a train (because she could not book a plane reservation at the last minute). By the time she reached the New Jersey hospital, his room had been filled with new patients as he had died. Only in reading through his personal papers, did she discover that Harry had lied about his age and was actually two years older than he had ever told her.

In typical fashion, Virginia fought to rebound from the trauma of losing her mate. Despite her maturity (as she phrased it, she "was on her third set of teeth") she was not ready to call it quits emotionally. She decided to have a major face lift because "my ego was feeling particularly in need of a boost." She moved from the Fifth Avenue coop where she and Harry had lived for eighteen years. ("I realized I was living with too many things of the past, so I threw them out and sold everything. Now, I'm making new memories.")

Above all, she went back to work in 1982. She played matron Stella Stanton on the NBC-TV daytime soap opera, "Texas," and also appeared in the feature film SLAPSTICK OF ANOTHER KIND with Jerry Lewis and Madeline Kahn, which received limited release in 1984. During that year she promoted a potential new cable TV program, "Growing Young" which was rejected by the networks as well. Despite this setback she continued lecturing around the country, doing charity fundraising chores, appearing briefly on ABC-TV's soap "All My Children" and keeping active.

A TRUE SURVIVOR

Her third autobiographical installment, *Life After Harry: My Adventures in Widowhood* (1988), was based on the premise: "Today I am a happy woman...a downright merry widow. I hope this book helps in a small way to open up that chance for you." She philosophized in the book: "You'll never stop remembering, but it's my belief that the greatest respect you can pay your deceased spouse is to go on living." The volume provided self-help tips including "The 10 Amendments for Widows" and offered sex advice: "If arthritis make some positions uncomfortable, try another. Be creative...."

Graham promoted the book on an extensive national tour. One of her many TV talk show appearances was on The Nashville Network's "Nashville Now." This led to her doing five one-hour talk shows for the cable network. Called "Virginia Graham: Never a Dull Moment," the programs were taped at her upper east side Manhattan apartment (decorated in shades of optimistic pink) and featured interviews with soap stars, home shoppers, achievers, etc.

Having survived a bad hip in recent years, Virginia still does "reruns" on the lecture circuit. In a reflective tone, she has admitted of her TV talk show career that her greatest ambition "always was to be a friend, a listening ear to the women of America." She is very outspoken about today's crop of talk show programs, insisting, "I don't believe you have to tell everything. I am very upset about public declarations about private affairs." She does acknowledge a partiality for Phil Donahue and his brand of talk show hosting.

With her spare time, the financially-secure celebrity thrives on impulse shopping and being extravagant with her daughter as well as her own friends. Still glib with one-liners, chipper Virginia concedes that her hair tone is not natural, "but my blonde personality was there all the time." On a more serious note, she confesses, "I may not be as happy without a man, but I'm content." She advises widows, "Look in the mirror and say, 'This is for me. Today, is my turn.'"

TV & CABLE SERIES:

Zeke Manners & His Beverly Hillbillies (New York City local, 1951-1952)
Virginia Graham and Food for Thought (Dumont, 1952-1957)
Where Was I? (Dumont, 1952)
Summer in the Park (Dumont, 1954)
Girl Talk (ABC, 1962-1969)
The Virginia Graham Show [Virginia Graham Talks] (Syndicated, 1970-1973)
America Alive! (NBC, 1978-1979)
Texas (NBC, 1982)

FEATURE FILMS:

A Face in the Crowd (1957)
The Carpetbaggers (1964)
A Secret Place (PBS, 1973) [TV movie]
Slapstick of Another Kind (1984) [made in 1982]

Merv Griffin interviewing guests (Don Rickles, Rose Kennedy and Harry Belafonte) on "The Merv Griffin Show" in the late 1960s.

Chapter 5
MERV GRIFFIN

In the 1970s, Johnny Carson once joked of his then TV talk-show rival, "Only three things in this world are certain. Death, taxes and Merv Griffin going 'Oooh!'" This was in reference to gee-whiz Griffin's growing habit through his years of TV hosting of being overly solicitous to his pampered chatter show guests. Years later, genre expert Larry King noted of Griffin: "I think he has come to rely too much on a steady stream of show-biz chitchat. He doesn't have that pleasing, slightly skeptical edge he once had." Despite these accurate observations, by the time "The Merv Griffin Show" faded from syndication in 1986, this self-styled "constant companion to housewives" had been shepherding celebrity notables on and off his show for three decades. Obviously, Merv knew exactly what he was doing in the highly competitive talk show arena.

Critic Kenneth Tynan characterized Griffin as "the most disarming of ego strokers." Merv smartly summed up his responsibilities in the field with: "My job is to get the best interview out of a guest, to find out what he's about, to be an X-ray machine, to ask the kind of questions the audience would ask if they could get their hands on the guest. I'm a catalyst, a traffic cop. Sometimes I play confidant to my guest to draw him out. Sometimes, I'm the devil's advocate. Sometimes I take him by surprise by being guileless, by asking him everything."

There are many facets to the complex individual known as Merv Griffin. Several of them are far afield from his easy-going persona as a talk show maven, a man who is best known to the viewing public as a "hip choir boy," "a sophisticated wit" and "the perennial boy-next door." Actually, a mid-1980s *TV Guide* profile of perfectionist Griffin pointed out, "His whole life has been about ambition, talent, gaining entrance to the power elite and having fun. And to those ends he has fashioned many masks."

A few decades earlier, his then wife, Julann had described Merv as "The staff of life—sort of like whole wheat toast." Twenty years later his now ex-spouse would comment, "I have never heard anyone say no to Merv." Peter Barsocchini, his show producer, would exclaim, "Merv would be a great guy to be around if there was a disaster, a war, if everything was destroyed in the village, Merv could figure out a way to get things going...."

MORE THAN MEETS THE EYE

During Griffin's many decades in show business, he rose from big band singer to movie studio contract player to TV game show host to the long-running star of several editions of his video gab fast. The public knew that he had developed and produced two of the most enormously successful TV game shows ("Jeopardy" and "Wheel of Fortune"), not to mention such popular TV entries as "Dance Fever." However, few home viewers were aware of the tremendous empire Merv had created by the mid-1980s through sharp business acumen and a killer instinct.

By then, his activities had moved from the entertainment pages of newspapers to the financial section. Here, readers saw the man who, in the late 1980s, battled successfully mega entrepreneur Donald Trump over resort casinos in Atlantic City and the Bahamas. Griffin's on-going big business wheeling and dealing led to his being dubbed "The Singing Billionaire." It caused him to quip, "I'm not a corporate raider. I am simply a man who constantly looks for new challenges." That he does.

Mervyn Edward Griffin, Jr. was born on July 6, 1925 in San Mateo, California, the second child (there was a two-year-older sister Barbara) of Mervyn, Sr. and his wife Rita (Robinson) Griffin. Mr. Griffin came from a long line of tennis champs, including his brother, the well-known player, Peck Griffin. By the time, Merv, Jr. was born, his 24-year-old dad had given up the tennis circuit to be a tennis pro.

In the 1929 Depression, the Griffins lost their house and had to move in with Rita's mother at her San Mateo house. The Robinson side of the family were all amateur singers/musicians. Sunday afternoons would be spent around the piano. Rita's sister, Claudia, who also lived there, taught young Merv to play the piano (and he later learned to play the pipe organ). This skill was kept secret from Merv, Sr. till Merv was fourteen and happened to play at a birthday party. Everyone was afraid that ultra sports-minded Merv, Sr., who now worked in a sporting goods shop, would object.

EARLY ENTREPRENEUR

By age eight, Merv was demonstrating his love of gossip. He published his own neighborhood newspaper, *Whispering Winds*, which was short-lived due to his printing a raucous joke which he did not understand. By now, he was also a seasoned producer of home shows to which he would invite neighborhood pals. Coming from a devout Catholic family, church was very much a part of his life, and he was a member of the church choir, singing as a boy soprano. (He would later be placed in charge of the church choir.) On a trek to Los Angeles, he visited with his bachelor Uncle Elmer ("Peck") who owned the Westside Tennis Club in Beverly Hills. While there, Merv met Elmer's tennis court buddy, movie star Errol Flynn. The star-struck young Griffin was mightily impressed.

Having attended Saint Matthew's Catholic grammar school, Merv went on to San Mateo High School where, as a defense against his being extremely overweight (a life-long battle), he became the class clown. More inspiring than the classroom was another summer trip to Los Angeles to visit with Uncle Elmer. By now, Elmer sold his tennis club and opened the Copa de Oro Club at the Beverly Wilshire Hotel.

In school, Merv participated in dramatics, but always hated to memorize scripts, so he would ad-lib. Having studied piano at a music conservatory in San Francisco, teenager Merv preferred pop music to classical, and thus abandoned any notion of becoming a concert pianist. He was already gaining a reputation through his piano playing at local dances.

When World War II broke out, Merv, who excelled at singing, organized USO tours with three girl back-up singers. He graduated from high school in 1942. He took a job as clerk in the provisions department at Hunter's Point Naval Shipyard. At night, he would enter talent contests and write songs. Briefly, he enrolled at the College of San Mateo, but soon quit, as he did mail room jobs at two different San Francisco banks. More challenging was his entry on "Budda's Amateur Hour" on KFRC radio in the Bay City, singing patriotic songs with an equally-heavy female partner. They won the first prize in that round, but lost in the finals.

DOWN AND OUT

Discouraged professionally, Merv was encouraged by a friend to audition at station KFRC again. This time he was hired to guest on "San Francisco Sketchbook" for $100. He did so well that he was soon given his own 15-minute daily program, "The Merv Griffin Show." He was billed as "America's Romantic Singing Star" with the listening audience totally unaware that this crooner was enormously overweight and boasted a 44 inch waist. (Whenever a contingent of fans came by the studio searching for Griffin, he was ordered by the station to hide.) During this time Merv and his friends put together an album for their self-formed Panda Records. To enhance his singing style, Griffin studied voice with Bill Stoker, whose other students would include Johnny Mathis and Guy Mitchell.

The year 1946 was a turning-point for the young entertainer. One day, screen star Joan Fontaine and her then husband, producer Bill Dozier, came by station KFRC looking for this romantic-sounding guy named Griffin. They had a notion that he might be right for the movies. When they caught sight of the very overweight Merv, they broke into laughter and left. Then, on another occasion, Joan Edwards, a singer on radio's "Your Hit Parade," was in town and decided to meet "America's Romantic Singing Star." She was impressed by his Perry Como-like voice, but bluntly told the brown-haired, blue-eyed young man, "the blubber must go!" Soon thereafter, Merv shed over 80 pounds, dropping down to 160, far more appropriate for his 5'"10 frame.

By 1947, 22-year-old Merv was earning $1,500 a week, but admitted he was spending it just as fast. He was dating entertainer Gypsy Ernst, but they never did marry. His daily San Francisco radio show aired in other cities as well. In Los Angeles, it was broadcast from 7:15-7:30 P.M., just the time orchestra leader Freddy Martin drove from his home to his nightly chores at the Ambassador Hotel's Coconut Grove Club. Martin heard the young singer and was impressed. Subsequently, when Martin's vocalist, Stuart Wade, announced he was quitting after their next San Francisco engagement, Freddy auditioned Merv. Griffin was hired on a five-year contract, starting at $175, with $25 raise each thirteen weeks. (Another applicant for the vocalist job was struggling Mike Douglas, who also would later become a TV talk show host.)

Freddy Martin and his group were frequently on the road. In 1948 they played 74 one-nighters. By November 1948, the Martin organization was back home playing at the Coconut Grove in Los Angeles, and four months later were settled in for a long San Francisco engagement. During this period, Merv became chummy with Judy Balaban, the daughter of New York-based Paramount Pictures executive, Barney Balaban. The friendship between Merv and Judy was long-lasting and the couple became an item in show business circles. However, nothing romantically serious ever developed.

FULL STEAM AHEAD

Griffin's career was rolling forward in the early 1950s as a member of Freddy Martin's team. Several of Merv's recordings with the group became big-sellers, including "Wilhelmina," "Never Been Kissed," "Am I in Love." However, the most notable record was the novelty tune "I've Got a Lovely Bunch of Coconuts" which sold over three million copies. (Unfortunately, Griffin's standard contract called for him to only receive $50 per recording.) There was no doubt that Merv was a popular figure; he even had his own fan club. The head of the Los Angeles chapter was future TV star Carol Burnett.

In 1950, Merv had made his motion picture debut with the Freddy Martin orchestra in a fifteen-minute short subject, singing "Tenement Symphony." That same year, Martin's organization did local TV appearances on the West Coast. Then in mid-1951, Martin contracted to do

"The Freddy Martin Show" for NBC-TV. The program was telecast from New York City from July to December 1951. On the half-hour program, Merv not only sang (*Variety* rated this crooner "one of the best in the business"), but did commercials. When not doing the weekly Thursday night TV outing, the orchestra played at the Roosevelt Hotel.

Accepting that the heyday of the big band/orchestra was over, Merv quit the Martin organization in mid-1952, hoping that his RCA recording contract would open show business doors for him. Besides, he expected to be drafted for military service in Korea. However, after his pre-induction physical, the Army decided it had filled its quota for his age group, and sent him home. In later 1952, Merv received a S.O.S. from Freddy Martin, begging him to take over as singer for a Las Vegas club engagement at the Last Frontier Casino. Griffin agreed. One night during the stand, Doris Day was in the audience, and was favorably impressed. Upon returning to Hollywood, she told her studio (Warner Bros.) about this appealing younger singer.

Meanwhile, Griffin's agent had been pitching Merv to several film studios, including Warner Bros. At the time, Bill Orr was casting director for the lot and he had been a pal of Merv's Uncle Elmer. This friendship led to Merv's screen test and him being signed to a $300 a week contract. His first feature film was not the hoped-for vehicle with Doris Day (he tested too young to play opposite her), but CATTLE TOWN (1952), in which he did brief duty as secretary to the Governor of Texas. Nevertheless, Griffin got to play in a Doris Day picture, BY THE LIGHT OF THE SILVERY MOON (1953), but his role was only a one-line speech as the announcer at an outdoor skating rink.

MERV IN THE MOVIES

His part was far larger (fifteen minutes) in SO THIS IS LOVE (1953), a loose biography of opera singer Grace Moore, starring Kathryn Grayson. Merv was cast as Buddy Nash, the actor-manager-fiance of Moore and got to sing "I Kiss Your Hand, Madame." In THREE SAILORS AND A GIRL (1953), Griffin was overshadowed by fat Jack E. Leonard, not to mention the singing lead, his rival, Gordon MacRae. Meanwhile, Griffin was invited frequently to the Sunday parties given by his studio boss, Jack L. Warner, where Merv would often play the piano and/or sing.

Being contracted to appear in THE BOY FROM OKLAHOMA (1954), a screen biography of Will Rogers, finally ended Merv's movie career. This role called for him to ride a horse, something he had never done before. It made him camera shy, and he decided the movies were not for him. Thereafter, whenever the studio casting department phoned, he would switch into a Chinese accent to announce, "O-h-h, Me-e-e-s-t-er Gr-e-e-f-in go away for a veree long time. I no can reach him." When Merv's next contract option came up, he asked for his release.

By now, Merv's RCA recording contract had fizzled. He accepted an assignment to be the opening act for Tallulah Bankhead at the Sands Hotel in Las Vegas. Next, in the summer of 1954, Griffin moved back to New York City. He found TV work appearing with Betty Ann Grove on "Summer Holiday" a twice-weekly CBS network outing. When that show faded, he turned to club work around the country. Later, back in Manhattan, he sometimes substituted for radio host Barry Gray who had a program aired from a Manhattan restaurant chatting with celebrities. For a 1955 City Center revival of "Finian's Rainbow," Griffin joined with Helen Gallagher. The engagement taught him he did NOT have sufficient discipline to ever do a major Broadway show.

Radio and TV proved to be the salvation of Merv's career. He hosted a Sunday morning CBS-TV religious program ("Look Up and Live") in mid-1955, was heard on radio in "Network Time" and was a guest vocalist on Robert Q. Lewis and Arthur Murray's TV programs. Now

Merv was living in an apartment on West 57th Street. He had a major assignment of appearing on CBS-TV's "The Morning Show" in 1956, singing, talking and trading quips with host John Henry Falk. When Will Rogers, Jr. came on as host, Merv left the project.

GOING PLACES

It was while appearing on the Robert Q. Lewis show as resident vocalist that Merv met Julann Wright of Ironwood, Michigan. She was a former actress turned secretary to Lewis. Griffin liked her sharp sense of humor; she was impressed by Merv's mix of affability and ambition. Meanwhile, after Lewis's TV show vanished, Griffin took on an ABC-TV variety series, "Going Places," which aired from a different Florida city each weekend. It was during this summer period that Merv's dad died of a heart attack at age 55.

ABC had faith in Griffin and, in 1957, hired him to star in a daily evening radio show, backed by a large orchestra and a eight-voice chorus. Merv cast Julann as his comedy foil. When that series expired in 1958, Griffin was signed to host the daytime game show, "Play Your Hunch." Ever-busy Merv was continuing his recording career and did well on the charts with "Banned in Boston" and "Charanga."

Meanwhile, in April 1958 he and Julann were engaged and, on May 18 that year, flew to Norfolk, Virginia, where they could get a blood test, marriage license, and ceremony all in one day. Their only child, Anthony Patrick, would be born on December 8, 1959. (The birth occurred on the same day "Play Your Hunch" moved to NBC-TV and Merv announced the happy event on his show.)

Merv Griffin with his wife, Julann Wright and their son, Tony in 1967.

Taking jobs wherever he found them, Merv moderated TV's "Keep Talking" which *Variety* termed an "ad-lib marathon" and demonstrated to the industry that quick-witted Griffin could handle such chores with ease. For NBC-TV, in October of 1960 he was co-host (with Bobby Vinton) of the short-lived Saturday night live program, "Saturday Prom." By now, the increasingly affluent Griffins had purchased a twenty-acre farm (complete with old mill and barn) in Califon, New Jersey, which they called "Teetertown."

LEAVE IT TO FATE

A quirk of fate launched Merv into the big leagues. He was doing chores on NBC-TV's latest rendition of "Play Your Hunch" in March 1962 at the network's Rockefeller Center headquarters. The game show and Jack Paar's "Tonight" show were temporarily sharing the same studio. Paar absent-mindedly walked onto the game show set taping and got caught in the act by Griffin and the cameramen. This encounter led to further conversation between Paar and Griffin and to Paar's invitaiton to Merv to substitute as host for Jack the next month.

The guest-hosting went so well that Merv was invited back on several subsequent occasions, heeding Paar's advice: "You always be prepared, but let the show unfold. Let it be chaos, but planned chaos." On one program, veteran British character actor, Arthur Treacher, (who had already appeared as a guest on Griffin's "Play Your Hunch") was a visitor. During a commercial break, Merv told the very proper, much older Arthur that if Griffin ever got a talk show, he would love to have Treacher as his sidekick. Treacher responded, "Why, you dear little fellow. I never knew anyone was interested in what I had to say."

By mid-year 1962, Jack Paar had decided to abandon his "Tonight" program. Among several candidates considered to replace him was Merv Griffin. However, it was Johnny Carson who began a thirty-year reign on the late night talk show as of October 1, 1962. On that same day, Merv premiered "The Merv Griffin Show." It was a 55-minute daily consolation prize provided by NBC-TV. His opening show guests included singer Patrice Munsel and comedian Shelley Berman.

Merv admitted that the program was a "borrowing" of the "Tonight Show" general format. In fact, one of his staff writers was Dick Cavett, who had formerly written for Paar on his talk show. As to his rivalry with Johnny Carson, Merv observed years later, "For some reason, we were mortal enemies at that time and we would insult each other on-air. When my show left NBC for syndication, I never appeared on his show. In later years, we got to be friends."

OFF THE AIR

After 26 weeks of struggling with ratings (some said the show was too sophisticated and needed more schmaltz), Griffin's daily TV program was cancelled. His last show was on April 1, 1963. For the finale he came out on a darkened stage, carrying a suitcase, raincoat and hat. He sat on the case and teary-eyed said, "I'm so sorry. Just hate ending this show. Haven't we had a good time?" Then he sang, "Lost in the Stars." After the demise, the Griffins vacationed in Europe.

When he returned, he hosted the summertime CBS-TV series, "Celebrity Talent Scouts," rejecting an NBC-TV offer for his exclusive, long-time services. To keep active, he did summer stock ("The Moon Is Blue" and "Come Blow Your Horn"). He reactivated his Merv Griffin Productions and packaged a TV game show, "Word for Word" (1963-1964). Always an avid word game player, Griffin was far more successful with the long-enduring "Jeopardy" which bowed on NBC in March 1964, with Art Fleming as the initial host. During the summer of 1964, Merv toured the strawhat circuit in the old musical "Broadway."

In 1965, Merv continued to build his game show empire with "Let's Play Post Office" which lasted a year. More importantly, on May 10, 1965 he starred on "The Merv Griffin Show," a daily afternoon talk show syndicated by Westinghouse. He was glad to be back in the genre format; the only type of TV he really enjoyed doing. The ninety-minute program was taped at Broadway's Little Theatre adjacent to Sardi's Restaurant on West 44th Street. At long last in control of his own project, he fulfilled his promise to make Arthur Treacher his confederate on the show.

The first guests on his new format, ninety-minute program was "Hello, Dolly!" star Carol Channing and comedian Dom DeLuise. A few months later, Merv enunciated his show's credo: "I long ago decided to be just Merv Griffin and let be what will. But I want this show to move out into the world, seek interesting people, explore ideas, find talent. If they can't come to us, we'll go to them." During the next four years of syndication, Merv provided a balance of show business, literary and political personalities.

CLOSE TO THE PRESIDENT

One of his best political guests, as even constant audience member Mrs. Miller would agree, was Bobby Kennedy in the fall of 1967. Going on remote, Griffin aired shows from England (with Leslie Caron, Julie Christie and Margaret Rutherford), from Ireland (with John Huston), from Spain (with Zero Mostel), from Paris (with Maurice Chevalier), from Cannes (with Sean Connery singing!) and from Monaco (with Princess Grace). One of his most controversial outings was a London-originated program on which Lord Bertrand Russell attacked the Vietnam War. By now, the Griffins were dividing their time between their elaborate Central Park West digs and the New Jersey farm. The staunch Roman Catholic Griffin, once a senior vice-president of the Catholic Actors Guild, was given the organization's Actor of the Year Award in 1966.

Merv Griffin Enterprises was big business even in the late 1960s. He employed over 125 people, had two separate Manhattan production centers, owned a music publishing operation, and was churning out several TV quiz show ("Reach for the Stars," "One in a Million, "Talk It Up"). Griffin had had several offers to make movies (THE CARDINAL, 1963, THE PRIVATE NAVY OF SGT. O'FARRELL, 1968), but it was in HELLO, DOWN THERE (1969) that he accepted a role playing himself.

The CBS-TV network had long coveted the revenue generated by Johnny Carson's "Tonight Show." The network now came to veteran Merv to host such a program for them. He told the giant network, "You can't afford me. I know Johnny [Carson]'s salary. You'd have to double it." To his amazement, CBS did! Merv left Westinghouse and moved his crew to the Cort Theatre on West 48th Street. He bought a dilapidated office building near the Cort to house his production staff, and installed a restaurant on the ground floor. It was called Pip's (after Arthur Treacher's nickname).

To get a beat on the fall TV season, the new ninety-minute "Merv Griffin Show" debuted on August 16, 1969, on CBS's 150 stations (in contrast to NBC's 212 station outlets for "The Tonight Show"). With Arthur Treacher continuing as sidekick, Mort Lindsay and his Orchestra, the premier show featured Hedy Lamarr, Woody Allen and Moms Mabley. It was Treacher who uttered nightly, "From the Cort Theatre it's 'The Merv Griffin Show.'... Look sharp now, here's the dear boy himself, M...E..R..V..Y..N."

Merv Griffin reuniting with his former co-host, Arthur Treacher on "The Merv Griffin"
in the mid-1970s.

TOUGH COMPETITION

Competing with other talk shows (hosted by Johnny Carson, Joey Bishop, Dick Cavett, David Frost), Merv found it tough going. He renovated his set to get a fresh look, removing the conventional desk and couch and switching to chairs so he could have program panels. He engendered great controversy in March 1970 with his program featuring Abbie Hoffman, a member of the Chicago seven.

However, whatever Merv tried, his ratings continued to slip. By the spring of 1970, a desperate CBS made Merv relocate the show to Los Angeles to have access to more glittery show business guests. Arthur Treacher did not make the trip westward; the network determined the eighty-year old was hurting the show's draw. The first Los Angeles-based program debuted on September 9, 1970. Temporarily, the Griffins (whose marriage was already shaky) moved into a furnished Beverly Hills home.

Despite his faltering talk show, Merv Griffin Enterprises now employed some 370 on their payroll, grossed $8.5 million in 1970, and had a variety of real estate investments including a Rockefeller Center office building. Merv drummed up ratings by focusing more on single theme shows (e.g. "Hollywood Couples," "A Salute to the Stars of the Silent Screen"). However, he received little support from his disenchanted network bosses.

Merv openly referred to the "funny little men at CBS" and feuded with CBS program chief Fred Silverman. The network continued its heavy meddling and program censorship, and Silverman insisted that Merv's show should be converted into a song-and-dance variety offering. CBS ended the impasse on December 2, 1971 when it cancelled his show as of February 11,

1972. Following his network departure, CBS erased all Merv's program tapes so they could never be reused.

ONE STEP AHEAD

Shrewd Merv had prepared for the CBS finale. He signed a five-year contract with Metromedia Broadcasting which called for 39 to 48 weeks of syndicated shows per year. More importantly, there would be no restrictions on the show format and he was to receive a far higher profit participation. The new project was to air from the renovated old Hollywood Palace Theatre on Hollywood and Vine. Dick Carson (Johnny's brother and former director of "The Tonight Show") was hired as director.

To present a new image, Merv trimmed down his bulky figure, and, to ease the pain of his disintegrating marriage, he began psychological therapy. The latest "The Merv Griffin Show" bowed on March 13, 1972 and his first slew of guests included Dinah Shore, Steve Lawrence, Milton Berle, Dom DeLuise and Dionne Warwick. The *Hollywood Reporter* printed, "It is a comfortable show. Merv is easy to watch, and he has entertaining guests.... Welcome home, Merv!"

In 1973, Merv formed Griffin/MGM Records, with the first release, "Happy to Know You," sung by Merv. On February 7, 1973, Julann filed for divorce. She insisted, "We grew in different ways. I still love Merv. He's part of my family, but I'm not 'in love' with him." (The divorce would be finalized in early 1976, when she received half of his estimated net worth of somewhere between $5 and $10 million.)

Griffin moved out of the family's newly-purchased Bel Air home and transferred to a luxurious Hollywood Hills "cottage." It became routine that every week after the final Thursday taping, he would pilot his own Beachcraft Super 18 plane to his lavish Pebble Beach home on Carmel Bay where one of his neighbor friends was Clint Eastwood. Merv's frequent date was now Eva Gabor, a perennial Griffin pal over the decades.

A WHEEL OF FORTUNE

While continuing his talk show hosting, Merv promoted new game show concepts. He came up with a huge winner with "Wheel of Fortune," which debuted in 1975. In 1976, Griffin taped three shows in Israel. While on a walking tour with the Mayor of Jerusalem, Merv got punched in the stomach by a midget Arab who thought it funny to hit an American TV star.

In early 1976, his program moved to the plush TAV Studios 2 south on Hollywood and Vine. TAV (Trans-American Video) owned by Merv, had assorted interests, including closed-circuit cameras/projection screens for horse/dog racing tracks and three East Coast radio stations. In October 1978, Merv took his show back to New York for the first time since leaving the Big Apple in 1970. In November 1979, he taped his 2,000th Metromedia show, and the same year, his newest creation, "Dance Fever" bowed on NBC-TV.

By now, his son Tony had formed the musical group, Karma Rock. Among his vast real estate holdings, Merv had added a southern California ranch where he lived. The year 1980 saw the publication of Merv's autobiography, *Merv*, written with Peter Barsocchini, producer of Merv's talk show. This book was followed the next year by *From Where I Sit*. Also in 1981, his show was the first daily program of its type to be syndicated by satellite, allowing for its programs to be beamed to stations on the same day they had been taped.

In both the 1981-1982 and 1983-1984 seasons, Griffin won Emmys as "Outstanding Host in a Variety Series." In between, he sandwiched in cameos in several movies, including two Steve Martin screen comedies, THE MAN WITH TWO BRAINS (1983) and THE LONELY GUY (1984).

A FOND FAREWELL

By 1985, Merv had been emceeing talk shows for 23 years. He estimated he had interviewed more than 25,000 guests, including Orson Welles, Richard Burton, Martin Luther King, Grace Kelly, Robert Kennedy and John Wayne. Merv's son, Tony, was now a member of the production staff. Merv had once said, "Without a doubt, I have always been enormously curious about people, and the day I stop being curious is the day my show goes off the air."

Well, in 1986, his syndicator King Features and Merv decided to call it quits. Not only had the fifty-year old host become extremely portly, lost his singing voice, but the joie de vivre had gone out of his chat sessions and his ratings. He had fallen victim to the competition (which not only included long-running Johnny Carson, but such newer entries as Phil Donahue and the latest new crop of talk show hosts, personified by Joan Rivers and Oprah Winfrey).

On September 5, 1986, chipper Merv showed clips from the "Best of Merv Griffin." At show's end, he told viewers: "I guess this is the first time on this last show I've ever said this. We will not be back after this message. The-the-the-that's all folks!" Later that night, Griffin was a guest (for the first time) on Johnny Carson's "The Tonight Show" and said with a wry smile, "You win." However, Merv was no loser. He was worth an estimated $235 million, which was increased when he sold Merv Griffin Enterprises to Coca Cola (later taken over by Sony) soon thereafter for a reported $250 million. He retained a hefty piece of his created game shows' handsome revenues.

Unable to stay away from TV entirely, he was back with an hour special ("Secrets Women Never Share") in December 1987 and the next week was co-host of the "12th Annual Circus of the Stars." Meanwhile, he had developed a pilot called "Coconut Ballroom" in which he would conduct his own singing group, The Mervtones. However the concept never sold.

MR. WALL STREET

Now an openly aggressive entrepreneur, he sought to buy the Beverly Hills Hotel. When that failed, he purchased the 578-room Beverly Hilton Hotel for $120 million. Merv reached his greatest visibility as a businessman when he went claw-to-claw with high profile corporate raider Donald Trump, seeking control of Resorts International, Inc. Merv won the highly-publicized stock battle, but, by 1990, had to admit that the enterprise had caused him to overextend himself financially. A court-approved reorganization of RI, Inc. soon followed, with an announcement in late 1991 that some of the corporation's assets might be sold.

Always the public bon vivant, the celebrity-surrounded Merv, who went on a crash diet to lose 40 excess pounds, said in 1991, "I don't have passions. That's for young people. I have diversification. And that's much better." However, in April 1991 he was hit with a $250 million palimony suit, instituted by 37-year old, former bodyguard Brent Plott. The latter alleged he had been the producer's gay lover for four years (1981-1985).

Now living in Florida, Plott spoke through attorneys that besides offering companionship, it had been his idea, years back, to select Vanna White as the new letter-pointer on "Wheel of Fortune." No sooner had this much-heralded court suit been dismissed on technicalities, than more headlines erupted. Deney Terrio, who had hosted Merv's "Dance Fever" from 1979-1985, filed an $11.3 million lawsuit against TV mogul Griffin, alleging that Merv was guilty of sexual harassment, defamation of character and breach of contract. By the next year, these allegations had faded from national headlines and public interest.

These days, Merv continues to devise new TV show concepts, hobnob with the rich and famous at his Beverly Hilton Hotel and at his various California homes. On December 31, 1992 he hosted his second annual New Year's Eve TV special, with the festivities again telecast from his Resorts Casino Hotel in Atlantic City. Meanwhile, glittery Eva Gabor continues to be Merv's favorite social partner. His girth may be almost as tremendous as his wealth, but silver-haired Griffin continues to look forward to new enterprises. As the ruddy-cheeked mogul stated when he quit the TV talk show rat race, "I was certainly not about to sit around clipping coupons. Retirement is something I may consider after death. even then, I doubt it."

TV & CABLE SERIES:

The Freddy Martin Show (NBC, 1951)
Summer Holiday (CBS, 1954)
Look Up and Live (CBS, 1955)
The Morning Show (CBS, 1956)
Robert Q. Lewis Show (CBS, 1956)
Going Places (ABC, 1956)
Keep Talking (ABC, 1959-1960)
Play Your Hunch (CBS; 1958-1959; ABC, 1959; NBC, 1959; NBC, 1962)
Music for a Summer Night (ABC, 1959)
Saturday Prom (NBC, 1960-1961)
The Merv Griffin Show (NBC, 1962-1963)
Celebrity Talent Scouts (CBS, 1963)
Word for Word (NBC, 1963-1964)
The Merv Griffin Show (Syndicated, 1965-1969)
The Merv Griffin Show (CBS, 1969-1972)
The Merv Griffin Show (Syndicated, 1972-1986)

FEATURE FILMS:

Music by Martin (1950) [short subject]
Cattle Town (1952)
By the Light of the Silvery Moon (1953)
I Confess (1953) [voice only]
The Beast from 20,000 Fathoms (1953) [voice only]
The Charge at Feather River (1953) [voice only]
So This Is Love (1953)
Three Sailors and a Girl (1953)
The Boy from Oklahoma (1954)
Phantom of the Rue Morgue (1954)
Hello, Down There (1969)
Two-Minute Warning (1976)
The Seduction of Joe Tynan (1979)
The Man with Two Brains (1983)
Slapstick of Another Kind (1984) [made in 1982]
The Lonely Guy (1984)

Jack Paar reminiscing with Merv Griffin on "The Merv Griffin Show" in the mid-1980s.

Chapter 6
JACK PAAR

Recently, Jack Paar, one of TV's earlier practitioners of the late night chatter show format said, "I hate the word 'talk show.' It makes it seem as if all I did was invent a davenport." What Paar did was to raise the art of conversation to a beloved national habit. This facile raconteur recalls, "We never put any guest on because they had a program coming up Tuesday. Absolutely never in my career did I do that. You didn't get on if you didn't have anything to say, if I didn't trust you." The self-effacing entertainer might have added that he possessed a marvelous ability to coax very colorful stories out of guests. As *TV Guide* analyzed once, "Somewhere along the line Paar had discovered that people like to see human beings being human. It is one of the sensational discoveries in the history of show business."

But there was also another reason that insured Paar's successful tenure on "Tonight." Genre purveyor Regis Philbin would note of his quirky idol, "Paar did something novel on television. He wasn't afraid to show his own emotions. He wasn't afraid of sharing his own life with the viewers." Newspaper TV critic Tom Shales agrees: "He brought out the best in everybody else, sometimes by bringing out the worst in himself. You may have been appalled; you couldn't be bored."

While Jack let the public eavesdrop on the private lives of celebrities and budding talent, he provided a great many details about his own domestic activities and laid bare his own paradoxical, seesawing emotions. When asked once if he had ever visited a therapist, brash Jack retorted, "I have no troubles that I can't tell standing up and to several million people at once." And that Paar did nightly. He was thin-skinned, as viewers soon understood. It did not take much to raise his hackles, especially if the alleged villain belonged to that prime group of Paar targets: Broadway nightlife gossip columnists such as Ed Sullivan and Dorothy Kilgallen.

However, no one was safe from Jack's wrath. When his bile was aroused, he would speak out frankly and frequently, letting the show's ratings fall where they may. If any of his semi-regular TV program troupe was guilty of some imagined slight, Paar was not above firing the person in a fit of pique. On the other hand, this arch sentimentalist could become so overwhelmed by a touching moment that he would break down into sobbing tears in front of the live cameras.

It was an expected (and demanded) bill of fare on Paar's TV show that he reveal (and exploit) any personal peccadillo. He would state, "although I make my living talking to millions of people at a time, I'm ill at ease meeting strangers whether it's the man checking the gas meter or a famous celebrity.... My dread of meeting people individually is as nothing to my terror at encountering them in groups." Hard to believe? However, in Jack's trademark expressions, "Every word is true" and "I kid you not."

NERVES OF RUBBER

On his nightly TV outings, Paar's extreme nervousness in front of the public caused him to pace, mumble to himself and wash his hands compulsively. It prompted him to fiddle (ineptly) with gadgets and toys continuously. Delivering his nightly monologue (which he memorized by writing it over and over in long hand) was a constant ordeal. One evening, for example, before going on the air, actress/model Suzy Parker grabbed Jack to tell him the details of her recent divorce. He became so distracted that he forgot his monologue. "I couldn't think of anything to say," he remembers, "so I simply looked at the audience and said, 'I've been drinking.'" Viewers accepted his explanation, for with Paar anything was possible.

With Jack's mix of barbed wit and gentle, little-boy manner, program guests never knew how the unpredictable host would react at any given moment. That was only fair because Jack Paar never knew either. In addition, the impish Paar delighted in smashing concepts of TV censorship by cutely telling mildly sexy jokes or using words like "buttock" without causing an apocalypse. However, if network heads did object and Jack found himself the "surprised" victim of overvigilant corporate censors, he was the first to cry foul. Such an event usually led to one of his famous on-the-air, "I quit the show" rejoinders. After the network soothed the ruffled little child lurking within Paar, he would return a few days or weeks later, ready to do battle on "Tonight" once again.

Jack Harold Paar was born on May 1, 1918 in Canton, Ohio to Howard and Lillian Paar. (There was a brother Howard, Jr. and a sister, Flora, as well as another brother who died very young.) Howard Paar was of Dutch-German extraction and worked for the New York Central Railroad as a division superintendent. During Jack's first years, the family moved from Canton to Detroit. As a youngster, Jack was enthralled with military uniforms and wanted to attend a military academy. However, the Paars could not afford that luxury. As a boy, he had a habit of stuttering which he overcame by stuffing buttons in his mouth and reading aloud.

When he was fourteen and in the ninth grade of Jackson, Michigan public school (the family had moved again), he developed tuberculosis. Later, he would joke of this difficult period, "I grew to like solitude so much I thought of joining a monastery, but I can't stand living in." During his convalescence, Jack read a great deal. Because Howard was a ham radio enthusiast, he nurtured the hobby in his offspring and set up a work bench by the boy's bedside.

A BUNDLE OF ENERGY

After eight months, including a stint working as a railroad laborer to toughen himself up, Jack recovered from his disability and returned to high school. He had missed so much time, he had to repeat his freshman year. His mother would recollect that he was always a restless youth: "He could never sit still long enough to fish with his father."

By the time Jack was sixteen, he knew he would never be a good student as he liked to daydream too much. One day, while strolling in downtown Jackson, he came upon a radio announcer who was doing a man-on-the-street program. The interviewer asked Paar his opinion of the Michigan penal system. Jack jabbered on at great length. The aired response gathered a great deal of attention. The next week, the local radio station, WIBM, hired Paar at $3 a week to work from 9 PM to midnight. A few months later, the station offered him a full-time job at $12 a week. Without much hesitation, he quit school. His parents were nonplused, especially his mother who had hoped he might become a minister.

After months at WIBM where he was an announcer, he accepted a position with radio station WIRE in Indianapolis. However, he soon quit and returned to Jackson and WIBM. Then, sometime later, he was fired for his irreverent attitude to management and tradition. He moved on to station WKBM (Youngstown, Ohio) and then to WCAE (Pittsburgh). At WCAE, he was fired for laughing at a slipup made by a station employee.

Next, he joined WGAR (Cleveland) making $60 a week. He was now twenty. Part of his work duties was to announce the big dance band shows from the ballrooms of Cleveland hotels. Thinking himself quite clever, he would use the evening's song titles ("All the Things You Are," "Who's Your Little Whoozis?") to send out messages over the airwaves to his girl-friend. Before long, CBS network headquarters sent the WGAR station manager a Teletype: "Tell Paar to stop making love on our network."

IT'S A DO-OVER

In the early 1940s, Jack dated an actress who had been in the road company of "Margin for Error," but that romance paled. Later, he married a woman named Irene whom he met when she auditioned at WGAR. However, they soon realized they were too young for such responsibility and divorced. Not satisfied, they repeated the marriage-divorce routine again.

By now, Jack who was working at radio station WBEN (Buffalo) had determined he wanted a more active role in show business and decided to become a comedian. However, before he could act on this career path, America entered World War II. In 1942, Paar volunteered for the draft. The Army sent him to a reception center in Battle Creek, Michigan. There, because of his radio experience, he was assigned to the 28th Special Service Company then based at the service camp in Indiantown Gap, Pennsylvania.

It was there he began entertaining the troops, as both master of ceremonies and comedian at servicemen shows. At a dance sponsored by the nearby Hershey (Chocolate) Company, he met Miriam Wagner, who was related to the dairy farmers branch of the Hershey family. On October 9, 1942 they married at the Dutch Reform Church in Hershey, Pennsylvania. Jose Melis, an Army buddy (who would become Jack's musical director on the "Tonight" show) played the organ at the ceremony.

Soon thereafter Paar was reassigned and, later, shipped out to the South Pacific. He was part of the convoy that landed on Gaudalcanal in March 1944. Once there, he set about his morale duties, hopping from island to island, with one day/night stands, often putting on three shows daily for the troops. At one point, Jack was assigned to a radio station of the "Mosquito Network" which broadcast to captured South Pacific isles. For a while, Paar (of the Army) and ex-child movie star Jackie Cooper (of the Navy) shared a tent on an Allied-occupied isle. Continuing his anti-establishmentarianism bent, part of Jack's standard comedy routine was to mock officers, much to the delight of the enlisted men in the audience.

WORDS OF PRAISE

During 1945, war correspondent Sidney Carroll wrote an *Esquire* magazine article praising Jack's comedic talents. ("He is one of the few G.I.'s who spoke out the gripes and groans the men themselves could never express. He did it with humor, and he did it with finesse.") This piece garnered tremendous attention in the entertainment sectors back home.

By the time Paar returned to California in February 1946, film studios and radio networks were already calling the Paar homestead in Indianapolis inquiring about this talented G.I. After a short visit with his family, Jack hurried to New York City where he appeared on a national radio show with Ethel Merman. He was so overcome by the moment, that he broke down and wept on the air. Soon thereafter, he was on a radio show with two of his comedic idols, Fred Allen and Jack Benny.

RKO Pictures signed the bright newcomer to a Hollywood contract. He used the paid-for train tickets to buy a used convertible to head westward with Miriam. Once in Los Angeles, RKO had his teeth capped and gave the comedian with the receding hairline a toupee to wear. Although he was being paid $350 weekly, studio executives could not decide what to do with Jack. "I did everything an actor does except act," Jack recalls. During the summer of 1947, Jack replaced radio's "The Jack Benny Program" with his own comedy series, and then ABC hired him for a short-lived radio entry that fall. Next, he hosted a quiz show, "The $64 Question," and later substituted for Don McNeill on "The Breakfast Club." Eventually, the studio put Paar into a trio of films (including Lucille Ball's EASY LIVING) with inconsequential results.

In 1949, the Paars became parents to daughter Randy, while living in a house above the Sunset strip. When RKO dropped Paar's option, he found radio soap opera work through his World War II pal Hans Conried, an actor now also a radio director. Twentieth Century-Fox thought Jack had movie potential and hired him to play opposite the rising Marilyn Monroe in LOVE NEST (1951). He would recall of the budding screen siren: "Since she was the object of constant sexual remarks behind her back and to her face, I felt some sympathy for her." The studio also cast Jack in DOWN AMONG THE SHELTERING PALMS, a lackluster musical set in the South Pacific. The outing was so bad that Fox held up its release till 1953.

THE OLD ROLLERCOASTER

With his film career effectively ended, Jack hosted a trice-weekly TV quiz show, "Up to Paar," which was also known as "I've Got News for You." The critics were unimpressed and jibed, "Up to Paar isn't." With no opportunities left, Jack and his family moved to New York City in the spring of 1953. That summer, he emceed the CBS-TV quiz show, "Bank on the Stars." *Variety* approved, noting: "Paar won over his audience with a mild introduction of himself and an exhibit of a blowup picture of his infant."

With his good notices building, CBS-TV hired him for a Friday morning show. Jack's rep company included Edie Adams, Richard Hayes and Jose Melis and the Pupi Campo Orchestra. By July of 1954, the Paar troupe had moved to a Saturday night time slot. On August 16, 1954, Paar took over CBS's "The Morning Show," formerly hosted by Walter Cronkite. For his efforts on "The Morning Show," Jack was paid $200,000 yearly. The revised cast comprised Betty Clooney (sister of Rosemary), the Baird Puppets, Jose Melis and the Pupi Campo Orchestra, along with commentator Charles Collingwood.

After a year, Paar switched to an afternoon program, a daily half-hour item which featured several singers (Edie Adams, Martha Wright, Jack Haskell) as well as Jose Melis's musical group. By May of 1956 (the year that Paar's father died) this series expired. Jack was reduced to being a radio disc jockey for ABC, aired from the rumpus room of his Bronxville home. The catch-as-catch-can cast included wife Miriam, daughter Randy, family dog Schapps as well as Jose Melis. However, it too got cancelled!

While Jack Paar's show business career was shriveling, the NBC network was suffering its own hardships. After Steve Allen left the hugely popular "Tonight!" program in January 1957, the network responded by cobbling together a hodgepodge known as "Tonight: America After Dark," part news, part entertainment, part talk show. The poorly-received late night offering plummeted in rating and cost the network a lot of lost sponsor revenue. After 26 weeks of tinkering with new participants, NBC admitted defeat. It decided to return to the "Tonight" show format. Reportedly, columnist Earl Wilson (involved with "America After Dark") suggested Paar as a likely hosting candidate to NBC.

BACK IN THE LIMELIGHT

Jack debuted on "Tonight" ("The Tonight Show") on July 29, 1957. Hugh Downs was the announcer, Jose Melis's Orchestra provided musical support, and the opening guests included fey screen character actor Franklin Pangborn. Paar would insist later, "Our debut was a disaster, and the reviews were terrible, but the show soon caught on." *Variety* had been one of the original doubters, noting of the host who had to carry almost single-handedly nine hours of weekly programming: "He's an original and sometimes brilliant wit, usually armed with good offbeat material and also an easy hand with the quick ad lib. But while pleasant, Paar seems to lack a certain warmth...his material is the type that has to be tight—it dissipates over the long pull."

Despite the odds, Paar saved the faltering "Tonight" showcase and his own career. When it debuted, only 62 stations carried the informal, impromptu program. However, soon the number was up to 154 stations and there were 30 million viewers for this gab marathon which utilized three writers and had a $50,000 weekly budget. The showcase program aired live from the Hudson Theatre on West 44th Street. It was not long before the show became famous for its faux pas.

There was the time when Jack got a headache while in the midst of his televised chores. He tried to get the wad of cotton out of a nearby bottle of aspirin, but couldn't. In desperation he poured water into the bottle and took a liberal sip. Then he absent-mindedly corked the bottle. The action of the water on the tablets was like a little detonator. It exploded, much to Paar's surprise and viewers' mirth.

Before long, iconoclastic Paar developed his own semi-regular "Tonight" show family. On July 31, 1957, Dody Goodman, a former dancer with a very naive comedy style, debuted on the program. Paar was quite taken with her unique brand of bird-brained comedy and had her return nightly till the end of the year. (She was the type of person who, when asked on the show what breed her dog was, replied, "He's a little m-u-t-t. I spelled it in case he's watching.")

FREQUENT GUESTS

Another frequent visitor was heavily-accented French chanteuse Genevieve. She initially came on the program as a singer, then stayed to do assorted chores, ranging from commercials to reading baseball scores. In the same league with Paar as an ad libber extraordinaire

Society observer Elsa Maxwell, a frequent visitor on Jack Paar's "The Tonight Show."

was acerbic Britisher Hermione Gingold, and she was swiftly made part of the proceedings. So was bosomy, aged social matron Elsa Maxwell, who enthusiastically reported on cafe society.

Later came British humorist Alexander King, who had had four wives and was a recovering drug addict. Paar described the cherished King as a "frail but fierce little man with the air of a delinquent leprechaun." King's appearances on "Tonight" launched him as a best-selling author. And not to be forgotten was zany comedian Peggy Cass. She was for Paar on his show what actress Teri Garr would be for David Letterman's TV program. Then there was Tedi Thurman the sexy weather lady who had a short tenure on the program.

Paar, also resurrected folksy comedian Cliff Arquette (Charlie Weaver), best known from the old "Fibber McGee and Molly" radio show. Finally, erudite Hugh Downs, a high brow who could prattle on any given subject, developed his own importance as Paar's sidekick. He was the one who said frequently on the show, "Well Kemo Sabe." These words were the signal that it was time for a commercial break.

Just as entertaining as Jack's guests, were Paar's fumblings to extricate himself from any given trap in which he had cavalierly thrown himself. There was the caper of Trish Dwelly, ostensibly a novice singer whom Jack extravagantly praised for being so practiced a "new" talent. Later, he admitted on air that he had learned just now that she was a professional; he apologized for his naivete.

IT'S NOT ALWAYS FUNNY

Sometimes he did not beg forgiveness for his actions. There was the occasion when former movie queen Gloria Swanson came on and began hawking her dress line. Jack snapped, "May I interrupt your commercial to do a commercial?" When Mickey Rooney walked onto the program inebriated and made a shambles of the talk session, a miffed Jack popped out with: "Would you care to leave?" Rooney did. When a feud arose between Paar and Ed Sullivan over the amount of money to be paid guests on their respective TV shows, Jack went public with his battle and demanded that Ed agree to air their differences on the "Tonight" show. When Sullivan failed to show up for the skirmish, Jack launched into a lengthy on-air diatribe. Finally, Jack's mentor, Jack Benny, shamed Paar into dropping the matter and even to saying in front of the cameras, "I'm sorry! I'm sorry!"

On the other hand, if Paar believed in a visitor, such as Robert F. Kennedy, then he was a staunch supporter of that person, no matter who objected, including Teamster leader Jimmy Hoffa (who threatened to sue Paar for on-camera derogatory remarks).

By 1958, Jack was earning $2,750 weekly, receiving a percentage of sponsor dollars and had six weeks of vacation annually. He soon began taking off Monday and Friday nights with substitutes hosts filling in on Monday and "The Best of Paar" being shown on Fridays. By now, "Tonight" had switched from live to live-on-tape telecasts and Paar was making annual pilgrimages to England to shoot on-location shows. Taped excursions to Hawaii, the Bahamas, Florida, Washington and Cuba followed.

There was a great uproar when Paar and company flew to Berlin to do a "Tonight" program focusing on the newly-constructed wall dividing the democratic and communist German city. Some viewers were taken aback by the featherweight chatter between Paar and Peggy Cass regarding the Wall; the U.S. Congress charged that Jack almost had created an international incident at the closed Berlin border with his troupe deflecting the U.S. Military from dealing with more important matters. While the ruckus was stirring up hard feelings on both sides, Jack trekked off to Moscow.

DIFFERENT TIMES

Leave it to Paar to get into legal squabbles when he wrote his first autobiography, *I Kid You Not* (1960). The book's "gimmick" was that this was the first time he was telling his own story. However, some months earlier he had done a lengthy interview with Maurice Zolotow that was to be the basis of a three-part magazine series. Zolotow suggested that the byline read, "by Jack Paar as told to Maurice Zolotow." To proceed with publishing his life story, Jack had to buy back the rights to his own life! About this time, Jack made a sentimental return to Hollywood for the first time in nearly a decade. He discovered that his Hollywood Walk of Fame star read "Parr" not Paar.

The peak or nemesis of Jack's "Tonight" show reign occurred on February 10, 1960. It was the (in)famous water closet anecdote that generated the turmoil. By today's standards, the story is mild; but the 1960s TV network censors were incensed. The lengthy joke revolved around an Englishwoman planning a trip abroad and who sends a note to her host asking about the "w.c." She was referring to a water closet (bathroom), but her host thought she meant a wayside chapel. The Britisher received a puzzling response which stated that the w.c. "is situated nine miles from the house you occupy.... It is capable of holding 229 people and is open on Sunday and Thursday only.... I would suggest that you come early." When NBC censors deleted it from the taped program, the next evening Paar told a flabbergasted Hugh Downs that not only was he quitting the show, but he was departing right then in the middle of the show. Downs was left to complete the program with comedians Orson Bean and Shelley Berman.

When both sides cooled down, the network suggested that Jack and his family take a paid vacation to Hong Kong. A few weeks later, however, Jack returned to the limelight of "Tonight." He admitted, "When I walked off, I said there must be a better way of making a living. Well, I've looked and there isn't. Be it ever so humble, there is no place like Radio City."

ENOUGH IS ENOUGH

By early 1962, after returning from a European jaunt, Jack advised the NBC brass that he was (again) quitting "The Tonight Show." Like Steve Allen before him, he found the pace too grueling. The network countered with a proposed new five-year contract at more than double his current $250,000 yearly salary. It offered him show ownership. However, Paar, who could be extremely stubborn, insisted he was too exhausted and that the continued censorship problems were too much. (For the record, future talk show maven Dick Cavett, who worked for Paar as a staff writer, would note that working for Jack "was a little like living at home with an alcoholic parent.")

The much-heralded finale was on March 29, 1962. The theme of the farewell program was a funeral tribute to Paar. Comedian Jack E. Leonard introduced assorted celebrities who dropped by to say goodbye to Paar. There were also taped messages from Bob Hope, Reverend Billy Graham, former Vice President Richard M. Nixon and Attorney General Robert F. Kennedy. Opera singer Robert Merrill serenaded Jack with an aria from the opera "Pagliacci." At the episode's end, Jack Paar departed the stage carried by a brace of famous pallbearers. A final title card read "No More to Come." While Merv Griffin, who had frequently substituted as host of "Tonight" was touted to be THE replacement for Paar, it was Johnny Carson who took over as host of the last night classic.

Now at liberty, Jack relaxed by taking a nostalgic trip to the South Pacific and chartering a 60-foot boat to revisit locales where he had been stationed during World War II. That summer he went to Kenya, Africa on a photo safari. He quipped of his trips, "I have about two million feet of home movies, so many inoculations that my arms look like the dart boards in an English pub and some colorful memories."

Like many other veteran show business personalities, Jack found that he missed the TV grind. That fall (September 21, 1962) NBC induced him to return with a Friday evening, hour-long variety show, budgeted at between $5-$6 million annually. José Melis's Orchestra provided musical backup, and recurrent guests were comic Jonathan Winters and "Tonight" regular Alexander King. Jack was his same capricious self, which led *Variety* to warn: "That 'I'm-a-pretty-swell-guy-and-love-everybody-but-if-you-cross-me-I'll-pin-your-ears-back' business is (or should be) behind him, part & parcel of post-midnight tv that Paar's now eschewed in favor of prime time exposure. His style and banter were particularly unique for the 'Tonight' ad lib shenanigans....."

HARD TO GIVE UP

Over the next three seasons, his guests ranged from Albert Schweitzer (visited on location in Africa) to a not-in-control Judy Garland, from Bill Cosby to Kate Smith. Paar's program show-cased footage of Jack's global jaunts, including a visit up the Amazon (where he stopped off en route to say hello to old pal Mary Martin), a pilgrimage to the Holy Land and a sojourn to Tahiti which included a talk with famed painter Paul Gaugin's son, Emile. By June 1965, "The Jack Paar Show" was history.

Once again a man of leisure, Jack purchased WMTW-TV in Poland Springs, Maine for $3.5 million. Having written volume #2 (*My Saber Is Bent*) of his life story in 1961, he next pre-pared *3 on a Toothbrush* (1965). The latter book detailed his adventures and encounters around the world. In this tome, he claimed that he was "the Typhoid Mary of travel, and I guess it's true that I'm a carrier of confusion." This was in reference to such exploits as jumping over a bull ring fence in Spain to escape a wild bull, being struck by a hit-run rickshaw driver in Zanzibar, losing the family's luggage in Africa and winding up with "three on a toothbrush."

In April 1967 when Johnny Carson returned to "The Tonight Show" after a highly pub-licized tussle with NBC network management, competitor Joey Bishop urged Jack Paar (then visiting Los Angeles) to make a special appearance on his ABC-TV nighttime talk show. Loquacious Jack obliged and babbled endlessly with co-guests Ethel Merman and Juliet Prowse. The overshadowed Bishop piped in to say, "You'll have to forgive me for eavesdropping." After this appearance, Jack returned to his quiet life in suburban Connecticut. The Paars' daughter Randy was in college, and, feeling at a loss for someone to care for, the Paars temporarily adopt-ed a lion cub named Amani. When asked if he thought the public missed his TV presence, Paar retorted, "frankly, I do not. I was never an entertainer for the masses, nor did I ever wish to be. It's a 'Gomer Pyle' world."

After eleven years away from the talk show forum, ABC-TV convinced Jack to give it another try in 1973. His resuscitated show was part of a revamping of the time slot held by Dick Cavett whose own chat program was fast dropping in the ratings. The plan was to alternate sev-eral talk show hosts (including Paar and Cavett) on a one-week-each-month basis. There was much talk about Cavett feeling he was being betrayed by his old boss, while Jack insisted that part of his deal was that the network must retain Dick's services.

THEY CAN'T ALL BE WINNERS

Jack's cycle ("Jack Paar Tonight") on the "ABC Wide World of Entertainment" premiered on January 8, 1973 with Peggy Cass as his announcer and sidekick. Relying on the old formula, Jack included home movies and much editorializing. Occasionally, he introduced fresh comedic talent, such as Freddie Prinze and Jimmie Walker. However, just like the old-fashioned bow ties Paar insisted on wearing, his format had too much deja vu. By the time it left the air on November 16, 1973, he had been reduced to airing three nights per month.

Later, Paar assessed of this flop: "I let them all down. I had lost interest in television. I couldn't seem to adjust to the new music...the big laugh subjects were mostly pot, dope, and deviant sex. I was underwhelmed." Blaming the format, not his personal appeal for the series' failure, he said proudly, "People used to tell me 'if you can't do it, it can't be done.'" Asked if he would consider any further TV excursions, he replied, "Everything I wanted to say I have said twice." Another time, he said despondently, "I guess the next event in my life will be my death."

Once again the country gentleman, he and Miriam resided in leisure at their New Canaan, Connecticut home where he grew vegetables and planted trees. After taping a segment of PBS-TV's "Over Easy," hosted by pal Mary Martin and former co-worker Hugh Downs, Jack told the press, "I'm not certain I could come back [now], but I'm asked all the time. When it's over, it's over. Anyone who doesn't know that is sad." As to his off-camera life, he had long ago sold his TV station but said he went to bed very early most nights to read and that "I'm thinking of selling my television sets."

Installment #4 of the Jack Paar book saga (*P.S. Jack Paar: An Entertainment*) was published in 1983. The overall tone of the book was downbeat (he insisted "I think the whole idea of talking to people [on TV] is kind of over"). The tome was often caustic, sometimes nasty, and the targets of his jibes ranged from Steve Allen to Groucho Marx. However, Paar was kindly disposed to successor Johnny Carson. That is, until "the misunderstanding." A mix-up (so it was claimed) occurred when Paar let it be known he wanted to go on "The Tonight Show" to promote his new book. The invitation was not forthcoming and he became indignant. He insisted, "He [Carson] has a thing about me. I invented that kind of TV."

A SPECIAL MOMENT

In May of 1986, NBC had a self-congratulatory TV Special honoring several decades of broadcasting and had all the hosts of "The Tonight Show" on the program, including Steve Allen, Jack Paar and Johnny Carson. To promote his own upcoming Special ("Jack Paar Comes Home" which featured kinescopes of past shows) on November 29, 1986, Paar finally made it to the other side of the desk on "The Tonight Show."

After exchanging compliments, Johnny led an emotional Paar to the visitors' couch and advised viewers, "We should lay a couple of things to rest. Jack and I are not what you'd call close friends...the longest conversation we had was maybe five or ten minutes, some years ago when we first met, and that was about it." Later, Jack got quite teary-eyed in describing the merits of his forthcoming TV project. A bemused Carson kept reassuring his predecessor, "Stay as long as you like" and Paar did, regaling the audience with anecdotes. This led Carson to quip, "Why do I feel I'm guesting on our show." Finally, Johnny asked, "Why'd you give up 'The Tonight Show'?...You could've been here today." Jack shot back, "Well, you needed the work.... Nobody will ever equal what you have done on this show." Finally, after admitting, "I talk too much," a much-moved Paar exited.

An overwhelmed Johnny noted, "That's the longest conversation I've had with Jack Paar in 32-years." Thriving on having the last word, the following week, Jack told the press, "I go to bed early. I've seen Johnny Carson ['s show] maybe five times in my life." On December 19, 1987, Paar returned with another—his most recent—TV special, "Jack Paar Is Alive and Well!" which again featured clips from his "The Tonight Show" years.

WELL DESERVED

In April 1991, Paar was honored at the Museum of Broadcasting's annual TV festival held at the Los Angeles County Museum of Art. That December he was coaxed out of retirement to lead a seminar at the Museum of Television and Radio in midtown Manhattan. He showed highlights of his old shows and talked about favorite guests.

Today, Jack prefers to devote his energies to his hobbies of painting and gardening. He is a grandfather (daughter Randy, a trial lawyer, married and became a mother with the birth of her son in 1985). When queried whether he would ever make a talk show return, he says, " I really don't know. The thing that would worry me is that audiences have stopped laughing. They now clap, whistle and yell 'Yo.' I don't know what the hell that means." When asked about the current crop of "Tonight Show" offshoots, he terms them "sleazy" and thinks Phil Donahue is "a disgrace."

As to the recently-retired Johnny Carson, Paar quips, "I should never have given the 'Tonight Show' to him; I should have rented it or married him." He admits, "I am from a different age, when conversation was not on a cue card" and that "I have little or no talent. I can't sing and I can't dance. But I can be fascinating." In further self-assessment, he claims, "I'm a feisty guy who fought for what I believed in" and that "If I've made any contribution to the medium... I like to think it's been in making conversation respectable again."

Whenever Paar is asked the $64,000 question of why he left his hit show in 1962 he responds, "I've never really had a good answer to that. Well, I guess I did a pretty amazing thing there, but we'll just have to put up with it." As to his tombstone, he insists whimsically that he intends the marker to read, "You had your chance, and now he's gone."

TV & CABLE SERIES:
Up to Paar [I've Got News for You] (NBC, 1952)
Bank on the Stars (CBS, 1953)
The Jack Paar Show (CBS, 1953-1956)
The Morning Show (CBS, 1954-1955)
Tonight [The Tonight Show/The Jack Paar Tonight Show] (NBC, 1957-1962)
The Jack Paar Show [The Jack Paar Program] (NBC, 1962-1965)
Jack Paar Tonight [Jack Paar Tonite] (ABC, 1973)

FEATURE FILMS:
Variety Time (1948)
Easy Living (1949)
Walk Softly, Stranger (1950)
Love Nest (1951)
Down Among the Sheltering Palms (1953) [made in 1951]

Chapter 8
DINAH SHORE

Like the late Kate Smith, another charming southern songbird, Dinah Shore is a beloved American institution. A staple of the entertainment scene, Dinah has been singing and talking professionally since the 1930s. In the 1940s she was Queen of the Jukeboxes (leading to 19 gold records); in the 1950s and 1960s she emerged as Queen of Television with her variety series. She started winning Emmy Awards in such abundance that, by the time she accepted her 8th (a record for a performer in TV history!) in the 1970s, the industry was quipping that if she "wins any more Emmys her house will sink." Over the years, the warm-hearted entertainer with the down-home personality has been frequently on the list of the ten most admired women in America and/or the world.

There are many sides to the ever-evolving Dinah Shore, once accused of having an "eternal smile." (In fact, cynical entertainer Oscar Levant once jibed, "I can't watch Dinah Shore. My doctor won't let me. I'm a diabetic.") Some of the public forever associates her with her trademark lip-smacking "m-m-m-m-m-mah" as, at the end of each of her 1950s TV shows, she would blow a kiss to viewers while advising them to "See the U.S.A. in your Chevrolet." Still others think of her as the wife of a handsome screen leading man (George Montgomery) who, after her divorce, had a much ballyhooed relationship with rugged, much younger movie star (Burt Reynolds). Then there is the contingent who admire Dinah the driven athlete, who excels at sports and has her own annual golf tournament.

Physically, 5'6", 110-120 pound Dinah has always been remolding her image, seeking a fresh look as times change. "Not being pretty really helped," she reflected once. "I never sat back and said, 'Look, I'm pretty.' Nobody every said I was. So I always worked on my appearance." Intellectually and emotionally, there are many contradictions to this bubbly star. She has admitted, "As a girl, singing never seemed more to me than something to fill the gap between school and marriage." However, as an ambitious performer/survivor, she has proved her inner strength time and again. *TV Guide* once assessed this complex individual as "an attractive and vivacious woman with an abundance of nervous energy, a quick mind and an instinctive knack for remaining very much the female while still holding sway in what is supposed to be a man's world."

She was born Frances Rose Shore on March 1, 1917 in Winchester, Tennessee, a small town on the western slopes of the Cumberland plateau. She was the second child (there was eight-year-older Elizabeth) of Solomon Aaron and Anna (Stein) Shore. Solomon was European-born, coming from a family of teachers. When he and his wife Anna settled in Winchester, he opened a small department store. Not only did the Shores have to cope with being the only Jewish family in town, but there were many on-going battles at home. Solomon was very stable, goal-oriented, while Anna had an artistic temperament, and was frustrated by her desire to be an opera singer (she had a rich mezzo soprano voice).

BLESSING IN DISGUISE

When Frances was eighteen months old, she contracted poliomyelitis, which led to paralysis in her right leg/foot. As recuperative treatment over the next several years, she was made to exercise strenuously and, later, to take ballet, swimming and tennis lessons. She would recall, "The early experience made me shy and ambitious at the same time.... I knew I had to do something to prove myself." Her mother pushed her hard. As a result of the illness, she felt ashamed. "I was constantly singing, dancing, and showing off in a desperate bid for attention and to prove I could do it." Most of the child's affection came from a black nursemaid Lillian Taylor ("Ya-Ya") who would take her charge to Church on Sunday to hear the congregation singing spirituals. (It was there that the future singer developed her love of, and talent for, singing the blues.)

In 1923, the Shores moved to Nashville, where Solomon became involved in a large department store concern. At public school, Frances still had a limp which caused her peers to make fun of her. By the time she was ten, Frances had almost overcome her handicap (through swimming and playing tennis daily), but had a hard time adjusting to the strong tensions at home. The shouting between her parents made her resolve never to be that way herself, vowing to be a compliant individual when she married.

As a teenager, Frances (her nickname was "Fanny") was skinny, awkward and rather unattractive. She had very black hair, a dark complexion and a prominent hooked nose. In a bid for positive attention, she learned to play the ukulele, but not good enough. The parental tug-of-war carried over into what sort of musical training she should have. Solomon hated anything to do with show business, while Anna wanted her to sing classical songs. Finally Fanny was allowed to take lessons from a professional teacher (John A. Lewis). It was Lewis who suggested she join the First Presbyterian Church choir for experience. However, she lasted there only a short time because she realized she was not equipped to sing in harmony. She was a solo act.

At fourteen, Fanny displayed her ambitious bent. She received $10 for performing at The Pines, a nightclub on the outskirts of Nashville. She did it secretly. However, when she arrived, in the midst of a rainstorm, and began singing "Under a Blanket of Blue," the dripping novice looked up to spot her shocked parents sitting in the audience. Ever anxious to fit in, Fanny was a cheerleader at Hume-Fogg High School, appeared in a Gilbert and Sullivan operetta and acted in class productions of "Little Women" and "Outward Bound."

PSYCHIC ABILITY?

In 1933, when Fanny was sixteen, she suddenly had a premonition at school that something was wrong with her mother. When she finally got to the principal's office and called home, the family maid told her that Mrs. Shore was indeed sick. Fanny ran home the fifteen blocks. Her mother died a few minutes later. Because Solomon was on the road so often supervising his chain of drygoods and notion stores, Fanny's sister, Elizabeth, married to Dr. Maurice Seligman, moved from St. Louis to Nashville to take care of her sibling. At age seventeen, anxious for her own life to begin, Frances planned to elope with the captain of the high school swimming team. However, she told too many people, her Dad intervened, and that was the end of the romance.

After graduating from high school, Frances attended Nashville's Vanderbilt University, majoring in sociology. During her years there, she played sports, did light musical shows with the Masque Club and was president of the Women's Student Government Club. By now, she had resumed vocal lessons with John Lewis and her singing style was reminiscent of Ella Fitzgerald. While a college sophomore, she went to the local radio station WSM where Lewis was performing.

Once in the studio, he told her to start singing, that the microphone was "dead." It was not and the audition won her a job singing on a five-minute, twice-weekly show ("Rhythm and Romance"). By now, she was calling herself Fannye Shore. The theme song for the program was "Dinah" which Fannye would sing in the style of Ethel Waters. In the summer between her junior and senior year, she visited New York for a convention of her college sorority. She remained for several weeks, making the rounds of radio stations, hoping to get a singing job, finally maneuvering an audition at NBC. However, when she arrived at the Rockefeller Center studio to sing, she developed a strong case of mike fright. No words would come out, and that ended her test. Her father convinced her to return home.

By the time she graduated from Vanderbilt in 1938, Fannye had three marriage proposals. However, she was determined to have a singing career. Mr. Shore was determined to crush her show business hopes and refused to advance her funds to return to New York City. Her sister and brother-in-law gave her moral support, but had no money to help her. Resolute Fannye sold her camera equipment for $250 and, with the proceeds, bought a one-way ticket to Manhattan.

SOMETHING FOR NOTHING

She soon realized how tough it was to break into radio. As the weeks passed, she moved to cheaper and cheaper hotel/rooming houses. One day, she auditioned at radio station WNEW, willing to sing on the air for nothing. She was heard by head disc jockey Martin Block and music director Jimmy Rich. She sang "Dinah." They said they would call her. They did, but forget her first name, referring to her as Dinah.

The new first name stuck (and in 1944 she legally adopted the name Dinah Shore). She began singing for free whenever there was an opening at WNEW. (Other vocalists doing the same thing at WNEW were Frank Sinatra, Dennis Day and Frankie Laine.) Later, NBC hired her at $50 a week to sing on a proposed Lennie Hayton's Orchestra radio show. However, the program never got on the air. Next, it was auditioning and being rejected by Tommy Dorsey that caused Dinah to alter her appearance. Reacting to adverse remarks about her skirt, sweater and bobby socks outfits, she developed a more glamorous image.

By now, perky Dinah, who sang wherever the opportunity arose, was being sponsored by George T. Simon of *Metronome* magazine as well as by the editor of *Down Beat*, and was becoming known as "the darling of *Le Jazz Hot*." Nevertheless, by New Year's Eve of 1938, she was

Clint Eastwood chatting with Dinah Shore on "Dinah's Place" in 1974.

broke. She called home to admit defeat. Her sister came on the phone and convinced Mr. Shore to send Dinah some much-needed funds.

The year 1939 started out far better. Dinah got a $75 a week job singing with Leo Reisman's Orchestra for two weeks at the Strand Theatre in Brooklyn, although the first week she lost $60 of her pay to a pickpocket. Soon thereafter, using her soft cooing soprano, she began recording with Xavier Cugat's Orchestra for $20 a record, performing such tunes as "The Thrill of a New Romance" and "The Breeze and I." In March 1939, she joined Ben Bernie for a CBS network program, but was fired two weeks later because the sponsor (American Tobacco Company) thought she sang too softly, slowly, and with a funny accent. (Ironically, years later she performed on "Your Hit Parade," sponsored by the American Tobacco Company and received $2,500 weekly for that stint.) Later in the year, she signed with RCA Victor to make recordings, was now heard on NBC network radio programs, and sang at Nick's Club in Greenwich Village.

MAKING AN IMPRESSION

For a few months of 1940 Dinah was billed as "Mademoiselle Dinah Diva Shore" singing on NBC's "The Chamber Music Society of Lower Basin Street," a lampoon of serious music programs. Then show business giant Eddie Cantor asked Dinah to audition for his "Time to Smile" NBC radio program. After singing in her sentimental style for well over an hour, the diminutive Cantor sauntered onto the stage and said to the exhausted Dinah, "Forgive me for making you sing so long. But I figure it's the last time I'm ever going to hear you for nothing." Under Eddie's tutelage, Dinah learned to slow down when performing. By now, her sister and brother-in-law had moved to New York to live with Dinah in Forest Hills.

In 1941, *Motion Picture Daily* conducted a poll for the country's best female vocalist, and Dinah won. Edgar Bergen wanted her to join his popular "Chase & Sanborn Comedy Hour" but she was still under contract with Cantor, who raised her salary to keep her happy. By the fall of 1942, Dinah had been proclaimed the Queen of the Juke Boxes. She was earning over $115,000 a year, but due to poor business advisors, she had to regroup financially.

Before the year was over, Eddie Cantor had used his film connections to negotiate for her a screen assignment at Warner Bros. Dinah and her relatives moved to Los Angeles; the Seligmans settled in Beverly Hills, while Shore moved into a Hollywood duplex with big band vocalist Kitty Kallen and others. When not working at the Hollywood Canteen or singing on "Command Performance" or her own radio show, Dinah was undergoing a transformation. Her black hair became honey blonde and she got rid of her pompadour hairdo. She learned to lighten her makeup to compliment her dark complexion. More importantly, she had plastic surgery to restructure her face (especially her nose) and had her teeth capped to remove the gap between her two front teeth.

By 1943, Shore could be heard on radio's "Dinah's Open House" (*Variety* rated her "one of the top emotional ballad singers") and then on "Paul Whiteman Presents." That August she made her movie debut in THANK YOUR LUCKY STARS, an all-celebrity outing in which she sang several numbers. And then she met handsome, Montana-born George Letz, better known as Twentieth Century-Fox contract leading man, George Montgomery. Dinah had first become aware of him when she had performed at the Steel Pier in Atlantic City.

Between shows, she went to a nearby movie theatre and fell in love with the star of the picture—George Montgomery. Time passed and she was singing at the Shrine Auditorium in Los Angeles when she spotted George in the audience. Her on-stage co-performer Bing Crosby would say later: "She may look like cotton candy wouldn't melt in her mouth. But, she knows what she wants, and she's harder than flint about getting it. I'd sure hate to be the man she sets her sights on! Poor George!" Eventually, Montgomery and Dinah met. However, due to his position as a Corporal in the Army Signal Corps, George was shipped to Alaska. Nevertheless, the two of them began a lively correspondence. Later, when he was shipped back to Los Angeles for reassignment, they decided to wed which they did on December 5, 1943 in Las Vegas at 3 AM. Three days later, he was transferred to San Antonio, Texas.

SECOND THOUGHTS

By now, Shore was the first lady of pop song with the G.I.s, a reputation enhanced by her three 1944 movies: co-starring with Danny Kaye in UP IN ARMS, singing in the all-star FOLLOW THE BOYS and joining with Randolph Scott and Gypsy Rose Lee in BELLE OF THE YUKON. The latter, a bad mix of satire and drama, suggested to Dinah (and the industry) that perhaps filmmaking was not the right medium for her. Like most show business people during World War II, Dinah did a great deal of entertaining the troops. She sang at local service camps and did a two-month tour in England and France, where she had a brief reunion with her serviceman husband. Then in May 1945 her father died.

Dinah signed with Columbia Records in early 1946. One of her first songs for that label was "Shoo Fly Pie" which did very well in the charts; even better-sellers were "The Gypsy," "For Sentimental Reasons" and "Doin' What Comes Naturally." By year's end, *Billboard* magazine had named her the top-selling female vocalist on the nation's juke boxes and over record counters. Domestically, she was determined to be the perfect, devoted wife. When not singing or filmmaking, she thrived on sports (tennis, golf, swimming) as well as her other hobbies (painting and photography).

She and George had purchased a two-acre lot in Encino (near Los Angeles) and Montgomery drew up plans for remodeling the existing ranch house there. He built all the furniture for the house. However, it was apparent already that the couple had very diverse personalities. She was a night person, he was a day type. She was very carefree about money, about being neat, and thrived on going off in many different directions; he was the opposite.

Along with fellow Columbia Records artist Frank Sinatra she recorded the duets "My Romance" and "Tea for Two" and her rendition of "The Anniversary Song" almost rivaled Al Jolson's hit version. Having dropped out of radio's "Birds-Eye Open House Show" she could be heard on "Ford Radio Show" with Peter Lind Hayes. After narrating a segment of Walt Disney's FUN AND FANCY FREE (1947) Dinah took a moviemaking sabbatical.

START OF SOMETHING NEW

Dinah found a new role, as mother, with the birth of daughter Melissa Ann, born on January 4, 1948. The next year she appeared at the Wedgwood Room at New York City's Waldorf-Astoria, where she had made her supper club debut eight years earlier. Her act was rated slick but aloof. That November, Dinah could be seen on NBC-TV on one of Ed Wynn's variety programs, which proved to be the forerunner of a new media career for her. Despite her negative feelings about her movie career to date, Shore felt a great affinity for the role of the mulatto Julie in SHOW BOAT and tested for the role at MGM. However, the part went to Ava Gardner for this 1951 screen musical.

At "loose ends," Dinah agreed to star in NBC-TV's "The Dinah Shore Show," a twice-weekly fifteen-minute offering, simulcast for radio listeners. The show was directed by Ticker Freeman who had been with Shore since 1938 as her piano accompanist. *Variety* enthused, "Miss Shore carries off the assignment with a charm and ease that established her right off as one of video's standout personalities." At the conclusion of her first TV show, she had a thirty-second gap to fill before the finale. She mugged with a hand to her mouth, kissed her fingers and blew the kiss out at the audience. She dropped the bit for show #2, but viewers wrote in to demand its return, and it became her trademark.

Being a live show, the program was full of unexpected moments. However, there was no doubt to anyone behind the cameras, that Dinah was in full charge. Increasingly a role model, Dinah was often asked to reflect on her dual professions. She said in the early 1950s: "I have only one fear, that if the time comes when the public no longer demands me and being a wife becomes a full time job, I'll not make as much a success of it as I have of the part-time one. Right now, I'm a successful career woman. In ten years, I'll tell you if I'm a successful woman."

Dinah and George had long wanted a brother for Melissa Ann, so in 1954 they adopted a son, John David who was nicknamed Jody. On March 7, 1955, Dinah earned the first of her eight Emmys to date, as Best Female Singer. On October 5, 1956, the very popular entertainer began her "The Dinah Shore Chevy Show" on NBC. The expanded air time to a full hour allowed her to do skits, invite top-name guest stars on the program, and to perform elaborate production numbers. For the first season, while she was still also starring in her fifteen-minute show, the hour program became a series of monthly specials. But then, in the fall of 1957, it became a weekly Sunday night affair. For its final two seasons (1961-1963), the program would be called "The Dinah Shore Show" and alternated with various specials on a rotating basis. Among the personalities Dinah introduced to the TV world, usually in song, were Maureen O'Hara, Yves Montand, Stephen Boyd, Gene Barry, Rosanno Brazzi and Craig Stevens.

ONE UP, ONE DOWN

Having sold their Encino ranch, the Montgomerys were living in Beverly Hills. When not doing her TV series, making recordings, or playing Las Vegas, Shore did volunteer work for the American Heart Association. As Dinah's career continued to grow professionally, George's was stagnating. "Hollywood's most successful marriage" was coming apart. He attempted a Western TV series ("Cimarron City") but it lasted for only one season (1958-1959). He next tried producing, writing and directing his own movies. In 1959 he went to the Philippines to make THE STEEL CLAW and was away for three months.

In 1960 he returned there to make SAMAR, taking with him a young Israeli actress, Ziva Rodann, as his co-lead. When Dinah was asked why she did not accompany George on location, she replied tersely, "I wasn't invited." There were rumors of a romance between Montgomery and Rodann during the shoot abroad, which both parties denied. During the summer of 1961, Dinah kept her children at their Palm Springs home, while George stayed at the Beverly Hills place. Reportedly, he began a relationship with one of the household staff, an aspiring actress. In November 1961, the employee was fired and, a few hours later, Shore announced that she and Montgomery were separating. He moved out of the house. The couple divorced in May 1962, which became final a year later.

With her TV schedule decreasing, Dinah moved to Palm Springs on a more permanent basis. She insisted she needed time "to think a little." She played a great deal of tennis and golf. (In 1970, she began the Colgate-Dinah Shore-Women's Circle Ladies' Professional Golf Association Tournament held annually in Palm Springs. By 1976, the Dinah Shore Tournament was pulling a very high TV rating and was soon boasting one of the richest purses on the women's professional golf circuit.) On May 26, 1963, Dinah married her tennis partner, Maurice Fabian Smith, a building contractor. Less than a year later (May 10, 1964) she filed for divorce, insisting "I couldn't make an independent decision because my husband criticized everything I did so much."

Although Dinah no longer had her own TV series, she continued to guest star in the medium, including a group of ABC-TV specials in 1964-1965. In 1966 she returned to New York supper club performing there for the first time in a decade.

TOO MUCH TIME

She did not realize how much "free" time she had until March 1969 when daughter Melissa Ann married and Jody returned to private school in Connecticut. Her long-time business associate Henry Jaffe evolved the idea of "Dinah's Place," after she spent a happy week co-hosting on "The Mike Douglas Show." Dinah's half-hour daily NBC-TV talk show debuted on August 3, 1970. Her first guests were two of her closest pals, Bea Korshak and Barbara Marx (later to be Frank Sinatra's wife). The studio set duplicated Dinah's own Beverly Hills home: large sun room, elegant living room, den, and a huge kitchen. The show's gimmick was to have Dinah on camera in the kitchen, making a favorite recipe as she chatted with celebrity guests. The program's underlying theme was to showcase the liberated new woman. *Variety* said: "Miss Shore made it all informal and friendly, showing a domestic ease.... The sets are fine, as are the prospects of this variety format." (In contrast, *Women's Wear Daily* complained that the guests were the show's backbone "because they relieve the tension Dinah creates by her forced, artificial casualness, the guests are really much more relaxed than the hostess.")

On "Dinah's Place," the segments ranged from Clint Eastwood showing Dinah how to pour and drink beer to Shore cooking after-tennis meatballs. George Hamilton might discuss the rise of mini bikes or Amanda Blake could be chatting about rug hooking. When former Vice President and Presidential hopeful Hubert Humphrey played around in Dinah's TV kitchen, he burned himself on a hot pot and cried out, "Oh, my God!" Then he groaned on air, "Well, I just blew the Bible belt." When Bishop Fulton J. Sheen was on the program, he sat there staring at Dinah, and she recalls, "I could only sit there and stare back." Frank Sinatra came on to cook spaghetti and sing, Leslie Uggams made sweet potato pie, Burt Lancaster made a superior Italian spaghetti sauce, Ethel Kennedy played the piano, and Joanne Woodward did beautiful needlepoint.

Often, Dinah would sing on the show and a week's worth of programs were usually taped in two days. Frequently, she would tape an extra show in case she wanted a long weekend vacation. As to dealing with her on-TV guests, she explained: "I can't stand to embarrass anyone, even my own kids. My first reaction when people say something embarrassing is to help them cover. I admire people with strong convictions. I listen to all sides here, and I've learned that people with real convictions aren't that far apart in basic philosophy.... That's why I can talk comfortably with people who hold totally divergent views. What I don't question is their sincerity and that's what moves me...."

Shore admitted, "We don't have the time or luxury to probe. What we are is a *do* show, not a *talk* show. Almost everyone who comes on has something he wants to do...." The viewing public thought of "Dinah's Place" as a cooking show, which led the star to comment, "I don't like to dispel that notion, because it has enhanced my myth, but it really isn't a cooking show at all. In fact, the cooking is quite simply an obstacle course." (Shore would go on to author four cooking books, including *Someone's in the Kitchen with Dinah,* 1971, and *The Dinah Shore American Kitchen: Homestyle Cooking with Flair,* 1990.)

BACK ON HER HORSE

Riding a fresh crest of popularity with an Emmy Award for the show itself in the 1972-1973 season, Shore acknowledged her new career high: "I have what must be a growing ability to roll with the punches. I find I can put down any guilt that might come out of constant self-examination. I *feel* so many marvelous things. I wouldn't trade that for all the soul-searching in the world!" Part of Dinah's new joy was her rapport with macho actor Burt Reynolds, nineteen years her junior.

She first met him when he appeared on "Dinah's Place" in 1971. There were many similarities physically, in background and in personality between Reynolds and George Montgomery. The tabloids thrived on the Dinah-Burt relationship, constantly emphasizing the age gap and the fact that she was far better known than he (a fact that changed after his April 1972 nude layout for *Cosmopolitan* magazine). When Reynolds, previously married (1963-1966) to actress Judy Carne, was asked about possible nuptials with Shore, he responded facetiously, "I believe in good marriage. I also believe in the Tooth Fairy. I couldn't ever go through another marriage. That would just wreck me." Outspoken Carne said that she thought the Burt-Dinah thing was "strange and weird. Frankly, I think the whole relationship is a bit of a hideaway from people for Burt."

"Dinah's Place," despite its loyal following ended its run on July 19, 1974, a victim of shifting network politics. On October 21, 1974, Shore launched "Dinah!," a ninety-minute syndicated talk/variety show that was condensed to sixty minutes in some marketplaces. *Variety* predicted that the program, also with a living room setting, would establish itself as "solid competition to Mike [Douglas] and Merv [Griffin]." The forecast proved correct, for the show had a six season run, in the last year being known as "Dinah and Friends" when she added the gimmick of a weekly co-host. Although her singing voice was starting to wobble, her charm continued unabated, and she maintained her rule "I don't back people into a corner."

WINDING DOWN

Meanwhile, Shore's relationship with Reynolds was winding down. In 1973, while he had been filming THE MAN WHO LOVED CAT DANCING in Arizona, there were dramatic headlines when young business agent David Whiting killed himself, supposedly despondent over the film's co-star, Sarah Miles (then married to producer Robert Bolt) for showing too much interest in leading man Reynolds. At the time, Dinah flew out to be with Burt and to share his motor home.

When Burt flew to Mexico in early 1975 to film LUCKY LADY with Liza Minnelli, Dinah visited him frequently. By April that year, gossip columnists insisted the romance was *kaput.* However, in the fall of 1975 the couple reunited, and he moved into the $300,000

Malibu beach house she had leased. After filming GATOR (1975) in Georgia, for which Dinah sang the title song, Reynolds returned that December to be with Shore at her Beverly Hills home. Soon thereafter, the couple split for good. However, they remained on extremely friendly terms, even though he groaned, "It's like breaking up with the American flag." He would explain later of the parting, "Once you get past the fireworks stage, it's really difficult to pass on to the next stage gracefully...." (In 1988, he would marry actress Loni Anderson.)

Now a free agent, Dinah began dating a variety of eligible men: actor Ron Ely, rock star Iggy Pop and former pro tennis star Joe Iacovetta. Besides her TV activities, she was on the board of directors of the May Department Store Company, where her main task was to keep her finger on the public's pulse. Her friend and publicist Charles Pomerantz assessed candidly: "It's very difficult for Dinah to make a decision. And as far as knowing how to handle money, she's always had some sort of business manager. I know there have been stories about Dinah being an excellent businesswoman, but actually she isn't..... You only have to walk into a department store with her—it's like the locusts have arrived. She loves to buy things for herself, friends and relatives. No—handling money is not her thing."

Actress Marisa Berenson, comedian Joey Bishop and actor/game show host Bert Convy visit Dinah Shore on "Dinah's Shore" in 1976

STAYING BUSY

Dinah made her TV dramatic movie debut in the telefilm DEATH CAR ON THE FREEWAY in September 1979, and the next spring she was at liberty when her syndicated TV talk show went off the air. She and another talk show veteran, Dick Cavett, both made cameo appearances in HEALTH (1980) directed by Robert Altman. When Burt Reynolds was the subject of a 1981 Friars' roast, willing Dinah was aboard to toast her former beau. She teased, "Burt Reynolds has done more for little old ladies in tennis shoes than anyone else I know." She then raised her long gown to reveal sneakers. Burt responded, "Lady, I don't know what I've done for little old ladies in tennis shoes, but you knock my socks off."

Throughout the 1980s Dinah enjoyed her leisure. She did a good deal of painting, having studios in both her Beverly Hills home and her Malibu retreat. She played a lot of golf, especially when she stayed at her Palm Springs home which was on the grounds of the Mission Hills Golf Course. In 1986, between doing TV commercials, she returned to Winchester, Tennessee after a thirty-year absence for a homecoming event. Over 35,000 people showed up for the gala, proving Dinah had not lost her charisma. In 1987, she toured the U.S. and Japan, singing with a jazz group. Occasionally, she would be a guest star on a teleseries such as "Hotel" (1987) or "Murder, She Wrote. (1989). When asked the inevitable question, she would reply, as in April 1989, "Yes, I would like to do another television show. I belong in television and I'm not doing that now. It's a medium that I understand and enjoy and respond to. I guess it's the hambone in me."

On July 10, 1989 she returned to TV, this time to The Nashville (Cable) Network with "Dinah Shore: A Special Conversation with Burt Reynolds." The ninety-minute outing was taped in Los Angeles. This led to a sporadic series of "A Conversation with Dinah" between 1989 and 1991 on TNN, including one with Tennessee Ernie Ford.

ON HER OWN AGAIN

In October 1992, Dinah's sister Bessie passed away, and now with her son Jody already married, Shore was again fully on her own. She insists, that contrary to her reputation, she is not a Pollyanna. "I feel deeply and, of course, I get depressed. We all do. You're not a floating vegetable...." As to her current existence out of the TV grind, which includes partying with such pals as Frank and Barbara Sinatra and Steve and Eydie Gorme Lawrence, she admits, "There are some people who feel they owe every moment of their lives to the people who buy their services. I don't think of it that way. My private life is lovely and it's mine. I don't court it, I don't flaunt it, and I don't hide it." Her reaction to the current rash of TV talk shows is: "I'm not a prude, but some of the tasteless things I see and hear today in television are appalling. They're reaching for the bottom of the barrel and they're trying to see who can get there first.... You know, television is a microscope. You cannot be untrue to yourself. Eventually it finds out who you are.... I couldn't assume a different personality on camera. I wouldn't know how."

It should be noted that the energetic Dinah Shore of today does not remain idle professionally. She does concerts, many no-charge benefits, including events to support Israel. "Work's my blue blanket. That's who I am. I am a singer who thinks and feels and I don't want to lose that anchor."

TV & CABLE SERIES:
The Dinah Shore Show (NBC, 1951-1957)
The Dinah Shore Chevy Show (NBC, 1956-1957; 1957-1961)
Dinah Shore Specials (NBC, 1961-1963; ABC, 1964-1965)
Dinah's Place (NBC, 1970-1974)
Dinah! [Dinah! and Friends] (Syndicated, 1974-1980)
Dinah and Her New Best Friends (CBS, 1976)
A Conversation with Dinah (TNN, 1989-1991)

FEATURE FILMS:
Thank Your Lucky Stars (1943)
Up in Arms (1944)
Follow the Boys (1944)
Belle of the Yukon (1944)
Make Mine Music (1946) [voice only]
Till the Clouds Roll By (1946)
Fun and Fancy Free (1947) [voice only]
Aaron Slick from Punkin Crick (1952)
Gator (1975) [title song vocal only]
Oh, God! (1977)
Death Car on the Freeway (1979) [TV movie]
Health (1980)

Dinah Shore at work in the 1990s on "A Conversation with Dinah" with guests Ricardo Montalbam and Carol Burnett.

TODAY'S FAVORITES
OUR LIVING ROOM GUESTS

Chapter 8
DICK CAVETT

In the late 1960s, the TV talk show host "stable" included Johnny Carson, Merv Griffin, Mike Douglas, Virginia Graham, David Frost, Phil Donahue, etc. etc. Cheeky rival Dick Cavett insisted that "you could tell his show from the others because he didn't have Zsa Zsa Gabor on it." However, several other qualities set whimsical Dick apart from his videoland confreres. Not only was he a university trained stage actor, but, as one contemporary publication described him, he was "TV's most articulate and sophisticated host."

Veteran talk show participant Larry King said of this media intellect: "Cavett is a conversationalist—he is as much the subject to the interview as the guest. But this works for Cavett because he's clever and witty and gives listeners the sense that they are the third person at a dinner party." Clean-cut Cavett himself agreed, explaining once, "It's so much nicer when it's more of a dialogue; it's so much easier when you have that break-through, and you get into something that resembles actual speech as it would be spoken away from the lights and the camera.... When that happens, I feel that I'm in it as an equal, rather than as somebody who is standing aside."

However, there is considerable complexity behind this puckish picture of sartorial splendor. At 5'6" he has always been sensitive about his height and slight build. Also, beneath his mild-mannered Ivy League demeanor lurks a sharp temper and a short fuse when he feels anyone is giving him a difficult time, whether it be a network executive, a TV audience heckler or a taxi driver. As a show business participant/devotee, he has long combatted his undying awe of celebrities. "I get very, very nervous when I think that all that separates me from them is air."

When asked in the early 1970s to elaborate on his star-worshipping, he explained his mixed feelings in typically erudite fashion: "For 90 minutes someone I've always admired is totally in my hands and it's up to me to help that person get through the show. There's a sense of power in that, but there's also a sense of 'When am I going to grow up and do whatever it is that this is preparing me for?' The thought of doing this for the rest of my life is just unthinkable.'"

A HIGH INTELLECT

Like his peer Merv Griffin, Dick has always been fascinated by word games. However, in true Cavett form, he celebrates this enthusiasm on a purely cerebral level, terming himself a "word prig." In another bit of self revelation, he has admitted he "uses language as a mask, a weapon and a distraction." He confesses that he employs word games as conversational icebreakers. ("Anything that fights despondency is something I like very much.").

In retrospect, there were many hints that wiry Dick Cavett was coping with great emotional pressure over decades of parading through the limelight. Even when he was at a career peak, there would be a pessimistic flavor to his conversation. He would state publicly that the strain of doing his TV talk show was a lot to be "endured" and that, to compensate, he sought to keep in physical shape.

He disclosed that the fear of doing a bad show always lurked in the wings, spoiling the pleasure of his success: "when I feel the talk is good, I can almost enjoy myself." When pressed, he confessed his great professional dichotomy: "I sometimes wish I had made a clear decision that I was going to be strictly commercial or that I was going to provide a radical alternative." He joked that even having guests for a dinner party would be a form of Chinese torture.

He and his actress wife Carrie Nye were great loners, always more content to be off by themselves. Cavett felt tremendous insecurity about the future, masking his concerns in urbane self-mockery: "Gawd I wish I knew where I was going. I often wonder what the hell kind of future I have. Of course, I exert a lot of influence over myself."

Dick Cavett of the 1990s.

Only in mid-1992 would Cavett bravely divulge what family and close friends had known for a long time. Over the years, he had been suffering from great bouts of depression, ranging back to his student days at Yale University. He indicated that he had undergone extensive shock treatment therapy in the early 1980s to stabilize his emotional vacillations.

CAVETT THE CORN HUSKER

He was born Richard Cavett on November 19, 1936 in the tiny town of Gibbon, Nebraska. (This only child would kid later, "The fact that I come from the Corn Belt contradicts my air of academia, though if I keep talking like this it won't.") Both his parents, Alva B. and Eva (Richards) Cavett were school teachers. His maternal grandfather was a Baptist preacher. During Dick's first years, the Cavetts moved to nearby Grand Island where they lived close to the railroad tracks. A few years later, they relocated to much larger Lincoln, Nebraska. The Cavetts existed on a tight budget, which improved a bit by the early 1940s.

Even as a toddler, Dick was precocious. Alva, then a high school English teacher, would read Shakespeare to his youngster. By the age of four, Dick was reciting A.A. Milne poetry. What made the youngster stand out especially from his friends was his short stature and the fact that, from a very early age, he possessed a booming, deep voice. (Cavett reflected once: "I have a feeling that about 90% of my life has been shaped by my voice, both as an embarrassment and as an advantage.")

By the time he was in the fourth grade he was correcting his teacher's spelling errors. Once when a teacher warned her students not to be stubborn as a German or sneaky as an Indian, little Dick retorted, "Don't foist your prejudices on us." Many of Cavett's summers were spent in Greeley, Colorado where his parents were each working on their individual master's degree at Colorado State Teachers College. Young Dick may have been advanced intellectually, but he had his limitations. One time he went swimming with a neighborhood friend, Mary Huston. The only problem was that he could not swim. When he stepped into too deep water, she had to drag him to safety.

In 1946, when Dick was ten, his mother died of cancer. A year later, Mr. Cavett, remarried, this time to a math instructor named Dorcas. While Dick had a reputation for aloofness and snobbery in school, he did his best to hide the fact that his parents were teachers, fearful that his classmates would think he had special tutoring sessions at home (he did not) or was given good grades as a professional courtesy to his parents (he was not).

FLIPPED OUT

Once Cavett overheard his father saying that he hoped his son would someday get a letter in sports. This remark prompted teenager Dick to participate in gymnastics and to later win two gold medals as state champion. However, he much preferred his solitary hobbies: magic, stamp collecting, theatrical makeup. He was an avid TV viewer, and particularly enjoyed watching stand-up comedians. He felt an instant identification with these professionals. He also had a passionate interest in Indian history and would spend hours at the old Historical Society in the basement of the state capitol at Lincoln, gazing at artifacts of the Plains Indians.

By age fourteen, the fledgling entertainer was participating on a local Saturday morning radio show. One of the fifteen-minute offerings was an abridgement of "Macbeth." Already an enthusiastic amateur magician, Cavett was overjoyed when he was hired at $100 to perform his magic act at a stadium in Omaha. However, only three people showed up for the unpromoted show and Dick never was paid his fee.

However, on the way home, Mr. Cavett cheered his son with "We had a $1,000 worth of fun." The episode encouraged Dick to stick by his ambitions. One day the budding prestidigitator was waiting in the wings to do his magic act at the Lincoln Lions Club. The announcer told the audience, "We have a disappointment for you. We couldn't get Johnny Carson today. But we have a young man who someday is going to be just as good." (By this time, Carson was doing both radio and TV shows from Omaha, earning extra money doing his magic act. On a later occasion, Dick would meet Johnny who was appearing in a church basement in Omaha.)

As a self-assured teenager, Dick was convinced he was the world's next Bob Hope. Naturally, when Hope came to perform at the University of Nebraska Coliseum, Cavett had to get a special audience with his idol. At the stage door, as Hope emerged to get into a waiting car, Cavett offered, "Fine show, Bob." Hope replied, "Thanks, son." (Years later, Hope would be a solo guest on Dick's TV talk show and, in 1977, Cavett would host the Lincoln Center Tribute to Bob.)

ONE WAY TO GET THE LADIES

Cavett was a natural high achiever in school. Although he had no real interest in student government, he got elected to the state-wide presidency of student councils. Also in high school, it occurred to him that one way to compete with the jocks (and to attract girls) was to perform on stage. Thus, with the dramatics club, he appeared in "Arsenic and Old Lace" and "Our Town" and would do a one-act play ("Soldadera") with future Academy Award-winner Sandy Dennis.

In the summer of 1953, a new stock theatre opened in Lincoln and Cavett was hired to play the title role in "The Winslow Boy."

Although still an adolescent, Dick was making subconscious career decisions. In 1952, he had attended his first International Brotherhood of Magicians convention in St. Louis. There he won a "Best New Performer" trophy. At the winners' banquet, each victor was to take a bow. In a flash, Cavett stood on a chair when it came to his turn. ("Some instinctual thing had told me how to get that laugh.")

Later, as student council president, he had to introduce a speaker, who slowly made his way toward the stage from the back of the auditorium. En route, the speaker apologized, "I'm sorry for this long entrance. I didn't mean for it to be dramatic." Impulsively, Dick shot back, "Don't worry. It's not." Cavett would recall, "The laugh hit like a thunderclap, and again I knew that I wanted to be a comedian."

Dick graduated from Lincoln High School in 1954 and received a scholarship to Yale University. Immediately upon arriving at the New Haven campus he realized the great contrast between himself (a country rube and poor) and most of the other students (urban sophisticated and wealthy). At college, Dick did not gravitate to any do-gooder groups or even to try for membership in a fraternity.

When not in classes, he played in and directed radio dramas on WYBC, the campus station. He participated in formal entertainments provided by the Saybrook Players, a troupe from the residential college where he lived as an upperclassman. He would appear in several major productions of the Yale Dramatic Society, including playing Reverend Hale in "The Crucible" and participating in a musical version of "The Great Gatsby" (in which future TV star James Franciscus had the lead).

STAR CRAZY

Admittedly pretentious and snobbish, uninhibited Dick continued his habit of celebrity-meeting. When Maria Riva (daughter of Marlene Dietrich) was starring in a touring production of "Tea and Sympathy" in New Haven, he went backstage after a performance to chat with the actress. He conversed with her in German and invited her to visit the campus the next day. She did!

On one of his frequent treks to New York City to see Broadway plays and to star gaze, Cavett spotted comedian Fred Allen on the street and stopped him to chat. He thought nothing of worming his way backstage after a performance of "My Fair Lady" to meet Rex Harrison or, on another occasion, to talk his way into a brief audience with Judy Garland. A few years later, the unquenchable admirer of the famous learned of the pending service for playwright George S. Kaufman at Campbell's Funeral House in Manhattan. Cavett rushed over to page homage and there encountered Groucho Marx, with whom he began a long-standing acquaintanceship.

During the summer after his sophomore year of college, Cavett worked at the Oregon Shakespeare Festival in Ashland. After the season finished, he took the bus back east. En route, he stopped off in Las Vegas. He walked into one deserted casino lounge and stood behind the standing microphone, imagining an enthusiastic audience listening to Dick Cavett, comedian. The summer after his junior year at Yale he worked at the Stratford Shakespeare Festival in Connecticut. He had one line in "The Merchant of Venice," a production starring Katharine Hepburn.

One of the actresses Dick met at Yale Drama School was Carrie Nye McGeoy, a banker's daughter from the Delta country of Mississippi. She would recall of her then future husband,

"His idea of a good time was to go drink sherry in his room and read Dr. Johnson's dictionary." Cavett graduated from Yale in 1958 with a B average. That summer he and Carrie worked at the Williamstown, Massachusetts summer theatre. Among the shows they played in were "A Streetcar Named Desire," "Auntie Mame" and "Cyrano de Bergerac." During their next summer there, Dick worked two weeks in a local lumberyard to earn money to buy an engagement ring for Carrie, but the nuptials were still to be a long way off.

AN EMOTIONAL BATTLE

By the fall of 1959, Dick and Carrie were each living in New York City. Having recovered the previous year from a severe bout of mononucleosis, he had now begun the ritual of having one of any number of (imaginary) fatal diseases. It was also the start of his first serious emotional low, a condition that had first surfaced during his Yale years.

The creative team of PBS-TV's "The Dick Cavett Show" (1978-1982): Clockwise: producer Jackie Craig, director Richard Romagnola, producer Robin Breed,] and host Dick Cavett.

In retrospect, Cavett says, "I think now that those hypochondriacal episodes were the beginning of depression for me." What was getting Cavett down was the sudden downslide of his budding career. In his first New York days he had won a role as a foppish cadet in a Signal Corps movie being shot on Long Island and was paid $100 for the two-day assignment. He had a walk-on bit on TV's "Sergeant Bilko," did extra work on a TV revival of "Body and Soul" and later played a young Nazi on a "Playhouse 90" production of "The Hiding Place" starring James Mason. Then his career fell apart. To support himself, he took office temp jobs doing typing and filing. For a spell, he wrote reports based on his undercover observations of department store workers.

At times, Cavett, then living in a fifth floor walk-up apartment on West 89th Street, grew so dispirited that he remained in bed for days at a time. When he would go out, it would be to take a part-time job or make the rounds of actors agencies. "During that time," says Cavett, "I did nothing but watch Jack Paar on 'The Tonight Show.' I lived for the Paar show. I watched it from my bed on my little black-and-white set on my dresser, and I'd think, 'I'll go brush my teeth in a minute,' and then I'd go to sleep and wake up at 3 the following afternoon."

One of Dick's temp jobs was being a copy boy for *Time* magazine. One day in 1960, learning that Jack Paar was searching for new material for his "The Tonight Show" monologues, he devised some dialogue for Paar. He put it in a *Time* publication envelope and sought out Jack

Paar at the Rockefeller Center TV studios. Through his *Time* credentials, Dick got through security and ran into his idol in a building corridor.

Later that day, Cavett would be sitting in "The Tonight Show" audience and was able to hear Paar working some of his jokes into his routine. After the program, Paar encountered Cavett in the elevator. "Thanks pal," the star said. "You should do that again sometime." A week later, Dick did. It earned him a job on Paar's staff and he soon rose to the post of talent coordinator. (Cavett found it ironic that he could put anyone on "The Tonight Show" except himself.) In his capacity of discovering fresh talent for Paar's daily outing, Dick would visit the local clubs. At the Blue Angel, he heard and liked Woody Allen, who soon became a good friend of Cavett's.

A HOT COMMODITY

As a Paar show staff member, it was Dick who wrote the special introduction for buxomy film star, Jayne Mansfield, allowing host Jack Paar to advise viewers "And here they are!... Jayne Mansfield." On one occasion, Paar had as his shapely guest Miss Universe, a German woman who spoke NO English. Dick, who knew both German and French was ushered on stage to interpret for the visitor.

In the translation to English, Cavett's version of the lady's remarks received big laughs. Years later, Paar would recollect that during this "Tonight Show" period he once walked into his dressing room and found Dick Cavett standing on a chair. He was looking into the mirror and with his right arm raised (in the typical Paar salute) was repeating over and over, "I kid you not! I kid you not!"

In the early 1960s, Dick developed a reputation as a useful talk show writer. After Paar's late night show left the air, Cavett worked for Merv Griffin and then for Johnny Carson. He and fellow Nebraskan Carson never became pals, but they got along all right. Once Carson remarked about a new Cavett monologue,"I think you're capable of better work than this." In contrasting Paar to Carson, Cavett found the biggest difference to be "Paar's willingess to commit emotional hara-kiri on camera and Johnny's reserve."

In the later summer of 1963, Dick quit working for Johnny Carson to fly to Los Angeles to write for Jerry Lewis's new ABC-TV talk show. He was to be paid $1,250 weekly, three times what he had ever earned before. The largess was short-lived, for the Lewis outing was gone by late December 1963. A humbler Cavett returned to New York and to writing for "The Tonight Show."

NEW BEGINNINGS

The year 1964 was a watershed mark for Cavett. On June 4, 1964 he and Carrie were finally married in New York City. She was then appearing (to favorable reviews) in an off-Broadway production of "The Trojan Women" and the couple were wed between performances. The next month, Dick's idol, Groucho Marx, was guest host on "The Tonight Show."

Also that year, Cavett finally began his stand-up comedy life at try-out night at the Bitter End in Greenwich Village. It was Woody Allen who encouraged him to take this career step. ("Without Woody," insists Cavett, "I might have stayed too long as a comedy writer...and I would have felt frustrated and not known why.") The next year, having honed his performing skills, he went on the road to perform stand-up comedy at clubs in Chicago and San Francisco. In July 1965, he was a guest on Merv Griffin's TV talk show, still exhibiting a great many of Woody Allen-type mannerisms. Nevertheless, he was a hit and signed for several additional appearances. Also that year, he made it onto "The Tonight Show," hosted by Johnny Carson.

In the next few years, Dick kept quite active professionally, thanks to his agent, Jack Rollins (who was also Woody's). He made several game show appearances, was on a "Kraft Music Hall" TV show with Groucho, did a pilot for NBC ("The Star and the Story") with Van Johnson, and appeared on segments of ABC-TV specials ("Where It's At") devoted to new talent.

THE BIG BREAK

Finally, he received his big break when ABC-TV hired him to host "This Morning" a ninety-minute daily talk show that utilized the gimmick of having a late night format in the daytime. *Variety* found the host "wry" and "low key" and advised: "The whole thing could just work if Cavett doesn't let his natural reticence prevent him from taking charge more. He got off some humorous asides, but his questions of guests were too often on the lines of 'Tell me Pat Neal—may I call you Pat?—who helped you most during your illness?"

Dick's foil on this program was announcer Fred Foy. Cavett was soon doing battle with the demanding network who insisted they, not their star, knew best how to shape the project. Behind the scenes, Dick was coping with his on-going depressions. He recollects, "Most of the time I'd feel fine and function normally. Then, with no warning, I'd go into a slide. I was still experiencing dips in 1968 after I got my talk show on ABC. I would be doing the show and thinking, 'Dammit, here I have this witty guest and I wish I were at my best.'"

Before long "This Morning" became known as "The Dick Cavett Show." It went on hiatus in Janaury 1969, being unable to succeed in the arid morning time slot. However, it returned on May 26, 1969 as a prime-time series seen three-times weekly. When ABC dropped Joey Bishop's talk show in December 1969, the network replaced him with Dick.

The new host brought along announcer Fred Foy and orchestra leader Bobby Rosengarden from his past endeavors. For his premier outing on Decmeber 29, the guest lineup at the West 58th Street facility included Woody Allen and opera singer Beverly Sills. *Variety* judged that Cavett's "approach represents a step upward in sophistication, away from the more show business oriented style of Bishop, and holds much promise as welcome relief from the shopworn formulas of late night shows in general." Soon, Cavett was being touted as "Television's Most Tantalizing Talkmaster" and "The Talk Show Host for People Who Don't Watch Television."

DOING WHAT'S NECESSARY

Appreciating that ratings were everything, Dick was not above being an oncamera ham. On one show, he got in the ring with a wrestler and managed to throw his oversized guest. On another occasion, the curtains opened to reveal a trapeze strung from the studio rafters. Dick swung out on it and did a pull-over swing. ("I was sore for a week afterward," admits Cavett, "but God, it was worth it.")

Several of Cavett's segments were devoted to single-guest shows, featuring the likes of Woody Allen, Charlton Heston, Fred Astaire (who gave Dick a dancing lesson while on the air), Jack Lemmon and Anthony Quinn. At times, Cavett could be overly reverential as on the telecast spotlighting acting legends, the Lunts and Noel Coward. On the other hand, Cavett would just as quickly tell a guest (in this case Timothy Leary): "I think you're full of crap."

It was not beyond him to tell a subject who was lying, "I find that very hard to believe" or "I simply think you're wrong." During one interview with a son of the late President Franklin D. Roosevelt, the guest had promised to be forthright, but ended by being overly evasive. Cavett turned sarcastic: "Do you think you can bring yourself to answer something resembling the question I asked you?" When prime egotist Gore Vidal was holding forth one night, Vidal drew his chair apart in a demonstration of his "intellectual superiority" from the other visitors. Host Cavett promptly asked him whether he might need another chair to hold his oversized intellect.

The highlight during the reign of "The Dick Cavett Show" occurred in December 1971 when former Georgia Governor Lester Maddox walked off the show in a fit of temper. About a year later, he returned to Dick's forum. As a joke, this time, Cavett walked off the stage. Dick's action led Lester to cuing the orchestra and to begin singing, "I Don't Know Why I Love You Like I Do." Dick was back on stage to join in the second stanza. On another famous evening, Norman Mailer came close to punching Gore Vidal in the nose. And not to be forgotten was the occasion when publishing mogul J. I. Rodale died of a heart attack during a show taping.

COMFORTABLE TIMES

For his efforts to please viewers and the network, Dick was well paid (grossing about $15,000 weekly). He and Carrie had a handsome six-room East Side Manhattan apartment and a beach house retreat at Montauk, on the eastern tip of Long Island. He had his own production company known as Daphne Productions.

To boost ratings, he fought to get top guests and sometimes went on location, such as his London trek in May 1971. To attract viewer attention, he guest-starred on other ABC shows (the series "Alias Smith and Jones" and the pilot "Nightside"). However, ABC at the time was the weak sister to the other major networks, CBS and NBC. Dick not only had fewer outlets than his talk show competitors, but the promotion was not as intensive, despite Cavett's superior reviews. (At the time, Johnny Carson was getting an estimated 7.7. million nightly viewers compared to Dick's 3.4 million.)

Finally, in April 1972, ABC announced that if ratings did not improve by July 28, the show would be dropped as of October 3. The network's statement led to startling results. During the next few weeks, the network received an estimated 15,000 letters from the public, most of whom demanded that Cavett be retained. A good number of ABC affiliate stations conducted campaigns to "Save Dick Cavett."

The controversy kept "The Dick Cavett Show" on the air, but the ratings never really met with ABC's demands. By January of 1973, Cavett's show was cut down to one week a month in order to fill out his contract. (Jack Paar came out of retirement to fill another week of the cycle, now known as "ABC's Wide World of Entertainment.") Some of Dick's guests during this period were Laurence Olivier, Orson Welles, Katharine Hepburn and Marlon Brando. By late 1974, Cavett was on the air only two nights monthly and by New Year's Day, 1975, he had vanished from the airwaves.

A QUICK FILLER

In the summer of 1975, CBS gave him a short-lived (4 weeks) hour-long variety show. Doug Hennings and Liza Minnelli were guests on the series, but the show "lacked conviction; it was not persuasive" (*New York Times*). Cavett produced the misadventure which earned him $440,000 but cost him $500,000.

On the surface, Dick, who loved to scuba dive, play tennis, etc. seemed to be coping well. His marriage, thought the public, was going well. Carrie explained glibly how they avoided professional rivalry: "I don't try to be a talk show host and he doesn't try to be an actress." Little known was the fact that Cavett was undergoing severe depression.

After pointing out to her husband that he had been sitting in their bedroom most of the day for several weeks reading the same book, he agreed to seek help from one of his former talk show guests, Dr. Nathan Kline. The latter was a psychiatrist who was an early pioneer in the use of anti-depressants. After two weeks of treatment, Cavetts says, "the curtain lifted.... My dosage was tapered after six weeks, but later I stopped taking the drug because I thought I was doing okay. Worse still, I irresponsibly denied the return of the symptoms."

In 1976 he was doing occasional specials such as "Dick Cavett's Backlot" where he interviewed John Wayne, Mae West and Gene Kelly. In October 1977, he started the new "The Dick Cavett Show" on PBS-TV, a half-hour interview program, with Sophia Loren and Marcello Mastroianni among his first guests. For this go-round, he made his programming far less controversial, to keep in tune with the times.

He sighed with relief that "There's a blessed lack of pressure" on this non-commercial network. The PBS series extended through 1982. Much later, he would confess that during this period he endured his severest bout of depression. "Everything turns sort of colorless.... You lose all sense of self-esteem. Your manhood is a casualty...." He even began to feel suicidal. Then one psychiatrist suggested a new, stronger anti-depressant. Finally, one day, as he said later, "It was as if I woke up and a curtain rose and there was color in the world, and I could think of at least three reasons to live."

DICK DOES SOAP

Besides his various talk show chores, in 1979, he was on segments of the daytime TV soap opera, "All My Children" (returning again in 1983). Later, he would guest on "The Edge of Night" (1983). During the summer of 1979, he starred at the Williamstown Playhouse in Massachusetts in "Charley's Aunt." He would also perform there in "Room Service" and Noel Coward's "Nude with a Violin."

Looking back, Cavett targets May 1980 as his worst emotional period. He had boarded the Concorde at a New York airport, waiting to take off for England to tape TV interviews. Suddenly, he burst into a sweat. He had to be assisted off the plane and dispatched in a limousine to Columbia Presbyterian Hospital. Dick recounts, "They tell me I was in such a state of agitation that I kept trying to get out of the limo in traffic and that my assistant...literally had to wrap her arms around me and brace against the door to keep me from bolting."

Within a few hours of arrival at the hospital he was given electorconvulsive therapy (ECT). Cavett says, "ECT was miraculous. My wife was dubious, but when she came into my room afterward, I sat up and said, 'Look who's back among the living.' It was like a magic wand." He remained hospitalized for six weeks and from that time onward, has been treated with medication.

For four months in 1983 Cavett took over on Broadway for Tom Courntey in Harold Pinter's serious comedy, "Otherwise Engaged." In 1974, Dick and Christopher Porterfield (his Yale roommate and later executive producer of "The Dick Cavett Show") had co-authored *Cavett*. As a sequel to that very successful (auto)biography, the team wrote *Eye on Cavett* (1983). That year he also hosted an HBO Cable Network series, "Magic Moments," and had a wry guest appearance on the sitcom "Cheers." He was again at the helm of the one-hour "The Dick Cavett Show" (1985-1986) on the USA Cable Network which fell victim to poor ratings.

A FEW BAD TURNS

On September 23, 1986, he returned to major network TV with "The Dick Cavett Show," an ABC talk/discussion outing on Tuesday and Wednesday evenings from midnight to 1 AM. To avoid his old "house intellectual" image, he stated at the start of the new TV run, "We're going to dumb it up! We're going to bring out a fat Columbia [University] professor and make him dance by shooting at his feet!"

On the first telecast he showed the audience an Emmy (the one won by "The Dick Cavett Show" for the 1971-1972 season). While clutching it in his hands, the trophy fell apart. The "new" Dick Cavett promised viewers the show would have "no gimmicks and we won't do prizes...And if we do, they'll be tasteful." He then told guest Lily Tomlin that he had not yet seen her "brilliant" Broadway show, "The Search for Signs of Intelligent Life" (which had been playing for nearly a year) and then discussed the time fifteen years ago she had walked off his talk program. After thirteen weeks, "The Dick Cavett Show" was cancelled.

In 1987's A NIGHTMARE ON ELM STREET 3: DREAM WARRIORS Cavett did a cameo, ironically finding himself in the company of Zsa Zsa Gabor, the pseudo-celebrity he had always avoided having on his talk shows. From September to December, on the Disney Cable Channel, Dick hosted "College Bowl '87." He had a fun brief role in BETTLEJUICE (1988) and, in July 1988, took over as narrator in the Broadway musical, "Into the Woods." In this Stephen Sondheim-composed show, he got to sing a little at the end of Act One. It was a mild way of fulfilling a hidden, life-long ambition to be a song and dance man.

Also during this period, he had a Saturday radio show on WABC and appeared again in "Charley's Aunt," this time at the Burt Reynolds Theatre in Jupiter, Florida. He also wrote several magazine pieces on the state of the TV industry as well as doing audio tapes ("Oliver Twist," "Shane"). In the documentary FUNNY (1989), an art house release, Dick, Eli Wallach, Alan King, Henny Youngman, et al discussed the art of comedy.

COMING OUT OF THE CAVE

For the 1989 fall season, he began yet a new series of "The Dick Cavett Show." It was a three times weekly interview show on CNBC (Consumer News & Business) Cable Network. On this low-key outing, typical guests included Alan King, Marvin Hamlisch, Gore Vidal and Dennis Miller. The atmosphere on this latest show was extremely relaxed, far different from the current-day flash of proceedings hosted by Arsenio Hall or Jay Leno or the trash subjects exploited on the programs commanded by Sally Jessy Raphel, Montel Williams, Jenny Jones, Jerry Springer, Geraldo Rivera, et al. In July of 1992, Cavett could be seen as an evil disc jockey on a few episodes of the ABC-TV soap "One Life to Live."
For the same network, that October, he was a guest on Linda Lavin's sitcom, "Room for Two."

Coming out of the closet, in mid-1992, about his lengthy emotional tribulations has liberated this talk show veteran. Today's mature Dick Cavett seems far more at at ease with himself and life and it shows on his TV forum. He admits, "I haven't been incapacitated since the Big One...[in 1980]. There have been some dips, but with my daily medication and weekly therapy I have the means to battle it. I also have the support of my wife, who never threatened to throw me out or to take a walk. When things were bad, she would wisely say, 'That's the disease talking.'...I feel

Dick Cavett visiting on "The Merv Griffin Show" in the late 1970s.

really well, have lots of energy and am fully functional. I came out of a dark mine, and I know that if I ever go back in there again, I will be able to get out of it."

TV & CABLE SERIES:

This Morning [The Dick Cavett Show] (ABC, 1968-1969)
The Dick Cavett Show (ABC, 1969-1972)
ABC Late Night (ABC, 1973-1975)
The Dick Cavett Show (CBS, 1975)
The Dick Cavett Show (PBS, 1977-1982)
Magic Moments (HBO, 1983)
The Dick Cavett Show (USA, 1985-1986)
The Dick Cavett Show (ABC, 1986)
College Bowl '87 (Disney, 1987)
The Dick Cavett Show (CNBC, 1989-   )

FEATURE FILMS:

Annie Hall (1977)
Power Play (1978)
Health (1980)
Simon (1980)
A Nightmare on Elm
Street 3: Dream Warriors
          (1987)
Beetlejuice (1988)
Moon Over Parador
          (1988)
Funny (1989)

Chapter 9
PHIL DONAHUE

"Is the caller there?"
"Help me out with this."

These catch phrases are synonymous with Phil Donahue, the dean of TV talk shows. So are his patented gestures: running his hand through his hair, fiddling with his shirts buttons or racing pell mell up and down the studio aisles thrusting a microphone at vocal audience members. Phil of the baseball cap and sneakers was one of the first (in 1967) and certainly the most enduring TV host to rely on the interactive TV talk show format. (In this framework, both the studio audience and home viewers, by phone, are an integral part of the show.)

In a way, each "Phil Donahue" episode is like a Town Meeting on the Air, focusing on emotionally charged issues. And the more controversial the subject matter is, the better Donahue and his advertisers like it. Donahue has often reminded his program staff that "I want all the topics hot. Not even lukewarm. Hot!" This thrust once led *Newsweek* to observe: "One sometimes suspects that Donahue's idea of the perfect guest is an interracial lesbian couple who have had a child by artificial insemination." (Believe it or not, Phil would have such a duo on his show in 1979.)

To meet the increasing media competition and retain respectable ratings, frequently Phil has adopted an "almost anything goes" attitude. It led to his (in)famous 1988 segment on male transvestism in which he paraded on air in a bright red skirt, as well as another program that year dealing with the baldness mystique in which he shocked viewers by sporting a bald dome latex skull cap. (It was also in 1988 that he had the controversial segment on dwarf tossing.) But beyond the glitz of Donahue's quasi-trash theme shows (especially during rating sweeps weeks), he is a thoughtful commentator on the human condition.

Early in his TV career, Phil enunciated his basic belief: "The average housewife is bright and inquisitive, but television treats her like some mental midget." Humorist Erma Bombeck (once Donahue's neighbor in Centerville, Ohio) suggests, "he's every wife's replacement for the husband who doesn't talk to her. They've always got Phil who will listen and take them seriously." Genre rival Oprah Winfrey says, "I absolutely could not have accomplished what I have in this business if not for Donahue. He established the fact that women were interested in more than mascara. He set the standards." In fact, Donahue who admits shamefacedly that he once was a male chauvinist (blaming his sexism on his Roman Catholic upbringing), has long been a fervent feminist. He is also an extreme liberal, supporting full equality for all races, creeds, genders and sexual orientations.

Donahue is many things to many people. For some, hyper-active Donahue is "Father Confessor." To others, he is the husband of TV star Marlo Thomas and son-in-law of the late comedian, Danny Thomas. (Warning, do not expect to find Marlo sitting in Phil's studio audience, nor him to discuss, like Regis Philbin would, intimate details of his home life.) To yet others, like consumer activist Ralph Nader, Phil "really is a kind of First Amendment in action. He has celebrities on the show, but his great contribution is the participation of ordinary people."

Despite decades of such praise, Donahue is honest in his self-assessments. He admits openly, "Whatever insecurity problems I've had, I've never been short of chutzpah." He also is level-headed about his chosen profession: "Nobody needs to take a test to be a journalist. Nobody needs to have a college degree. Nobody needs to appear before a board. Nobody needs to give a urine analysis. Nobody has to do anything. Everybody can be a journalist, including moi." Despite his lack of "credentials," he feels a strong moral duty to viewers. "I don't feel obligated to walk down the center of every issue. But at the same time, I think it's really important not to preach. It's arrogant, and in a pragmatic sense, it's not good television."

Phillip John Donahue was born on December 21, 1935 in Cleveland, Ohio, the son of Phillip and Catherine (McClory) Donahue. (There would be a second child, Kathy, born when Phil was five.) Mr. Donahue, who had once wanted to be a professional musician, was a furniture salesman. By 1943, the family moved into their first-owned house on Cleveland's Southland Avenue. Phil's childhood was much influenced by Roman Catholicism. He went to Our Lady of the Angels Grammar School and was an altar boy at Our Lady of Angels parish. As a youngster, Donahue was combative, "I believe I fought because I was scared. Fighting proved to others that I wasn't scared." He was also an enthusiastic Cleveland Indians baseball fan, but not so great as a player on the church school team. When he was ten, he took tap dance lessons briefly because his dad thought it would give him confidence. Phil went along with the classes because he thought it would improve his baseball coordination.

In 1949, Phil attended the newly-founded all male St. Edward High School in suburban Lakewood, accepting that he did not have the scholastic drive needed to attend St. Ignatius, a Jesuit high school. He was a cartoon artist on the first edition of the school paper, and had a small part in the first class play, "An American Living Room." "Little Philly," as he was known, played the clarinet in the school band, but academically, he was, in his own words, "mediocre."

AN OUTRAGEOUS CHARGE

Because Notre Dame University, like St. Edward, was operated by the Holy Cross religious community, he was accepted there. A "highlight" of his first year on the South Bend, Indiana campus, was being summoned back to Cleveland to disprove a charge by a local girl who insisted to the Father at St. Ignatius that she had been married to Phil. It was later proven than she was mentally disturbed. While theology and philosophy were his favorite subjects in his sophomore year, he chose to be a business major. He acted in college plays; in his senior year playing Biff in "Death of a Salesman." When he was a junior, he met Margaret Mary Cooney, the sister of a classmate, who was then attending Marquette University. During the summer after his junior year, Donahue got a job at WNDU-TV, the NBC network affiliate station for South Bend. He kept his $1-an-hour job through his last two semesters at Notre Dame. His tasks included reading station break messages and doing commercials.

During the Easter vacation of his senior year, he auditioned for KYW-TV in Cleveland and was hired as a summer replacement announcer. Thus, the day after he received his B.A. degree in June 1957, he began employment at KYW. Donahue soon realized that being an announcer was boring. That October, armed with audition tapes, he went to Albuquerque, New

Phil Donahue in the 1980s.

Mexico where his girlfriend Margie Cooney was living with relatives. None of the local TV/radio stations would hire him, so he accepted a job sorting checks at the Albuquerque National Bank. On February 1, 1958, he and his sweetheart were married at the San Felipe de Neri Church in the Old Town section of Albuquerque.

By mid-1958, Phil was rehired at KYW-TV in Cleveland, but again it was only a summer assignment. When no other media offers were forthcoming, it was back to banking, this time counting money in the basement of the National City Bank in Cleveland. Fortunately, two weeks later, he received a job lead from his former South Bend, Indiana station manager. The position was at a small radio station in Adrian, Michigan (then a town of 23,000).

For $500 a month, Phil was the new Program/News Director. who also covered news in the field. In doing an investigative piece at the local dairy, the owner, who also was a city commissioner, threw him out of the office. It shattered Phil's idealism and caused him to realize, "Even in small-town journalism, it's not so much the nature of the material you are dealing with as the nature of the egos involved." The episode taught Phil to question the establishment, a novelty for a child of the '50s.

HIS FIRST COUP

After ten months in Adrian, Phil moved on to WHIO, the TV and AM radio station in Dayton, Ohio. By now, the young Donahues had become parents (Michael was born on January 30, 1959; Kevin was born on December 9, 1959). His WHIO salary was $6,700 a year. When ambitious Donahue obtained a brief interview with visiting teamster official Jimmy Hoffa, the hot news footage was used on the CBS Evening News with Walter Cronkite. A jubilant Phil regarded this as a coup, even though only his right hand showed on TV. Another first, filming former Presidential advisor Billy Sol Estes preaching at a church revival in Dayton, led aggressive Donahue to shipping the footage off to Walter Cronkite, but this episode was not aired.

As time passed, Phil developed a growing reputation as a respected street reporter and news anchor determined to be anything but a mushy-mouthed media newsman. As part of his station chores, he hosted a monthly Technology for Tomorrow show dealing with projects underway at Dayton's largest employer, the Wright Patterson Air Force Base. In retrospect, Phil could kick himself for having been so naive at the time about the TFT show (generated by the station, according to Donahue, to play up to the Pentagon). Looking back, he is amazed that his overwhelming desire to please his bosses caused him to lose sight of asking the hard questions or questioning interviewees' stock responses.

As he continued onward with WHIO in the early 1960s, Donahue sought to handle more far-reaching news stories. He went far afield to cover a mine disaster in Holden, West Virginia, but convinced the station manager to let him and his cameraman go on location. Once, when interviewing presidential candidate Richard Nixon, he got so vociferous in his interrogation, that he accidentally spat in Mrs. Nixon's eye. By 1964, the Donahues had four sons (now including Dan and Jim) and, in 1965, their only daughter, Mary Rose, was born. He was earning over $15,000 yearly and they had sold their first home and moved to a bigger house. Besides anchoring the 6 and 11 PM news, Phil found great satisfaction in moderating a daily afternoon radio show, "Conversation Piece." It utilized a telephone call-in talk show format, and it quickly developed high ratings.

By 1967, Phil was earning $20,000 yearly and had added a daily TV business program to his hectic schedule. Typically, he would be gone from home from noon to midnight, except for a brief return for dinner. It was little wonder that his wife felt abandoned and began hating his job and the TV business. Years later, Donahue admitted, "The fact that Margie's unhappiness grew without my even noticing it is itself evidence of my consuming professional ambition and only one indication of how little energy I was really giving to my responsibilities at home." Also in hindsight, Phil would realize that what had drawn him to Margie was her beauty not her inner person.

WANTING MORE

In June 1967, Phil quit WHIO ("My enthusiasm was dying as my job became routine.... I wanted out and up.") He went to work in the sales division of the E. F. MacDonald incentive/trading stamp firm. He had to take a cut in pay, but at least the hours were regular. This position lasted three months. By then, he had an offer from WLWD, a VHF-TV station in Dayton to do a "Conversation Piece" type show on television. The project offered him a guarantee of $24,000 during the first year of his two-year contract. Needless to say, he accepted the position immediately. Meanwhile, the growing liberal within Phil burst forth. He became involved in a heated controversy whether the Church of the Incarnation in Centerville, Ohio (where the Donahues resided) should build a huge expensive church. He was a dissenter, but the church was dedicated in 1969. Later, he would stop going to church altogether. He had also grown increasingly anti-Vietnam and was busing his oldest son, Michael, to an inner city school.

"The Phil Donahue Show" debuted on WLWD-TV on November 6, 1967. His first guest, setting the trend of shock TV, was atheist Madalyn Murray O'Hair. On the fourth show, the guest was a funeral director (and featured Phil actually reclining in a coffin). On the final show of the first week, Donahue exhibited a new, anatomically correct male doll (without a diaper). He asked viewers to phone in, if they approved or disapproved of the doll for children. Later in 1967, Donahue had an openly gay man on his pathfinding program. On January 4, 1968, Phil's father, age 64, died of a heart attack, having been too ill ever to see his son's new TV program. Eager to draw "big" name stars to his program to increase ratings, Phil relied heavily on celebrities like Phyllis Diller or Paul Lynde who were passing through Ohio or performing on the Kenley theatre circuit in the state.

The year 1969 was a watershed mark for Donahue. By then, he had moved away from Roman Catholicism reasoning, "The church was paternalistic and hardly on the cutting edge of social change. The church had become a hurdle that was not worthy of my energy." Now, after two years as local programming, "The Phil Donahue Show" was being picked up by other stations and, later, syndicated nationally. (However, some outlets, even in the more sophisticated New York City marketplace, dropped the fast-paced program as being far too controversial for its viewers.) *Variety* analyzed that the key to Phil's success was "a handsome, Kennedy-like wit and intelligence which is always restrained but is quick to interject for the benefit of viewer clarity or understanding."

ANYTHING GOES

In the early years of "The Phil Donahue Show," some of the most contested programs that were censored by stations around the country included those dealing with such subjects as: film of an actual abortion, the birth of a baby on air, lesbian mothers who won custody of their children, mistresses anonymous, parents of gays, a discussion of expandable penile implants, etc. Ever anxious to be hard-hitting and reality-driven, Phil taped a week of shows in November 1971 from inside Ohio State Penitentiary. By now the talk show was being syndicated to 38 stations, many of them in the midwest.

As Phil's career accelerated, his marriage disintegrated. He and Margie separated in the summer of 1973. She rented an apartment in Albuquerque and lived there with two of the couple's five children; Phil had "custody" of the others. After ten months of separation, they attempted a reconciliation. However it failed, and four months later, she left for New Mexico with all the children. Six painful months thereafter, in later 1974, the couple reached a voluntary agreement in which he obtained custody of the four boys. They were divorced in 1975.

In the midst of his domestic crisis, it was decided to move "The Phil Donahue Show" to Chicago. Having reached a plateau from its Dayton, Ohio base it was estimated that being situated in a far bigger city would attract more important guests and give the show a more cosmopolitan veneer. Meanwhile to generate publicity for his TV forum, Phil rode an elephant at Niagara Falls in May 1974; a week earlier he had belly danced on air with Zia.

By 1975, Phil was being produced at WGN-TV in Chicago. It had a new set and was now known simply as "Donahue." To house himself and his four sons, he purchased a three story, six-bedroom house in Kenilworth, a very upscale North Shore community for Greater Chicago. That year, he did a new interview with Teamster figure Jimmy Hoffa, shortly before he vanished (and mysteriously, so did the tape of that program). In 1976, Avco Broadcasting sold "Donahue" to Multimedia Broadcasting for $425,000. With his increasingly lucrative income, Phil moved his household to a five-bedroom house in Winnetka, with a special apartment for domestic help.

THE SWINGING SINGLE

Since his divorce, Phil, a very eligible single father, had been dating heavily. Then along came Marlo Thomas, most famous as the star of the TV sitcom, "That Girl" (1966-1971). They had first met briefly when she was in Dayton, Ohio promoting a TV special ("Free To Be You and Me"). Then, on January 26, 1977 she came on "Donahue" to promote hew new movie, THIEVES. The wonderful chemistry between interviewer and interviewee was extremely obvious. Their eyes sparkled, and they gushed compliments to one another. At one point, Marlo said pointedly, "You are loving and generous and you like women. It's a pleasure [to be here] and whoever the woman in your life is, is very lucky."

Donahue, who can be amazingly shy in his private life, called her hotel that afternoon, hoping to ask her out. He heard nothing. Next day, she was in the same TV station building taping another show. Phil mentioned to the host of "Book Beat," that he had a crush on Marlo. Later, the emcee hastened over to tell Phil that she had a crush on him. That night she returned his call and mentioned that she was leaving for Denver. Maybe, hint, hint, he could meet her there for dinner. He did, and it was the start of their courtship.

In the fall of 1977, "Donahue" was about to celebrate ten years on the air. Although he had won the first of several Emmys in the 1976-1977 season, the show still had no Los Angeles or New York outlet. After failing to sustain itself in the Big Apple market on three past occasions, the show premiered on WNBC-TV in New York in October 1977. It was another milestone in the growing success of "Donahue." On June 7, 1978 the program won a national Emmy Award as Outstanding Talk, Service or Variety Series. The following year, Phil signed a new six-year contract with Multimedia Broadcasting at a reported $500,000 per year. His show was now seen in 200 cities by an estimated 8 million people.

Also that season, he contracted with NBC-TV's "Today Show" to provide three compact segments per week for "Today," starting in the spring of 1979. (This assignment lasted until 1982.) Now a national celebrity and a full-blown media commodity, Phil was on the cover of *Newsweek* in October 1979. The publication praised his program as "the hottest talk show on the dial" and described it as "part psychodrama, part street theater, part group therapy and always...'pure television.'"

The dean of TV talk shows celebrating his 25th anniversary on TV in 1992.

IN THE PUBLIC EYE

As the chief of the #1 syndicated talk show on U.S. TV, Phil had great visibility (except in the world of commercials where he did not tread). He hosted his first prime-time TV network special ("TV Guide: The First 25 Years") in October 1979 and was the subject of several major magazine features. All this publicity inspired him to set the record straight with *Donahue: My Own Story* (1980). The autobiography was authored by Phil "& Co.", the latter being key members of his staff. He dedicated the book to his children ("who taught me things I should have known") and to Marlo Thomas ("who taught me things I thought I knew"). *TV Guide* reviewed, "He claims to care deeply for the disconsolate in his audience, yet one suspects he cares more deeply for a lofty Nielsen rating." The *New York Times* decided, "the book jumps from one anecdote to another...as disconcertingly as—well, as a talk-show host trying to keep his conversation zippy."

Three months after the publication of *Donahue*, Phil, 44 and Marlo, 36 (or some said, 43) were married on May 21, 1980 in Beverly Hills at her parents' home. The wedding party included just members of both families. In 1982, the long-running "Donahue" switched its base of operation to WBBM-TV, the station in Chicago owned and operated by CBS. In October 1982, Phil added to his chores by becoming co-host, with Greg Jackson, of "The Last Word," an hour-long news analysis program, aired week nights at midnight. The following April, when the lead-in program, "Nightline," was expanded to an hour, "The Last Word" was dropped.

To accommodate both their careers, Phil and Marlo (who was based primarily in New York City) owned a penthouse apartment at 875 Fifth Avenue. In July of 1983 they bought an adjoining unit, then spent the next several years renovating their expanded duplex. The result of the renovations, as other owners in the coop alleged, was a great deal of damage done to the building, amounting to $221,859. Finally, just before the couple were to move into their new digs, a fire broke out in their premises, causing more noise, dirt and dust. All these problems led several of the building's tenants to refer to the Donahues as "the neighbors from hell." Meanwhile, in January 1984, Phil who had gained a reputation as a politically concerned TV host, co-moderated (with Ted Koppel) the Democratic Presidential Debate aired on PBS-TV.

NEW COMPETITION

By 1984, "Donahue" had been based in Chicago for nearly a decade and, for most of that time, had been the Windy City's most popular talk show. (In fact, to many viewers Phil was Mr. Chicago.) This unique situation changed early in the year when ex-Baltimore TV personality Oprah Winfrey began hosting "A.M. Chicago." Within a few weeks, that program had risen from the lowest-rated program of its format to being on par with "Donahue" and then soon out-ranked it. "Coincidentally," by the end of the year Phil had relocated his program to a base in New York City. Thus, by January 1985, his daily show was coming from Studio 8G in Rockefeller Center. Buoyed by the new atmosphere, his ratings escalated.

On December 29, 1985, Phil and New York-bred Soviet journalist Vladimir Pozner co-hosted the first "Citizens' Summit." Via satellite, audiences in Seattle, Washington and Leningrad in the Soviet Union discussed current human rights issues from different cultural viewpoints. The follow-up special was "Citizens' Summit II: Women to Women," bringing together women in Boston and in Leningrad. In 1987, Donahue and Pozner would be honored by the Better World Society with a Global Communication Award. The media duo would also embark on a lecture tour of the U.S. as well as four cities in the then Soviet Union.

In the mid-1980s, Donahue had peaked as a TV celebrity, but unlike many in the face of increasing numbers of rivals, he maintained a steady following. (By then, the program had won 18 Emmys.) He remained refreshingly direct about himself, bragging, "I'm a pretty spoiled brat. For [over] 19 years now, I've had my own name on my program. And no one in this business has more editorial freedom than I do."

On the other hand, Donahue, who could be quite the sentimentalist, was still subject to outbursts of Irish temper. That was reflected in an early 1986 tussle at LaGuardia Airport when right wing Lyndon LaRoche backer William Ferguson spotted Phil and Marlo in the terminal. Ferguson screamed epithets at Donahue, insisting, "You should be in jail." The talk host recalls, "I didn't call a meeting. I just dropped my bags and went for him." On the home front, his son

Michael was selling TV ad time, Kevin was in sports management, while Dan, Jim and Mary Rose were still students. Phil said of parenting, that if he had it to do over again, "I would work harder to be as demonstrably loving with the boys, as I was with my daughter."

HARDER THAN IT LOOKS

Despite his golden touch, not every project came easily for Donahue. One case in point was his five-part NBC-TV miniseries, "Phil Donahue Examines the Human Animal." It aired in August 1986, but it was a three-year battle to get the massive project packaged for telecast. It went into production in early 1985 with location filming in Europe and the Middle East, utilizing taped interviews with fifty experts in the fields of biology, anthropology and behavioral sciences. However, in September 1985, 3/4 of the material was scrapped as the series' focus was revamped. By then, a hardback book version of the envisioned special had been published. When finally aired, the TV product was well received as thought-provoking.

Ever-vigilant Phil was the first Western journalist to visit Chernobyl in the Soviet Union (now situated in the Ukraine) in 1987 after the horrendous nuclear accident. Because of his past "Citizens' Summits" specials he was well known by Russian TV viewers. On his ten-day visit, he taped four segments worth of material. To celebrate his show's twentieth year on the air, he (and Marlo) took his staff on an eight-day cruise to the south of France. For the occasion, he chartered the Concorde to fly the team to France where they transferred to *The Sea Goddess*, one of Europe's most luxurious yachts. That November, he telecast a two-decade retrospective.

Keeping up the pace, Phil co-hosted "Today" for a week in April 1988 with Jane Pauley. That May, the Donahues spent their wedding anniversary at their completed New York apartment, finally abandoning their Central Park West rental apartment. This on-going renovation saga was only matched by the couple's purchase of a mansion on Beachside Avenue in Westport, Connecticut. They had been renting this manse on Millionaire's Row for several seasons and purchased it in the spring of 1986. In typical fashion, Marlo envisioned massive overhauling. The restructuring, due to expensive changes of mind, pushed on through 1988, excluding the month of August, when Phil took his annual show vacation.

With her fear of being kidnapped, Marlo insisted on an elaborate alarm system being installed, which created endless electrical problems. No sooner had they completed the rebuilding than they decided the vacant mansion next to theirs was an eyesore which spoiled their view. Afraid that the lot would be sold and subdivided, they purchased the property for several million dollars. By this point, the local preservation society and many neighbors had became incensed at this "landmark" being destroyed.

Nevertheless, a determined Marlo and a compliant Phil went ahead with the demolition of the home and added the new acreage into their estate, rebuilding their tennis court to be more fashionably out of sight of the main house. Obviously, such actions did not endear the Donahues to the locals, who taught the celebrities they could not always have their own way. For example, they had to moor their 42' Grand Banks powerboat at a Norwalk, Connecticut marina because the far closer Pequot Yacht Club refused to accept them as members.

LOOKING GOOD IN RED

In June 1986, silver-haired Phil did a galvanizing show out of the heart of Brooklyn's Bedford-Stuyvesant from a black church where in-the-news Glenda Brawley sought refuge from a grand jury subpoena. Having donned a red dress and hose for a November 1988 ratings sweeps show, he admitted that Marlo "got upset about the cross-dressing show" feeling it "would give critics a big opportunity to take potshots." She was correct, but Donahue defends himself: "sometimes you have to tapdance a little faster to draw a crowd. It worked: I got myself on the cover of *USA Today*."

Although he was trailing behind "The Oprah Winfrey Show" and "Geraldo" in the syndicated talk show race, Phil had a healthy new program contract at the start of 1990. While he had a lot to say on many subjects, he had little comment for a new book, *That Girl and Phil*, published in November 1990. It was co-authored by Desmond Atholl, a Britisher who had been the major domo/butler to the Donahues from 1986 to 1988. The scathing "expose" presented an extremely unflattering portrait of Marlo.

It provided several tantalizing episodes involving her super perfectionistic nature, and self-absorption. Atholl claimed her wild personality swings could switch her from "monster to Madonna in less than a minute." Atholl had no unkind words for Phil, whom he found to be just as decent in person as he was on the air. However, the ex-employee wondered how or why he coped with his amazing wife. (Reportedly, the Donahues quietly separated briefly in 1990, with according to wags, Phil seeking a respite from their allegedly, at times, stormy marriage.)

In addition to "Donahue," Phil, in 1991, began co-hosting the syndicated TV program, "Pozner & Donahue" (which was also heard on radio in the spring of that year). Following the path of talk show giant Larry King, Phil focused a great deal of TV time in 1992 on interviewing various presidential candidates on his program. One seg-

The Phil Donahue of today.

ment was devoted to a Bill Clinton-Jerry Brown debate, and was unique for Donahue in that he did not use a studio audience and had no phone call-ins.

DON'T GO TOO FAR

That format departure received no outcrys from his fans. However, there was a loud complaint when, in late July/early August 1992, he aired a few weeks of "ghost" host shows, taped without Phil actually being present. He had taped introductions and inserts for the program, and it was staff members who, unseen on camera, raced around the audience holding out mikes for audience feedback. Occasionally, this format led to mayhem, because their was no guiding force to moderate out-of-control audience members or viewers phoning in their heated opinions. *TV Guide* censored Phil: "We'd like to remind one of our favorite daytimers that his show is 'Donahue,' not donnybrook, for a reason."

On September 22, 1992, "Pozner & Donahue" returned for a new TV season, this time on CNBC cable. Aired twice weekly in prime time, the show had the co-hosts discussing current events with one another, and taking phone calls. When asked why he was doing this additional project, Phil responded, "Why wouldn't I want the chance to speak to really important issues, and to listen to what the callers have to say about those issues." The *Hollywood Reporter* warned: "the political slant was definitely liberal, with Donahue writhing in sympathy with left-wing causes and Pozner brutally comparing certain Republicans to hard-line advocates in his own country."

As co-host with Susan Lucci of the 19th Annual Daytime Emmy Awards in June 1992, a segment of that NBC-TV special had included a 25th anniversary salute to Donahue, the talk show maven. Better yet, was the two hour special on November 6, 1992 devoted to Phil's quarter century as a genre specialist. Taped at a Broadway theatre, Phil quipped to the invited studio audience, "It took 25 years and 6,000 hours to make it to Broadway." He proved his versatility by doing a tap dance to "Me and My Shadow," with a troupe of youngsters made up to resemble him.

Phil also did a skit with fellow talk show hosts (including Oprah Winfrey, Geraldo Rivera, Montel Williams, Jerry Springer and Sally Jessy Raphael). Between showing highlight clips from past shows, he introduced from the audience his first TV show guest, Madalyn Murray O'Hair, as well as his mother and five children. Marlo Thomas, then starring on the Los Angeles stage, taped a video valentine for Phil, insisting "he's a great cook and a great slow dancer."

OUTRAGEOUS IS GOOD

In late 1992, Phil made guest appearances on network TV series, in Donahue's case, "Blossom" and "LA Law." It was part of a new routine for talk show hosts, who were both being exploited for their wide audience appeal and to extend their visibility to other types of TV audiences.

When asked not long ago, where he would draw the line on the choice of sensational topic shows, Phil Donahue admitted to *TV Guide*: "I don't know. We got here by being outrageous. We've televised an abortion, and the birth of a baby. I've wrestled women, belly-danced, and was thrown out of a roller-derby ring. I've been body-wrapped, acupunctured.... We are tabloid—I'm happy to wear the label. I believe that there is a check and a balance. Our problem is not that we go too far, but that, generally speaking, the media don't go far enough. Those who go too far, too often, will fall of their own weight. People won't watch politicians or male strippers five days a week."

In recent years, it has been touted frequently that Phil might one day quit the TV show arena to tackle politics, even running for U.S. President. However, he cautions, "I have no exaggerated notion of my own electability. I've criticized the church, the government—I have my baggage. I'm not at all sure I'd politically survive the first negative ad by my opponent."

Now in his late 50s, Donahue insists "I'm at a very good part of my life. I'm very happy. I'm probably not the jack-in-the-box I once was, but I've got lots of energy. I'm very blessed."

TV & CABLE SERIES:
The Phil Donahue Show [Donahue] (Local/Syndicated, 1967-)
The Last Word (ABC, 1982-1983)
Pozner & Donahue (Syndicated, 1991-1992; CNBC, 1992-)

Chapter 10
DAVID FROST

It is quite unique for an entertainer to connect successfully with both British and American audiences. This is particularly true in the specialized spheres of satirical humor, talk show hosting and political commentary. David Frost is that rare bird who has bridged the cultural gap between the two countries. This media Renaissance man says offhandedly, "Versatility is no crime, but it is a source of adrenaline." Explaining his phenomenon, Frost assesses, "Independence helps. When I did the [Richard] Nixon interviews [1977], I didn't come with a set of allegiances. Secondly I spend so much time here [in the United States]. When I'm on British television, I'm a British TV personality. When I'm on American television, I'm an American TV personality."

The British-born son of a Methodist minister, Frost could have been a soccer star. Instead, he chose to use his outstanding intelligence and sharp wit to become a stand-up comic. Later, with an entrepreneurial flair, he developed television series and a TV network at home, while becoming a successful TV talk show star and commentator cum interviewer on the other side of the Atlantic Ocean.

To accomplish his chaotic, around-the-clock schedule, he learned to treat lengthy plane flights in the same way most people regard a simple taxi ride. (Frost holds the Guinness world record for the most transatlantic travel.) For the five-foot, eleven-inch Frost, "I don't need to do anything to relax because my work relaxes me."

David Frost examining his likeness being unveiled at Madame Tussauds Waxwork Exhibition in London in 1969.

Because of his overwhelming desire to discover what makes people tick, Frost has devoted much of his lifetime to molding interviews into his livelihood. (Of the many famous subjects he has interrogated, his favorite has been playwright Tennessee Williams because "from the very first answer, it was a totally seamless interview.") Before going on air with his trademark "Will you welcome now...." this seemingly casual prober has already done exhaustive preparation, using both U.S. and English-based research teams.

NICE AND INTIMATE

The New Republic once judged that a typical David Frost interview program resembles "a long warm bath." But, cautioned N.R. Kleinfield (*New York Times*), "Mr. Frost's technique can be deceptive. His interviewing style seems so harmless, and often it can be infuriatingly docile. His strongest talent is for being able to put someone so at ease they practically forget they're awake." And that he has, getting former President Richard Nixon to say that he had "let down the country," or Hugh Downs admitting to a hair transplant or Arthur Godfrey revealing that he had been sterilized.

What lies behind the dinner party charm of David Frost, the solicitous, consummately cheerful man with prominent white teeth, a slightly nasal voice, perpetually raised eyebrows and an ever-present small cigar? At one stage in life, before settling down belatedly into marriage, he was touted as one of the world's most eligible playboys. (His romantic attachments ranged from Diahann Carroll to Carol Lynley to Liv Ullmann.) When in New York City, he would often be found spending the noon hour sipping French wine and nibbling on goodies at Sardi's Restaurant as he mingled with show business greats.

When in London, and not preoccupied with his English companies operating from elegant offices in the Mayfair district, he would most likely be seen hobnobbing with royalty and high political figures. John J. O'Connor (*New York Times*) rates Frost an "unflappable fellow and a "bon vivant, never at a loss for an amusing anecdote" and having "a remarkable enthusiasm." However, O'Connor warned, "never underestimate the shrewdness beneath the bubbling surface." Kay Gardella (*New York Daily News*) found David to be a man who has "a ready answer for any question, supplying his own questions, digressions and witty asides" She reacted to David: "Frost is a facile, quick person, skilled in the media. He is quick on the uptake, fast and bright, and one has a tendency to equate that with a lack of depth.... That could be an unfair evaluation. Still, there's always that question mark." In contrast, media watcher Malcolm Muggeridge was not impressed, insisting that "David Frost represents modern mediocrity."

JUST THE FACTS

David Paradine Frost was born on April 7, 1939 in Tenterden, England. He was the third child (there were two older sisters, Margaret and Jean) of Wilfrid John Paradine Frost and Maude "Mona" Eveline (Aldrich) Frost. As a young man, Wilfrid, the son of an ironmonger, had been a mining engineer whose work took him around the globe. Wilfrid was twenty-two when he met nineteen-year-old Maude and married her in 1922. When he was twenty-seven, Wilfrid got the calling to God and decided to become a Methodist minister, as was Maude's brother, Kenneth.

Thereafter, the Frosts led a transient life, constantly moving around and suffering from a poor income. By 1938, they were in Tenterden, a small town in Kent county, where David was born the next year on Good Friday. By the time David was nine months old, the family had relocated to Kempston, a suburb of Bedford. At age four, young Frost was sent to kindergarten in Bedford at a very progressive school. Later, the family settled at Gillingham, also in Kent county, where Mr. Frost earned the equivalent of $25 a week. Years later, Frost recalled, "My father was a true pastor in terms of caring for his flock, and life at home was fascinating because there would be all kinds of people there—even once an escaped convict. My father always told me, 'Even a stopped clock is right twice a day.'"

When David was fifteen, Wilfrid was transferred to Raunds, a little Northamptonshire town. There he reached the peak of his salary, earning about $40 a week. David entered Wellingborough Grammar School where he was an avid soccer player. About this time, David and his family were among the thousands attending Reverend Billy Graham's Greater London Easter Crusade. David was so inspired by Graham, that it led to a period of greater religious belief and he began lay preaching. In pursuing this course, he discovered he was a natural entertainer. He joined the church youth club which did dramatics.

One evening in 1956, the teenaged Frost attended the cinema. While watching NOW AND FOREVER (1956) in which popular young British actress Janette Scott received her first screen kiss, he fell in love with her. It would be a few years before he could act on this feeling. While waiting for a state scholarship to Cambridge, Frost taught at a secondary school at Irthlingborough near Raunds. By then, he had decided against accepting a professional soccer contract with the Nottingham Club and knew he wanted to become a show business performer and producer.

HIGHLY EDUCATED

In October 1958, David entered Cambridge University. Bright by nature, he spent more time on extracurricular activities than on his studies. (As a result, he almost lost his scholarship.) He contributed to several university publications (*Granta, Varsity*) and joined The Footlights, a campus revue and cabaret club which featured the older John Bird, Peter Cook and Eleanor Bron. In his performances, it became clear that quick-witted Frost was best at satirical monologues. During the spring of 1961, Richard Armitage, a leading London theatrical agent, visited Cambridge on a talent hunt. He sat through a revue given by The Footlights and was much taken with David's talent.

Frost graduated from the University with honors in English in the summer of 1961. By then, he had already made his TV debut appearing as a student performer in programs telecast from Norwich via Anglia Television. He followed through on his initial dramatic work by contacting Richard Armitage and, through the Noel Gay Agency (where Armitage worked), wrote several satirical magazine pieces for *Queen* and *Strand* magazines.

Soon he began an apprenticeship on the "This Week" program at Associated Rediffusion, Ltd, a London-based TV production company. He was earning fifteen pounds a week, but not impressing his bosses who found him too unphotogenic. Meanwhile, he was performing in nightclubs and cabarets, sometimes substituting at the Establishment for his university chum, Peter Cook. He was most successful at doing monologues. At Rediffusion he switched from "This Week" to "Let's Twist," a dance show with David as master of ceremonies. Later in the year, he made his debut as a cabaret comedian at the Blue Angel. He was booked for a week, but stayed for two months. One of his best routines was conducting a bizarre press conference.

Ned Sherrin, a producer at the British Broadcasting Company (BBC), saw Frost's work at the Blue Angel and was tremendously impressed by his bright, impish humor. Sherrin felt David would be just right to help the BBC expand "Tonight," a news magazine format show. (Actually Peter Cook and John Bird were the first choices to anchor the program, but they had other professional commitments). Frost left Rediffusion and contracted with the BBC.

David Frost and his then frequent companion, singer/actress Diahann Carroll, in 1971 at London's Heathrow Airport.

GETTING THE EDGE

The new fifty-minute Saturday night entry focused irreverently on political satire. It was titled "That Was the Week That Was" (TW3). Full of ad-libs, parodies, musical numbers and lots of anti-establishment humor, it debuted on British television in late November 1962. *Variety* reported of the live proceedings, which included such regulars as Millicent Martin, Kenneth Cope and David Kernan, "David Frost was fine as emcee, showing few signs of fluster and himself giving an edge to the comment."

The fractious, facetious show was a phenomenal hit with Britishers. who delighted in the show's mockery of sacred cows and its sharp barbs on current governmental and moral issues. Viewership soon jumped from three million to twelve million. Frost's "Seriously, though, you are doing a grand job!" became a national catch phrase. David's salary tripled from its fifty pound beginnings.

Almost immediately, David Frost, the compere of "TW3," became a national figure, and basked in the limelight. About this time, he reencountered actress Janette Scott, now a panelist on TV's "Juke Box Jury." She was still married to Canadian actor-singer Jackie Rae, although they had been living apart for a year. She and David began a long-term on again-off again romance.

Americans had their first glimpse of David when he played a reporter (with a few lines of dialogue) in THE V.I.P.s (1963) starring Elizabeth Taylor and Richard Burton. Then, when it was announced that the NBC network in the United States had bought the rights to "TW3," David was offered a guest spot on the American version. To promote the forthcoming spin-off, Frost came to New York and was a guest on "The Tonight Show" with Johnny Carson. By September 1963, David was back in London for the second season of the British "TW3."

However, after a few weeks, the show was cancelled due to the pending British election. The BBC was nervous about what might be said or done on the unpredictable "TW3." Back in America, Frost was on hand to participate in a preview Special of "TW3" in November 1963, which featured Henry Fonda as a guest star. Two months later, on January 10, 1964, NBC debuted the half-hour weekly program. Regulars included Elliott Reid (emcee), David Frost, Henry Morgan, Buck Henry, vocalist Nancy Ames and Skitch Henderson's Orchestra. In the translation from England to the U.S., the show's irreverence became blunted and never gained the requisite popularity. The series lasted till May 4, 1965. (Two decades later, on April 21, 1985, Frost would host a "TW3" revival special on ABC-TV.)

NO TIME TO WASTE

While "TW3" was struggling in New York, David was also starring on another program for the BBC, "Not So Much a Programme, More a Way of Life," a satirical followup to their "TW3." This was the start of Frost's transatlantic commuting, a Herculean schedule on which he thrived. A few weeks before "TW3" faded from American TV, the controversial "Not So Much" passed from the British scene, pulled from the airwaves reportedly because of an in-bad-taste parody involving the Duke of Windsor (whose sister had just died).

During 1965-1966, David did a series of five-minute religious broadcasts. By March of 1966, David was part of another BBS series, "Frost Report," a talk show with a different slant, including quick-fire sketches each in its own setting. The program, which lasted through 1967, featured a repertory company (John Cleece, Ronnie Barker, Ronnie Corbett, as well as Mexican-American folk singer, Julie Felix) and focused on different aspects of British daily life. During this period, David formed David Paradine Productions to sign up artists (such as Cleece, Barker, Corbett) and place them in showcase TV programs.

When not doing "Frost Report," David found time for a series of six late night shows, "An Evening with David Frost," which were telecast from Edinburgh. After tinkering with several pilots, David inaugurated the "Frost Programme," distributed by Rediffusion for the Independent Television Authority. The series bowed on September 28, 1966 with actor Robert Morley as the main guest. The purpose of the thrice-weekly program, which lasted for two seasons, was to be spontaneous and intimate, and, most of all, spotlight controversial guests. And that they were!

On one show, American Gore Vidal took issue on air with Sir Cyril Osborne, a member of Parliament who supported corporal and capital punishment. Tommy Thompson (*Life* magazine) described the series as a "crisp and controversial confessional booth where the great, the notorious, and the weird come to bare their souls, live, before the nation." With unquenchable energy, Frost also served as disc jockey for "Frost on the Phonograph" a BBC radio show.

WIELDING INFLUENCE

The year 1967, in which his father died, saw David adding to his resume. He launched a new British series, "At Last the 1948 Show" and did "David Frost's Night Out in London" an American-distributed TV special. With Antony Jay, he wrote *To England with Love*, an assessment of English morals, prejudices and peculiarities. Using his financial and business connections, David put together a consortium, which obtained a prized franchise to create the producing corporation, London Weekend Television. (He would also be involved with founding TV-AM.)

Not that Frost was ignoring his social life. His relationship with Janette Scott had cooled (she later married singer Mel Torme), and his more recent romances included club performer Jenny Logan and Anne de Vigier, the daughter of a wealthy manufacturer. As a media darling, and a much sought-after social figure, Frost often hosted "intimate" dinners for well over a hundred guests. (The synergism of his TV interviews was remarkable. These public tete-a-tetes often led to private conversations, personal friendships and lucrative business associations.)

By early 1968 when Rediffusion merged with Thames Television, David's "Frost Programme" had concluded. While in New York plugging his newest book, *The English*, he was the substitute host for Merv Griffin on his syndicated TV talk show. With his droll charm and facile talents, he turned a potentially conventional interview with actress Susan Strasberg into an absorbing account of her experiences with psychiatry.

His talent was duly noted by the TV industry. In March of 1968, he was host/interviewer for "The Next President?" a syndicated series of interviews with U.S. presidential candidates, including Richard Nixon, George Wallace, Eugene McCarthy, Ronald Reagan and Robert Kennedy. The gimmick of these intelligent, timely sessions was going on location wherever the candidate might be at the moment.

IN STEPS FROST

On July 4-5, 1968, Frost sat in for Johnny Carson on "The Tonight Show" and was well-received. By now, Merv Griffin, planning to move over to CBS, had told Westinghouse Broadcasting that he would not renew his syndicated talk show contract. The syndicator thought of hiring Bob Newhart, Henry Morgan or Steve Lawrence to replace Merv. Instead, they chose David, renown for his scathing interviews which were a happy mix of conversation and confrontation. They suggested a five-year contract for 250 shows per year. The agreement would be worth at least $2.5 million to Frost. After a refinement of terms, he agreed, adding this new talk fest to his workload which included doing three weekend shows for London Weekend Television.

Enthusiastic rather than harried by his new duties, David based himself in New York at the Lombardy Hotel on East 56th Street in a three-room suite on the seventh floor. (In mid-1971 he would relocate to the Plaza Hotel.) His new talk show was to be produced at the Little Theatre off Times Square and next door to Sardi's. Frost established his production office in facilities on a higher floor of the building. The ninety-minute entry bowed on July 7, 1969, featuring a mix from both sides of the Atlantic: Prince Charles (in a taped segment), the Rolling Stones, Ed Sullivan and journalist Jimmy Breslin.

Billy Taylor was leader of the studio band, while Frost abandoned the familiar host desk to sit in an easy chair opposite his guests. Now and then he would·glance down at his clipboard filled with massive background notes. While early shows were filled with embarrassing technical botches, *Variety* acknowledged that David was a "skilled questioner and listener." In contrast, Jack Gould (*New York Times*) reacted adversely at first. He labeled the Britisher "a visitor in search of a format...seldom very amusing, and deferential enough to be an assistant to a television vice president."

However, after a few nightly installments, Gould, as well as a portion of America, looked more kindly on this newest entrant in the talk show sweepstakes, even if his accent was too "odd" for middle America. Before long, urban audiences were appreciative of his caustic wit, and had become well aware of David's catch phrases ("Wonderful stuff!" "Marvelous!" "Smashing!" "That was just lovely" "It was a joy having you") and his closing routine ("All the best for now. God bless.")

INVITE THEM ALL

His "The David Frost Show" guests would range from Bing Crosby to Artur Rubinstein, from Sir John Gielgud to Raquel Welch. He also enjoyed having political figures on his program, whether they be Vice President Spiro Agnew or Mrs. Lyndon Johnson. Most so than any other talk show host, he had most of his genre rivals on his stage, including Johnny Carson and Merv Griffin.

By 1970, globe-trotting David had been a millionaire for years. His new American TV show had already won an Emmy and would repeat this initial victory the next season. He was finishing a book, *The Americans*, dealing with his U.S. interviews. He had received an honorary doctorate in the U.S. and was awarded the Order of the British Empire. In his "spare" time he was doing additional record albums (such as his "David Frost and Billy Taylor—Merry Christmas").

In the spring of this year, he went to California to tape several shows featuring Jack Benny, Carol Burnett, George Burns, et al. He started dating film actress Carol Lynley whom he had first romanced in London in 1965. Then, he went to see Diahann Carroll sing at the Ambassador Hotel's Now Grove Club in Los Angeles. Before long the white Britisher and the chic black American were a "hot romantic item," seen together in Hollywood, Hawaii, Las Vegas and Manhattan. Diahann would be on his TV show in June 1970. However, Frost, the perennial bachelor, could not commit to settling down with Carroll or any of the other women he dated. She would marry, briefly, a Las Vegas businessman in 1973. (A few years later, Burt Reynolds, then still dating talk show host Dinah Shore, would announce, "I've formed a society called Marriage Anonymous. The charter members are Warren Beatty, David Frost and myself. If any of us is tempted to get married, we ring up the others and they come around and get us drunk till the idea passes." Eventually, each of the trio would abandon bachelorhood.)

Westinghouse/Group W had so much faith in Frost that they launched his "David Frost Revue" in September, 1971. The syndicated half-hour show had a resident troupe which included Jack Gilford, Marcia Rodd and George S. Irving. Following in the steps of his "Frost Report," the show's focus was again on social satire. However, many viewers found the "Revue" frolicking lame, not at all in the same league with TV's far funnier "Rowan and Martin's Laugh-In." The series only lasted one season. Not long after it vanished so did Frost's talk program in July 1972. Ironically, it was a victim to competition from Merv Griffin's new syndicated talk show from Metromedia. The latter had arisen after Merv's CBS-TV venture had failed to outdo Johnny Carson's "The Tonight Show" ratings.

NEVER COUNT HIM OUT

Once relieved of his U.S. TV shows, Frost, who was also doing Las Vegas club performing, cut back temporarily on continent-hopping. He devoted more time to British (and sometimes Australian) TV series, specials and enterprises. His luxurious existence then and later certainly qualified him for "The Lifestyle of the Rich and Famous." By the mid-1970s, just when David was being forgotten by Americans, he made a remarkable comeback. He carried off the industry coup of contracting with former President Richard Nixon to do extensive interviews, dealing in part with the controversial Watergate scandal.

When the major U.S. networks had refused to meet Nixon's expensive demands, David stepped in and closed the headline-making deal. Under the terms, Frost agreed to pay Nixon $600,000 for six hours on the air. Frost's research team prepared for a year in advance of the event. The interviewing occurred over a twelve-day period in San Clemente, California. In all, Frost and Nixon taped 28 3/4 hours of discussion. According to David, during the first day's get-together, Nixon sidestepped any head-on discussion of the Watergate affair.

As Frost recalls, "When he came back on the second day, having realized the total stonewall did not work, he was prepared to volunteer something —not enough, as it turned out—and then suddenly the atmosphere became more of the confessional." When the once chief executive admitted he let the country down, even the unflappable David was flabbergasted. "At the end, I was drenched and wrung out, as much as he was. I sensed that at that moment he was more vulnerable than he had ever been." If the public still had questions whether Frost was a personality or a journalist, the tremendous viewership that watched the four ninety-minute telecasts in May 1977 knew differently.

This remarkable set of candid interviews reestablished David in the U.S. as a major media force. Frost's contract with Nixon permitted him a seventh hour of TV programming to be culled from the lengthy interviews. That additional segment was put into syndication in September 1977. With Nixon receiving 20% of net earnings, the ex-President alone realized at least $1 million from the telecasts; Frost earned even more. In November 1992, the tapes were packaged for home video distribution. (When David wrote his *Book of the World's Worst*

Decisions, 1983, he claimed that Nixon merited the "Order of the Golden Boot" for "his decision to order voice-activated Sony tape recorders for the Oval Office in the White House.")

A GOOD STEPPING STONE

The huge success of the Nixon interviews led to further TV specials for Frost, including interviews with Henry Kissinger and the deposed Shah of Iran. The latter conversation prompted a $3 million project and eight-part docudrama, "Crossroads of Civilization," produced in cooperation with Iran's Ministry of Culture and Arts. The following May the celebrity interviewer was the host of "Headliners with David Frost," an hour-long NBC summer show. The program was a mix of name subjects (ranging from the Bee Gees and John Travolta to ex-C.I.A. chief Richard Helms). It boasted a recurring segment called "Headliners Forum" where the host would postulate a question (e.g. "What is the secret of a happy marriage?") and several notables on tape would respond with pithy, facetious remarks. In addition, gossip maven Liz Smith provided weekly tidbits on this program, which finally went off the air as of July 5, 1978.

David's playboy reputation continued to sustain itself, with his global dating now including American socialite Caroline Cushing. Then, in 1981, Frost married. His bride was actress Lynne Frederick, most noted for being the fourth and final wife of screen star Peter Sellers who had died in July 1980. Within a year of their matrimony, the Frosts separated and divorced. Much happier was his courtship of the blonde, humorous Lady Carina Fitzalan-Howard, thirteen years his junior. She was the second daughter of the Duke of Norfolk, a Roman Catholic peer. "We'd known each other socially for years," David recalls, "but when we saw each other at a party in 1982, suddenly it was dot-dot-dot-different." (Supposedly when a nun asked Lady Carina if her prospective groom was religious, she responded, "Oh, yes. He thinks he's God.")

At the time of their marriage in early 1983, there was much controversy about the union because of the mixed religions. In 1984, the Frosts would become parents of Miles; in 1985, Wilfrid would be born; and George arrived in late April 1987. Speaking of parenthood, proud father Frost would say, "For me to have this new adventure now is fabulous. It's even more fun than I expected."

David continued to tinker with TV programming, producing feature films, as well as turning out novelty books like *David Frost's Book of Millionaires and Really Rich People* (1984). For the telefeature AGATHA CHRISTIE'S THIRTEEN FOR DINNER (1985), starring Peter Ustinov and Faye Dunaway, David played himself in a cameo. In 1987, David returned to a familiar forum with his syndicated American television series, "The Next President?" Co-produced with *U.S. News & World Reports*, the venture required nine months of preparation.

JUST A HOP, SKIP, AND JUMP

Once again, David commuted weekly on the Concorde between the U.S. and London, where the family now lived in a huge Victorian house with a country garden. Each program hour of "The Next President?" focused on a different candidate, and included Vice President George Bush (reflecting on the leukemia death decades ago of his three-year-old daughter Robin), Governor Michael Dukakis (captured on tape on the explosive day that two of his staff were dismissed for improper behavior against a rival candidate) and Reverend Jesse Jackson (acknowledging his wife's role as "Vice President of their marriage").

David also talked with former President Jimmy Carter, who blasted Reagan for "the bribery of kidnappers" in the Iran arms deals. After interviewing President Ronald Reagan at the White House, Frost admitted, "I would have loved to have pinned him down in Irangate, but nobody else has either." In contrast to his 1968 and other presidential series, Frost's new edition included conversations with the candidates' wives and were usually taped at the subjects' homes.

By this point, Frost was special London correspondent for U.S. TV's "Entertainment Tonight." With his many business activities, he was being referred to as a one-man international conglomerate. He was producing/packaging such TV shows as "The Spectacular World of Guinness Records" and, in late 1987, put together "A Royal Gala," a benefit featuring Princes Charles and Princess Diana. Observers found it amusing to note that bon vivant Frost was now so chummy with the pillars of the British institutions he had once satirized on "TW3." In September 1988, he was a substitute host for Bryant Gumbel on NBC's "Today Show," a tactic to keep his image and name alive in the American marketplace.

"Inside Edition," a new syndicated daily tabloid informational show, received much ballyhoo from its producers. The syndicator claimed the new program would

David Frost in the 1980s.

focus on "compelling human dramas and celebrity interviews." In contrast, anchorman Frost insisted a day before its debut, "All the crap that's on television, now, these sleaze programs, are going to make anything *we* do look like William Shakespeare."

However, "Inside Edition" turned out to be more along the exploitive lines of "A Current Affair." *Variety* found David's commentary "boring" and his presentation as "somewhat pretentiously" handled. After five weeks of being overly-intense on air, Frost disappeared from the show; some rumor-mongers said he had been bounced, others claimed he had quit. He was replaced by Bill O'Reilly for the show's run. Frost said later, "It just wasn't my scene." He added that the bad experience "twas but a 'hiccup,'" in his lengthy media career.

BACK TO BASICS

Glad to have more time for his wife and three children, Frost devoted himself to his British TV series ("Frost on Sunday" and "Through the Keyhole"), socializing, writing a newspaper column, wine tasting and playing golf. Then in later 1991, PBS-TV convinced him to star in "...Talking with David Frost." He admitted to being pleased at returning to the long-form TV interview format which he felt was "somewhat an endangered species." He thrived on having conversations with "unpredictable people," and that "Dealing with politicians is a particular challenge."

The new program, which was simulcast on National Public Radio, debuted on January 2, 1991, with an hour-long conversation with President and Mrs. Bush. Later guests on the once monthly show included Robin Williams, British Prime Minister Margaret Thatcher and General Norman Schwarzkopf. In 1992, like fellow talk show hosts Larry King and Phil Donahue, David's programs frequently became question-and-answer sessions for presidential candidates. Frost ended 1992 by being awarded knighthood in a New Year's honors list. He was among 940 Britons and members of the British Commonwealth so recognized with this distinction.

When asked not long ago what mistakes he has made in life, David judged, "I would say, in general, I have been lucky. I can think of hiccups. Two or three spring to mind. When I did 'The David Frost Show' in this country, the BBC wanted to show highlights six months later and that ruled out all the topical shows and just left the entertainment show. I had to spend two years in Britain explaining that I hadn't given up politics. ... I suppose "Inside Edition" was a five-week mistake. Starting TV-AM, we made mistakes... The first year was mayhem. But that's all changed for the better.... And in terms of the reverse of mistakes, marrying Carina was the outstanding nonmistake I made."

SECRETS OF THE TRADE

When prodded about the key to good interviewing techniques, the shrewd practitioner listed the following qualifications: "Mutual respect is important. The other key thing is to help the person forget what are the avowedly artificial circumstances of the situation, in that there are lights and cameras. I don't know how that happens. It's instinct. It's eye contact. It's asking questions they've never been asked before... With tough questions, it's usually easier to ask them in a civilized manner."

David Frost once admitted, "At the age of 50 I might want to be Prime Minister or I might want to be running a leper colony. I have no idea, but I'm keeping every option open." More recently, he has amended his ambitions: "The truth is I couldn't imagine the political life. It involves so many years on the back benches marking time. I think life is improvements on a theme. And the theme is, things you enjoy and that give you a buzz....One would hope [in life] to have made a contribution. Wasting time is what I hate the most. People say, 'Oh, very Methodist, very Methodist.' But in terms of staying fresh, I'm going to be trying to look for the new frontiers without knowing where the frontiers will be. I'm still keeping my options open. Very much so."

Finally, when once asked if there was anyone he still wanted to talk to, but could not reach, he thought and then replied in typical Frostian jocularity: "Well General de Gaulle promised me an interview on the third morning when he rose again, but he never showed up."

TV & CABLE SERIES:*
That Was the Week That Was (NBC, 1964-1965)
The Next President? (Syndicated, 1968)
The David Frost Show (Syndicated, 1969-1972)
The David Frost Revue (Syndicated, 1971-1973)
Headliners with David Frost (NBC, 1978)
The Next President? (Syndicated, 1987-1988)
Inside Edition (Syndicated, 1989)
...Talking with David Frost (PBS, 1991-)
     * U.S.-originated series only

FEATURE FILMS:
The V.I.P.s (1963)
Agatha Christie's Thirteen for Dinner (1985) [TV movie]

Chapter 11
KATHIE LEE GIFFORD

Like comedian Rodney Dangerfield, all Kathie Lee Gifford wants is a little (okay, a lot) of professional respect. "Just because I act silly," she reasons," doesn't mean I am silly.... Lucille Ball was a very serious woman behind the laughs. It takes a lot of confidence in oneself to seek the comedic moment, even at my own expense." She has another concern. Many people are cynical about her overwhelming sweetness and sentimentality. It has prompted her to say, "I really want people to think of me as a kind person. If anything hurts me, it's when people think all I care about is things that don't matter—houses, clothes, money and jewelry. People make a big deal out of my ring." She also resents being labeled perky. "To me," she defends," perky means you have no opinion on anything, and I'm an extremely opinionated person and quite irreverent at times."

Kathie Lee Gifford with her sportscaster husband, Frank Gifford, and their son, Cody in 1990.

There is yet another fly in the ointment. Kathie Lee has an inner need to run off at the mouth, which far outweighs her ability to bite her tongue. In typical fashion, she blurts out whatever is on her mind, often embarrassing herself rather than hurting others. ("I don't have a malicious bone in my body," she notes. "I would never on purpose hurt anybody or misrepresent somebody.") Thus, there is good reason why she titled her bestselling autobiography *I Can't Believe I Said That!* (1992). It has also led her to an important morning ritual, a brief prayer to God: "Lord don't let my mouth get me in trouble today!"

Kathie Lee Epstein Johnson Gifford is something of a 1990s media phenomenon, a latter day Mary Tyler Moore (with whom she shares a physical resemblance). Kathie Lee's evolution is a marvel unto itself. She is a half-Jewish girl born in France who became a Christian gospel singer (and married one!) and spent a long TV apprenticeship ("Name That Tune," "Hee Haw Honeys," "Good Morning, America"). Finally, she became a national celebrity as the prettier half of "Live with Regis & Kathie Lee," currently one of the hottest syndicated TV talk shows in the United States. En route, the divorcee married her dream hunk, ex-football star, now turned TV sports commentator Frank Gifford, with whom she had her first child.

There is much more to pert, bubbly Kathie Lee than meets the eye initially. Not only is she a better than competent singer and dancer who has recorded several albums and done club acts, but she has a presence and comedy timing that makes her a natural for TV sitcom. While part of her is spontaneous and ever eager to make fun of herself, she has her serious side. Her religious background governs her threshold of where wholesomeness stops and tastelessness starts.

MORE THAN MEETS THE EYE

She can be thin-skinned, especially if the offender has slighted her husband or their beloved son, Cody. Such situations make her extremely combative. She is also: (1) very ambitious (she still hopes to star in a Broadway musical); (2) a celebrity dabbler (having dinner at the White House, hobnobbing with Donald Trump); (3) very shrewd (merchandizing herself as a highly-paid TV spokesperson); and (4) an astute businessperson (with her own clothing line). As she analyzes, "I'm only a perky cupcake half the time. That's my secret." She also says of her career evolution, "I did it the long, hard, *nice* way."

Kathie Lee Epstein was born on August 16, 1953 in Paris, France to Aaron and Joan Epstein. Her dad, a chief petty officer, was stationed with the U.S. Navy in France. The Epsteins were already the parents of David (born in 1950, he would become a minister) and Michele would be born in 1955 (she would become a singer). When Kathie Lee was born, her mother sent out birth announcements reading, "A STAR IS BORN."

Aaron was a non-practicing Jew, while Joan was a Methodist. When Kathie Lee was four, the family, who had been living in Germany, returned to the United States, first based at Annapolis and then settling permanently in the Belair section of Bowie, Maryland. Aaron retired from the Navy to became an insurance agent. In his free time, he played the alto saxophone in a jazz band (The Five Moods). Occasionally, Joan, who had a pleasant voice, sang on local radio programs.

Kathie Lee recalls her childhood as being "normal and happy" and that her parents were like "Ward and June Cleaver crossed with Billy and Ruth Graham." She took piano lessons for four years and hated it, but says her mother, "As a child she loved to perform with her little microphone." Additionally, she played on the Little League softball team and attended Methodist Sunday School in Bowie.

PRAISE THE LORD

A major turning point came when Kathie Lee was eleven. One evening, Joan Epstein watched Billy Graham preach on television. The next day, the teary-eyed woman announced that she was "born again." Soon thereafter, both Kathie Lee and Michele rededicated themselves to the Lord, as did Aaron in his own fashion. Not until a few years later did Kathie Lee learn what had prompted her mother's spiritual renewal. In 1957, Mrs. Epstein had had an abortion, rather than have a fourth, unwanted child.

By 1967, when she was fourteen, Kathie was an active born-again Christian. Over the next few years, she and Michele organized a folk music group (Pennsylvania Next Right), influenced by Joan Baez and Bob Dylan, as well as Peter, Paul and Mary. They performed at charity functions, hospitals and a few local coffeehouses. In 1971, she was a pretty seventeen-year old senior at Bowie High School and a cheerleader. She had won the Kraft Hostess Award which led to her first TV commercial. (She was flown to Chicago to film it for Kraft Foods.) She had also won a $1,000 college scholarship (and a dark brown wig) in Maryland's Junior Miss Pageant. As a result, she qualified for the nationals. However, she was disqualified at that level for unknowingly breaking pageant rules by merely talking to a boy on the staff. More importantly, she had made the acquaintance of singer Anita Bryant, the contest's co-host. (Bryant would recall, "She kind of reminded me of myself when I was younger. She was fun and bubbly.")

After completing high school, Kathie Lee spent some months in Key Biscayne, Florida, serving as Anita's girl Friday and baby-sitting the celebrity's four children. Convinced that Kathie Lee could have a career in Christian entertainment, Bryant campaigned secretly to get her protegee a music scholarship to Oral Roberts University in Tulsa, Oklahoma. In college, Kathie Lee became part of Roberts's World Action Singers, which performed at concerts, made gospel recordings, and were featured on his TV evangelical show. Although she was caught up in the University's program to a degree, Kathie Lee began having some serious doubts. "They tried to cookie-cutter all of us. I wanted the diversity of life, God went to the trouble to make us unique. They wanted us to believe the same way, think the same way."

STRIKING OUT

As a result of her new-found individuality, Kathie Lee quit school a semester before graduating as a voice major. She moved off campus to her own apartment in Tulsa. During this period, she began a soul-searching diary, which eventually would be published as *The Quiet Riot* (1976). Meanwhile in 1975, she moved to Los Angeles, hoping for a show business break.

She auditioned for commercials, did gospel recordings, and, for a brief time, was a nurse on the NBC-TV soap opera, "Days of Our Lives," yelling "Dr. Horton. Dr. Horton!" She had initially come to the set to visit a costumer friend, but within one day, she was hired as a show extra. Then she began doing bit parts and lots of voice-overs. "I was the most minor regular they've ever had!"

During this phase, she had begun dating Paul Johnson, 29, a gospel composer whom she first met at a taping of Oral Roberts's weekly TV program back in 1974. Later, Paul was in charge of her Bible study group. Their on-again, off-again relationship was due primarily to Paul's ambivalence about their romance. Kathie Lee was far more certain of their great love, and her assurance led to their eventually marrying in 1976. They spent their honeymoon in Acapulco, Mexico. However, it was a painfully unfulfilling experience for both. As she would note euphemistically in her autobiography, "we just couldn't seem to get relaxed with each other."

Convinced that their marriage vows were sacred and forever, both partners started a very painful period for both of them. In turn, the situation led to a platonic, polite life together, being based at their small ranch house in Los Angeles. Religious and psychological counseling did nothing to improve their loveless, anguish-filled union. Meanwhile, professionally, under Paul's guiding (or goading) and Kathie Lee's talent and prettiness (not to mention her sublimated frustrations), the couple became increasingly well-known on the gospel circuit. They performed together at concerts, did recordings (including her album "Kathie Epstein, The Quiet Riot"), and were featured as a model Christian couple in religious magazines.

PAYING HER DUES

As they had gone separate paths emotionally, so did they split professionally. While he was away a great deal of the time on the gospel circuit, she continued auditioning for TV programs. In the fall of 1977, she joined the cast of the syndicated show, "The $100,000 Name That Tune." With Tom Kennedy as host, she would sing the songs that contestants had to guess, substituting "la la" for the actual lyrics. She remembers having to learn, or so it seemed, two hundred songs in five days. She remained the "La La Lady" for a season.

Kathie Lee Gifford and Regis Philbin in publicity poses for their "Life with Regis & Kathie Lee" in the 1990s.

Meanwhile, she had been appearing on "Hee Haw", the corny but quite successful country-western syndicated variety series. Under her maiden name, she had also filmed a pilot for "Hee Haw Honeys," a spin-off of "Hee Haw." In the new series which went on the air in the fall of 1978, she and Misty Rowe were the attractive waitress daughters of Kenny Price and Lulu Roman in their Nashville restaurant. At this small roadside diner (Honey's Club), they not only served food but also entertained customers by vocalizing. *Variety* applauded Kathie Lee for having "a perky, brisk, Sandy Duncanish quality that she could parlay into better things." "Hee Haw Honeys" lasted through 1979.

Professionally, Kathie Lee had appeared first in Las Vegas when, shortly after arriving in Hollywood, she joined a singing group performing in the gambling capital. A few years later, after her TV work had made her a far better known personality, she got another break. Sandy Duncan was scheduled to open for impressionist Rich Little at the MGM Grand Hotel, but her grandmother died. Kathie Lee was summoned to pinch hit. Arriving at Duncan's casino dressing room, she found a bouquet of flowers with a note from Sandy: "Dear Kathie Lee, if you're better than I am, I'll kill you! Love, Sandy." This appearance guaranteed Kathie Lee the opening act in Las Vegas and Reno for such performers as Bill Cosby and Bob Hope. She says, "If there was an opportunity, I took it."

One day in 1981, Kathie Lee, who was a wife in name only, came home to find that her spouse had left for good. According to her, "I felt like I had presented myself as a gift to my husband that had been given back." Badly wounded, but now free to support only herself, she continued on with her show business career, including three days as substitute host on TV's "A.M. Los Angeles."

EVERYONE'S DREAM

In October, 1981, while performing as an opening act in a Reno casino club, she was spotted by a producer from "Good Morning America," the long-running ABC-TV magazine-style program. She was asked to do a few days of fill-in hosting, and then was hired to do field reporting for this major program. The job required her to relocate to New York City, where she established herself in a small basement apartment on the Upper West Side.

Despite a bumpy marital and professional life to date, Kathie Lee had never lost her effervescent personality, nor her spontaneity. The latter often got her into difficulty on "Good Morning America." For example, one day early on in her tenure as special correspondent on the show, Kathie Lee strayed from the script she was reading from the teleprompter. She was reporting on Princess Diana and her impact on the British fashion industry, and quipped suddenly, "Maybe she could help the Queen." In retrospect, Kathie Lee says, "Nobody was going to fire me or anything like that, but I knew that was not the right place."

As substitute co-anchor on "Good Morning America," Kathie Lee often filled in for Joan Lunden. One day in this capacity, she was rushing out of her backstage dressing room when she noticed someone bending over a sink fixing his contact lens. She admits that she liked the view, but was not so certain whether she cared for the man, Frank Gifford, who was subbing for David Hartman that day. He rememberd that while on the air together that morning, he noticed her neck was craning "like a turkey" because her seat was too low. He later called her to suggest she raise it.

Before long, she and Gifford, the ex pro-football player who had become a highly popular network sports announcer (especially of "Monday Night Football") had become good friends. At the time, he was involved in a second marriage turning sour. Frequently, he fixed Kathie Lee up with his bachelor friends. She, in turn, during this period, got involved in another doomed relationship after her divorce from Paul Johnson became final in 1983. Thinking back to these years, Kathie Lee quips, "Let's just say I was not the best little girl in the world anymore."

A FREQUENT FLYER

Between 1982 and 1985, Kathie Lee estimates she logged in a half-million miles searching for human interest features on "Good Morning America." Meanwhile, she participated in network TV specials, such as "The Funniest Joke I Ever Heard" (1984) and "The Guinness Book of World Records" (1985). In early 1985, Ann Abernathy left her assignment as co-host of "The Morning Show." That local New York area TV talk program was anchored by feisty genre veteran, Regis Philbin. He had seen Kathie Lee on "Good Morning America" and thought, "My God, she is so alive! She makes David Hartman look like a young guy." Kathie Lee was asked to join the show as Philbin's new partner.

It was a major career decision to leave a network show for local programming. She explained once, "Regis is the main reason I left 'Good Morning America.' Everybody thought I was crazy because Regis was doing just a local show in New York and I was already on network.... But I'd always felt extremely confined at 'Good Morning America.' Because of the format, I just wasn't allowed to be myself. And the fact is that I've never once regretted leaving. It turned out to be the best thing I ever did." For several weeks, until her "Good Morning America" contract ended, she literally sprinted back and forth between shows. Naturally, uninhibited Regis kidded her about the moonlighting on their first "Morning Show" together.

While "The Morning Show" featured cooking segments, how-to tips, celebrity guests and light chatter, the program's highlight was always Regis's trademark opening "Host Chat." In this 15 to 20 minute time slot, Regis and his vis-a-vis would prattle on about their latest offcamera activities, with seldom anything considered too personal upon which to report. Philbin describes it as "totally spontaneous. That's what makes the audience want to watch. There's no safety net. You never know how far it will go." Studio audiences and home viewers immediately reacted favorably to the professional chemistry between cantankerous Regis and spirited Kathie Lee, she nineteen years his junior. As she says, "We're the two most uncool people in the world.... Regis and I bring out the naughtiness in each other."

It had long been a familiar TV sight for Regis to expound from his prop stool about the world at large, local news headlines, or the latest tomfoolery of the show's executive producer Michael Gelman. Now, there was Kathie Lee to react in mock exasperation, "Oh Reege!" as she rolled her eyes heavenward. In turn, when she gabbled on nonstop about anything (in)consequential, he, with arms folded and a stern look of disbelief at her latest "oinkers," would turn to the cameras and ask "ARE YOU READY FOR THIS?"

A CLEAR UNDERSTANDING

In retrospect, Philbin says of his partner in success, "she knew right from the beginning what I was all about, what the [show's] opening was all about—it was a freefall exchange, and it had to be fresh, and she fell right into it. Right from the beginning I knew she was going to be great." Jeff Jarvis (*TV Guide*) would agree: "She is his perfect foil. Sometimes, I admit, she can charm even me. And sometimes, when she talks Big Issues, she still makes me want to shoot my TV. But that's why it's good to have wry Regis around. He puts her in perspective."

By 1986, Kathie Lee's TV career was flourishing. It was then that she acknowledged finally what her mother had seen years back on her early TV appearances with Frank Gifford; i.e., that there were love sparks between the couple. By now, twice-married Frank, the father of three, had divorced his second wife, Astrid Naess. Since neither she nor Frank were "wounded birds" anymore, it was the right time for the couple to fall in love, despite a 23-year age difference. (They both share an August 16 birthday.)

She remembers saying when accepting his proposal, "I'm marrying you because I adore you, flat out adore you, and I'm not a money-grubbing bitch." They wed on October 18, 1986 in Bridgehampton, New York. The new Mrs. Gifford admits, "He totally changed my life. I was really lost at the time. My career was thriving, but I was personally unfulfilled." On the show, she began relating personal incidents about their married life, and how she was redecorating their 232-year-old Greenwich, Connecticut farmhouse. Frank would awake each day, wondering what new intimate episode of their private life would bubble forth from Kathie Lee on air. However, he insisted, "I'm not in the business of censoring her. I respect her ability to edit herself, although frankly, she has said things that are embarrassing."

After three years of building solid ratings on the local level, "The Morning Show" went coast-to-coast on September 5, 1988, syndicated by Buena Vista Television. The format remained essentially the same, but it was now known as "Live with Regis & Kathie Lee." At first, the program was ignored by national critics. Regis explains this with "the sleaze factor was really taking over [in the TV talk show genre]. Geraldo [Rivera] got his nose broken; Phil [Donahue] was wearing a dress; Sally [Jessy Raphael] was walking around with hookers; Oprah [Winfrey] lost 65 pounds." Kathie Lee would add: "We've always felt like the Little Show That Could.... We've never had the critical acclaim. We've only really had strong word of mouth."

ONE WAY OR ANOTHER

Before long, however, the talk show began attracting major reviewers as fans. Tom Shales (*Washington Post*) said it best: "'Live with Regis & Kathie Lee' is that horse of a different color you've heard so much about. Not racy, not freaky, not remotely tawdry, the syndicated daily hour of small talk and tomfoolery has become one of television's least disheartening hits, and the reason it's succeeded has everything to do with the two wacky cranks at the heart of it.... They amuse each other to bits. And us too.... It's what daytime television is all about, or was before the quadrasexuals and spouse beaters and exhibitionistic tell-alls took over."

Not content with their daily morning TV forum, Regis and Kathie Lee began performing a club act together in the tri-state area, including Trump Plaza in Atlantic City and the Garden State Arts Center in New Jersey. Their on-stage routine included bantering about current events, comedy routines, and showcased their singing talents. In another venue, both Philbin and Gifford expanded their income by doing TV commercials, with Kathie Lee extremely active in this regard.

Faithful viewers of "Live with Regis & Kathie Lee" soon came to know that Kathie Lee very much wanted to have a baby. Her biological clock was running, but Frank, who already had three grandchildren, was not anxious to become a father again at this mature point in his life. However, as chronicled on the show, Kathie Lee conceived her child-to-be while on a Carnival Cruise (for whom she was a spokesperson) with Frank.

Soon she was discussing her morning sickness, the expanding size of her breasts, etc. on her TV outing. Her pre-natal period became a major show focus. On March 22, 1990, she gave birth to Cody Newton Gifford, named after Cleveland Brown tackle Cody Risien. While on maternity leave (Regis's wife, Joy, filled in as co-host), Kathie Lee had her studio dressing room done over as a nursery. Later, when she brought the infant on the show, the program's rating hit the roof. Until Cody was fifteen months old, she took him to the studio each morning with her.

SOMETHING TO TALK ABOUT

Now a proud mother, each day she had some fresh anecdote to relate about Cody, including announcing when she had stopped breast-feeding Cody. However, Frank was not left out of the limelight. In December 1990, she titillated viewers with the revelation that her husband, who slept in the nude, sleepwalked and that the past night he had ended up accidentally in bed with the nanny.

Increasingly, Regis and Kathie Lee were becoming one of television's most popular couples. Capitalizing on this, they co-hosted the televised "The Miss America Pageant" in 1991, a task they repeated in 1992. (She had been a special guest star on the contest for several years in the mid-1908s when Gary Collins was host.) They continued their separate and joint club appearances, playing as a duo at Manhattan's Rainbow and Stars Room and New Orleans' Saenger Theatre. "Live with Regis & Kathie Lee" rose higher in the ratings.

Meanwhile, the Giffords enjoyed the good life on their five-acre Connecticut estate, which housed, as every loyal program viewer knew, two bichon frise dogs, Chardonnay and Chablis. Kathie Lee was the first recipient ever of the Woman of the 90's Award from the American Anorexia and Bulimia Association. She was active in charity work for Variety Clubs International, Multiple Sclerosis and the Special Olympics (one of Frank's causes). Her parents, who operated an inn in Rehoboth Beach, Delaware, said of their famous daughter, "My husband and I consider ourselves Kathie Lee's groupies."

ONE IS NOT ENOUGH

Kathie Lee had made it no secret that she wanted a second child, but that Frank was resistant because of his age. As viewers came to know, in early July 1992, while vacationing in Colorado at their condo near Vail, Kathie Lee conceived. In mid-August the Giffords returned to Vail to celebrate their joint birthdays. The next day she had a miscarriage. On August 31, 1992 she choked back tears as she told viewers about losing her baby. Regaining control of her emotions, she put the tragedy into proper perspective for the TV audience by proceeding to discuss the recent Hurricane Andrew in Florida. On a November 1992 TV special with interviewer Barbara Walters, Kathie Lee noted she still would like to try for another baby. The next month, a few days before Christmas, Kathie Lee, let it be known on "Live with Regis & Kathie Lee," that she, age 39, and her husband, age 62, were expecting another child in the summer of 1993.

The Kathie Lee Gifford of today has reflected, "Who needs this? I have a great husband, a terrific little boy. Sometimes it gets to the point that I think about giving up the business and going home to them." However, the reality of her life contradicts that stated anti-career attitude. Her autobiography, *I Can't Believe I Said That!*, written with Jim Jerome, was published in November 1992 and quickly became a commercial hit. Her new Warner Bros. album ("Sentimental Journey") of standards, part of a new recording multi-album pact, was released in early 1993. She continues to be paid exceedingly well to do commercials for Revlon, Slim-Fast and Carnival Cruise Lines. Moreover, she has her Signature Fashion Label clothing line to supervise and she and Regis have completed a cookbook.

Will she remain a part of "Live with Regis & Kathie Lee" in years to come?. She admits that "We're better together than apart" and that no matter what happens, she and Philbin will always be friends. However, in another mood, she added not too long ago: "I get bored easily. I'm not bored here and I'm not bored with Reege, but if they don't start to give me opportunities here to do some of the other things that are offered me, then it will be upsetting to me." As to juggling her career and home life, she admits, "My challenge is to balance it all in a healthy way. And I'm not always successful at that."

TV & CABLE SERIES:

Days Of Our Lives (NBC, 1975)
$100,000 Name That Tune (Syndicated, 1977-1978)
Hee Haw (Syndicated, 1977-1978)
Hee Haw Honeys (Syndicated, 1978-1979)
Good Morning, America (ABC, 1982-1987)
The Morning Show (New York City local, 1985-1988)
Live with Regis & Kathie Lee (Syndicated, 1988-)

Kathie Lee Gifford and Regis Philbin with the reigning Miss America, Marjorie Judith Vincent, at the 1991 "Miss America Pageant."

Chapter 12
WHOOPI GOLDBERG

Leave it to Whoopi Goldberg to do something different when she joined the talk show hosting marathon in the fall of 1992. Rather than follow the crowd by utilizing a big set, a raucous back-up band and a frisky sidekick, she wanted something simple. Her heart told her to try a one-on-one approach, with a single guest. Her visitor might be from the world of show business, sports, politics, etc. Her theory was "I believe if you promote interesting conversation for more than five minutes, something great might happen." Viewing the new program, syndicated gossip column Liz Smith judged, "She is so forthright, so downright upright, so down to earth and appealing, that the show is both invigorating and relaxing—a joy to watch."

Whoopi said once, "I think I was fated to be in the public eye." Certainly, she has traveled a long path from a minority youngster in a New York City housing project to the Hollywood superstar of today who works nonstop in several mediums. Currently, she is one of the film industry's top-paid performers, and her "recognition quotient" places her at the top of female personalities in the entertainment industry. However, it hasn't been an easy transition for the once teen-age welfare mother, who, now in her mid-forties, is a grandmother with a love life of her own.

She is one of those unique performers who is always breaking new ground and has had to pay a price. With her wild zigzag of "do-do" braids (her dreadlocks are even longer in 1993) and gape-tooth smile, she is not your conventional beauty. Instead, she is the type of person who grows on you. Funky Whoopi has always relied on inner radiance, energy and, most of all, innate intelligence to win over audiences.

Similarly, her comedy is not that of the average standup comedian with a fast patter of one-liners which are dirty for filth's sake. (Not that Goldberg is a purist by any means. As *Time* magazine analyzed her, "raunchiness isn't part of her act; it's part of her nature.") Her stage routines are an extension of herself, full of sly humor and energizing originality. This is true whether she is performing a monologue on the human condition in today's troubled times, or presenting one of her several full-bodied characterizations that she developed over the years. (Her personality extensions include the little girl who wants to be white so desperately that she bathes in bleach, and the young male drug addict with a Ph.D in literature). Her unconventional stage work is Whoopi's way of reaching out, of being true to herself. It is the only way she can be.

"I AM WHO I AM"
Whoopi has always been a "one of a kind" personality. According to her, "I don't set out to shock people. It's just who I am, and I guess I'm somewhat shocking. I get in trouble speaking out, but I'd be in trouble with myself if I didn't." She has admitted, "I have my foibles. But I also have a great belief in the human spirit." Those who want to bend her to their will often accuse her of being

"troublesome" on a movie or TV set. Goldberg has a different perspective: "I'm difficult when you're not prepared to do your job and I'm there ready to do mine and I watch you blame other people for you not being prepared. And I don't like being lied to; it makes me nuts." Movie co-star and good friend Ted Danson analyzed recently, "some people might say she's stubborn, and she is stubborn to the line she wants to walk, to the truth she wants to say. She doesn't roll over. But if she were a man, you'd say she's clear, not stubborn."

Reviewing HOMER & EDDIE, one of Whoopi's three 1990 theatrical films, Janet Maslin (*New York Times*) stated, "Whoopi Goldberg remains one of the great unclassifiable beings on the movie screen." That she is! However, the enigmatic Whoopi likes it that way. After her memorable screen debut in THE COLOR PURPLE (1985), everyone expected great things of this 35-year-old black actress. But thereafter, she paraded through a series of stinkers, some of which even she couldn't salvage. Then, she rescued her career with an Oscar-winning performance in GHOST (1990) and a mega hit, SISTER ACT (1992).

Having overcome so much to reach her present successful status, Goldberg refuses to "go Hollywood," nor does she want to be a MOVIE STAR. She says, "I try not to. Sometimes it's fun, but sometimes it's a pain. And it's a lot of work—get dressed up, present yourself as a star is supposed to be presented…. And when you go out, you're going out as Whoopi Goldberg, and that's a bit wear-

ing. But, you know, if you have to get milk, you have to get milk. I don't want to be trapped in my house."

She was born Caryn Johnson in New York City on November 13, 1949. Soon thereafter, her mother, Emma Johnson, who already had a baby boy, would be deserted by her husband. As a result, Emma, a nurse and a Head Start teacher, had to raise her two children alone. The Johnsons lived in a housing project in Manhattan's Chelsea district in the West 20s. Caryn attended elementary school provided by the St. Columba Church on West 25th Street.

ALWAYS DREAMING

Even early in her life, Caryn had a vivid imagination, stimulated by watching old movies (especially 1930s screwball comedies) and sitcoms on television. Her childhood idols and "teachers" were such far-ranging performers as Gracie Allen, Claudette Colbert and Carole Lombard. Years later, she would explain, "I'm a real sponge in terms of seeing things and absorbing them. And, with the people I have admired over the years, I've stolen from them and added the things that I know instinctively.

From age eight to ten, an enthralled Caryn performed with the Helena Rubinstein Children's Theatre at the nearby Hudson Guild. From the start she liked acting because "I could be a princess, a teapot, a rabbit, anything." She remembers, "I was a very quiet and very dull child. I liked things other kids weren't into at the time—movies, theater, ballet. When you grow up in Manhattan, all these things are accessible."

As a distracted teenager, Caryn recalls her mother having to prompt her to get on a bus to attend a Leonard Bernstein concert, visit a museum, etc. However, by then, having dropped out of high school, she had become involved in civil right marches and student demonstrations. She had turned also to recreational drugs. According to the actress, "I got into drugs because they were there and everyone was doing them. I hate to say this, but it was a safer time to do them. You could be high in the street and not be worried about being clonked over the head. Acid was something you did with lots of people in the park." Looking back, she claims: "Those times were not tragic and terrible for me because it was part of the whole picture of what was going on. Of course, I would not recommend anyone go through that, because the safety nets are gone."

In 1971, Caryn wed her drug counselor, a man named Martin. By then, she had refocused her life and had began pursuing a show business career. She found work singing in the choruses of such Broadway shows as *Hair*, *Jesus Christ Superstar* and *Pippin*. By 1973, her marriage had ended. Caryn divorced Mr. Martin only to discover that she was pregnant. Her daughter, Alexandrea Martin, was born in 1974.

FROM CARYN JOHNSON TO WHOOPI GOLDBERG

In the fall of 1974, Caryn and Alexandrea flew to California, courtesy of a one-way ticket provided by a friend. Once in Los Angeles, she was offered a ride to San Diego. The short visit extended to a six-year stay. Professionally, she helped to found the San Diego Repertory Theatre, appearing in such productions as *The Grass Is Greener*, *Getting Out* and *Mother Courage*. Anxious to expand her career horizons, she became part of the Spontaneous Combustion, an improvisational troupe, as well as teaming with Don Victor. With the latter she did a sort of Elaine May-Mike Nichols routine. By now, she had changed her stage name. At first, she thought Whoopi Cushion sounded cute (or the French version Whoopi Cushon). Then, on her mother's prompting to pick a more respectful name, she decided on Whoopi Goldberg, claiming that somewhere in her heritage a relative had had the surname Goldberg.

(In the early years, the shock of discovering the German-Jewish sounding Whoopi Goldberg was actually born a black American Catholic, had its own special affect on audiences.)

In between acting assignments, Whoopi got by financially through a series of jobs, ranging from bank teller to bricklayer. When she graduated from beauty school, she used her cosmetology license to work dressing the faces and hair of corpses at a local mortuary. At least, she reasoned, they couldn't talk back. Sometimes she had to rely on welfare to make ends meet for herself and her daughter. However, she always reported income she made to the social workers, because 'I didn't want my daughter seeing mom lying." Thinking back to her years as a sometimes welfare mother, she says: "Yeah, I get pissy thinking about it, because it shouldn't be so degrading. But I'm not bitter. That takes too much time."

It was 1980 and the team of Victor and Goldberg had negotiated a San Francisco engagement. However, by the time she flew to the Bay City, Victor had decided not to join her. She was frightened about doing her routines alone, but went through with the commitment. "I did an hour. At the end of it, I knew that I could do a solo performance." Deciding to remain in northern California, she settled in with Alexandrea. Whoopi teamed with comedian David Shein and together they joined the Blake Street Hawkeyes, an experimental theatre troupe in Berkeley. Partnered with Shein, she wrote "The Last Word," which the duo performed in Berkeley. It was for this production that she created "Surfer Chick," a thirteen-year-old girl from THE Valley who uses a coat hanger to abort her own baby. As a single mother who was busy performing and being active in women's abortion rights, Whoopi had little time for paying work. As a result, the single parent had to rely again on welfare.

A SOLID HIT

Goldberg's self-written "The Spook Show" was created, she said, "To get work. That was my biggest intention. That show grew out of desperation." It was first presented in 1983. Before long, this one-woman show was playing to standing room only crowds throughout the San Francisco Bay area. The program consisted of four to six characterizations, including: the strung-out druggie, Fontaine, a college graduate; the coat hanger-carrying California Valley girl; the badly crippled woman who lives through her dreams; and a young black girl who wants to be white because "You have to be white to be on 'The Love Boat.'" Whoopi did not use makeup for her contrasting portrayals. Each night the roles would be redefined according to the rapport between she and the audience. Whoopi toured the U.S. with this project and, later, went to Europe, calling the show "A Broad Abroad or Whoopi Goldberg Variations."

By February 1984, she was in Manhattan performing her tour-de-force at the Dance Theatre Workshop. Producer/director Mike Nichols saw a performance and was so overwhelmed he told her he wanted to bring the show to Broadway. Whoopi agreed to his plans. However, first she returned to Berkeley to star in "Moms," a show she co-wrote about black standup comedian, Moms Mabley. Back in New York once again, she starred in "Whoopi Goldberg," the show opening on Broadway on October 24, 1984. She and the presentation received rave reviews. This one-woman showcase was later turned into a HBO-Cable special, "Whoopi Goldberg-Direct from Broadway" (1985) and also released as an album which won a Grammy Award.

Ever since reading Alice Walker's *The Color Purple* (1982), Whoopi had been intrigued with the Pulitzer Prize-winning novel. She wrote Walker that if a film version was ever made, she wanted to be a part of it. The author responded that she had seen Goldberg's stage work and already had her in mind when and if a movie adaptation happened. When Steven Spielberg agreed to produce and direct it. Whoopi auditioned eagerly, admitting, "Honey... I'd play the

Whoopi Goldberg in perhaps her most famous role, as Celia in THE COLOR PURPLE (1985).

dirt." Although she preferred the subordinate role of Sophia (which was assigned to Oprah Winfrey) she agreed to take on the demanding role of Celia at a $250,000 salary. Among the eleven Oscar nominations chalked up by THE COLOR PURPLE, was a Best Actress one for Whoopi. She lost to Geraldine Page of THE TRIP TO BOUNTIFUL.

As a result of the hoopla over her stage show and her motion picture debut, *People* magazine labeled Goldberg one of the 25 most intriguing people of 1985. (*Newsweek* applauded, "Whoopee for Whoopi!") Goldberg became so highly visible on the social and entertainment scene, that someone quipped "she'd even go to the opening of an envelope." In actuality, she was still living in San Francisco in an unpretentious home (which she called "the real world"), going to PTA meetings and periodically teaching acting classes. Jokes about "Whoopi sightings" hurt Goldberg "very deeply. I guess no one realized how new all of this was to me."

QUESTIONABLE CHOICES

At the time, it was assumed that THE COLOR PURPLE would launch her on a marvelous film career. Such was not the case. As Whoopi explains, "I did the pictures I was offered. Do you think I would sit around and say, 'Here's great scripts, here's crappy scripts; I'll do the crappy ones?'" She became known as "Miss Second Choice" or "Ms. Replacement" in Hollywood. She substituted for Shelley Long in JUMPIN' JACK FLASH (1986), for Bruce Willis in BURGLAR (1987) and for Cher in FATAL BEAUTY (1988). (One of the roles she most coveted, but lost due to her color, was that of the title figure in THE PRINCESS BRIDE, 1987.)

The one class project Goldberg did during this time was CLARA'S HEART (1988), where she was a Jamaican maid who becomes the substitute friend/mother for a confused, upper class, white adolescent (Neil Patrick Harris). Ironically, that movie made little or no money, while her Eddie Murphy-type action pictures were box-office winners. For FATAL BEAUTY, after Cher dropped out, singer Tina Turner was considered next, then it fell into Whoopi's domain. She notes that "the movie was written with a beautiful woman in mind, and they resisted me. When they finally did come to me, they had to pay an ugly woman's price [reportedly $2.5 million]." Plans for Goldberg to co-star with Walter Matthau in a remake of the classic comedy, BORN YESTERDAY, evaporated.

Throughout this period, energetic Whoopi was busy in other forums. She received an Emmy nomination for an appearance on the TV series "Moonlighting," in May 1986. In the same year, she did the first "Comic Relief" with Billy Crystal and Robin Williams, a charity fundraiser for the homeless. The event, made into a HBO-Cable special as well as being released as an album and video cassette, became an annual happening. In February 1987, she teamed with Carol Burnett, Robin Williams and Carl Reiner for an ABC-TV special. *TV Guide* raved, "A very special hour of laughter and song with four of the funniest people on earth." She also found time for romance. On September 1, 1986, she married a Dutchman named David Claessen in Las Vegas. He was a cinematographer and filmmaker, nine years her junior.

In 1988, Whoopi bounced from comedy specials on cable TV ("Whoopi Goldberg's Fontaine...Why Am I Straight?") to record albums to doing her one-woman show (now known as "Living on the Edge of Chaos") at the Universal Amphitheater in Universal City, California. On regular television, she could be seen recurringly as the advice-dispensing Guinan, the alien humanoid hostess, on "Star Trek: The Next Generation" ("When else am I going to get to outer space?" the actress jokes.) Additionally, she did a guest shot on "Pee-Wee's Playhouse Christmas Special."

ROAD BLOCK

She was so unhappy about the final results of her next film, THE TELEPHONE (1988), that she instituted a legal action to prevent its distribution. The art house entry later found limited release and a disgruntled Goldberg said of her string of bad movies: "Yes I'm disappointed, but I take no responsibility for them. The studios take this nice, gritty script and turn it into pabulum."

People wondered how Whoopi could survive stretching herself so thin professionally. Actually, the pace had an adverse effect on her domestic life as well. Because of their separate careers, Whoopi and her husband were frequently apart. Due to her busy acting schedule, Goldberg had to rely increasingly on her mother and others to bring up her daughter Alexandrea. She treated her offspring like a roommate, "like we were pals, without realizing that somebody has to take the responsibility."

In retrospect, Goldberg admits, "You make specific choices with children. I didn't make the mother's choice. I chose my career. I should have cared more. I was selfish and I am selfish. But I just felt that when opportunities came up, I had to take the ball and run. I would have become very angry and bitter otherwise. I've learned since what being a mother means, what those responsibilities entail. I know that I have to care more." Meanwhile, Goldberg's marriage to David Claesson fell apart. She filed for divorce in October 1988 which became final in 1989. By then, she was dating (and/or engaged) to camera operator Eddie Gold, and, later, was seen frequently with Brent Spiner, who played Lieutenant Commander Data, an android on "Star Trek: the Next Generation."

Whoopi seemed to be everywhere in 1989. She made her TV movie debut with KISS SHOT, playing a single mother who employs her skills as a pool shark to support her family. She headlined the HBO-Cable special "Whoopi Goldberg Live" (August 6, 1989) and was the narrator/host of the syndicated TV documentary "The Truth About Teachers." As an on-going key member of the Comic Relief fundraisers, she was part of the released videocassette versions of the annual Comic Relief comedy shows. She also hosted AIDS: EVERYTHING YOU SHOULD KNOW an educational video made for the home market. Additionally, she became a grandmother on her fortieth birthday (November 13, 1989). Her daughter, fifteen-year-old Alexandrea, gave birth to Amarah Skye Martin in Berkeley. Although respecting her daughter's right to make her own choices, the pregnancy caused a rift between Whoopi and Alexandrea that took years to heal.

MENTAL PATIENT TO HIT PSYCHIC

In February 1990, Whoopi was seen in HOMER & EDDIE, a little movie co-starring James Belushi. Says Goldberg, "When I saw the first cut of this movie, I thought, 'I'm not going to talk about it—ever! I don't want to know from it. I mean, it sucks. I don't know why they ever released it.'" She played an escaped mental patient with a brain tumor who has a month to live. Belushi was a mentally-retarded dishwasher. The movie was a commercial dud. Brushing off this defeat, Whoopi appeared live on stage in Stateline, Nevada at the Circus Maximus Club, did Gap commercials with and without her mother, daughter and granddaughter, and co-hosted the AIDS fundraiser TV show, "That What's Friends Are For" (April 17, 1990). Never resting, she was in Australia, New Zealand and Tasmania in the summer of 1990 with her one-woman show. When asked on CBS-TV's "This Morning" how it felt during those rare times when she was out of work, down-to-earth Whoopi responded "it's like having a period all of the time."

Her career took a giant step forward with the summer 1990 release of GHOST. (She would say later, "I didn't know my career was so far down the toilet until I read the reviews for GHOST.") In that major box-office hit, she played a fake psychic living in New York City. She is the eccentric soul who discovers that she has real communication skills with the hereafter and helps ghost Patrick Swayze get in touch with his bereaved young widow (Demi Moore). *Newsweek* championed: "thank God Whoopi finally has a part that lets her strut her best stuff." With almost $200,000,000 in domestic grosses, GHOST became the year's top moneymaker. She won an Academy Award, a Golden Globe and a British Academy Award as Best Supporting Actress for being Oda Mae Brown in this romantic drama.

The fall 1990 entertainment season seemingly belonged to Whoopi. She was among the celebrities on hand that September at Los Angeles's Wiltern Theatre to boost the fundraising efforts for "Commitment to Life," an AIDS project. When the TBS-Cable cartoon series, "Captain Planet and the Planeteers" bowed on September 15, 1990, she was the voice of Gaia, the Earth's spirit who is awakened from a deep sleep by worldwide pollution. Meanwhile, her TV series, "Bagdad Cafe," which co-starred Jean Stapleton, returned for its second season, having premiered in March 1990.

The project's comedy quotient was sadly lacking and the series gained more publicity for on-set problems than for its entertainment values. Goldberg was so perturbed by the meandering project that she quit the CBS-TV venture. It went off the air as of late November 1990, but two further episodes would be telecast in July 1991. On December 1, 1990, Goldberg was named Entertainer of the Year at the annual Image Award ceremonies, sponsored by the Beverly Hills/Hollywood chapter of the NAACP.

ON A MORE SERIOUS NOTE

THE LONG WALK HOME (1990) was a noble attempt at recreating the civil liberties strife of 1955 Montgomery, Alabama and the bus boycotting by blacks. Whoopi was the maid who teaches her spoiled employer (Sissy Spacek) the meaning of human dignity. Much more successful was SOAPDISH (1991), a wacky comedy about the bizarre inside world of TV soap operas. When Goldberg was a jury member at the Cannes Film Festival in May 1991, she got slack from filmmaker Spike Lee because she voted for BARTON FINK over his JUNGLE FEVER. To erase the bad taste of her "Bagdad Cafe" TV work, she did a guest-starring episode of the sitcom "A Different World" (for which she was Emmy-nominated) and was in a segment of the HBO-Cable horror anthology series, "Tales from the Crypt."

From November 1991 through early 1992, Goldberg was on location in Soweto, South Africa, filming SARAFINA! (1992), which had been an acclaimed Broadway musical. She played a Soweto teacher, a kindly, principled revolutionary who "disappears" because of her political views. Upon arriving for the shoot, she discovered that some South African radical black liberation groups thought Goldberg, the Hollywood star, should have stayed home.

She found herself threatened in newspapers by groups angered that they had not been consulted and that the cultural boycott of the Apartheid-torn country should be continued. The situation was full of potential danger for Whoopi, but she refused to be cowed. She met with the dissidents and straightened them out as to her motives and the situation. Explaining her "bravery," Goldberg says this perilous situation was nothing new for her. "A lot of people say they're going to kill me. I can't run and hide every time somebody says they're going to do something to me, because it happens a lot."

Her 1992 movies proved to be quite a mixed bag. Besides SARAFINA!, which proved to be very uncommercial, there was the all-star THE PLAYER, a satirical study of behind-the-scenes Hollywood. The plotline involved a homicide and Whoopi appeared as a tampon-wielding police detective investigating the case. WISECRACKS was a minor league documentary, a tribute to the world of female comics. However, the surprise hit of the year was SISTER ACT, a project intended originally for Bette Midler.

The comedy presented Goldberg as a gangster's moll on the run who hides out at a convent. Once in a nun's habit, she not only revises and changes her own values but injects fresh spirit into the decaying monastic order. She coaches the parish's choral group and turns them into a media sensation. As the sleeper of the year, SISTER ACT grossed over $140,000,000 domestically and over $100,000,000 abroad.

BEHIND THE SCENES

Everything was not all sweetness and light during production of SISTER ACT. Goldberg came to loggerheads frequently with the Walt Disney Studio. She had several disputes with the comedy's director as well as with management over the shaping of the movie and her characterization. It led her to say, "Working for Disney, I do feel like a nigger again, and I'm not afraid to say it." However, later she and Disney's upper echelon bosses made up. At one point, she sent a hatchet to the top brass on the lot, suggesting, "let's bury this, we've got a job to do." They, in return, sent her a pair of brass balls and said, "Always keep these with you in case you lose one." Months later, it was Whoopi who had the final laugh. SISTER ACT was so successful, that she was lured into agreeing to star in a sequel, SISTER ACT II, at a reported $6.5 million salary.

Progressing naturally from all her activities thus far, it was not a novel idea for Whoopi, who had been a guest on several TV talk shows over recent years, to headline her own gab program. In fact, once before she had almost been a host. During Pat Sajek's year-long stab (1989-1990) in the medium, she had been asked to guest host on his program. She agreed to do it, if her guests could be three former First Ladies: Rosalynn Carter, Betty Ford and Lady Bird Johnson. The request was denied and Whoopi went off to other business.

Then, in late 1991, Genesis Entertainment suggested she star as the host of a syndicated half-hour talk show—to be done her way. Goldberg enthused: "We won't have an audience; there's no 'posse' and no band. I'll be able to spend 22-minutes each evening having a great conversation with one guest. It's a terrific way to find out who each guest really is and why this person has become so important to us." Warming to the project, she said later, her talk show philosophy would be to talk to the people "who I think are amazing, politically, socially and in entertainment. And talk about *them*, not just their newest project." She added, "We'll probably have lots of people I don't agree with and wouldn't want to go to dinner with. I want the show to be what the U.S. is supposed to be—a melting pot with different ideals and beliefs." In short, said the irrepressible Whoopi, the format is "let's hang out and shoot the   s—-."

Promoted with "It's Whoopi Time!" the TV program debuted on September 14, 1992. Her first week of guests included Elizabeth Taylor, Ted Danson, Tom Metzger (the White Supremacist), Elton John and Robin Williams. Others in the visitor lineup thereafter were Billy Crystal, Cher, Burt Reynolds, Jack Lemmon, Luke Perry and Garry Shandling. (Among those who turned down requests to be on her show, were George and Barbara Bush, Richard Nixon, Sally Field, and General Norman Schwarzkop.) When scheduled to chat with the likes of Tom Metzger, Goldberg insisted there would be no fireworks. "I'm not about hostility. I just want to understand how they got to be who they are. I want to know: 'Is this how you were raised?'"

MIXED REVIEWS

The reviews for the ultra low-keyed "The Whoopi Goldberg Show," in which she fawned over her guests, were mixed at best. *Entertainment Weekly* rated it a C+ and called it "the warmest, most buttery new talk show on television." The magazine added that she "is doing her share to bring civility to the talk-show wars." However, cautioned the publication, "the atmosphere on her set is so humid with respect and reassurance that this normally hard-headed performer seems to have gone all soft and squishy."

Rick Sherwood (*Hollywood Reporter*) decided, "given the gregarious nature of its star, 'The Whoopi Goldberg Show' is a surprisingly staid affair...the result is a show that displays little personality and only marginally more style." With very disappointing ratings, it was doubtful that all of the 205 stations who had carried the syndicated program, would continue. However, Goldberg, having signed for 115 segments, touted, "I don't have any big expectations. If we last an entire season, I'll be happy." Her syndicator, meanwhile, was already suggesting that the show's format should be altered to include her doing a bit of standup comedy, be more "confessional," as well as having more than one guest per episode and to perhaps rely on theme programs. After the first batch of shows were shot for the fall/winter 1992 season, a determined Whoopi took a break to regroup before the new TV shows were to tape in early 1993.

Goldberg has not placed all her eggs in this one talk show basket. In the summer of 1992 she returned to the stage (doing "Love Letters" with Timothy Dalton) as well as appearing at the Hurricane Relief Concert in Miami (duetting with Gloria Estefan on "Shout"). She authored a children's book, *Alice*, published in 1992 to much acclaim. She co-starred with Ted Danson, in the Richard Benjamin-directed MADE IN AMERICA, a romantic comedy set for 1993 release. She signed to do "animal voices" for Martin Scorsese's NAKED IN NEW YORK (1993) and to provide voices, along with Leonard Nimoy and Macauley Culkin for THE PAGEMAKER (1993).

For the AIDS-crisis film, AND THE BAND PLAYED ON (1993) being made for HBO-Cable, she was set to join a cast which included Richard Gere, Matthew Modine, Alan Alda and Anjelica Huston. However, due to health problem, she dropped out of the made-for-cable documentary feature. Goldberg continued with her recurring guest appearances on TV's "Star Trek: The Next Generation" (which merged into a new spin-off, "Star Trek: Deep Space Nine," in 1993) and "Captain Planet and the Planeteers." She also has her "Tales from the Whoop" specials for Nickelodeon Cable and has signed for three upcoming HBO-Cable comedy specials.

GETTING HER HOUSE IN ORDER

In September 1992, Whoopi placed her Malibu beachfront house on the market at $3.35 million, preferring to live in her other Los Angeles home when in town. (She also has a

Connecticut farm where she keeps a few horses.) More recently, she has been linked romantically with her MADE IN AMERICA leading man, Ted Danson, he recently separated from his wife of many years. She met the "Cheers" TV star on the "Arsenio Hall Show," when they were both guests. Hall had noted that most comediennes are not physical knockouts. Danson replied, "You're wrong," citing the talk program's next visitor, Whoopi. Later, Ted told Goldberg that he had always wanted to make a romantic comedy with her.

According to the Whoopi of today, "It's a good time in my life. I'm feeling pretty good about myself these days." When asked about her old marriages, she replies, "They seemed like a lifetime." As to living alone since her daughter moved out on her own, "I've got family; I'm surrounded." As to racism and sexism in Hollywood, she admits, "Occasionally I get annoyed, but you can waste a lot of time doing that, or you can go on and do what you have to do. [It] doesn't stop me from doing anything." The costliest career lessons she has learned are "That art and business are two different things. They really truly are. It was only art for me until the business stepped in. The business aspects can be wonderful—because it means you can make more money. but there's a price—you lose control of things."

As to who is the real Whoopi Goldberg, the star describes: "When I go out in public, I go out as Whoopi Goldberg. But when I'm in the house, it's Caryn Johnson, Caryn Johnson parent; Caryn Johnson grandmother. It's a whole different gig.... the mask is 'Everything's fine, everything's copacetic. No stress, no fuss, no muss.' But when I get home and I turn into a real person who has to deal with bills and family crises and whatever, there's no room for Whoopi Goldberg in that."

TV & CABLE SERIES:

Star Trek: The Next Generation (Syndicated, 1988-1993)
Bagdad Cafe (CBS, 1990; 1991)
Captain Planet and the Planeteers (TBS/Syndicated, 1990-) [voice only]
The Whoopi Goldberg Show (Syndicated, 1992-)

FEATURE FILMS:

The Color Purple (1985)
Jumpin' Jack Flash (1986)
Burglar (1987)
Fatal Beauty (1988)
Clara's Heart (1988)
The Telephone (1988)
Kiss Shot (1989) [TV movie]
Homer & Eddie (1990)
Ghost (1990)
The Long Walk Home (1990)
Soapdish (1991)
The Player (1992)
Wisecracks (1992)
Sister Act (1992)
Sarafina! (1992)
National Lampoon's Loaded Weapon I (1993)
Made in America (1993)
Naked in New York (1993) [voice only]
The Pagemaster (1993) [voice only]

Whoopi Goldberg with her then husband, David Claessen, in 1986.

Chapter 13
ARSENIO HALL

"I want to create a party with America looking through the keyhole," says 6' tall Arsenio Hall, he of the long elastic face, bulbous eyes and jaw full of teeth. And that this wunderkind does on his informal late evening talk show. When the syndicated TV program emerged in the late 1980s, it quickly gained the enthusiasm of younger viewers who felt a generation and culture gap with the likes of Johnny Carson's "The Tonight Show" or even "Late Night with David Letterman." With mercurial Arsenio at the podium, revving up the audience with his "Wooh! Wooh! Wooh!" (as he and studio viewers crank their arms in a circular motion), he would immediately establish the night's game plan. Next, he'd race over to show bandleader Michael Wolff, leader of the studio musicians (The Posse) and greet Wolff by touching fingers. Now, with everyone in high gear, he would shout the magic words, "Let's get busy!"

A typical lineup on "The Arsenio Hall Show" usually includes guests who are young, offbeat and untried. Generally, there is an emphasis on showcasing black talent, ranging from rapper Ice-T to choreographer/director/actor Debbie Allen to screen star Wesley Snipes. Or such Arsenio pals as Eddie Murphy, Mike Tyson or Magic Johnson might drop by for an oncamera chat. But no matter whom the guest, one can rely on the host to be impulsive, emotional, and huggy-huggy with visitors. (He is also likely to go "mmm-m-m" if he thinks a guest is being unresponsive.)

Show producer Marla Kell Brown said once of Hall, "He'll do and say things no other host would dare utter." She is quite correct. Arsenio, flashing his gummy smile and widening his large eyes expectantly, is the type to ask Brooke Shields if she'd retained her publicized virginity (to which the actress just laughed), or inquire of sex therapist Dr. Ruth Westheimer if she'd ever faked an orgasm (she didn't answer). As Hall says, "I just ask what y'all are thinking anyway."

Arsenio has a rule of thumb for his program: "When I'm on the air, if I'm too worried about ratings or bookings, that takes you out of your game. You miss an obvious follow-up question.... I don't want to have [background research] cards. That takes away from the ability to have a real conversation. You can't *listen* with cards." He also determined from the start: "Unlike most talk shows, on my show, the audience in a sense becomes the co-host of a late night party. They are to me what Ed McMahon...[was] to Johnny [Carson.]...." For Hall, "My philosophy is to leave my ego at the door and get the best out of my guests." Thus, "that [TV stage] set is my place. I invite you to it, and I'm a nice host. I'm here to entertain and to treat you like I would if you were in my home."

A WELL CONCEIVED PLAN

However, this TV fun-meister also has a particular agenda: "When I used to watch [Johnny] Carson as a kid, I couldn't understand why a black artist like Joe Williams, who sang as well as Mel Torme, only got a wave from Johnny. Why couldn't Joe tell his stories about touring with Count Basie? I thought, 'When I come through, I'm going to make sure I don't mess with little white kids the way this is messing with me. We're going to have a party and everyone's going to be invited.'"

Who is this slick, hip party-giver? On the surface, Arsenio Hall is the type of show business personality whose expansive Paramount studio suite is full of high tech equipment, professional memorabilia and a great many teddy bears. His off-hour duds include a Reebok T-shirt, slacks, unlaced sneakers and a baseball cap. However, in public, he is far different. Mr. Blackwell recently named Arsenio one of TV's best dressed men because his "bold, busy" outfits "set the contemporary standard every 24 hours." On the other hand, fashion forecaster David Wolfe decided that Hall's "style overshadows his personality, which is big enough."

As to Arsenio the private man, his show producer, Marila Kell Brown, states, "Arsenio is a very private person.... He's the son of a minister; it all begins with that." Hall himself has said, "I give you all of me as an entertainer. I give you none of me as a private person. I have to have something that's all mine, and that's my love life, my home life." As a famous, wealthy bachelor, Hall admits, "My fear is that if I had a wife, I'd be a terrible husband to her; I would not give her what she needs and deserves. Because right now, I've got another woman called show business, who will leave if you neglect her. You have to make her number one, or she'll be outta here. I haven't found a woman yet who wants to be the chick on the side."

As a workaholic ("I work when other people sleep") he describes himself as "this entertainment and show-biz machine, and clearly, I should go out and purchase a life." He concedes, "I change every day. One day I have a heart of gold. The next day, I want to march with Al Sharpton the rest of my life. I'm America's most schizophrenic entertainer." Most of all, Arsenio Hall is a man driven by a dream. At a People's Choice Awards a few years ago, he stated, "They told me I didn't have the talent, that I was too black. If there's anything you want to do, don't let them take your dream away."

AN ONLY CHILD

Arsenio Hall was born on February 12, 1955 (some sources list 1957) in Cleveland, Ohio. He was the only child of Reverend Fred Hall and his wife Annie, who was twenty years his junior. Mrs. Hall recalls that she saw the name "Arsenio" twice while she was pregnant with him, and thought it was an omen. She says the name comes from the Greek, meaning "strong male." "But," jokes Arsenio, "I always say it's the Greek word for Leroy."

He grew up on 79th and Kinsman in Cleveland, living in the corner of a block in a terminally-ill housing project. Growing up in the ghetto, it was not uncommon to find a rat running around the bathroom floor or for the next door neighbor, as was the actual case, to be shot during a pickup football game. (Years later, when Arsenio returned to Cleveland in 1989 for a visit, he discovered that several boyhood friends were either dead or in jail. At the time, he said, "Yo man.... Nobody got out but you.")

When Arsenio was around three or four years old, his father, pastor of the Elizabeth Baptist Church, gave him his first taste of show business. Reverend Hall would tape his sermons to analyze his speech. Often, he would let his son add his thoughts on the tape. (Hall still has the recordings.) When Arsenio was five or six, his parents broke up. They had been disagreeing for years and would get into fierce arguments.

"It wasn't unusual for me to see my dad go for a gun during the arguments....It wasn't just screaming—much deeper and more traumatic. I developed a rash and started sleepwalking. They'd find me in the garage in the morning, sleeping in the car.") Having decided to end the trauma, Mrs. Hall, with Arsenio in tow, moved in with her mother who lived around the corner. Thus Arsenio was raised primarily by women: his mother, grandmother and godmother.

PULLED FROM ALL DIRECTIONS

In these formative years, the Halls used their son as an emotional tug of war. One time, the future star recalls, he wanted a pair of Coach Converse sneakers. His parents made it a traumatic issue for their own purposes, with their son the victim. (Nowadays, Arsenio has a horde of such tennis shoes.) As a growing youngster, Hall remembers "playing catch with my mother and the ball hit her in the head because she couldn't catch. I needed a dad for that."

With only a single parent, Arsenio's role models were not the usual ones (e.g., singer James Brown or civil rights leader Martin Luther King, Jr.), but a local black professional. "I was just a kid at the time my mom worked for him," says Hall, "but it really impressed me to see this black lawyer, this black man, in a position of prominence and power." When he would visit with his father, Reverend Hall was always preoccupied with his clergy work, but was very protective and very strict with his child. (Years later, when his son had decided on a show business career, the Reverend would advise him, "I don't care what you do, just stay close to God. Being a man of God as an entertainer, you'll probably be able to reach more people than I will, and that means something.")

As a youngster, Arsenio had an active imagination. He would cut apart newspapers to make his own papers and crossword puzzles. A magician since he was seven, it was not long before Arsenio the Magician was performing at birthday parties, talent shows, and weddings. ("Most kids had a paper route and mowed lawns to make a little money, but I was allergic to grass, so I did magic.") Active in the church choir, he was always on the go, always thinking of the future. His Sunday School teacher would reminisce years later: "when you talked to him, he'd see you and yet he didn't see you. His mind was always on something else."

As an adolescent, Hall was a fanatic devotee of TV talk shows, especially those of Johnny Carson, Dick Cavett and Dinah Shore. He would critique those programs for his mom, and insist that someday "I want to do what Johnny Carson does." Early on at school he was a class clown. According to Hall, "I was who I was because at home there was no one to laugh at me, there was no one to play with me. For me, it was like, 'Fuck this learnin', I come here to party, 'cause ain't nobody at my house.'"

MARCHING TO A DIFFERENT BEAT

At Warrensville High School, Hall was a drummer in the marching band and orchestra and started his own musical group. When his school basketball coach asked the lanky athlete to devote more time to court practice, he said no. He preferred to be home perfecting his magic tricks, or learning new dance steps by watching favorite groups on TV such as the Temptations and the Miracles. Most of all, he dreamed of the future, far away from the ghetto and quarreling parents.

After graduating from high school, Arsenio went to Ohio University in Athens, Ohio, majoring in communications. After his sophomore year, he transferred to Kent State University in 1975 to be closer to his family in Cleveland. (His grandmother was ill at the time.) In a speech class at Kent State he announced, "I plan on making my living with my oratory skills, and I'd like to be a talk-show host." This revelation merited lots of laughs from classmates.

He worked on the campus radio station (WKSR) as a disc jockey, did his magic act for fun and profit, and worked in school drama groups. When he auditioned for *Purlie Victorious*, to be staged by the Black Drama Workshop of the Institute for Afro-American Affairs, the tryout earned him the role of Reverend Purlie. ("I played Rev. Purlie and just fell in love with the whole process.") When comedian Franklyn Ajaye performed on the Kent State campus to promote a movie, CAR WAR (1976), Hall introduced himself. Ajaye promised to take Arsenio to the Comedy Store, if and when he came to Los Angeles.

Hall received his B.A. from Kent State in late 1977. He went to work in Detroit for Noxell, makers of Noxema. One night after tuning in "The Tonight Show," he decided to quit his job. He moved to Chicago, to a suburb called Rosemont, to be with his mother who was working there. One evening, he drifted into a club called the Comedy Cottage and was intrigued by its roster of performing comedians.

The visit inspired him to perfect his own routine. After signing up for amateur night, he developed a severe case of mike fright. There followed many evenings when he refused to go on at the last minute. Finally, he made his debut. He was good enough to be hired to work there for $10 a night. On a dare, he entered a competition at the local Playboy Club and won two bookings. At the time, he thought his act was funny, but in retrospect he has decided he was "terrible."

THE LEAN YEARS

Hall struggled for many months as a Chicago-based entertainer. Meanwhile, his father died in 1979. Hall's turning point came that December 25, when he emceed a show for singer Nancy Wilson. She was late and he had to do stand-up comedy to keep the audience entertained. She was impressed sufficiently to hire him as a regular warm-up act the next week, and he went on the road with her. Next, he did his comedy routines for Aretha Franklin, then later for jazz keyboardist Patrice Rushen and singer/composer Neil Sedaka.

Finally, it was Wilson who financed Arsenio's move to Los Angeles. He arrived in town in his beat-up Pinto car, and soon found work. He opened for more singers, including Robert Goulet, impressionist Jim Bailey and Tom Jones. For Tina Turner, he provided the warm-up when she appeared at Caesar's Place in Atlantic City in 1983. Hall says, "She was the only artist I opened for that I never met."

Meanwhile, he had begun hanging around Los Angeles' comedy clubs, including the Comedy Store and The Improv. It was there that he met fellow young comic, Eddie Murphy. According to Hall, "Eddie's the brother I never had. We share intimate secrets. We cry together. There's no competitiveness between us." Another comedian whom he did NOT meet was John

Belushi. Arsenio had gone there to meet the famed funster, but he had left by the time Hall arrived. The next day Belushi died from drug overdosing. According to Hall, "It shook me into saying, 'That's a warning.' That was a sign as far as direction was concerned."

By now, Arsenio had auditioned several times for "The Tonight Show Starring Johnny Carson." However, the talent coordinators found his comedy "too barbed" and/or too "sophomoric." So it was back to being the opening act on the road, now performing with the likes of Patti LaBelle. Her only guideline to him for his gig was: "Honey, that's your act. You do what *you* want to do." For Hall, "Patti turned me loose. As much as I love Nancy [Wilson], she kept me conservative. She used to tell me, 'Please, don't ever be nasty. You're so wonderful' I kept telling her, 'Nancy, I'm *not* so wonderful.' Patti told me to be myself because that's the only thing that'll ever work for you. My career changed because Patti is wild; she let me go. Her words became my personal philosophy that year; this is the year to be yourself."

REAPING THE REWARDS

All his apprentice work finally paid off. He was hired to co-star on "The 1/2 Hour Comedy Hour" produced by Dick Clark for ABC-TV. The network told Arsenio to "Pick a white guy!" as co-host and he selected Thom Sharp. The frenetic variety program debuted on July 5, 1983. *Variety* reported that Arsenio "was guilty of mugging too much for the studio audience." The summer show lasted only a month. Despite its quick evaporation, it taught Hall, "Trust yourself.... If I ever fail again, it will be based on my own sensibilities." Now a rising name in Hollywood, Hall was seen on the social scene, first escorting British actress Emma Samms and then being seen with sitcom star Mary Frann ("The Bob Newhart Show"). With part of his income, Arsenio bought new cars for his mother and himself.

After several guest appearances on "Thicke of the Night," the late night talk show hosted by Canadian Alan Thicke, Arsenio was asked to join the program as a regular. However, by mid-June 1984, that show had failed. The next year, Arsenio was among the troupe on NBC-TV's "Motown Review," a six-week summer variety show, starring Smokey Robinson. This, in turn, in early 1986, led to his becoming co-host with Marilyn McCoo of the syndicated TV musical revue program, "Solid Gold." With his velvet-toned bass voice, Hall supplemented his income by doing commercial voice-overs and providing a voice (1986-1987) for "The Real Ghostbusters," an animated series on ABC-TV.

If Johnny Carson had lumped Arsenio into the category of "too far out" for "The Tonight Show," then permanent substitute host Joan Rivers had no such reservations. Hall made it to "The Tonight Show" in March 1986. That September when she began her own rival talk program, "The Late Show" on the Fox network, Arsenio was a frequent guest on the show. In May 1987, Rivers was dumped by Fox. Until a replacement series ("The Wilton North Report") could bow, the talk program continued the same format, now using substitute hosts. Of the rotating guest emcees, flashy Arsenio proved to be the most popular.

However, Fox, feared to take chances having a black host as permanent star of the nationally seen program. Then, it changed its mind. Against a lot of advice (including his manager's), Hall accepted the challenge, receiving more than $100,000 for his chores which began as of August 17, 1987. Realizing he had nothing to lose, Arsenio decided to wake up late night America and give them something different than the typical Johnny Carson fare: "I figured I'd make a show for people who just didn't relate to the kind of show he's doing."

TREND SETTING

Wearing his trademark diamond earring and frequently garbed in leather, way-out Arsenio told his audience at the start of each program, "We be havin' a ball." Then he'd launch into a lively ninety minutes of comedy, music and chatter. Drawing on his friends, he had comedians Eddie Murphy and Robert Townsend on the show, several avant garde rock bands, and relied on stunts such as playing one-on-on basketball with visitors (like Elliott Gould).

One program found Mike Tyson, Magic Johnson and Emma Samms singing "When the Saints Go Marchin' In" with Little Richard. The unpredictable Arsenio was not above talking to the audience about his big rear end, or discussing fashion styles with guests. The way the brothers and sisters in the studio audience shouted at him, at times it seemed as if "The Late Show" was more of a church revival meeting than late night TV programming.

During Arsenio's tenure, the jivin' "The Late Show" gained respectable ratings, equaling those of Joan Rivers. "For the first time," stated Hall, "I let loose, just being myself and having fun. It worked." However, the network had little faith in this interim production, giving it scant promotion. Hall often had to purchase his own show wardrobe. One evening, Hall encountered media mogul (and Fox conglomerate head) Rupert Murdoch at a fancy Los Angeles restaurant. Hall remembers clearly: "I spotted...[him] waiting for his car. I introduced myself, and he started fumbling through his pockets for a ticket. He thought I was with valet parking. I told him, 'No, Mr Murdoch. I do your show,' and he mumbled, 'Nice to meet you.'"

After "The Late Show" left the air on November 6, 1987, viewers conducted a write-in campaign to bring it back. The network obliged with re-runs of Arsenio's shows. Then the long-

Victoria Principal and Ted Danson visit with Arsenio Hall on "The Arsenio Hall Show" in 1989.

anticipated "The Wilton North Report" debuted in December 1987 and bombed. It was gone by early 1988. By this point, Fox had been negotiating with Hall to return to their network in a talk show format at a $2 million fee. However, he refused, preferring to sign a multi-picture film and TV contract with Paramount, estimated to be worth $3 million. (Hall's buddy, Eddie Murphy, was already under a lucrative studio contract there.)

ARSENIO AND THE MOVIES

Arsenio already had appeared in his first motion picture, AMAZON WOMEN ON THE MOON, made in 1986 but not released until 1987. In this haphazard collection of disjointed comedy episodes, Hall played a contemporary man unable to cope with modern household appliances, including his bothersome VCR. John Landis had directed Hall's scenes in AMAZON WOMEN and he was in charge of the Eddie Murphy comedy, COMING TO AMERICA.

Murphy played an idealistic African prince, with Arsenio (in a counter-image characterization) played his cynical, materialistic pal, Semmi. Like Eddie, Arsenio was given the opportunity to play several additional roles in the comedy. Relying on heavy makeup, his cameos included a very unpretty woman in a singles bar, an enthusiastic preacher and an elderly barber. Unlike AMAZON WOMEN, COMING TO AMERICA was a huge hit, grossing more than $300 million worldwide. For his performance(s) in COMING TO AMERICA, Arsenio received the Best Supporting Actor Image Award from the NAACP. Also in 1988, he was the host of MTV Music Video Awards and continued to participate in charity telethons.

As part of his Paramount contract, Hall was next to do THE BUTTERSCOTCH KID, a period piece about a man left with the little boy belonging to an ex-girlfriend. However, the project was soon dropped. Arsenio explains: "I found out that I hate to do movies. It was a nightmare. Making movies is very complicated, tedious and tiresome. It is especially terrible for a comic, because you do a joke and you turn to people and ask, 'Was it funny?' They say, 'We'll let you know in eight months.' I wanted to get back into TV badly."

However, his previous contract with Fox for "The Late Show," forbad him from doing his own talk program for a year. He bided his time, but then almost decided not to attempt the challenge of hosting his own program. He claims his July 21, 1988 appearance on "The Tonight Show" changed his mind completely. During the commercial breaks he and fellow magician Carson did tricks for the studio audience. Hall recalls: "It was being out there that made me realize I was about to compromise my dream. I said the hell with 'too hard.' All my life, I've wanted to do what this man does."

FULL CONTROL

Hall and Paramount came to terms for him to host a new TV show. He insisted on being the program's executive producer with authority to build his own staff, doing the hiring and firing. He helped to design the set, wrote the show's theme song ("Hall Or Nothing"), picking the guest lineup, and began practicing to write his own monologues. He intended to be "the architect for a lot of my dreams." Under the Paramount pact, and (through his Arsenio Hall Communications), he was to receive an estimated $2.5 million yearly salary. With this largess, he bought a house on Mulholland Drive for $795,000.

Hall's syndicated show was scheduled to bow on January 3, 1989, six days before the debut of another new genre program, "The Pat Sajak Show." Said Hall of the "Wheel of Fortune" emcee, "As long as there's an alternative to Sajak, the public will always take it." In contrast, Hall was high on David Letterman's late night TV show for "forcing America to loosen its collar a bit and not take things too seriously." As for Johnny Carson, "he has an incredible understanding of when he's needed and when he's not.... Doing a talk show for him is like a snooze alarm on a clock: he can find it in the dark. He doesn't care about numbers of competitors." Regarding obnoxious Morton Downey, Jr, who was hosting his own gab marathon, Arsenio judged "Mort shows you what you don't want to be."

For Hall's first program, his guest lineup included Brooke Shields, Luther Vandross, Leslie Nielsen, and, for some unknown reason, character actress Nancy Kulp (of "The Beverly Hillbillies") sitting in with the band. Rick Kogan (*Chicago Tribune*) wrote of the opener: "The stage...was a seriously glitzy affair; filled with greens and blues, it looked like some sort of show business aquarium. It was fitting, however, since the entire setting seemed to mirror Hall's own double-breasted style and slickness." Kogan concluded, "there is no denying that the 'Arsenio Hall Show' is one babe capable of making some noise."

Arsenio would end each night's program with "See you in 23 hours." As promised, the next evening he would return with a new array of talent, including lots of sports figures (e.g. Kareem Abdul-Jabbar, Sugar Ray Leonard and Captain Lou Albano). At first, Hall, seated in a plush easy chair across from his guests on a matching couch, was ill-at-ease in his interview segments. There was a nervousness behind his loosey-goosey approach.

UNDER A MICROSCOPE

As the new kid on the block, everyone was analyzing the trendy, new show. Chuck Reece (*Channels* magazine) reported of Hall's property: "What he's doing is putting a lot of elements of black popular culture in front of the white part of his audience. The show is hip, hipper than anything else on late-night TV." Arsenio was also proving to be controversial with his on-the-air guests.

When film director/actor Spike Lee appeared, Lee criticized Eddie Murphy for not helping blacks enough in Hollywood. Arsenio defended his pal, leading to a verbal tussle. As a result, Hall cancelled Lee from appearing on a later show, but thereafter the two made up. There were other much-heralded feuds. Madonna teased her host about his "tired" hairdo, leading Arsenio to insist later that she has "borrowed our sound but not our sensibilities." When Hall showed unflattering honeymoon pictures of Roseanne Barr and Tom Arnold, the comedienne took offense. Eventually, she cooled sufficiently to return as a guest on Arsenio's TV forum.

Hall was sued for $10 million by Willis Edwards of the Beverly Hills-Hollywood chapter of the NAACP. Edwards claimed that Arsenio had labeled him an "extortionist" in radio and newspaper interviews. (The suit was dismissed later in Los Angeles Superior Court.) When Hall's former mentor, Joan Rivers, cancelled an appearance on his TV show at the last minute (claiming illness), Arsenio turned cool towards her. Through it all, Hall's "emotions on the shirtsleeve" approach pushed his ratings higher. Equally important, his program attracted younger viewers, the target consumer group advertisers love so well. "The Arsenio Hall Show" was nominated for three Emmy Awards in mid-1989.

Meanwhile, to fulfill an obligation to Paramount and Eddie Murphy, Arsenio appeared in Murphy's HARLEM NIGHTS (1989), in which Murphy starred, produced, directed and scripted. Hall was paid $900,000 for being in this dull gangster yarn set in 1938 New York. Critically lambasted, the lumbering comedy did quite well at the box-office because of the stars' drawing power. Meanwhile, on his TV venue, Hall appeared as his own brother, Chunkton Arthur Hall (better known as Chunky A), a 300-pound rap singer.

ALWAYS IMPROVING

The success of this sketch led to a later comedy album ("Large and In Charge") featuring Chunky A. Also in 1989, Arsenio was working with a New York City-based media consultant, Virginia Sherwood, to improve his interviewing skills. Due to his success, he now had high visibility with his anti-drug commercials. ("I'm kind of a role model now...and that means heavy responsibility.") Socially, he had been linked more recently by the supermarket tabloids with the music world's Paula Abdul.

However, he claimed that, in actuality, his one true love to date had been a woman with whom he had a long rapport. It had begun when they lived together during college. ("This was a six-year relationship that ended because I got in this business. She said, 'This is not for me. You're from Cleveland with dreams of being a star. I'm from Cleveland.'") Hall was still living in his relatively modest San Fernando Valley home. He had purchased a condo for his mother in West Hollywood, but she insisted on getting a job, and was working in the sales department of a sporting goods concern.

With his increasing popularity, in April 1990, Paramount signed a new contract with "The Arsenio Hall Show, extending the studio's commitment from five to six years, through 1995. As part of the deal he was to be executive producer of another late night program ("The Party Machine with Nia Peeples" came and went in 1991), as well as star in future Paramount theatrical films. By June 1990, 205 stations carried his TV show and his ratings had increased 23% over the first six months of 1989. The next month, he was named first national ambassador for the Drug Abuse Resistance Education program (D.A.R.E.) and, that fall, he again hosted the MTV Video Music Awards.

In December 1990, Arsenio was stirring up the mix again, this time in combat with Queer Nation, a high-profile gay rights organization. They took Hall to task for his alleged anti-gay humor and staged a protest during one of his telecasts. Arsenio retorted by claiming he would be "the last person" to discriminate against another minority, insisting that he often had gay friends on the TV show. However, said Hall, it was no one's business what his guests' sexual orientation were.

EVER POPULAR

In a 1991 *Time* magazine/Cable News Network poll, Arsenio was named "Favorite Late Night Host" and his episode (November 8, 1991) which featured Roseanne Barr and Magic Johnson (who had been diagnosed as HIV positive) was his highest rated program of the year. Once again, he hosted the MTV Video Music Awards and, besides his D.A.R.E. duties, he was involved deeply with Make-A-Wish and Starlight Foundations, both of which benefitted terminally ill kids. It was estimated that Hall's gross income in 1991 was over $21 million.

Now a permanently entrenched talk show maven, Hall had established his own ground rules for what made his program zip. When criticized for being too soft in questioning his guests, he retorted: "I'm throwing a party on my show. And when you invite people over for a party, you don't cross-examine them." He also insisted that he did not want his series to be rehashes of performers repeating what they had just done or said on other such programs. "I don't want to be the second person to hear stories."

Fellow standup comic and one-time pal Jay Leno began his reign as permanent host of "The Tonight Show" on May 25, 1992. There was immediate speculation as to whether Jay, up against Arsenio in overlapping time slots, could outdraw him. The two stars are quite different in their professional images. Whereas Hall is a finger toucher and a hugger, Leno is more of a hand shaker, at the very best an arm patter. Arsenio could be quite emotional publicly, in contrast to Jay who, by his own assessment is "not the roller-coaster type, crying one day, laughing on a mountain the next." While Hall enjoyed offending, clean-guy Leno always avoided blue, rude jokes. Arsenio was from the street ("I'm from the clubs, I'm from the smoke and the dope. I'm from the g-h-e-t-t-o"). On the other hand, Jay was much more a sidewalk type of guy ("Being hip just means some people don't get it"). In financial terms, Hall was earning $12 million for his hosting chores; Leno was drawing $3 million.

Before long in 1992, there were industry rumors that "The Tonight Show" was using hard-nosed behind-the-scenes tactics to pressure guests from appearing on other talk shows, especially Arsenio's and Dennis Miller's. The situation infuriated Hall and he let it all hang out. He told *Entertainment Weekly* magazine that he would "kick Jay's ass" in the ratings. When Dennis Miller's show was cancelled, Hall verbalized: "He should be staying and punk-ass Leno should be going."

LETTING IT ALL HANG OUT

When taken to task about his outspokenness, Arsenio explained. "I have no problem about saying good things about my competitors, but Jay Leno and I aren't friends! And you know what? I wasn't anointed, okay? No one put the late-night silver spoon in my mouth. I earned every drop of mine." It was no accident that Arsenio persuaded two "Tonight Show" alumnus, Ed McMahon and Doc Severinsen to appear on his talk show. Doc said in his appearance (and in other interviews) that the new "Tonight" crew was "a bunch of screwballs. Jay Leno is running around...trying to figure out 'How can I get them to like me?'... Frankly, I haven't seen anything that makes me want to stay tuned in."

In September, Helen Kushnick, executive producer of "The Tonight Show" was let go, amid industry charges that she had spearheaded the aggressive booking wars to insure Jay Leno's high ratings. At a later press conference, Leno insisted that Kushnick's firing was "unwarranted." He acknowledged that it was his show and he took full responsibility, despite his disclaimer of not knowing what was going on behind the scenes in the grab-the-hottest-guest marathon. In a moment of self-styled magnanimity, he suggested he and Hall should make peace and get back to work. Arsenio refused and, in a November 1992 issue of *TV Guide*, was quoted as saying" "Now I am trying to close this chapter of my life, though it will never be forgotten." Ironically, by the time Arsenio made this statement, his TV show's ratings were slipping as Leno's was rising.

Meanwhile, Hall expanded his role as concerned citizen. When the late April 1992 Los Angeles riots broke out, he did his best from his TV platform to cool hot tempers, including allowing Mayor Tom Bradley to appear and speak on his program. Appreciating the good-will influence generated by Hall's humanitarian approach, Bradley declared July 21, 1992 as Arsenio Hall Day, lauding the celebrity for such deeds as donating $165,000 to transform a crack house into a community center. (Hall also had participated in TIME OUT: THE TRUTH ABOUT HIV, AIDS & YOU, 1992, an awareness home video he produced for the Magic Johnson Foundation.) The next month, Hall threw a party for press agents, managers, etc. "who supported me while journalists were trying to position me as the black host. Sure, I'm a black host, but I'm doing a show for all people."

According to the rumor mill, his latest romantic attachments include actress Maria Conchita Alonso, as well as 28-year old Trisha Cados. The latter, then separated from her husband (later she filed for divorce), was a publicist for the public relations firm handling "The Arsenio Hall Show." Professionally, besides supervising his TV talk show, making occasional TV guest appearances (such as on Tom Arnold's new sitcom, "The Jackie Thomas Show" in late

December 1992), Arsenio also served as executive producer of BOPHA (1993), a Paramount feature directed by Morgan Freeman and starring Danny Glover and Alfre Woodard.

In the current audience rating sweepstakes, Arsenio had dipped noticeably as Jay Leno's "The Tonight Show" and other newcomers, including long-time friend Whoopi Goldberg, have competed for viewership on the talk show circuit. Things will get even tougher in the rating wars come the fall of 1993 when Hall must compete on the late night talk show battleground not only with Jay Leno on NBC and David Letterman on CBS, but with Chevy Chase's new TV talk show on the Fox network. There is also industry rumor that Arsenio's syndicated show might be moved by many local stations to a new 12:30 AM berth, rather than its current 11 PM time slot. Despite the soon-to-heighten battle for viewership, Hall insists, "I don't make any changes. No changes. It's a bad move. When you start making changes, it makes you insane."

As to his career future, Hall insists: "I have no intention of going beyond my Paramount contract.... I never want to allow myself to get comfortable." However, concerning his talk show hosting, he confesses, "I was born to do this. When I'm in the spotlight, I'm gone. I love it more than anything in the world. When everyone is barking and screaming, it's the best feeling I've ever felt, like a three-point jumper with one second left in the championship game against Boston. Better than an orgasm."

TV & CABLE SERIES:
The Half-Hour Comedy Hour (ABC, 1983)
Thicke of the Night (Syndicated, 1984)
Motown Revue (NBC, 1985)
Solid Gold (Syndicated, 1986)
The Real Ghostbusters (ABC, 1986-1987) [voice only]
The Late Show (Fox, 1987)
The Arsenio Hall Show (Syndicated, 1989-   )

FEATURE FILMS:
Amazon Women on the Moon (1987)
Coming to America (1988)
Harlem Nights (1989)

Chapter 14
LARRY KING

Larry King is far more than the affable Brooklyn-born Jewish boy who made good. He is a very direct man with a fantastic ego, famed for his striped shirts, suspenders and swept-back hair style. He is the star-crazy guy whose condominium walls are loaded with celebrity photos and who regales visitors with non-stop funny anecdotes laced with extensive name dropping. *TV Guide* ranks this slightly-built individual with large glasses as the "hardest-working interviewer in the broadcast business." The *Hollywood Reporter* labels him "the foremost purveyor of New News." He insists of his life's work, "I do a form of journalism. It results from my interviews."

For this high-achieving Type A personality, his "lets slow down" schedule includes his daily hour-long TV talk show, his daily three-hour phone-in radio program, and a weekly *USA Today* column. Over the decades, he seesawed from modest beginnings to luxuriant overindulgence, down to bankruptcy and back up to a $2 million dollar yearly income. During these jarring lifestyle changes, he authored five autobiographical books, married five or six times which produced a daughter and an adopted son, suffered a near fatal heart attack requiring bypass surgery, and just barely managed to stay out of jail.

Industrious Larry admits to being a control freak and characterizes himself as "TV's 'Street Guy.'" He explains, "I never went to college, I'm fascinated and curious about everything.... I'm still Larry Zeigler, as I was, starting out in Brooklyn, asking, 'Why did you do that?'" He amplified on this trait for the *New York Times*, "If you think about it, my curiosity is something that is a part of me, that is inside of me, that lives with me. I am curious, curious. The average person is curious and what I help that average person do is tweak that curiosity to provide some answers. There is no such thing as soft or hard questions. It comes from good listening."

As a veteran talk show host, sometimes criticized for being too soft on guests, he says, "I like questions that begin with 'why' and 'how,' and I listen to the answers, which leads to more questions." For him, "The only thing worse than a silly, argumentative, or boring guest is one who doesn't show up at all." (Mike Tyson was one Larry King guest who did not show up in 1989; another was comedian Mort Sahl who failed to show up twice.)

NEVER AT A LOSS FOR WORDS

One thing about King, a liberal Democrat, is that he is never shy. "I don't want to be defensive," he once cautioned *TV Guide*, "but I'm damn good at what I do. I know criticism comes with it, especially when you're in the middle of a hunt." He adds, "I'll go longer than anyone. I'll get more information than anyone, I'll do better."

Lawrence Harvey Zeigler was born on November 19, 1933 in Brooklyn to Eddie and Jennie Zeigler. A six-year-old son had died of a burst appendix shortly before Larry was born; Martin would be born when Larry was four. Mr. Zeigler, a Russian emigre, owned Eddie's, a bar and grill in the Brownsville section of Brooklyn, located under the tracks of the elevated train. When World War II started, Eddie hoped to enlist in the Army, but was rejected for being overage.

To demonstrate his patriotism, he sold his bar and went to work in a defense plant in Kearny, New Jersey. He worked the night shift helping to build warships. On June 10, 1943, Eddie Zeigler, age 44, died of a heart attack. Larry, 10 and Martin, 6, were shipped off to Camp Eden in Kingston, New York following this tragedy. However, their stay was short-lived. Larry was too unhappy about losing his dad to cope with the new environment.

Later that summer, Jennie and her two sons moved from their third-floor Brooklyn walk-up to the Bensonhurst section of the borough. They found an attic apartment across the street from Mrs. Zeigler's sister, Bessie. The family went on welfare. Jennie did unreported seamstress work to supplement the income; later she found work in a garment industry sweatshop. Shattered by his dad's passing. Larry

Larry King, the lecturer of the 1990s.

developed a paranoia about his father's "desertion." He began wondering if everything else he loved (e.g., his family, sports, radio-listening) would desert him as well.

ALWAYS OBSESSED

Once an astute student (he skipped the 3rd grade) he now became lazy about school. However, his native curiosity could not be long suppressed. At Sam Maltz's neighborhood candy store he developed a life-long thirst for newspaper reading. Then too, he became increasingly obsessed with sports. He also recalls, "When I first moved to Bensonhurst, before I got to know anybody, the radio was my only friend. It was the first thing I saw in the morning, and the last thing I heard at night." Larry worshipped radio personality Arthur Godfrey, almost as much as he loved to go to Brooklyn Dodgers baseball games.

Larry meandered through Brooklyn's Junior High School #128 and then moved on to Lafayette High School. From ages fourteen to nineteen he belonged to the Warriors, more a social and athletic group than a street gang. He was known to fellow members as Zeke. Larry, had a vivid imagination and a thin sense of the "truth."

He was not above playing antic jokes. On one occasion, a pal left the neighborhood to undertake a tuberculosis cure in Arizona. Zeigler told everyone that their friend had died and that he was raising money for a memorial in his honor. Having amassed a tidy sum, Larry and his cohorts splurged the funds on themselves. Their scheme backfired when the boy in question recovered early and reappeared suddenly at school.

Having graduated from high school, Larry knew he wanted to be in the broadcasting industry. However, he had no idea how to break into the business. Marking time, he worked at odd jobs, including delivery boy and mail room clerk. In 1951, at age eighteen, he married. He asserts the union lasted for about fifteen minutes, was never consummated, and was annulled. (Thus he does not claim that as the first of his several marriages.)

THE BIG BREAK

In 1957, at age 23, Zeigler went to Florida by bus because he was told that Miami might be a good place to start in broadcasting. A small wattage AM station (WAHR) hired him, not because of his good speaking voice, but to sweep floors. However, when the morning disc jockey quit, Larry was asked to take over his job. In his first day on the air, he was so full of mike fright that he could barely open his mouth. The manager yelled, "This is a communication business. Communicate!" Larry did, as well as following his boss's suggestion to change his surname to King.

After about a year there, he was also put in charge of a half-hour nighttime radio sports show. One evening, when subbing for the station's all-night dj, King received a breathy call from a sexy-sounding female who insisted she "wanted him." Always a fast thinker, he slapped the double album of Harry Belafonte at Carnegie Hall on the turntable and rushed over to her house. Just as he and this married woman were getting comfortable, the record jammed at the line, "where the nights...where the nights...." King raced back to the studio, just in time to accept a great many calls from disturbed listeners. He was quickly learning the power of the airwaves.

By late 1958, he had received an offer from a larger radio station (WKAT) to handle a morning dj show. Too unconventional to be normal, he diverted from the tried-and-true routine. He would interrupt his record-spinning with bizarre news alerts, inventing characters such as Captain Wainright of the Miami State Police. His quirky Captain Wainright, who once advised listeners to consider placing horse track bets with policemen as a time-saving device, brought a devoted audience to King.

As a result, Pumpernik's, a popular Miami restaurant, hired Larry (age 25) to host a radio talk show from its busy dining room. Handling this chore taught King a lot about the art of interviewing. From his beginning days of question and answer sessions with waitresses, or plumbers (if a convention were in town), he rose to conversing on air with celebrities such as Bobby Darin and Jimmy Hoffa. Two regulars on the show, when they were in Miami, were then unknown Don Rickles and cult figure Lenny Bruce. From this restaurant show experience, Larry learned, "I had an ability to draw people out in an interview. The key to my success as an interviewer is in the fact that I am truly interested in a person's craft, in his or her work."

ON TOP OF THE WORLD

Within the next year, Larry was also doing a weekend feature segment on WLBW-TV, hosting a Sunday night talk show. In the radio field, he moved on to WIOD, one of the city's biggest stations. After some months, they suggested he switch the program's locale from Pumpernik's to a more casual ambiance of their choice: a houseboat (in fact, the one used for the popular TV show "Surfside 6"). One of King's frequent guests was actor Alan Alda who was starring a great deal of the time at the Coconut Grove Playhouse. One of Larry's most special nights on the air occurred when Joe DiMaggio, Jr. recounted how he never really knew his celebrated sports figure father, and that the closest they ever came occurred while driving together to Marilyn Monroe's funeral.

Meanwhile, Larry had married Alene Akins in 1961. He was 28; she was 21. She had had a son (Andy) when she was fourteen, and then had dropped out of high school to care for him. She was self-educated and a very private person, in complete contrast to Larry. King met her when the Miami Playboy Club was about to open and he invited six of the Bunnies onto his radio show. Alene, then under 21, was the cousin of one of the Bunnies and came along to the interview. When of age she would become a Bunny herself, earning $450 a week compared to Larry's $135 weekly on radio. By 1963, the couple divorced, she leaving for Iowa with a another talk host (whom she later married) from WIOD to whom Larry had introduced her.

To increase his TV exposure, in 1964, King jumped from WLBW to WTVJ-TV where he was assigned a weekend talk program. He also married Mickey Sutphin, who was his wife from 1964-1966. In 1965, the *Miami Beach Sun* hired Larry to write a weekly column in the vein of Walter Winchell's celebrity spotting pieces. Although King was earning close to $70,000 by 1966, thanks to his three jobs, he was already in trouble with the Internal Revenue Service. His indulgent life style left insufficient funds to pay his taxes. As King says in retrospect, "At my most egotistical moments, of which there were many, I felt as if I owned Miami—and I lived as if I did, too."

It was at this juncture that he first met financier Lou Wolfson. Wolfson, in his late fifties, had once controlled a $400 million industrial empire and was known as "the great raider." Now he had turned his energies to philanthropy. Larry met Lou at Hialeah Race Track. It was Wolfson who agreed to back King in packaging a new show ("Profile") he had devised.

Under a corporate umbrella, Larry taped a few of these half-hour one-guest interviews shows, but the concept never sold. Neither did a different style talk show that Lou sponsored and for which King did the narration. Meanwhile, once having divorced Mickey Sutphin, Larry rekindled a romance with ex-wife Alene. By this time, she had divorced her post-King spouse. Larry and Alene married a second time in 1967, remaining together until they split in 1971.

POOR DECISIONS

During this period, Lou Wolfson was undergoing federal investigation for the alleged selling of unregistered stock. Later, Lou was indicted and the case went to trial. Meanwhile, Wolfson had decided to donate $5,000 in cash to Jim Garrison, the New Orleans district attorney who was making a crusade of investigating the John F. Kennedy assassination. Larry used a portion of these funds he was suppose to give Garrison (who had been on his talk show) to pay off IRS back taxes.

Later, King offered to intervene on Lou's behalf with government figures. He claimed he had a special contact with top administration officials, because he had met newly-elected President Richard Nixon when he had been a guest on King's radio show. Similarly, he also knew Nixon's close associate, Miami-based Bebe Rebozo. Thereafter, Larry persuaded Wolfson that Nixon's pal, attorney John Mitchell, was working on Lou's behalf in the legal tussle. As such, Wolfson gave Larry money to pass on to Mitchell for legal·fees, etc. Instead, Larry used the dollars to prolong his financial musical chairs. Shortly, the situation snowballed out of hand.

In 1969, soon after King had confessed the truth to a flabbergasted Wolfson, Lou was sentenced to prison. When he was released in 1971, the still-infuriated financier pressed charges against Larry for grand larceny, despite King's offer to somehow repay the money. On December 20, 1971 King was arrested. However, he spent less than ten minutes at Dade County Jail before being released without having to post bond. The trial was set for January 1972, but the judge had a heart attack the night before the case was to be heard. Three months later, the same judge was scheduled to hear the case. At that point, it was discovered that the statue of limitations had run out and the charges were dropped against Larry.

Throughout this entirely bizarre period (1966-1971), Larry had become quite a local hit in Miami. Besides the radio talk show, a TV interview program and his weekly newspaper column, he also did background features on the Miami Dolphins for airing during the team's football games. In his fast-living phase, King played the horses a great deal, drove a Cadillac, and tossed money around freely, refusing to consider the consequences. He was behaving, according to him, "as if I didn't have to live by the same rules others live by." Despite assorted marriages, he persisted in having affairs on the side, typically with luscious models. He reasoned: "I felt that Larry King deserved to be seen with beautiful women."

ROCK BOTTOM

After the arrest scandal, and despite the charges being dropped, he suffered a nearly four-year banishment from the media. In retrospect, he admits, "I was a pushy, business-oriented person who was so stuck on himself he couldn't see sideways, so I hit rock bottom." He and Alene, who had a two-year old daughter, Chaia, again divorced. In was now 1972 and he was finished at WIOD radio station and WTVJ-TV. Down to his last $42, he bet it at the track and won nearly $8,000. However, within three months he had spent it all. Next, a small Miami radio station offered him pittance to handle special sports commentary. He accepted. To keep afloat, King turned to a millionaire acquaintance he had met in 1971. Over the next few years, this individual advanced him $90,000. Later, when King had to declare bankruptcy, this benefactor was Larry's largest creditor.

The next several years were tough for King. Through Larry's friendship with jockey Bill Hartack, he traveled frequently to races around the country. On a stopover in Shreveport, Louisiana, King accepted a public relations job for a racetrack due to open there soon. That fall of 1974, he was hired to do color commentary for the World Football League's Shreveport Steamers, broadcasting on the city's largest radio station. Larry began joining the Steamers for their away games. The next year, the new owners of the race track brought in a new crew, and fired Larry. At liberty, he drove to San Francisco where a racetrack pal was living. After a month in the Bay City, he accepted a job as Saturday announcer for University of California football games.

Before his new sports announcer's post was to start in the fall of 1975, he drove cross country to Miami to spend time with his ailing mother. (She would die in 1976.) Once in Florida, he learned that radio station WIOD had a new general manager. The new executive was willing to hire him back to continue his same-format show, in which he would interview a guest and then answer phone-in questions. The first night back in front of the microphone, the nervous King began his show with "As I was saying...."

In 1976, the *Miami News* hired him to write a weekly feature column, and additionally, he obtained a new TV show. He also met Sharon Lepore, who was in the midst of divorcing her junior high school sweetheart. She had two daughters, then age 13 and 10. King's daughter Chaia was eight and was living with her mother. Larry was earning $28,000 annually, when he and Sharon wed in September 1976.

TOO MUCH MONTH AT THE END OF THE MONEY

It was in 1978 that Larry, now earning $50,000 yearly, declared bankruptcy to cope with outstanding debts of over $350,000. Having learned his lesson finally, he quit track and card gambling, and hired financial advisors to establish his weekly budget. A few months earlier, the Mutual Broadcasting Network negotiated with King to host a new late night radio talk show that would be distributed nationally. Although the network had failed with previous attempts at this format, King reasoned,"I just didn't have that much to lose."

"The Larry King Show" bowed on January 30, 1978, with only 25 stations around the country signed for the new program. For the first few months, the show originated from Miami, but as of that April was relocated to the network's Arlington, Virginia studios. King was not opposed to a fresh start in a new region, especially since the facilities' proximity to Washington, D.C. meant that he could invite prominent politicians onto his forum. King's wife Sharon, who had been a teacher, began working in the production department of "The Charlie Rose Show, a syndicated talk program emanating from D.C. Then she worked on a local cable talk show, as well as local radio offerings.

Thanks to Larry's charisma, by 1982, "The Larry King Show," which aired from midnight to 5:30 AM nightly, was being heard on 250 stations and far outshone the competition in the ratings. With his magnetism, he was able to attract a wide variety of program guests which include such diverse personalities as Frank Sinatra, Reverend Jerry Falwell, Miss Piggy, former President Gerald Ford and porno movie star Marilyn Chambers (who took off all her clothes— but remember this was radio).

His show, for which there was no script nor any studio audience was divided into three segments. King claimed he never prepared for the show and never met the guest till they went on the air. It was his way of making the air time as spontaneous as possible. There was an opening interview segment with the guest, followed by two hours for the visitor to take calls from people all over the country. The final 120 minutes were devoted to "Open Phone America," with King on the air solo accepting calls on any and every topic. (According to Larry, "Money is far and away the subject most on people's minds." On the other hand, King insists, "Religion is not the opiate of the masses, sports are. Sports are a worldwide opiate.")

LOYAL FOLLOWING

Among Larry's legion of faithful radio listeners were a "stock company" of recurrent phoners, such as the "Portland Laughter," who did nothing but display his infectious laugh. Then there was the "Miami Derelict," who never worked, just devoted himself to amassing a huge collection of radio and TV taped shows. The "Brooklyn Scandal Scooper" was an unemployed dishwasher who wanted to get into radio. Sometimes, the show would get a bit out of hand, such as the occasion when the guest (a psychic) walked off the show because he refused to let her chat with the listening audience on the phones until she answered some tough questions.

Undaunted, King stood in for her, fielding questions on the world of psychic phenomena. As the years passed, the show developed a weekly audience of three to five million listeners coast to coast. In 1982, King's program received the Peabody Award, which he rates a crowning achievement. Also that year, he authored, with Emily Yoffe, his autobiography, *Larry King*. It was the first of several installments, followed by *Tell It to the King* (1988) with Peter Occhiogrosso, *Tell Me More* (1990) also with Occhiogrosso, and the nostalgic, soft-focused *When You're Brooklyn, Everything Else Is Tokyo* (1992) with Marty Appel.

Now, in 1982, a media success and a national figure, Larry told his wife Sharon that his daughter Chaia might be coming to live with them. Sharon balked and suggested he take a separate apartment. Once he had moved out to his own Alexandria, Virginia condo (which he would purchase in 1985), she filed for divorce.

A workaholic, Larry not only thrived on his nightly marathon radio show, but was also writing a weekly *USA Today* column. Then on March 13, 1983 he added to his chores by hosting "The Larry King Show" ("Sunday Night Live"). It was a Sunday night nationally syndicated TV talk show (to 110 stations at the start), telecast from downtown D.C. It used the same format as King's popular radio offering, but allowed for a studio audience. *Variety* described Larry as the "owl-faced talker" with interviewees "grilled by King's machinegun style of asking questions."

Variety complained, "the problem with the [new] King show was that viewers need not watch it, only listen. It just didn't visually grab the audience's attention. but it does provide intelligent conversation...." The show lasted only until July 10, 1983. In 1984, Larry made his feature film debut in the mega hit GHOSTBUSTERS. For playing himself, he was paid $2,500. (He would make another cameo, as himself, in the Dudley Moore comedy, CRAZY PEOPLE, 1990.)

HIGH GEAR

In the spring of 1985, King signed a new five-year pact with Mutual Broadcasting for $1.85 million. Almost simultaneously, he signed with Cable News Network (CNN) at $250,000 a year. For the latter, he was to do a new television version of his talk show ("Larry King Live!" which debuted June 3, 1985), plus do background commentary for Baltimore Colts and Washington Capitals football games to be aired on a sports pay channel. This was on top of other radio assignments and column writing (which now included the *Sporting News*). Moreover, there was a weekly Washington, DC. TV show, "Larry King, Let's Talk" aired from WJLA-TV. Apparently, up to any challenge, the buoyant King insisted, "I'm on a roll, but even though the schedule is tough, the shows aren't."

In 1987 Larry King was keeping up his usual high pace. He was living in Alexandria with his daughter Chaia, 19, who was attending the local American University. Larry appeared to be on top of the world. However, he had underestimated the toll of his workload, a situation further aggravated by being twenty pounds overweight and a chain smoker. On February 24, 1987, he had a heart attack. (Ironically, it was the morning following an interview with Surgeon General Everett Koop, who had advised him to stop smoking.) The attack was a climax to King's accelerating coronary artery disease first diagnosed in March 1981 when he developed a peculiar shortness of breath. He rushed to George Washington University Medical Center for treatment.

By the beginning of that March, he was released from the hospital and vacationed in Miami for a few weeks. By March 24, 1987 he was back at work. Actress Angie Dickinson, his special friend and frequent date over recent years, was on hand to provide encouragement. (King claims he never seriously thought of wedding Dickinson because their liaison was "not fireworks." Her version, reportedly, was her inability to cope with his womanizing and career addiction.) Thinking his life was now back in order, he began pursuing his ex-wife Sharon.

They had had several reconciliations in the five years since their divorce, but could never reach a comfortable compromise for a joint lifestyle.

Then, on December 1, 1987, with his heart condition worsening, he underwent bypass surgery at New York Hospital-Cornell University Medical Center. One of the many notables who visited his hospital room during the recovery period was media peer Phil Donahue. On December 9, 1987, King left the hospital, determined to follow through on the prescribed regimen of restructured living habits. The trauma of Larry's heart attack, bypass surgery and new life style (e.g., treadmill exercise, becoming a permanent non-smoker, etc.) formed the basis for *Mr. King You're Having a Heart Attack* (1989), written with B. D. Colen. Meanwhile, in 1989, King married Julie Alexander, who operated a placement service. The next year, she filed for divorce. However, in 1991, they reconciled and then finally divorced in 1992. She blamed the split on Larry being still too much in love with ex-wife Sharon.

BEST JOB IN THE WORLD

Now, a reformed man professionally, Larry cut back—a bit—on his work schedule. He refused to do a recurring segment on TV's "Entertainment Tonight" or host television's "Crime Watch." However, he did "Sunday Night with Larry King" (October 28, 1990). The hour special was a NBC-TV network pilot for a weekly variety show a la Ed Sullivan. *Variety* observed that "King seems a bit ill at ease removed from his usual straight-interview setting" and that "his usual shoot-from-the-hip style is somehow more abrasive on network TV than on CNN...." Although this concept failed, Larry was still earning well over $2 million annually. On the lecture circuit, alone, he commands $35,000 per appearance, and he also did several sports and healthy living audio/video tapes.

In the 1992 U.S. presidential campaign, the major candidates turned frequently to the TV talk show forum to gain visibility and air their views, all at no cost. One of the surprise entrants to the election race was eccentric Texas billionaire Ross Perot who ran on an independent ticket. He received so much exposure on "Larry King Live!" that viewers soon wondered whether it was Perot or King who was actually running for public office. When Perot confirmed on King's CNN show that he did indeed intend to run against incumbent George Bush and favorite son, Bill Clinton, Larry gained a new title, "Kingmaker." The very visible talk show host moderated several 1992 specials ("From the Heart of America: Larry King Town Meeting").

He gained tremendous coverage when Vice President Dan Quayle said on "Larry King Live!" that he would support his daughter should a situation arise that required her to have an abortion. There was equal controversy concerning a pre-election "Larry King Live!" show visit by entertainer Cher, spouting her views about the state of the world. At a conference at the National Press Club (Washington, D.C.) in October 1992, Larry King was introduced as "the political pundit of the year." It was also this year that he was inducted into the National Association of Broadcasters' Hall of Fame. As a result of King's increased popularity in 1992, Mutual Broadcasting decided, as of February 1, 1993 to move Larry, the "king of late night" from his 11PM to 2AM radio talk show shift to 3-6 PM EST. The radio network hoped to take advantage of King's high profile by moving him to the afternoon drive time.

Never bashful about his professional self, King insists, "I've got the best job in television today. Phil Donahue told me that he would change places with me—but I wouldn't change place with him; or with [Ted] Koppel, Barbara Walters, or Oprah [Winfrey]. I've got an hour of TV, worldwide, live. I make well into seven figures—more money than I'd ever dreamed. There are no other talk shows in my time. I never get hassled by [CNN headquarters in] Atlanta. Don't hear, 'We went down a ratings point in Chicago—why don't you do more sex?'"

Regarding future dreams, he admits that someday he would like to cut back a bit, taking off a summer, perhaps, to be a baseball announcer, to do a little acting. "I never want to give up my TV show" he insists. "If—God forbid—I ever became President, I'd keep right on doing 'Larry King Live' from the White House."

TV & CABLE SERIES:
The Larry King Show (Miami local, 1962-1971, 1976-1978)
Sunday Night Live [The Larry King Show] (Syndicated, 1983)
Larry King Live! (CNN, 1985-)
Larry King, Let's Talk (Washington, D.C. local, 1985-1987)

FEATURE FILMS:
Ghostbusters (1984)
Crazy People (1990)

Chapter 15
VICKI LAWRENCE

If you were choosing party guests from the world of show business, bubbly Vicki Lawrence ought to be among the very first you'd invite. This lithe 5'6'" redhead, who went from teen to mature woman while performing in front of the TV cameras, knows what comedy is all about. Both on the long-running "The Carol Burnett Show" and the equally successful "Mama's Family," she proved to be a zany funster who could provoke laughter from even the most dedicated sourpuss. Want someone to sing? Lawrence is ready, willing and most able (she had a #1 hit with "The Night the Lights Went Out in Georgia.") How about organizing parlor games? Try Miss Vicki, she hosted TV's "Win, Lose or Draw" game show for three years. Need to bring the best out of those wallflower invitees? Lawrence is your salvation. She's proving daily on her new TV talk program ("Vicki!") that this warm-hearted host can loosen up the most wooden guest.

Already in her fourth (!) decade as a TV celebrity, Vicki "has it all" to paraphrase "The Lifestyle of the Rich and Famous." She has passed through several tough emotional phases, enough to have caused a person of less mettle to drop out of the limelight permanently. However, she is far more than just a talented entertainment industry survivor. Beneath her image as a very physical comedian, she boasts a great deal of common sense and inner radiance honed from her long-time assignment as wife and mother. As Lawrence confesses, "I was very shy when I started on 'The Carol Burnett Show.' Becoming a person has been a long, slow process. But I've grown up. I'm not afraid to say what I think."

She was born on March 26, 1949 in Inglewood, California a community located a few miles southwest of Los Angeles. Howard Axelrad and Ann Alene (Lloyd) Lawrence were already the parents of another daughter, Joan. Howard was a C.P.A. for the Max Factor Cosmetic Company, while Ann was a very determined housewife. Ann decided quickly that her younger daughter was too energetic and had too much potential talent to waste her time being a mere child. From the toddler stage onward, it was drummed into Vicki that she could and would be a high achiever. Vicki recalls that, almost from the start, her strong-willed mother "had me singing for company. I hated it. As soon as I could walk, she made me swim."

To please her mother, as soon as she was old enough, Vicki agreed to take ballet, tap and modern dance lessons. Almost as quickly as she left the baby-talking phase, she began vocal lessons. When her fingers were long enough, she was being instructed on the ukulele, guitar and then the bass. (Later, she would be taught trumpet, drums and tambourine.) Seemingly more a curse than a blessing, Vicki proved to have natural talents in all these areas. Spiritually, Vicki was raised a Christian Scientist and said as an adult, "I never had to get involved in the I-must-find-myself bit. I take care of myself. I can heal myself if I work at it."

NOTHING OUT OF REACH

Not only was Vicki pressured into honing her performing skills, but she also proved to be a high achiever in school. In the eighth grade, she won a national writing contest. (She reflects, "I was always bored when I was a youngster. So, to keep myself busy, I'd enter contests, any kind. They were things for me to do. I think contests and pageants are great for young people. They're an education.") At Inglewood's Morningside High School, pert Vicki narrated a class film, was a song leader and vocalist, played in the student orchestra and was also a cheerleader.

By her teen years, the very proficient Vicki was singing with two local groups of folk singers. In 1964, she auditioned for the Young Americans, composed of 36 teens from southern California. The non-profit group was begun in 1962 by music teacher Milton C. Anderson. This wholesome assemblage of young professionals toured the country during school vacations, performing at concerts, doing TV appearances and making recordings. To stay in the organization, each member had to maintain a B scholastic average or better. Vicki would remain with the Young Americans for three years, and would make her theatrical film debut with them in the documentary feature, THE YOUNG AMERICANS (1967).

With her seasoned stage presence, it was natural that Lawrence should be in school plays. In a production of "Macbeth" she was cast as Lady Macbeth. Local newspaper reviewers noted a strong physical likeness between Vicki and Carol Burnett. During her senior year, when she was seventeen, Lawrence was encouraged to send a letter (enclosing a snapshot and review clippings) to Carol Burnett. In her note she told the TV/stage star about the uncanny resemblance they shared. In her nervousness, Vicki forgot to include a return address. Some weeks passed before she received a phone call from Burnett. By then, a very curious Carol had tracked down Vicki through her father's name mentioned in the article and had called phone information for the number. They chatted for a while and Vicki mentioned her upcoming appearance in a local area talent contest. Lawrence was convinced that would be the last time she would hear from the celebrity.

Days later, Vicki was at Hollywood Park race track where she was named "Miss Fireball" in a contest sponsored by the Inglewood Firemen's Association. A quite pregnant Carol Burnett came to the occasion with her producer husband, Joe Hamilton, and came backstage to say hello to Vicki. The star mentioned briefly that they should get together sometime soon for a girl-to-girl chat. However, Burnett left early (according to some accounts) because she was not feeling well. A disappointed Vicki heard nothing further.

Then, says Vicki, "About a month later, I heard on the radio that Carol had had her second baby, Jody, at St. John's Hospital in Santa Monica. I decided to go over there and bring her some flowers. I told the maternity nurse that I was looking for Mrs. Hamilton and she thought I was Carol's sister, Trixie. Before I had a chance to explain, the nurse led me into Carol's room."

Lawrence recalls that the new mother was nice about Vicki's pushiness. She promised to call the high school student when she got home. Three weeks later Hamilton phoned to invite Vicki to audition for Carol's upcoming CBS-TV variety series. Not sure whether their daughter had been successful or not, the Lawrence clan were about to start a vacation trip east when Hamilton called to say that Vicki would indeed be part of the fall TV series.

JUST A NORMAL LIFE

Until the television offer came, Vicki insists that she had planned originally to go to college at UCLA, become a dental hygienist, marry a rich dentist "and spend the rest of my life shopping." She claims that show business as an adult profession "never dawned on me."

The hour-long "The Carol Burnett Show" debuted on September 11, 1967 on CBS-TV. Besides Carol, the resident company included comedian Harvey Korman, utility leading man Lyle Waggoner and, as fourth banana, Vicki. In a skit on the first show, Lawrence played the trouble-prone daughter of Carol and Harvey. In later program episodes, she was featured in sketches involving Carol and her rambunctious kid sister, Chrissy. Because the program was a variety offering there were plenty of opportunities for Vicki to display dancing and vocal skills. All the while, she perfected her ability to do comedy and light drama.

The first seasons were not easy for Vicki, who had been such an extrovert in high school. She admits that she was shy and overwhelmed by performing with such high-powered professionals. As she explains, "Actually I was scared to death to be there, because I didn't feel I deserved it. My career was more or less a gift from Carol, rather than something I suffered for. I was embarrassed to say Hi to anyone, for fear they would start laughing at me. Really." Looking back, she says "I was awful. I was the worst. I had trouble finding the ladies' room."

Not only did Vicki have to cope with the strains of doing a weekly series, but she insisted as well on enrolling in UCLA (as a backup in case she and/or "The Carol Burnett" did not work out). On a personal basis, she had a very difficult time adjusting to being a budding celebrity. "It didn't take very long before I just didn't get along very well with my old friends from school. We had nothing to talk about."

NEW FOUND FAME

In the spring of 1968, with "The Carol Burnett Show" a rating hit, the Lawrences moved into a new home near Beverly Hills, so Vicki, now earning around $800 a week, would be closer to work and school. During the summer of 1968, Vicki capitalized on her new fame by going to the Dallas Music Hall in Texas to play Carrie Pipperidge in a production of "Carousel." A far more sobering experience was flying to Vietnam that year on a handshaking tour that lasted 21 days. Sometimes she would visit 17 fire bases in one day. "You could hear the shooting all the time. It didn't hit me until I got home. It's hard. I would think about it at night, when I got home—I wrote to a lot of guys. It tore me up."

For the first two seasons of "The Carol Burnett Show," Vicki continued her studies at UCLA. However, by the end of her sophomore year in 1969, she realized she couldn't keep up the dual existence of performer and student. Firstly, she found that she would no longer be able to arrange her class schedule to work around her rehearsal schedule. Secondly, she realized that it was becoming impossible for her to be just a "normal" student. Lawrence says, "I still remember one professor, I'd come into class and he'd start with the compliments, 'Just loved you on TV last night!' Or, he'd say to the class, 'She's terrific! Most of the kids never watched TV and had no idea what in the world he was talking about. It was embarrassing."

From June to September of 1969, Vicki and Lyle Waggoner were both regulars on "The Jimmie Rodgers Show," a CBS-TV summer variety hour replacement for "The Carol Burnett Show." The program allowed Lawrence more opportunity for exposure and to refine her talents.

The Carol Burnett showcase returned on September 24, 1969 for its third season, with Burnett's good friend Jim Nabors again the opening show's guest star. By now, Vicki was given increased prominence in the proceedings. *Variety* acknowledged that she "is an okay song and dance gal in her right and acquitted herself acceptably with the funnies on the preem [premiere]."

Of her social life in the late 1960s and early 1970s, Vicki reflected later that her shyness and growing pains caused her "to date guys who weren't nice to me, because I didn't have a very high opinion of myself." It was in this period that she met country-western singer Bobby Russell. As a songwriter, he had gained prominence with "Honey" and "Little Green Apples," and would jump onto the pop charts himself with vocals of tunes like "Saturday Morning Confusion." In the summer of 1972, during her hiatus from "The Carol Burnett Show," Vicki and Russell married. They had a 300-acre spread near Nashville, Tennessee where they raised cattle and horses and grew soybeans and tobacco.

Vicki Lawrence in the early 1970s and in the 1990s.

HIT SONG, FLOP MARRIAGE

Ironically, it was Bobby's writing of "The Night the Lights Went Out in Georgia" that led to domestic turmoil. When another vocalist bowed out, Vicki, who had already recorded singles for various labels, agreed to record the song. It broke onto the industry charts in late 1972 and remained there for fourteen weeks, reaching the #1 position for two weeks. The song became a gold hit and led to further recordings for Lawrence. However, admits Vicki, "Bobby couldn't deal with his wife being a record star and, in his mind, more important in the music business than he was." In December 1973, divorce papers were filed. At the time, Vicki acknowledged at the time, "It just didn't work out. I'm glad it happened now rather than later, when there might have been kids." (Bobby Russell would die in November 1992 at the age of 52.)

By this point, Vicki had gained her personal independence from her parents through her marriage and then her divorce. (However, she would never entirely resolve her anger about her parents "My mother pushed me. She also wanted total credit for everything I've done, including my Gold Record....") By now, Lawrence had developed a very warm stage presence. No longer the novice, she felt she should be treated on a more equal footing on "The Carol Burnett Show." Her business dealings at this time with Burnett's demanding husband, Joe Hamilton, still rankles.

She remembers that after five seasons on the show, she marched into Hamilton's office and told the executive producer: "You know, I really feel I have spent enough time on the show and I pull my weight and I think I should be paid what Lyle [Waggoner] is making.' He said, 'Lyle has a family to support.' I said, 'Oh, all right.' I turned around and left and didn't even get mad until about 5 years later when Carol got really involved in the ERA [Equal Rights Amendment]. I said, 'Well, clean up your back yard first.'"

During the 1974-1975 TV season, Carol Burnett introduced a new skit, "Ed and Eunice," dealing with a warring middle-class southern couple (Harvey Korman, Carol Burnett) who must cope with her cantankerous mother (Vicki Lawrence). (Originally, Carol had planned to play Mama, but then changed her mind.) The routine would become so popular that, over subsequent seasons, there would be thirty "Ed and Eunice" sketches. The highlights of these domestic burlesques was Vicki as the widowed, feisty Thelma Harper. Because the farce was but one segment of the fast-paced hour show, it was decided for expediency that Mama's senior citizen character should be etched without special makeup. Through the use of a gray wig, outrageous stomach and hip padding and a pair of granny spectacles, Vicki became the screeching matriarch with a bowlegged strut.

BAREFOOT AND PREGNANT

By the start of the 1974-1975 "Carol Burnett" season, Vicki had met and married show business make-up artist Al Schultz, who had worked on PLANET OF THE APES (1968), and later became a chief make-up artist at CBS. Lawrence credits him with "making me proud of myself." However, It was Schultz who almost cost Vicki her TV series job. When Vicki became pregnant and it could no longer be hidden, producer Joe Hamilton fired her from the program, citing the "deformity clause" in her contract. Lawrence was flabbergasted by the harsh decision.

As she recalls painfully, "It wasn't like I was some bimbo twit out of wedlock." She went to Hamilton and reasoned, "Lucy [Ball] had her baby on her commercial break." To which he replied, "Yeah, but that was Lucy. She was married to her leading man. You should be home knitting booties with your feet up." Lawrence was forced to do just that and, in 1975, gave birth to Courtney Allison. Later, Burnett who was too much under her spouse's control, spoke up and demanded that Vicki be brought back to the series in the fall. Vicki claims she has never discussed the matter with Carol (who later divorced Hamilton just a few years before he died). "I don't want to dredge up any more pain for her," says Vicki. On her part, Burnett would once voice, "We started out as mother-daughter, we soon matured to big sis-little sis. Now we're peers, because Vicki's a grown-up woman. Besides, I don't think anybody owes their career to anyone. People can open doors for you, but unless you can walk through, you're not going to last.... Vicki owes her career to Vicki."

"The Carol Burnett Show" returned for its ninth consecutive season in the fall of 1975. Lyle Waggoner had departed and comedian Tim Conway, who had been a program guest several times before, signed on as a regular. The show was now in its golden age. For her supporting role on the series, Vicki won an Emmy Award for the 1975-1976 season. In 1977, Vicki gave birth to her second child, Garrett Lawrence. This time there was no question about dropping her from the program.

Because of the special chemistry between Carol and Harvey Korman, the industry was skeptical of any further success for the long-running variety show when Korman did not return in the fall of 1977. His replacement was Dick Van Dyke, who, after just three months, decided to leave the show. Feeling she had better quit while she was ahead, Burnett determined this would be the program's final season. On March 28, 1978 a special two-hour entry aired, featuring clips from past seasons.

SHIFTING GEARS

By the point this series ended, Vicki was appearing in the West Coast stage production of "My Fat Friend," making the rounds as a quiz show celebrity guest, and co-hosting "The Junior Miss America Pageant" from Mobile, Alabama. In the early summer of 1979, "The Carol Burnett Show" regulars reunited (along with newcomers Kenneth Mars and Craig R. Nelson) to tape four new segments, this time, for ABC-TV, which showed them in August-September of that year.

Having always been too busy professionally, Vicki and her husband (who had retired from the make-up field to be his wife's manager and to operate a leasing business), now decided to move to Hawaii permanently. They traded in their small vacation condo in Maui for a larger one near to Carol Burnett's home. However, after a year of semi-retirement, the family returned to California. "I really found out that I needed more than just being 'mom,'" says Vicki. "It seems like it doesn't matter how much time you give the kids, you can give them 24 hours a day, it's still not enough, and I started to lose Vicki somewhere in there. I was turning into just 'mom.'"

Initially, Vicki had rejected offers to take on a TV show of her own, fearful that she could not carry the burden. But now, she tried a sitcom pilot for ABC-TV. The choice was "Mr. and Mrs. Dracula," in which Dick Shawn and Lawrence were the nocturnal blood-thirsty couple who move from their Transylvania castle to a Manhattan apartment. The unsold pilot aired on September 5, 1980. (Later, a second pilot for the same projected series would be produced with Paula Prentiss replacing Vicki.)

To keep busy, when not on the TV game show circuit, Vicki appeared on "The Love Boat" and a few episodes of "Laverne and Shirley." The Schultzes were now living in Hidden Hills in the west part of the San Fernando Valley and had sold their Hawaiian condo. In their free time, they entered their 45' yacht in various races (The Lipton Cup, The San Francisco Big Boat series) and won several trophies.

WHEN IN DOUBT. . .

Following the rule that when in doubt try something familiar, Carol Burnett, Harvey Corman and Vicki reunited for the March 15, 1982 CBS-TV special, "Eunice," dealing with further bittersweet misadventures of the bickering family. (Vicki was nominated for an Emmy for her supporting work in this offering.) The next day, CBS announced it planned to turn the property into a spin-off series, but nothing concrete happened. Other networks also rejected the format, because the pilot had been prescreened and the audience's reaction was negative.

The show was rethought and rewritten and NBC agreed to make it is a mid-year candidate for the 1982-1983 TV season. "Mama's Family," produced by Joe Hamilton, debuted on January 22, 1983 with Harvey Korman as the pompous host, Alistair Quince, who introduced each episode. Vicki was the buxom, no-nonsense Thelma Harper living in Raytown with her sensitive sister (Rue McClanahan). Almost immediately, Thelma's dim-witted son, Vint (Ken Berry), whose wife had run off, moved into the crowded blue-collar household with his two teenaged children (Eric Brown, Karin Argoud).

Before long, Vint was romancing a floozie neighbor, Naomi (Dorothy Lyman). Much to crabby old Mama's disgust, Naomi marries Vint and moves in. Occasionally, Ed (Harvey Korman), Eunice (Carol Burnett) and Mama's other daughter, the snobbish Ellen (Betty White), would make token surprise visits. The *New York Times* reported, "Miss Lawrence's delivery of her one-liners is sharp enough to make one wish the lines were better. They are about as original as the laugh track." Despite critical reservations, the series lasted through the 1983-1984 NBC season.

Again at liberty, Vicki had to overcome her well-etched image as the matronly Thelma Harper. She rued, "the world in general is far more willing to accept you as you really are than the people in this business. I run into producers and industry executives and there's always this great 'Gee, you're young' surprised look in their faces." She also revealed, "I've got a bit of an identity problem of almost being a cartoon character when people see Mama.... I could dress like her forever and not ever be myself. I'd get lost in the shuffle totally. But I've found that without a script, it goes nowhere. I just feel like a fool." Lawrence also had another identity problem: forever being compared to Carol Burnett. It caused her to sigh, "I love Carol as much or more than anybody, but it's tough to be constantly compared to her. 'Cause I ain't her.'... It's like they think I can't do anything without Carol standing beside me. It takes every single job to convince people I am an entity of my own and not an extremity of Carol."

JUST BEING HERSELF

Next, Vicki hosted "The Great American Homemaker" show for USA Cable. The 1984 program featured segments on cooking, gardening, home organization, child rearing and consumerism. What was she doing starring on such an informational entry? "Doing this show is a nice opportunity for me to be myself on camera, which I don't get to do too often. And I think I am a typical homemaker."

Once the cable show was behind her, Vicki tried another pilot, "Anything for Love," which co-starred Lauren Tewes and Marsha Warfield. ABC-TV aired the unsold entry in August 1985. All the while, Vicki was campaigning to get "Mama's Family" back on the air. She proved tenacious at playing industry politics. ("I had the best education in the world on Carol's show. It was like going to Harvard. And I graduated with honors.")

"Mama's Family" returned to the air in September 1986 as a syndicated sitcom. The revised cast/format found acerbic Thelma still ruling the roost in a house filled with her locksmith son, Vint (Ken Barry) and his low-class but dedicated wife, Naomi (Dorothy Lyman). To replace the departed teens (vanished from the storyline), there was Bubba (Allan Kyser), Eunice and Ed's neglected, rebellious teen-age son who comes to live in the Harper household. The revised show, sometimes directed by Harvey Korman, would prove to be a solid hit and lasted for four seasons through 1990.

Meanwhile, Vicki and her family had relocated to Long Beach. Because her spouse was also her manager, it led to too much togetherness, which, at times, caused household tensions. Never one to sit still, Vicki Lawrence Schultz (as she was sometimes billed), while still starring in "Mama's Family," became one of the few women to host a network daytime TV game show. As of September 1987, she began emceeing "Win, Lose or Draw" on NBC for two seasons. The show was co-executive produced by Burt Reynolds and Bert Convy (who was the first host on the program's syndicated version).

THE FAMILIAL DRY SPELL

Following the finish of her sitcom, Vicki went through a professionally dry period. She recounts, "After 'Mama' went off in 1990, I got knocked around by the networks. I was being advised what kind of shows I should do, who should write it, etc. It was an incredibly depressing experience, and frustrating. I was either going to flip my lid or do something constructive with my life." It eventually wound up with her being offered a syndicated talk show by Westinghouse Group W Productions.

With a solid project at hand, she "got on...[her exercise bike] and watched every talk show on television. I began to wonder if I was the last normal person on Earth. I always considered myself to be a pretty average person. I'm a wife, a mother, and lucky enough to be in show business. And I think I'm concerned about the same things other people are—the economy, education, ecology.... So, as I watched these shows, I wondered where they got all the strange people. I decided then and there they don't deserve any more air time—not on my show!"

"Vicki!," taped at the NBC-TV production facilities in Burbank, California, debuted on September 31, 1992. Her first episode was devoted to Teen Idols of the 50s and Early 60s, and had guests Fabian, Edd Byrnes, Frankie Avalon and (via satellite) Annette Funicello. Rick Sherwood (*Hollywood Reporter*) judged of the newest entrant to the talk show sweepstakes: "[she] has been able to adapt her winning personality to the demands of the talk show circuit with a mellowed, more mature approach that still keeps a watch on the comedic buzzer. Lawrence succeeds where others have failed because she plays fan and interviewer, a kind of anywoman asking the questions fans might ask. She is at once interested and a bit gushing, but she also is able to guide the conversation smoothly even when it threatens to bog down."

Compared to another genre newcomer, Whoopi Goldberg, "Vicki!" quickly developed an avid following and adequate viewer rating. What made the show so much fun was Lawrence's enthusiasm for clowning around. She might join Radio City Rockettes in a high-kicking routine, or learn, along with Dame Edith (Barry Humphries), the proper etiquette for formal dining. On one show, she had a reunion of "Mama's Family" and, through trick camera work, had herself interviewing the opinionated Thelma Harper. Determinedly keeping her show folksy and focused on positive subjects, "Vicki!" remains wholesome and fancy free. She insists "I'd love to be the Dinah [Shore] for the '90s."

When not hosting her program (or working on TV specials such as the 25th Anniversary Reunion of "The Carol Burnett Show" aired on January 10, 1993), Lawrence and her family (including two springer spaniels) live quietly at their Long Beach residence by the water. In recent years, she has been the celebrity spokesperson for the Long Beach chapter of D.A.R.E. as well as having hosted the Long Beach Police Department's Celebrity-Sports Classic which raises money for D.A.R.E.

A few years ago, Vicki insisted, "I'm not really a workaholic. If they cancelled show business tomorrow, I don't think I would be disappointed. I'd just find something else to do."

TV & CABLE SERIES:

The Carol Burnett Show [Carol Burnett & Company] (CBS, 1967-1978; ABC, 1979)
The Jimmie Rodgers Show (CBS, 1969)
Mama's Family (NBC, 1983-1985; syndicated, 1986-1990)
The Great American Homemaker (USA, 1984)
Win, Lose or Draw (NBC, 1987-1989)
Vicki! (Syndicated, 1992-)

FEATURE FILMS:

The Young Americans (1967)

The Vicki Lawrence of today with husband Al Schultz and their two springer spaniels.

Chapter 16
JAY LENO

It's their first week on the job and they want to make a good impression.

SCHEDULED TO APPEAR THIS WEEK!

MONDAY BILLY CRYSTAL

TUESDAY TOM CRUISE

WEDNESDAY EMILIO ESTEVEZ

THURSDAY SIGOURNEY WEAVER

FRIDAY MEL GIBSON

THE Tonight SHOW WITH JAY LENO
MUSICAL DIRECTOR BRANFORD MARSALIS

11:35PM 4^{cc}

Advertisement for the May 25, 1992 debut of "The Tonight Show with Jay Leno."

It's a dirty job, but someone had to do it—replace Johnny Carson, the long-running host of TV's "The Tonight Show." For a time, it seemed that David Letterman, Joan Rivers or even Garry Shandling would be Carson's prized successor. Then the mantle fell to Jay Leno, the burly comedian with the lantern-jaw and the sheepish grin. The question was (and still is for some), does he have charisma to develop a sizeable audience following over the long haul?

In his "before Carson's replacement" years, Jay had a reputation as a sterling standup comic. He was (and is) the type of comedian who wants everyone to like him and who has a horror of appearing pretentious. Interestingly, although his humor has never been either dirty or malicious, he has always gotten laughs from the most sophisticated crowds. (Jay explains this with: "It's a matter of doing what's essentially true.") The *Hollywood Reporter* once praised him: "Jay Leno is shtickless. He is not neurotic, self-deprecating, crazed or raunchy. He doesn't pace across stage, scream like a banshee or deliver his lines in a monotone stupor—and he doesn't play the accordion. The guy is just plain funny."

Time magazine painted this nasal-voiced funster with, "his style is simply to take an everyday premise, then explore it with rigid logic until it becomes ridiculous. He is the voice common sense teased out to the absurd." Jay described his act with "I always liked the funny things that women liked. You grow up trying to make your mother laugh. I enjoy making women laugh more than men." He also says, "I talk about things adults talk about. Marriage, buying a house, a car. I'm always amazed that 'adult' has come to mean the most immature type of behavior possible."

When Jay crossed over into becoming Johnny Carson's (permanent) guest host on "The Tonight Show," talk show veteran Larry King judged of his monologues: "Jay is one of the best at tapping the other source of material that has marked the great modern-day comics since [Mort] Sahl and Lenny [Bruce]—current events. When Leno works his way around from personal observation to the social and political stuff taken from the day's newspapers, he's in top form. He makes virtually no distinction between the Leno you see onstage and off."

WORDS OF PRAISE

Another genre expert, Regis Philbin, observed, "His monologues were the sharpest political commentary ever. He seems to have eased up. But he's got tremendous empathy with kids." (On the other hand, Leno, very liberal in private life, insists that he is no more political than most late night hosts: "Political implies ideological, and my comedy is not ideological.")

Jay has often joked that his entry into show business's upper echelon was through the back door. "It was always, 'Can we get who we want? No. Then get Leno.'" Throughout his apprenticeship years, he claims, "One of the worst things was the fear that something might happen to my folks before I could make something of myself, that they might die thinking their kid's a bum." He has admitted he is a compulsive worker: "Vacations are fun, for a day or two. But they're not as much fun as doing your act."

Now a success, Leno remains a very private person. He cautions people who analyze his comedy act to learn more about the "real" comedian, "My personal views should be no more evident than a newscaster's." It is well known that Jay does not drink or smoke and only will do commercials for American products. His wife, the writer Mavis Nicholson, has revealed that Leno is quite self-contained: "I could count on the fingers of one hand the times he has said, 'I don't know what to do about this.'... He's so complete in himself that it's frustrating." She has acknowledged also that "his important relationships are very few...."

On the road, Leno has always been extremely down to earth. "When I finish my act, I go back to my room and watch television, or I'll go out for pizza with a friend. I'm hopelessly American. If something doesn't come in a Styrofoam box with a lid on it, I'm lost." His traditional outfit is blue jeans, shirt and cowboy boots. He is most happy when he's tinkering with one of his several motorcycles. For Leno, "show business is my job and so I don't really have any interest in it. People sometimes give me show business memorabilia—like I would want that.... If you came over to my house, I don't think you'd know what business I'm in. I don't have pictures of Tony Orlando on the wall or anything."

SON OF ITALIAN IMMIGRANTS

James Douglas Muir Leno was born on April 28, 1950 in New Rochelle, New York. He was the second son (his brother Patrick was older by ten years) of Angelo and Catherine (Muir) Leno. Angelo was the son of Italian immigrants, whose own father ran a fruit and vegetable wagon in order to raise his ten children in Manhattan's tough Lower East Side. Angelo was a prizefighter when he met Catherine, who, as a child, had emigrated from Scotland. Once married, Mr. Leno became an insurance salesman to support his growing family. The Lenos were already in their early forties when they had Jay.

Early in life, the boy had to adapt to his parents being the age of other friends' grandparents. When he started grade school, he was soon nicknamed Jay by his classmates. When he was nine, his father was offered his own insurance office in Andover, Massachusetts, and that is where Jay grew up. He recalls: "It was a good life, standard middle-class stuff. No wife-beating or alcoholism, no gaping psychic wounds. Maybe that's why my material's not foul-mouthed or nasty or vicious. I'm not an angry comic."

Jay had two masculine influences in life. First was his father, who, long ago in the sales game, had learned to close a sale with a fast quip and had become a frequent master of ceremonies at company banquets. Secondly, there was his high-achieving older brother (who later would put himself through law school). In comparing himself to his sibling, Jay would say: "Patrick got what he wanted by being intelligent. I got what I wanted by being conniving or funny. We're polar opposites. He's quiet; I never shut up. He's patient; I'm impetuous. He'd do Rubik's Cube in five minutes. Me too, but I'd smash it with a hammer, then glue back all the pieces."

At school, Jay was not a good student. His fifth grade teacher wrote on his report card, "If James used the effort toward his studies that he uses to be humorous, he'd be an A student. I hope he never loses his talent to make people chuckle." Leno remembers: "I was the class clown, but the things I'd do—flush tennis balls down toilets, lock dogs in lockers—were not exactly career moves." While he did not particularly enjoy sports, he did enjoy the reaction he had on classmates with his pranks and his growing ability to tell jokes. "I've always been able to remember everything I said, good or bad, and the reaction it got. I was never particularly good at remembering names or spelling or adding, but I could always remember what made people laugh."

AND THE WINNER IS. . .

As a high school senior, he had a part-time job at McDonald's fast food restaurant and often came to class in his work outfit (apron, white shoes, hat, order pad and pencil). Whie he was considered by everybody to be a jokster, he was skeptical about his comic abilities. However, his opinion changed when he entered McDonald's talent show for the northeast region and won. "Until then, I just always thought I'd be a funny salesman." By this point, a guidance counselor at school had told his mother, he should quit school and work, "After all," he explained, "an education isn't for everyone."

After graduating from high school, he enrolled at Boston's Emerson College, majoring in speech. For a while, he worked with a campus comedy group, but it did not work out. When he auditioned for the college's comedy workshop, he was rejected. However, he found a way to vent his comic humor. He frequently was asked to emcee school talent shows and, thus, had an opportunity to work a good many funny remarks into his introductions. By stringing them together, he discovered he had the start of a comedy act.

His models in comedy were the up and coming comedians like George Carlin, Robert Klein and David Steinberg. Meanwhile, to earn spending money, he turned his hobby (tinkering with cars and motorcycles) into a vocation, and worked as a mechanic. When he thought ahead to what he would do after college, Leno remembers: "I still figured I'd end up working on cars, but something way down in the brain-pan began to say, 'Hey, these guys [his favorite comedians] are great. Maybe I can do what they do."

To earn additional money for his education and to hone his skills, Jay began working as a stand-up comic in the greater Boston area. Because there were few comedy clubs in those days, he had to dig to find exposure. At the beginning, he entertained at Bar Mitzvahs, church events and at the Kiwanis Club. Later, he turned to more demanding audiences at bars with stage shows. Sometimes he had to bribe a bartender to let him perform, on the condition that if he went over with the crowd he'd be reimbursed.

PROTECTIVE WOMEN

Once he did his comedy act at a whore house. Mostly, his gigs were in crummy clubs in nearby Revere or in Boston's combat zone. Although the ambiance was seamy, the experience was good and the pay not bad. He would recall with fondness, "I was twenty-two years old. I had six nude girls in my dressing room. I was a college student and I was making thirty, forty bucks a night. It was great! And the strippers were very protective. They'd say, 'Stay away from Joey, he's a drug dealer.' It was like traveling with my mom."

Jay graduated from Emerson College in 1973 with a degree in speech therapy. To keep afloat, he found work as a mechanic for Rolls-Royce and other luxury cars. Meanwhile, he continued plying his trade as a fledgling comedian. Sometimes, his daytime job required him to drive a fancy car he had serviced to New York City. He used the opportunity to audition at various comedy clubs there. Occasionally, on these Manhattan junkets, he slept in the alley near the Improv Club.

Throughout this period, his parents remained supportive. He also found an agent, or thought he did, until the man suggested that he become a wrestler whose gimmick was telling jokes. From making the rounds and appearing at Catch a Rising Star and the Bitter End, Jay became pals with such up-and-coming comedians as David Brenner, Robert Klein and Freddie Prinze. It was they who urged Leno to move to New York City. He did just that and continued to gain experience in the comedy club circuit, at coffeehouses and wherever else he could perform.

Leno insists that what brought him to California was catching a very untalented comedian performing on Johnny Carson's "The Tonight Show." If that was the competition, he was ready to try his luck. Having no responsibilities other than to himself, he bought a one-way plane ticket to Los Angeles. Almost directly upon arrival, he auditioned at the Comedy Store on Sunset Boulevard, a club that showcased new comedians. He was hired, but the nightspot did not pay salaries. Thus began the "rough period" in Hollywood.

IT'S NOT ALWAYS EASY

Sometimes he slept under the stairs of the Comedy Store or at downtown charity missions. Eventually, he would sleep in the back seat of a 1955 Buick Roadmaster he had acquired. Describing these lean years, Leno says, "It was tough. I'd meet a kindly waitress who would let me use the bathroom; then I drove across town to use someone else's shower. I figured it was handy training in the event I ever had to hide out from the police."

After working the Los Angeles club beat for a while, Jay came to the attention of comedian Jimmie Walker, then starring in the TV sitcom, "Good Times." He hired Jay to write special comedy material. (It would be Leno, in turn, who introduced another comedian, David Letterman, to Walker, which led to David getting a job on Walker's payroll as writer.) Another person who came to see Jay at the Comedy Club was Mavis Nicholson, a cool, cerebral daughter of an actor, who was a writer. She remembers, "I was seated front-row-center with my nose practically on the stage in the middle of this guy's routine. I'd never heard of him, but he was funny, tall and kind of cute. After seeing some of the other acts, I realized just how good he was."

During intermission, en route to the ladies room, she brushed by Jay. They hardly talked. The next week, she went to the Improv where a friend introduced her to a man with "the kind of hair most of us would die for. When I realized it was Jay, I thought, 'Great.... another chance.'" Mavis recollects, "I couldn't even envision having a relationship with Jay. It snuck up on me, when I realized one day what had happened, I was in love with him."

Another visitor to the comedy clubs was Helen Gorman Kushnick, three years older than Jay. She soon became his business manager and good friend. One night in 1975, comedian Harvey Korman came to the Improv and he was impressed enough with Jay's talents to urge Johnny Carson to see the newcomer perform. Carson did and, after the show, talked briefly with Leno. He told the aspiring comedy star to use less stories in his routines and more jokes. Reportedly, the very disappointed Leno went outside and thought about pelting Johnny's car in the parking lot with eggs. Later, upon reflection, he realized Carson was right.

MAKING THE ROUNDS

By 1977, Leno had already been making the rounds of talk shows, including those of Merv Griffin, Mike Douglas, Dinah Shore and John Davidson. It was through the intervention of comic master Steve Martin that Johnny Carson finally agreed to have Jay on "The Tonight Show." His debut appearance was on March 2, 1977. As Leno tells it, "Your first 'Tonight Show' is kind of like your first girl. I mean, it's real fast. It's over real quick. You weren't very good. But you never forget it. But you do know you want to do it again. And do it better the next time."

Not only did Jay have sufficient jokes in his repertoire for his first "Tonight Show" outing, but he had enough left over for several other occasions when he was asked back on Carson's TV program. However, his act got worse, not better. He was running out of material. After seven or eight stints, he was NOT asked back to "The Tonight Show" for many, many months. Meanwhile, he had been a troupe member of the short-lived "The Marilyn McCoo and Billy Davis, Jr. Show" a summertime CBS-TV variety program. He now returned to the road to ply his craft, reasoning, "the longer you're on the road, the more you see how real people have to live. It keeps your comedy fresh."

It was also in 1977 that Jay made his motion picture debut in FUN WITH DICK AND JANE. In that Jane Fonda-George Segal comedy, he had a walk-on. (Later, in Michael Caine's SILVER BEARS, 1978, he played the son of a Mafiosa. He was a squabbling chauffeur in AMERICAN HOT WAX, 1978, and a prizefighter in AMERICATHON, 1979. All of these assignments were character parts.) On the nightclub circuit, Leno was increasingly in demand as a warm-up act for Perry Como, John Denver, Tom Jones and Johnny Mathis.

What really stymied Leno's progress in these years was his unusual looks. At 6' tall, weighing 180 pounds, the blue-eyed, black-wavy hair Leno, of the unusual face, was not typically handsome like a Johnny Carson or a David Letterman. He was not even whimsical-looking looking like a Woody Allen or a John Ritter. That fact prevented Jay from gaining the career exposure that starring in a TV sitcom or in a feature film would have provided. As Neal Karlen (*Rolling Stone*) phrased it, "Leno projects an unsettling presence."

SETTLING IN

If he could not become a TV or movie comedy leading man, he could make a very good living on the road. By 1980, he was well settled into his Hollywood Hills ranch house with Mavis. Typically, when they were home, she would be reading a book, he would be fixing motorbikes. He insists that he decided to marry her when he noted that his insurance policy did not cover her. They wed in 1980, leading Leno to reflect later, "all the women in my life were responsible, respectable, just good people. It was a very sheltered environment, emotionally. So I could never understand the way men talked about women, and I definitely couldn't understand the attraction of a dumb, insecure woman." Marriage, however, did not alter their lifestyle. She still did not join him on his frequent tours. She explained, "I know wives who do accompany their husbands on the road. Their husbands make them sit there—and watch. You see them, they're like a dog that's been kicked too many times...they just want the guy to die or to lose his vocal cords. They're sick of it."

Once "Late Night with David Letterman" went on the air in 1982, Jay became a frequent guest on his friend's NBC-TV talk program. While he had been nervous with Johnny Carson ("I always called him Mr. Carson") he was on the same wave length with Letterman. According to Leno, David's show "is geared well to what I do, in the sense that a lot of jokes I do there wouldn't work on other

TV star Jay Leno in 1991.

shows, because the host wouldn't have the rapport I have with David and wouldn't know what I'm talking about."

By 1986, Jay was King of the Road, performing an average of 300 nights a year at comedy clubs/casinos throughout the United States. As part of a long-term contract with NBC, in February that year, he hosted "Saturday Night Live" and later co-hosted (with Arnold Schwarzenegger) "Friday Night Videos." For the network, he had his showcasing special, "The Jay Leno Show." Meanwhile, he did a sold-out appearance at Carnegie Hall on March 29, 1986. In May 1986, his hour-long special, "Jay Leno and the American Dream" was seen on Showtime Cable. The year was capped for Leno by being asked in September 1986 to be one of two permanent guests hosts (along with Garry Shandling) for Carson's "The Tonight Show." (This was after the debacle which had seen Joan Rivers leave that "Tonight Show" chore and move over to her own rival late night talk show.) For Leno, being the (guest) host was far easier than being a guest. In his new capacity, he only was in the hot spot as a comedian for the opening monologue, thereafter he was merely an interested interviewer.

In 1987, Leno was riding a career crest. He was receiving $15,000 per club appearance. Now, even with time out to do "Tonight Show" hosting (which increased when Garry Shandling left to do his own TV program), he was on the road for, at least, 200 performances a year. These included a stand at the Sands Hotel/Casino in Atlantic City that June. Such a hefty performing schedule earned him around $3 million. In addition, there was income from his TV contracts and other outlets, including commercials (potato chips, etc.). Leno also made another bid to return to filmmaking. The Dino De Laurentiis Entertainment Group signed him to a three-picture deal.

He made the first, COLLISION COURSE, in 1987. It co-starred Pat Morita and cast the two comics as bumbling detectives on the trail of a homicidal killer in Detroit (although the film was shot largely in North Carolina). However, before it could be released, or other Leno projects go before the cameras, that organization got into financial difficulties which virtually removed it from the filmmaking business. (COLLISION COURSE would be released by HBO on home video in 1990.) Rounding out 1987, on Thanksgiving eve, Jay starred in "Jay Leno's Family Comedy Hour," a prime-time special.

Promotion for Jay Leno's November 1, 1986 TV special.

ALWAYS LEVEL HEADED

Remaining level-headed about his career success, Leno reflected: "I did this a lot longer not being famous without any exposure than I have done it with it.... I mean, it's fun, you have a good time with it, but you can't really take it too seriously." By the end of 1987, Jay and Mavis had moved from their 12-room Hollywood Hills home to a large Beverly Hills mock-Tudor residence. The new house included plenty of garage space for his assorted motorcycles and classic autos.

Leno was also now setting career boundaries. About doing commercials: "I draw the line at taking money for something I don't use." As to stretching his professional horizons: "I have no desire to sing, nor to play King Lear, nor to star in my own sitcom." He vetoed doing additional film comedy: "When you do a joke in the movies, people go 'Oh very funny. Now could you move a little this way....'" He also announced that he had no interest in cutting a comedy record. ("I don't want to hear my act all over town. That would drive me batty.") As for working with a comedy troupe, "That would be terrible! I'd much prefer to rise or fall on my own achievement." Regarding domesticity, "Mavis travels with me about half the time. The other times, we talk on the phone."

In 1989, Jay was represented in a new medium: publishing. He compiled *Headlines: Real But Ridiculous Samplings from America's Newspapers*, published by Random House. He was one of the voices heard in WHAT'S UP, HIDEOUS SUN DEMON, a revamping of the 1959 schlock film, THE HIDEOUS SUN DEMON. He had renewed his two-season contract as sole guest host for Johnny Carson. On the road, at $25,000-$30,000 a performance, he was doing 200 hundred plus appearances a year, including a stand at the Sands in Atlantic City that August. He still had a very clean act, explaining: "I'm not as offended by obscenity as much as I'm bored." When asked why he worked so much, he retorted: "I don't want to sit on a beach! This is what I do! But people think there must be something psychologically wrong with me."

Time magazine named Jay the most popular TV comedian of the 1980s. In the new decade he continued as before. Then in the spring of 1991, he was announced as the permanent successor to Johnny Carson on "The Tonight Show." He had beat out such other logical successors as his good friend, David Letterman. Jay confessed, "I don't think I would have this job if it wasn't for David" (who showcased Leno so often on the air). Leno also acknowledged that he had campaigned for Carson's job: "The thing that got me 'The Tonight Show' is that I would visit every NBC affiliate where I was performing and do promos for them. Then they would promote me in turn. My attitude was to go out and rig the numbers in my favor."

Another reason for Jay beating out David in "The Tonight Show" sweepstakes was that if NBC went with Letterman to replace Carson, it would be a lose-lose situation (i.e., the network would lose "Late Night with David Letterman" and it would lose Leno as a team player). Additionally, there was an industry perception, as reported in *Time* magazine that "Letterman's pervasive irony seems less suited to the 90s than Leno's sincerity."

GOODBYE AND HELLO

May 22, 1992 was the milestone night in TV history when Johnny Carson bid farewell to thirty years of hosting "The Tonight Show." The following Monday, May 25, was Leno's first evening as the new star of "The Tonight Show with Jay Leno." There were many changes from the Carson days. There was a new funky set and theme music for the show. Gone was the Ed McMahon type sidekick; instead there was former graphics coordinator Edd Hall as the show's announcer. The big band sound of Doc Severinsen and his crew was replaced by the solid jazzy tones of Branford Marsalis and his musicians. What did remain was the format of an opening monologue by the host who then presented an assortment of acts and interviews. Helen Kushnick, who had been Leno's manager for years, sold her personal management firm to NBC Productions and became executive producer of "The Tonight Show."

At the conclusion of his first "Tonight" show, Leno said, "Not bad if I do say so myself." The next evening he said concerning a very hip music group that had just performed (one that would never have been allowed on the far more traditional Carson show), "This is not your father's 'Tonight Show.'" On the following program, Jay beamed, "There are no more reruns!," a jibe at Johnny's penchant for cutting back his work week with frequent reruns. While initial ratings for Jay's "The Tonight Show" were good, Jeff Jarvis (*TV Guide*) insisted that Leno was "acting like a puppy in need of a tummy scratch."

He reasoned, "One minute, he plays inane audience games like Johnny. The next, he coolly quips with his jazzy bandleader like Dave Letterman. Then he turns to serious interviews, looking studious like Bill Moyers. He even looks like the giant, economy-sized Arsenio Hall when he fawns over guests.... When Leno...tells jokes—he steps over his punchlines and pleads for laughs with practiced sheepishness and aren't-I-cute grins."

Just when Leno had settled into his hosting chores, things turned tense. Industry observers wondered why Johnny Carson had failed to mention Leno on his last show, or why Jay had not acknowledged the past King of Late Night when he began his own reign. Then, David Letterman began grumbling publicly about being irked at having been bypassed as Johnny's successor. The worst was yet to come. Rival talk show hosts Arsenio Hall and, to a lesser extent, Dennis Miller, complained that the word was out in Hollywood that any guest who appeared on their TV shows would NOT be welcome on "The Tonight Show."

The often highly-emotional Hall began sharply criticizing Leno, suggesting he was a duplistic acquaintance posing as a friend. This led the upset Leno, who was packing on weight during these trying times, to inform the press regarding Arsenio: "I mean, what is this attitude? He makes $12 million a year! Are his monologues worth $9 million a year more than mine? What you have here appears to be two millionaires fighting it out. It's fine if it gets more people watching the shows, but why throw rocks at each other?"

AGAINST JAY

When Dennis Miller's TV talk show was cancelled in mid-summer 1992, he told his viewers he was "releasing his delegates" to Hall and Letterman. "I won't encourage any of my viewers to go to Leno." Some days after he was no longer a part of the talk show rat race, he said, "Jay and I were very good friends at one point. I don't think I'd talk to him again, nor would he want to talk to me." Soon thereafter, shock radio (and TV) host Howard Stern was on "The Tonight Show." The always controversial Stern blurted out, "This moron Arsenio, who couldn't even do stand-up comedy. Jay, true or false: Is Arsenio a good stand-up comic?" Leno was speechless. This prompted Howard to yell: "This is the problem with the show, Jay! You got no killer instinct!"

On August 10, 1992, after two weeks off the air due to telecasts of the Olympics, Leno returned to his forum. He said, "Oh, they've been taking shots at us. You know, sometimes people think if people say nasty things about you and you don't answer it, it's a sign of weakness. Well you don't get this far, you don't get this job, by being weak. And if you don't think that nice guys can finish first, just keep watching." In the rating wars, "The Tonight Show" had about 5 million viewers; Arsenio Hall had about 3.5-4 million and was slowly gaining. (However, with a younger host and having more hip guests and performers on "The Tonight Show," Jay was definitely cutting into Arsenio's turf.)

The week of September 14, 1992 proved a traumatic twist for "The Tonight Show" and the hotly-rumored booking wars. The turning point occurred when Hollywood personal manager Ken Kragen went public with charges that after he declined to pull country singer Travis Tritt off "The Arsenio Hall Show" to appear on "The Tonight Show" instead, Helen Kushnick allegedly told him that Tritt would no longer be welcome on the NBC program. Also, a scheduled appearance of another Kragen client, singer Trisha Yearwood, was cancelled. That opened the floodgates of denials and counterclaims from various industry camps.

Helen refuted Kragen's allegations on Howard Stern's nationally syndicated talk radio show via a call to his program. This led NBC to impose a gag order on Helen, as well as issuing an ominous statement that management changes on "The Tonight Show" were being discussed. Meanwhile, Kushnick was claiming that the ruckus was actually a case of the old boys' clubs versus an outsider. ("I've upset the balance of power. They don't like a woman doing this.") She sent the network a letter of intent to file a sexual discrimination lawsuit. On Monday afternoon, September 21, 1992, the expected happened. NBC issued an announcement that "Effective immediately, Helen Kushnick will no longer be the executive producer." She was asked to leave the premises by the end of that day, which she did.

BUM RAP

Following her discharge, Jay released a statement saying her removal was unwarranted. Later, on October 5, 1992, at an industry luncheon, Jay told the gathering, "Everything that happens on my show is my fault. The show has my name on it; I take full responsibility for everything that happens." As for Helen (who attended that get together), he insisted "she got a bad rap." He said he was not fearful of the genre competition. "They should come after me; that's what this job is about. Would I be lazy if there weren't other talk shows, you bet." He also acknowledged that he regretted not having paid homage to Johnny Carson on the first night he took over. He claimed he did not want to appear to be riding on Carson's coattails.

Some days later, Leno was questioned about rumors that NBC might replace him with Letterman if ratings did not pick up. Jay responded, "He should be breathing down my neck. If I drop the ball, pick it up, run with it. That's what it's about. I don't whine." When asked if he was bitter over the ongoing furor, he answered: "I'm in show business, and I make a lot of money, so I don't get bitter." In a later magazine piece, Helen Kushnick would respond to Leno's insistence that he was ignorant of the machinations behind the scenes on his show. In the article, she related that she once told Jay, "I've been serving you steak dinners for the last 18 years. I just haven't bothered showing you how I slaughtered the cow."

Thereafter, NBC insisted: "We're in it for the long haul with Leno. This is a marathon, not a sprint." On the other hand, Jay told *TV Guide*: "Yes, I feel like I have a sword hanging over my head, but I'm the one who's gone to NBC to say I'd quit if I began to do poorly, not the other way around." Thereafter, things quieted down temporarily, except for occasional potshots taken by Arsenio Hall against Leno, and visa versa. By mid-December, however, Leno was dragged into an escalating battle of power with David Letterman.

CBS-TV had offered Letterman a $14 million yearly bid for the comedian to take over the 11:30 PM time slot on their network. NBC had until January 15, 1993 to match the two-year offer, part of which would require giving Letterman the 11:30 "The Tonight Show" time period. (There was also talk of offering one or the other of the two NBC-TV talk show stars a 10 PM weeknight berth to solve the conflict.) During this much publicized tug-of-war, Leno remained calm, insisting, "Of all the things going on in the world right now, this is one of the sillier problem."

QUIET NO MORE

Leno's passive behavior, however, changed in late 1992 when NBC, who should have been happy with Leno's improved ratings, changed its official stance about backing Leno against Letterman. Now the network merely said "no comment" as to its current position on keeping Jay in the 11:30 PM time period. Suddenly, Leno, who currently was his own manager and TV agent and had to fight his own battles, became extremely vocal to the press. He admitted, which was a lot for him, that regarding NBC "I'm not mad. I'm just disappointed." However, he did insist, if he lost his 11:30 PM show hour "I'm gone.... I'm not being wimpy, I'm not being wishy-washy. My position is clear..... I was hired to do 11:30, and anything else would be perceived as 'You screwed up.'" (If Leno left NBC, the network would have to pay over approximately $10 million to Jay for "breaking" its committed deal with him.) As to his relationship with long-time friend Letterman, Jay insisted: "I understand that David is a very, very important commodity to this [NBC] network. I don't care if they pay him 10 times what I make. That's fine. This is not a feud. There is no problem between us."

During late December 1992 and early January 1993, as the final deadline drew near for NBC to choose between Leno and Letterman, Leno finally succumbed to the pressure of the highly-touted contest. At first subtly and then far more openly, he began to "joke" on the air and to the media about his unhappiness with the NBC brass for not coming forward to say once and for all that he, Leno, was their choice to host the vital 11:30 PM nightly show. After the decision was finally reached (and announced publicly on January 15, 1993) that Leno would indeed remain with "The Tonight Show," the beleaguered but now relieved Leno reverted to being Mr. Nice Guy. He told the press of his overall reaciton to the concluded TV network talk show war: "It's too easy to paint good guys and bad buys in this situation." However, Jay admitted to still not being 100% confident of his status with NBC. Wanting to mend fences with the NBC hierarchy, Leno acknowledged, "there were people within the network who perhaps felt David [Letterman] would have been the better choice. I would like to find out why they felt that way and what I can do to bring them around. I used a blanket statement saying, 'Look, the people lobbying heavily against me —it's nothing personal, I have no axe to grind—but come talk to me. Tell me what you like and what you don't like so we can do this right.'" Leno also admitted that what hurt worst about NBC's obvious fence-sitting during the ruckus was, "I can take anything but apathy in this business. Either applaud or boo. But just don't sit there. Give me some feedback."

The Jay Leno of today (named not long ago by Mr. Blackwell as one of the "best-dressed stars on television") emphasizes, "My career has always been like the hour hand of a clock— stare at it and it doesn't appear to be moving, but an hour later, you'll see progress." For him, "the real trick in this town is to make show-business money and live like a normal person." He adds, "I'm from the school that says happiness is a privilege, not a right. I hate when people whine because they're not happy at every given moment. You want to be happy? Fine, go earn it." On the other hand, he points out, "Think: I spend my life making people laugh, they applaud me, and I get paid for it. What could be better!"

TV & CABLE SERIES:
The Marilyn McCoo and Billy Davis Jr. Show (CBS, 1977)
The Tonight Show Starring Johnny Carson (NBC, 1986-1992)
The Tonight Show With Jay Leno (NBC, 1992-)

FEATURE FILMS:
Fun with Dick and Jane (1977)
Silver Bears (1978)
American Hot Wax (1978)
Americathon (1979)
What's Up, Hideous Sun Demon (1989)
Collision Course (1990) [made in 1987]

The musical director (Branford Marsalis) and the star (Jay Leno) of "The Tonight Show with Jay Leno" in 1992.

Chapter 17
DAVID LETTERMAN

A familiar show business cliche insists that beneath most every comedian's cheerful exterior lurks a sad soul (e.g., the Jimmy Stewart clown character in the circus movie, THE GREATEST SHOW ON EARTH, 1952). In today's world of television, one such prankster with a dour interior is TV funnyman, David Letterman. One of the elements that makes him unusual in the profession is that he makes little effort to hide his pessimistic outlook on life. He admits willingly, "I do things I'm very upset by, and not very many things I'm pleased by. But I just think that's part of the general neurosis that motivates people to go into show business." On another occasion, he expressed, "comedians by and large are not fun people to hang around with. They're dejected and depressed and sullen and nasty and back-biting and jealous, and I'm right in there...."

In fact, Letterman has exploited his cranky personality into a prized performing trait, frequently tossing zingers at his baffled TV talk show guests or taking pot shots at the absurdity of contemporary culture. His pal, comedian/talk show host Jay Leno, said once, "Dave is one of the few performers who can say something real vicious and have it come across as cute." Letterman himself contends, "I'm not malicious. I don't want to get a laugh at the expense of others.... Then again, if I see an opening, I go for it."

On another occasion, when confronted with the theory that his prevailing attitude behind the talk show desk is "condescending, smug, even mean," he admits, "I suppose I am all of those things, but we [he and his TV show staff] never invite somebody on to demonstrate condescension—or condensation. If somebody comes on and is a bonehead and is loafing through an interview, I resent that, and maybe I will go after them.... I'm stunned at the number of people in show business who come and don't seem to get that what we want from them is a performance."

Almost from the start of his late night TV talk show tenure, clean-cut Letterman attracted a particular type of young adult viewer, those with a jaded outlook on the Establishment. As biographer Caroline Latham observed in *The David Letterman Story* (1986), "The issue of feeling superior may well be a key to David Letterman's popularity. His fans are the viewers who join him in that feeling." Merrill Markoe, former writer for "The David Letterman Show" and once David's romantic interest, has another insight. She says, "His sensibility is, and was, 'You and I know he's nuts.' Dave and the audience are united in the knowledge that they're in on the joke. And he's been able to do that ever since I [first] saw him."

JUST A BIG KID
However, there is another telling aspect to this deadpan comic prince of darkness: his antic sense of childish humor. He is the type of guy who will cover himself with crushed alka seltzer tablets and fizz in a huge barrel of watermelons or who gleefully crushes a beloved Smurf cartoon character with

a steam roller. He is also the game comic who has had his asbestos space suit peppered with marshmallows and then had staffers aim blowtorches at it.

Letterman's humor is a direct descendant of the Steve Allen brand of impish comedy which made the latter's 1950s TV shows so unpredictable, so full of juvenile physical humor, and so entertaining. There is also a linkage between David and talk show pioneer Jack Paar. They both are bright men with a gift for a conversation and who abhor sham and any foolish regulation. They each wear their fragile emotions on their shirt sleeves, ready to erupt at a given moment.

David Letterman was born in Indianapolis, Indiana on April 12 1947, the second of three children born to Joseph Letterman and his

wife. Joseph was a florist and Mrs. Letterman worked in the shop to help support the household, which included two daughters and a son. Finances were tough for the Lettermans, but David would say later, "It was a solid 'Father Knows Best' or 'Leave It to Beaver' type of lower middle-class family." A more telling aspect of David's childhood was his later recollection when asked if he received sufficient attention from his parents as a child: "I got too little. I clearly got too little."

David claims that as a youngster and a young adult he was a hypochondriac and his fantasy as a shy youth was to be the next Arthur Godfrey. He rates TV stars Steve Allen, Johnny Carson (especially on "Who Do You Trust?") and Jonathan Winters as great influences in his teen years. Looking back, decades later, he would state, "They're the three I really paid attention to. With those three, I see myself—and I catch myself doing things that I feel are an amalgam of their influences. But that's subconscious, and maybe everybody does it."

BAG BOY

By the time he entered Broad Ripple High School, he had an after school job at the local Atlas Supermarket bagging groceries, a position that lasted for three years. He was also tall, skinny and what he terms "a basic geek." In 1990, he would reminisce: "There was a period in high school...when you sort of had to figure out who you were....you start to examine your own inventory and think, 'Is there anything I can do that is going to make me desirable or make me different?'"

For Letterman, the light bulb of self-illumination lit up during a public speaking class. He recalls, "For the first time in my formal academic experience there was a subject that seemed to come easily to me, more easily than algebra or geometry or shop. I was not very bright...but at that time it was clear to me that this was something to remember. That was a valuable lesson."

He also acknowledges, "In high school, I was never with the really smart kids, I was never with the really good-looking kids, and I was never with the really great athletes. But there was always a small pocket of people I hung out with, and all we did was make fun of the really good-looking people and make fun of the really smart kids and make fun of the great athletes."

After graduating high school, Letterman attended Ball State University in nearby Muncie, Indiana. He was a speech, radio and TV major, a member of Sigma Chi fraternity, and his ambition was to become a great disc jockey on WLW in Cincinnati. During his senior year, when he was 21, David married his college sweetheart, Michelle Cook.

In 1968, now a college graduate, he and his wife settled in Indianapolis. For the next few years, he worked at a local TV station, Channel 13, where he was a jack of all trades, doing everything from announcing to movie reviews. (One evening, to relieve the tedium of his mundane chores, after the late night movie was over, instead of allowing a conventional sign-off, he had the camera zoom in on a cardboard replica of the TV station which he then demolished.)

ONE FUNNY WEATHERMAN

On weekends, David was the substitute weatherman, and the boring task drove the rebellious young man daffy. Letterman explained, "You can only announce the weather, the highs and the lows, so many times before you go insane. In my case, it took two weeks. I started clowning. I'd draw peculiar objects on the cloud maps, and invent disasters in fictitious cities. I made up my own measurements for hail, and said hailstones the size of canned hams were falling." Such an unorthodox approach to TV newscasting had its affect. As Letterman would recall, "Management was always sending down notes to keep it [i.e. the weather forecast] straight—until, of course Happy News hit the Midwest, after which I was urged to be even funnier."

In his fifth year of working for the ABC affiliate in Indianapolis, he also did a radio talk program. He felt far more comfortable in this freer-form format. However, he still had to deal with a lot of "beanheads." According to Letterman, "I did a radio show where I talked to morons on the telephone—people who had found a way to make tires out of cheese; folks who could prove that someone was building a giant brain magnet on Neptune."

Late in 1974, while still working for the TV/radio station, he had his first brush with a Hollywood personality. Actress Teri Garr was touring the country promoting her new movie, YOUNG FRANKENSTEIN. Garr, who later would become a perennial guest on David's network TV talk show, still remembers her first meeting with the young Letterman at this backwood station: "He was exactly the same [then as now]. He said, 'So, you live in Hollywood. What kind of car do you drive?'"

By early 1975, Letterman was going through heavy emotional changes. The previous year his father had died. By now, David had decided that professionally and personally he could no longer stay in Indianapolis. According to him, "I was too unhappy with myself to stay there. If you're secure with yourself, then regardless of where you are, you're happy and you lead a productive life, and have kids and go to Rotary meetings and you have, you know, just a great life. But if you're insecure like me and millions of other young airheads, you move to Los Angeles and entertain drunks in bars. Or try to."

MAKING THE MOVE

In June 1976, he and his wife loaded their possessions (including two cats and a hide-a-bed) onto his red pickup truck and headed west to Los Angeles. Michele got a job as a department store buyer. David had brought along six TV sitcom scripts that he had drafted, and he peddled them to the television networks, but there were no takers. The agent who had shown initial interest in promoting him as a writer faded out of the picture. Letterman realized, "I found I didn't have the patience to be somebody who gets up and really writes. So the quickest way to any kind of reinforcement was working at the Comedy Store—I'd find out immediately if I was funny or not." One of the performers whom he saw and liked at the Comedy Store was Jay Leno. (Letterman said later, "I thought to myself, 'Ah, I should go back to Indianapolis,' because he was doing it [i.e. comedy] the way I wanted to, and I thought that I probably never would do it as well."

Seeking security behind his big red beard, 6'2" David got up the courage to appear at the Comedy Store on their Monday night Amateur Night. He eventually got to perform and soon began to be noticed. One of those who found his sense of comedy amusing was Jimmie Walker, then starring in the TV sitcom, "Good Times." He hired David to write material for his show. ("I guess," says Letterman, "he felt that I more than anyone reflected the black point of view.") This assignment led to work on a Jim Stafford TV show which never aired. David also wrote special materials for Bob Hope, John Denver and Paul Lynde. As a stand-up comic, he made appearances on "Don Kirschner's Rock Concert," "The Gong Show" and, for a time, was the warm-up comedian for TV's "The Barney Miller Show."

As Letterman's show business career rose, his marriage fell apart. From the perspective of time, Letterman views this period: "It seems odd to me now. I was married for a long time, like nine years. My life is so different now from what it was then that it does seem strange there was this other person with whom I was very close for all that time who now plays no part in my life."

It was in 1977 that David earned his first TV series. The members (Bill Danoff, Taffy Danoff, Margot Chapman, Jon Carroll) of the music group, The Starland Vocal Band, had had a hit recording with "Afternoon Delight." This led CBS to give them a half-hour summer variety show which debuted on July 31, 1977. Three of the program's writers (Peter Bergman, Phil Proctor and David Letterman) also appeared on the show, which was shot on location in a variety of locales (Washington, D.C.; Great Falls, Virginia). When the fall season began, Letterman was again back to scuffling for jobs. One assignment was a pilot for a projected TV series, "Leave It to Dave." The set for the offbeat concept was constructed to resemble the inside of a pyramid, with Letterman's chair as a throne. He hated it; so did the networks.

DAVID AND MARY

Having developed a reputation as a reliably funny man, boyish David with the gap-tooth smile was asked to join the repertory company of Mary Tyler Moore's new variety series, "Mary," which premiered on CBS-TV on September 28, 1978. Other regulars on this hour-long show included Michael Keaton, Dick Shawn and Swoosie Kurtz. Reporting on the debut presentation, *Variety* noted, "David Letterman is going to be the heavy of the cast, a snobbish manipulator everyone dislikes but somehow puts up with, and a couple of his routines were terrific." However, after three episodes, this expensively-mounted show was cancelled. Meanwhile, thinking his career was on the fast track, David had purchased a Malibu house.

Fortunately, Letterman's work on "Mary" had not gone unnoticed. Talent scouts from "The Tonight Show" caught his act on that program and invited him onto Johnny Carson's talk show. He was so successful in his debut appearance that after a few return visits, executive producer Fred De Cordova asked him to be a guest host on the show. This occurred in January 1979, and within the next year, he returned in that capacity twenty more times. Contemplating those early hosting chores on "The Tonight Show," David has admitted that it was a great learning experience: "My instinct in the beginning was to try and make everything I said hilarious; now I can sit back and let everybody else do their bit."

In March 1979, David made his TV feature film debut in "FAST FRIENDS," a NBC-TV movie focusing on a young divorcee (Carrie Snodgrass) involved in the backstage world of a TV talk show. The next month, when Johnny Carson made one of his recurring announcements that he intended to quit "The Tonight Show," the NBC-TV network signed Letterman to an exclusive two-year contract, with an option for a third season. This action prompted the industry to regard David as Johnny's successor, an unofficial status that would both please and haunt Letterman to this day. To keep busy, David performed in the casino clubs in Las Vegas and Lake Tahoe, usually on the bottom half of the performing bills.

However, club work was not David's forte. As Jack Rollins, his business agent/manager and, later, TV show producer would explain, "His standup was okay, but if there was anybody right for television, it was Dave. He's a guy who grew up with TV, he cut his eye teeth on it and he is a Midwesterner. That seems to give him this universal appeal." Fred Silverman, president of NBC (1978-1981) agreed that David was the ideal TV personality: "From the very beginning, I found him very witty. He knew where the jokes were, and he had a very distinct point of view."

THE ORIGINAL SHOW

With Silverman's backing, the network formulated a daytime TV program to highlight David's humor and to be, in Silverman's words, "folksy and family, a kind of Arthur Godfrey for the 1980's." "The David Letterman Show" bowed on June 23, 1980 in a ninety-minute format. It was an odd mongrel of a live program, filled with celebrity interviews that sometimes were mock serious, other times straightforward, and sometimes embarrassingly dull.

Aired from New York City, the show featured a house band, news reports (by Edwin Newman) and a large assemblage of comedy regulars (including Edie McClurg, Bob Sarlatte and Wil Shriner). Its biggest claim to originality was the goofy humor of its star, who relied on (some insist exploited) his studio/home audience. At a drop of a smirk, he might send an audience member out for snacks for the cast/crew or ask an unsuspecting studio visitor to take over hosting the show while he disappeared for a while. Letterman loved to go on remote, one time making the rounds (with his TV camera crew) to several different shops, each of which had a sign, "World's Best Coffee." One of the driving forces behind this new-style TV offering was (head) writer Merrill Markoe with whom David had a long-term romance. (They had met on the set of "Mary" where she was a writer and he a performer.)

Despite the innovative, unpredictable humor of "The David Letterman Show," it did not win over enough TV watchers, for morning viewers expected, and wanted, blander entertainment. The show was chopped down to a sixty-minute format in August 1980. Then, as additional affiliate stations dropped the show, it was taken off the air as of October 24, 1980, replaced by "The Regis Philbin Show." Ironically, several months after it vanished from daytime programming, "The David Letterman Show" won two Emmys for the 1980-1981 season.

As his starring vehicle crumbled, David understandably became very stressed out. He remembers, "It was very painful. The morning show went away, and you never know whether you'll be back again." However, NBC, now under a new regime headed by Grant Tinker (who had produced "Mary" for his wife, Mary Tyler Moore), had faith in Letterman. The network placed David under a new $1 million per year contract, and insisted he not do anything else until they found a new vehicle for him. This non-working phase became the worst fallow period of his life. He drank a good deal of beer, got too fleshy, and wallowed in boredom.

THANKS JOHNNY

In a way, Letterman owed his next TV venture to Johnny Carson. In September 1980, Carson had cut back his "The Tonight Show" from ninety minutes to sixty, leaving an empty time slot after 12:30 AM, which, per the contract between Johnny's production company and NBC, gave Carson approval of whatever show followed "The Tonight Show." After tinkering with that air period for several months, the network, with Carson's consent, debuted "Late Night with David Letterman." This would result in a production credit on Letterman's show for Carson Productions. However, there was little contact between the two programs save for a liaison who insured that the back-to-back shows did not duplicate guests.

"Late Night with David Letterman," produced in New York City, premiered on February 2, 1982. According to Letterman, to gain inspiration for their new project, he and the staff "looked at some early Steve Allen shows and some really early Ernie Kovacs.... One thing the shows we liked all had in common was a casual kind of liveliness, an un-slick, see-the camera-cable/see-the-mistakes kind of things. See, what we try to do is pure Television.... We go into the studio, use the cameras, invite the people in—we do a television show. Whereas what most other people do is produce things to be shown on television, but they're not Television—they're dramas, comedies, musicals, whatever. They're at the slick end of things and we're at the bargain basement end."

From the start, regulars on "Late Night with David Letterman" included bespectaced Paul Shaffer, the self-styled hip bandleader, who became to Letterman what Ed McMahon was to Johnny Carson. Another family member was short, roly-poly, Larry "Bud" Melman (Calvert DeForest) whose bizarre duties included going on remote as straight man on ridiculous "Candid Camera"-style segments to show the gullibility of passersby.

It was head writer Merrill Markoe who dreamed up such gimmicks as loopy video remotes and conceived such features as "Stupid Pet Tricks," "Viewer Mail" and "Stupid Human Tricks," all geared to provide the show with a whimsical charm. David called on buddies (e.g., Jay Leno, Richard Lewis, Jeff Altman, George Miller) from the Comedy Store to appear on his program. However, it was Letterman who provided much of the offbeat humor as he indulged his penchant for juvenilia, such as dropping a typewriter (and other objects) out of an office building window to see how they would explode upon impact.

DAVE'S ANTICS

From his trademark sneakers to his Levis slacks and baseball cap, David was at once antic and irreverent. He would frequently take his program notes and toss them over his shoulders through the backdrop window (to the sound effect of glass breaking). He thrived on calling unsuspecting victims, picked at random from phone directories, or going on location to hassle John Q. Public out of his complacency (i.e. trying to force a night security guard to let Letterman gain entrance to an office building after hours). Such escapades, along with his own tart brand of humor, soon gave Letterman and his nightly capers a reputation for being mean-spirited and disrespectful. This upset traditionalists among TV watchers, but it pleased his younger viewers (especially the Yuppie set) who thrived on his anti-establishment behavior.

After two years on the air, "Late Night with David Letterman" rose from being a cult favorite to a successful alternative entertainment success. While Johnny Carson's show reached 9 million (on a good night), David's program typically had a viewership of 3.7-4.4 million. However, the type of young, affluent consumers who watched Letterman's offering attracted major advertisers. Letterman's show began showing up regularly in the annual list of Emmy-nominated programs.

As in the good old TV days of Steve Allen and Jack Paar, one never knew what Letterman's twisted sense of humor might prompt him to do next on air. One time, he heard that Sophia Loren was in the Rockefeller Center studio building and did an impromptu on-location visit with her. He met with far less successful results when, in 1985, he tried the same thing with (ex) President Jimmy Carter, then across the studio hall where "Live at Five" was taping.

Another innovation on his show that year was the (in)-famous "Top 10 List" segment, which began with "The Top 10 Things That almost Rhyme with Peas." A favored visitor to the show was sportscaster Marv Albert, with whom David could converse on his favorite subject—sports. Another frequenter was actress Teri Garr who seemed to bring out the best/worst in antic Letterman, as did comic Steve Martin ("he understands exactly what the show is about. He's nice and he's smart," says Letterman).

CLEANING UP HIS ACT

By 1985, Letterman had stopped chain-smoking (but still puffed on cigar) and no longer used alcohol, caffeine or other stimulants. He lived in suburban Connecticut, not far from one of his idols, Jack Paar. In true Letterman form, he remained a very private person, especially regarding his offcamera relationship with Merrill Markoe, no longer part of "Late Night." (Even Jay Leno, a best friend and favorite Letterman show guest, admitted he had never been invited to David's house for dinner.)

Reflecting back on the early days of "Late Night," David told *Rolling Stone* that year: "In the beginning, I thought the closer to your actual self you were on the show, the better it would be. But now...I realize you definitely have to be more than yourself. You have to pretend that you're bigger than you are, that you're enjoying it more than you really are. It all has to be blown up, and you have to say and do things that you wouldn't normally have the scantest opinion on. It's just show business, you know." To keep his humility, the talk show star had a review framed over his office desk which read: "THE DAVID LETTREMAN SHOW IS LIKE GARBAGE—IT STINKS." And the fidgety comic admitted, "The most pressure I'm under is when I do 'The Tonight Show.' My deep fear is that Johnny won't think I'm funny." As to the evolution of his career, he joked, "I had to be a talk show host. I can't sing or act."

In February 1986, to celebrate the fourth anniversary of "Late Night," the cast/crew taped the show from a Boeing 747 en route from New York to Miami. When David, along with Shelley "Cheers" Long, co-hosted the 1985-1986 Emmy Awards, he used the opportunity to take a jibe at General Electric, the conglomerate that had purchased RCA, the parent company of NBC which owned Letterman's show. David wagged to his mentor, Grant Tinker, who had resigned from NBC after the buy-out and was in the audience that night, "Your commitment to quality was an example to us all...and if you need anything to help you get back on your feet, don't be bashful."

In the fall of 1986, there was new late night competition on the talk show circuit from Joan Rivers and David Brenner, but neither survived. David did on his own turf, but he was always wondering about and being asked that inevitable question: would he one day replace Johnny Carson on "The Tonight Show." In a moment of candor, Letterman confessed in 1986: "In the back of my mind, if I weren't asked someday to do it, I'd feel kind of sad, Yet, doing it— that's my worst nightmare. That I'd be foolish enough to take Carson's position if offered to me, that I'd die a miserable death in that time slot, and meanwhile NBC had given my old show to someone who was quite happy to keep doing it. Maybe the prudent thing would be to let some other poor bastard walk into the fray for several months, and *then* try doing the show."

OPTIONS

To keep Letterman's options open, Jack Rollins, his agent and show producer, admitted he was looking for film roles for David, but that his client would NOT do commercials. "You have to grow or you won't exist," Rollins explained. Letterman said himself: "It's not like I'm burning to do a film. I would only want to do a movie just to see if I could do it." Later, after signing a deal with the Walt Disney Studio, he stated, "So I guess my own insecurity for my position in show business is what led me to...take them up on their offer." So far, nothing concrete has resulted from this motion picture agreement.

For the first five years of "Late Night," the program was seen from Monday through Thursdays from 12:30 to 1:30 AM. As of June 1987, the show was additionally aired on Fridays at the same time. (Beginning in September 1991, the hour-long series started five minutes later, at 12:35 PM.) To promote the program's sixth anniversary, Letterman hosted a star-studded ninety-minute spectacular taped at Radio City Music Hall on January 4, 1988. He had now become part of the Establishment. As a sign of affluence, he had a fancy loft in the upscale TriBeca area of Manhattan, as well as his $1 million home in New Canaan, Connecticut.

If 1988 had stated off auspiciously, it soon turned sour. An industry writers' strike that summer almost killed "Late Night," but the show struggled through until the settlement occurred. David's beloved dog, Bob, died that August. Letterman made news when his driving license was suspended for assorted speeding tickets. He and Merrill Markoe, his girlfriend (and partner in comedy) of nearly ten years, broke off their romantic relationship. Crowning the year for David was the horror of being subjected to the Celebrity Fan from Hell.

Margaret Ray, 33, who insisted that David was the dominant figure in her life, was caught by the police driving David Letterman's $60,000 Porche. She identified herself as the talk show host's wife and her son as David Letterman, Jr. Subsequently, she would be apprehended at least six times inside Letterman's New Canaan, Connecticut home. (In June 1992, she would be sentenced to six months in prison for this first degree criminal trespass.) Little wonder that in 1988 David would tell the press: "I just don't allow myself the luxury of being optimistic about anything. It's really hard for me to understand that anything we do has any kind of effect or bearing on anyone anywhere in this country. It's just like we entertain 240 people nightly in the studio audience and then we go about our business."

FEELING THE HEAT

To celebrate the eighth anniversary of "Late Night," David hosted a TV special (February 1990), taped at the Universal Amphitheater in Universal City, California. At nearly 43, Letterman was no longer the young Turk on the TV block. He was feeling the pinch of heated rivalry from younger Arsenio Hall who was attracting to his TV talk show what once had been exclusively David's audience. Industry insiders suggested that David had a realistic fear of becoming "the hipster's Perry Como" or, as another observer quipped, Letterman was beginning to suffer from "Incipient uncoolness brought on by a bad case of the Nineties." In response to the growing competition, Letterman said, "ultimately, you can only do what you're equipped to do, and I think you can make a mistake letting yourself become distracted."

But TV viewers noted that the Letterman of the 90s was a kinder, gentler host. (His nadir had to be the 1988 show visit of actress Nastassja Kinski who almost burst into tears on air when he insisted that her spiky, unique hairdo closely resembled a bonsai tree.) In talking to GQ magazine, David reflected, "I've had this job longer than any other job I've ever had. When you do that, you become more focused and more introverted than maybe is a good idea. So I think that's caused me to change a bit."

Upon being told that he seemed to have toned down his antipathy to anything or anyone that was too conventional, he replied, "Christ, I didn't go into this [TV show] to be hated, you know." When interviewers asked about his offcamera activities, David would ramble at length about yearly visits home for the Indy 500 race. However, when it came to discussing his social life, he admitted: "I've found that the one area I'm always uncomfortable talking about is...female companions...."

In May 1991 came the news that Letterman had been awaiting with mixed feelings for twelve years. Johnny Carson was definitely quitting "The Tonight Show" in another year. However, it was Jay Leno who had been given this prize plum as his replacement. What amazed a disgruntled David most was the fact that he learned the major news, like everyone else, through a public announcement. It led to speculation that Letterman and NBC/General Electric (with whom he had an increasingly bad relationship) would come to a falling out sooner rather than later. Meanwhile, on January 30, 1992, David had his 10th anniversary special on NBC, filmed over two nights at Radio City Music Hall.

THE RACE BEGINS

By April of 1992, Letterman's current three year NBC pact with NBC had another year to run. Obviously, he was an unhappy camper and made no bones about it. He began speculating aloud, in every available forum, whether he would renew his network pact. It was already known that one syndicator had offered him a $40 million deal for two-years' worth of a proposed talk show. Matters became more prickly at the end of May 1992, when Jay Leno officially took over "The Tonight Show."

Adding fuel to the fire was a publicly distributed memo from Helen Gorman Kushnick, then Jay Leno's business manager and executive producer of "The Tonight Show," who let it be known that if Letterman's show vanished, she could easily have Jay expand his sixty-minute format to a ninety-minute show. (Ironically, for a time in the early fall of 1992 after Helen Kushnick had been ousted from "The Tonight Show," there were rumors that, if Leno's late show rating did not pick up, he might also be ousted and replaced by Letterman.)

As 1992 proceeded, Letterman (and his support staff, including the very powerful Creative Artists Agency who replaced Jack Rollins as his personal manager) became increasingly vocal about his grievances against NBC/General Electric: (1) he was still unhappy about the way the network had told him about Leno becoming Carson's successor; (2) he was offended that the network, in a cost save, wanted to utilize the "Late Night" studio in off-hours for other programming; (3) he was irked by the network's initial refusal to budget the tenth anniversary "Late Night" special for Radio City Music Hall or to preempt its "Wings" and "LA Laws" for its ninety minute primetime airing; (4) he was still disturbed by NBC's decision in 1991 to repackage his old talk show programs to the A&E Cable network without consulting Letterman (eventually the pact was altered from a five- to a three-year duration with a right of cancellation).

When David was one of Barbara Walters's guests on her new ABC-TV interview special (September 9, 1992), his future with NBC, naturally, was a prime topic. In a more expansive mood than usual, Letterman allowed that he was shopping around for other forums for "his" show. In November 1992, he and NBC (whose top executives David sarcastically referred to on air as "boneheads," "pinheads" and "programming geniuses") agreed to extend his network pact for two additional months (until June 1992). They, in turn, allowed him the option to begin formal talks with interested parties about hosting a new talk show.

The network retained the right to meet any bid offered Letterman. By then, it was understood that if Letterman left NBC, "Saturday Night Live" comic, Dana Carvey, most likely would inherit David's late night show spot. As far as the persistent rumor that Letterman was angling with ABC to take over its late night hours, that was squelched for good in late November 1992. Letterman, who had earlier stated he would never pressure that network into handing him Ted Koppel's "Nightline" (11:30-12:00 PM) time period, cut off negotiations with ABC when they suggested he do his show for them immediately *following* "Nightline."

WHAT A DEAL!

The bidding wars steamed up again in December 1992 when CBS-TV publicly offered Letterman approximately $14 million a year (more than twice his current NBC deal) to move his show—practically in tact—to their network. As part of the deal, Letterman would gain such additional benefits as ownership of his show and the opportunity to produce a follow-up show in the 12:30 AM time spot.

Per David's revised NBC contract, the network had until January 15, 1993 to make a parallel counter offer. Meanwhile, throughout this much-discussed contract negotiation, David (or sometimes show guests such as Steve Martin) would remind the 5 million viewers of "Late Night" of the latest wrinkles in the continuing war between Letterman and NBC. Needless to say, this situation led to a strained relationship between David and his long-time pal, Jay Leno.

Finally, the much-publicized tug-of-war ended on January 15, 1993 with a triumphant CBS announcing that Letterman would indeed join their network lineup in mid-1993 in the cherished 11:30 PM time spot. NBC countered that after David vacates his late night NBC berth on June 25, 1993 it will fill the hour period with a new series to be developed by "Saturday Night Live" creator Lorne Michaels, possibly to star Dana Carvey. With the furor finally over, Letterman told the press of his new CBS series: "This. . . [will be] a show for adults. Now's our chance. I didn't get to do 'The Tonight Show.' This will be the show that I think I could have made 'The Tonight Show.'" As to the format of his "new" TV project, David said that after eleven years of "Late Night" he and his staff had played out "fistful after fistful of ideas that we thought would be great to try on television. . . . We're pretty much tapped out. So we want to try something else. I just want it to be the best possible version of a new show that we can make it. I'm not saying it will be sterile and cold and nothing like the old show."

Looking back on his own already extensive show business career, Letterman observed a few years ago: "I was always amazed at the number of Major Entertainment Figures who'd done things that just seemed to be so obviously silly. But then I think of the stuff that I myself have done—not that I'm a Major Entertainment Figure—but I sure did a lot of idiot stuff that could be held up to ridicule. But I think that's true of anybody. You try something and it doesn't work and you say, 'Well, I'll never be doing that again!' But too bad, you've done it once and it's already on record somewhere."

As to his medium of choice, David assesses, "I think television stinks, and I think it's supposed to stink. I don't think we want it to be good. There are exceptions, of course, but by and large, I don't think we want it to be so good that people spend any more time watching it. I think it's just about the way it ought to be."

Regarding his professional future, the one-time stand-up comic confesses concerning his talk show hosting career: "I like doing this. This is all I ever really wanted to do—have my own TV show. It's not like this is a way station or this is a stop along the way.... I know how unhappy and sad I would be if I didn't have a show to do every night."

TV & CABLE SERIES:
The Starland Vocal Band (CBS, 1977)
Mary (CBS, 1978)
The David Letterman Show (NBC, 1980)
Late Night with David Letterman (NBC, 1982- 1993)
The David Letterman Show (CBS, 1993—)

FEATURE FILMS:
Fast Friends (1979) [TV movie]

Chapter 18
REGIS PHILBIN

All talk show hosts have their particular shtick. Beneath Johnny Carson's impish grin always lurked a smart put-down of any of his feisty guests; David Letterman of the benign smile could and can turn downright hostile if he's in a rambunctious mood. Then there is street-wise, New York-bred Regis Philbin. Now in his fourth decade as a talk show host, Regis (better known as "Reege") has made a fine art of being the lovable curmudgeon who lives to kvetch.

On his TV turf, he thrives on complaining and carping, whether it be about the weather, politics, his daughters, the unfairness of life, a clunker of a rented car, or about the latest shenanigans of his current TV partner in crime, Kathie Lee Gifford. She, in turn, has said of her smart aleck media alter ego: "He's got a very peculiar charm. And I do mean peculiar.... It's unique, it's endearing, and there's nobody like him in the whole world..... He can be charming, he can be frustrating and he can be infuriating. But he's always funny."

With Regis nothing is left to moderation as faithful viewers can attest. When he gets wound up on a pet peeve, his voice rises several decibels and his hands begin chopping the air as he launches into a talkathon on his newest grievance. Philbin's approach to life, as well as to his show's parade of guests, is as basic as his trademark prop, his talk program stool. Seated on his "throne," he is fully prepared to unwind non-stop, at least until a commercial break. As such, let the show's guests and audience beware!

Despite being an irascible elfin personality, Regis on air is not vicious in the mode of a Morton Downey, Jr. or a Howard Stern. Instead, he is an enthusiastic cracker barrel

Regis Philbin, the TV talk show host in the early 1980s.

Regis Philbin and Kathie Lee Gifford, the co-hosts of "Live with Regis and Kathie Lee."

philosopher, totally in love with the sound of his voice and his own views on life. In his blunt way, he is a Will Rogers for the TV generation. James Brady (*Parade* magazine) judged recently of "Live with Regis & Kathie Lee": "it's bargain-basement television, and it works—thanks to Regis Philbin, maybe the most relaxed talk-show host ever."

PLAIN OLD GROSS

On a different slant, the TV Regis can be very graphic, such as when, in 1991, after recovering from a hospital stay, he held up his removed kidney stones for the audience's inspection and then lurched into a graphic lecture on the size and use of a catheter. In rationalizing such behavior, he insists, "The audience doesn't want to know how wonderful your life is. What's going to keep them tuned in is the other side of life—the aggravations, the slights, the family stuff. Sometimes you really gotta suck it up and tell the most embarrassing things." Regarding this facet of Philbin, his TV cohort, Kathie Lee Gifford, has voiced, "He has the ability to make a viewer feel that he's talking directly to you, that he's a friend of yours who's telling you a story. Many TV personalities want people to think that they're perfect, but Regis allows his imperfection and his human frailties to show."

As with Sally Jessy Raphael and Larry King, prattling Regis Philbin has "always wanted to be a TV talker" and he also spent many apprentice years rising to his current position. He admits freely that many times en route he botched his career momentum. Discussing the many twists of Regis's professional life, Phil Rosenthal (*Los Angeles Daily News*) has championed the veteran yakker: "When the inevitable Big One hits and California slides into the sea, we would all do well to be with Regis Philbin. Philbin survives everything.... Many are funnier and quicker. Others are more attractive and smoother. But few are more successful.... Philbin isn't just surviving anymore. He's thriving."

Regis Francis Xavier Philbin was born to Frank and Florence Philbin on August 25, 1933 in Manhattan. He was named after his father's alma mater, Regis High School, a local Catholic boy's institution. His dad was the personnel director of the old Sperry Gyroscope Company. Philbin recalls, "I came from a family of crazy characters. Many of them, particularly my mother, were great story tellers and a great audience for each other. There were many, many laughs on my mother's—the Italian—side of my family."

SPORTS NUT

When Regis was four, the devoutly Catholic family moved to the Bronx and lived on the 1900 block of Crugar Avenue. He attended Our Lady of Solace Grammar School where "Sister Mary Frances used to rap my knuckles for talking too much." As a young teen, he had an after school job at Max's Candy Store. However, his real interest was sports, which he played with a passion and which remains a prime enthusiasm. In 1949 he graduated from Cardinal Hayes High School and then enrolled at Notre Dame University (where a few years later another future talk show host, Phil Donahue, would matriculate).

Regis graduated from college with a degree in sociology. Actually, by this time, he wanted to go into show business as a singer. But for Philbin, "Manhattan seemed like another world. New York was a glittering place with Broadway at its peak. It was exciting but seemed totally unattainable to me." Temporarily squashing his ambitions, he enlisted in the Navy where he spent the next two years.

By the time Philbin was a civilian again, he had determined that he wanted a television career. What inspired him was his idol Jack Paar. "Jack Paar is who I always wanted to be. I mean, I really wanted to be Jack Paar. The next best thing was to be like him. So I learned just by watching him." What enticed Regis was that "With Jack Paar, you never knew what was going to happen. He had you transfixed. Whether it was all planned or not, it seemed spontaneous." Soon Philbin had maneuvered a job as an NBC page in New York City. One of his tasks was ushering people to seats for "The Tonight Show," hosted by Steve Allen.

MARRIED AND MOVING

In 1957, he married TV actress Catherine (Kay) Faylen, the daughter of actor Frank Faylen (best known as the father on TV's "Dobie Gillis"). By then, Regis had decided there were greater professional opportunities in Los Angeles, so the couple moved westward. His first "break" was working at local TV station, KCOP. He was hired to work in the film shipping department. He soon tired of this mundane job and, to relieve the monotony, began writing tongue-in-cheek reviews of the station's programming. He signed his literary creations "The Phantom" and posted them liberally around the premises.

It did not take the station manager long to track down the culprit. After reprimanding Regis, he relented and allowed the novice a chance to do some real writing, contributing to the news scripts for TV newscaster Baxter Ward. One night, the station's sportscaster failed to appear, and since sports nut Regis was on hand, he was pressed into service. "I threw a shirt, tie and jacket on, and sat down with my heart pounding and beating. I thought I was going to die right there.... I delivered the sports. My first legitimate on-air experience. And I almost didn't get through it, believe me!"

And then, it was back to writing news copy. However, as part of the deal with the station manager, he had to still deliver the films during the morning, driving the station's truck around Los Angeles. The menial task began aggravating Regis. He told his boss "You know what I'm doing. You could train a gorilla to do this job." Then he quit. However, Regis then, as now, could be as endearingly earnest as he was annoying. So the station manager helped Philbin get a position as news reporter at KSON radio in San Diego. After a year, Regis moved over to local KFMB-TV as a feature reporter, substitute anchorman and sportscaster. By now, 1959, the Philbins were the parents of a daughter, Amy (who, as an adult, would become a singer).

In 1960, San Diego's KOGO-TV hired Regis as a feature reporter for their 6 PM news and anchorman for the 11 PM news. In October of the next year, he realized his ambition of getting his first talk show. "The Regis Philbin Show" aired from 11:15 PM to 1:30 AM on Saturday. Because the program's budget did not allow for writers, a band, or any of the typical talk show accoutrements, Regis had to improvise.

TALK, TALK, TALK

Out of necessity, he developed his trademark "Host Chat" segment in which, at the start of each program, he would sit on a prop stool and tell the audience about what he did that past week. While his rambling monologue seemed to have no limits, Philbin always monitored himself from "going too far." His chitchat format created a strong rapport between himself and the viewers, gaining him a loyal following. As the *San Diego Union*'s TV reporter observed, "Philbin has obviously made his mark on local television."

The San Diego version of "The Regis Philbin Show" lasted from 1961 to 1964. For most of the run, the host with boundless energy and a staccato rhythm delivery was almost a one-man production staff. He would book the acts, make the calls to insure their appearance, arrange for lodging, etc. (Meanwhile, he was still doing his 11 PM nightly news show for the TV station, chasing down features, etc.)

For a local offering, "The Regis Philbin Show" attracted quite a roster of name guests during its tenure. One night Regis invited Jerry Lewis on the show and the two had such fun that the comedian stayed on the air with Regis till 3:30 AM, with other late night programming being preempted. Richard Nixon made an appearance during his 1962 campaign for the governership of California and played the piano.

Others notables on Philbin's showcase included Nancy and Ronald Reagan, Bill Cosby, Pat Boone and Liberace. Regis's best break came when veteran newspaperman Walter Winchell promoted Philbin in his column. He endorsed: "He is show-biz from head to toe nails. Plus style, class, dignity. The only late-show personality around, we believe who matches Johnny Carson's way with a guest or a coast-to-coast crowd."

THE BIG TIME

With such praise, it was not long before Regis was promoted to the TV big leagues. Westinghouse Broadcasting was phasing out the syndicated "The Steve Allen Show." The network promised the declining number of stations carrying that program that it would offer a new show from Los Angeles which focused less on talk and more on music and comedy. So Regis left San Diego to host the syndicated "The Regis Philbin Show," which first aired the week of October 26, 1964.

To create audience appeal, he used the gimmick of a guest star of the week, the first being Ann Sothern. However, everything worked against Philbin. Only a few stations carried his series and it had to compete with the larger-budgeted Johnny Carson's "The Tonight Show." Then too, in most markets, Philbin was on a two-week tape delay. "What could I possibly talk about that would have relevance two weeks from now?" Philbin said later. "I have to be live, and be able to relate something that has happened in my real life. I don't know how to use writers, so I failed miserably."

By early 1965, with more stations dropping "The Regis Philbin Show," it was inevitable that Westinghouse would drop Regis. A few months later, in April 1965, the syndicator had a new replacement, "The Merv Griffin Show," which became a substantial hit. Although Regis would outlast Griffin professionally and eventually have his own successful TV forum, that turn of events still galls Philbin. "That was my big shot and I blew it. Merv followed me and became a multimillionaire! And I'm fighting with HER [i.e. Kathie Lee Gifford on 'Live with Regis & Kathie Lee'] every morning! That's how LIFE IS!"

It was also in 1965 that the Philbins became the parents of their second child, Danny. Tragically, their baby boy was born with two malformed legs which later had to be amputated. Thereafter, the boy would be confined to a wheelchair. In 1989, the supermarket tabloids would exploit Danny as Regis's forgotten son who lived with his mother in a Los Angeles housing project. Regis would retort to this with, "It was all lies" and suggested that his ex-wife had misconstrued the situation to the overly eager press. He also insisted that his son lived comfortably in suburban Van Nuys and that he and Danny talked "every week."

SECOND BANANA

In 1966, Regis was doing a local show for KTTV-TV in Los Angeles. During this stint, among the many guests he interviewed was controversial talk show host Joe Pyne. Comedian Joey Bishop appreciated how Philbin handled the abrasive guest. Months later when Bishop was signed to star in "The Joey Bishop Show," ABC-TV's latest threat to Johnny Carson and "The Tonight Show," he hired Regis to be his second banana. It was a strange role for Regis, but he handled the subordinate situation well. Bishop's talk show debuted live on April 17, 1967 with

Governor Ronald Reagan (who arrived late) and Debbie Reynolds as the first guests. *Variety* reported that Regis was "Hollywood's subdued answer to Ed McMahon" who "brings Bishop on sans vocal exclamation, to wit: 'And now...it's time for Joey.'"

As "The Joey Bishop Show" settled into its run, Regis was given more opportunities on the program to be his "tactless" self. He was an unbridled contrast to the dry humor of the star with whom he got along well. On the nationally seen program, Regis was allowed finally to fulfill his dream of being a singer. It happened when Bing Crosby was a show guest in 1968. Becoming aware that Philbin was a frustrated crooner, Der Bingle asked him during the gab fest to sing "Pennies from Heaven." Regis obliged.

Philbin's performance led to a Mercury Records LP album, "It's Time For Regis," in which Philbin vocalized on several old Crosby standards. It was also in this year that Regis and Kay divorced. In a polite mood Philbin will say it was "a marriage that didn't work or last" but there were many domestic problems over the years: Kay's failure to make a name in show business, the ongoing health problems of their son, her enjoyment of social drinking. And then there was the matter of Joy Senese, Joey Bishop's attractive assistant. Regis was falling in love with her.

By mid-summer 1969 it was no secret that "The Joey Bishop Show" was failing. It died on December 26, 1969. On the last installment of the program, astrologer Sydney Omarr told Regis that he would become a household word. When Regis asked when, Omarr responded, "It's going to take 20 years."

CRITICAL ACCLAIM

Before the Bishop assignment ended, Regis the survivor had found another opportunity. In August 1969, he began "Philbin's People" on KHJ-TV in Los Angeles. It was a ninety-minute Saturday night local program which attempted to blend talk, politics, music and comedy, using a round-table discussion forum. The first night's guests included comedian Phyllis Diller, Los Angeles Mayor Sam Yorty and basketball star Bill Russell.

Rick DuBrow (*United Press International*) applauded the series as "one of the best talk shows I have ever seen on television.... It was what video should be." During its several months' run, the program won a local Emmy. Later in 1970 when the host of KHJ's three-hour live morning show, "Tempo" left, Regis stepped in as the replacement.

It was on March 1, 1970 that Regis and Joy Senese married. She recalls, "When Regis and I were married...I knew that life would never be dull. How could it be when Regis' idea of a surprise honeymoon for me was not to make any plans or reservations, but to just get in the car and 'wing it.' It's a good thing Regis is a lot of laughs, it made up for some of the hotels."

While still fulfilling his chores with "Tempo," Regis made his club debut at the original Playboy Club on the Sunset Strip. (In later years, Regis would continue on the club circuit, being the opening act for Tony Bennett, Steve Lawrence and Edie Gorme and Don Rickles.) He also made the first of a few movie appearances, playing himself in the Woody Allen comedy, EVERYTHING YOU ALWAYS WANTED TO KNOW ABOUT SEX BUT WERE AFRAID TO ASK (1972).

ONE MAN SHOW

When Regis first started doing "Tempo," Ruta Lee and then Sam Born were his co-hosts, but mostly it was Regis carrying the ball himself. He found the job taxing and boring. Then an industry friend came to the rescue. Tom Battista was general manager of KMOX-TV (later KMOV-TV) in St. Louis and invited his pal to do "Regis Philbin's Saturday Night in St. Louis."

So he could do both jobs, he would commute to Missouri one weekend a month. He would tape one show on Friday night, a second one on early Saturday evening, then do a live show at 10:30 PM and finally tape the last one on Sunday afternoon. By 1973, he not only was exhausted by the pace, but he also totally burned out with "Tempo." As a result, he quit the latter project.

By 1975, Regis and Joy were the parents of two daughters: Joanna and Joy. His "Saturday Night in St. Louis" had been cancelled during a station budget crunch. However, in typical Philbin fashion, he had a new job already. He had been hired by KABC-TV in Los Angeles to serve as entertainment reporter and film reviewer for the 6 PM and 11 PM news. He also hosted an ABC-TV game show, "Neighbors" (1975-1976) and. for a few months in 1976. was part of "Almost Anything Goes" a live Saturday evening show for the ABC network. Shot on location, this latter show required him to fly to different parts of the country each weekend.

Later in 1975, Regis moved over to KABC-TV's popular "A.M. Los Angeles," a magazine format offering. At the start, his wife Joy was the part-time program co-host and together they displayed wonderful chemistry. She was followed by Sarah Purcell (1975-1979) and then by Cyndy Garvey (1979-1981). By the time Cyndy was his partner in mayhem, Regis had refined his on-the-air routine so that, at the show's opening chat session, he would cross his arms and stare at her. To prompt Cindy to spill the beans on her private life, he would jibe, "Come on, Garvey woman.... You don't have a boring life!" (It was a routine that would be used again and again by Philbin with future co-hosts.)

By now, Regis had become famous for his "anything goes, but boy are you going to hear about it" modus operandi on "A.M. Los Angeles." For example, one time he was scheduled to interview an instructor teaching babies and small kids how to swim in a pool. It was the fall and the swimming pool's water heater had malfunctioned. Regis jumped in, and when he made contact with the icy water, he began yelping. Nevertheless, he did do the interview.

TIME TO CLEAN HOUSE

Another feature of "A.M. Los Angeles" was the show's trivia question. One day the puzzler was "Who gave Deanna Durbin her first screen kiss?" Film buffs know that was Robert Stack but Philbin despaired that any of the callers phoning in would guess the right answer. Finally in (playful) exasperation, he raised the ante by vowing he would clean the house of the caller who answered it correctly. (P.S. He ended cleaning the successful caller's entire house and, of course, taped the expedition for later airing on the program.)

In the fall of 1981, Regis's "A.M. Los Angeles" contract was expiring. Just at this time, Grant Tinker who had taken over as head of NBC programming, called and offered Regis a talk show, the still unfilled slot to replace David Letterman's cancelled morning program. Philbin was flattered that he did not have to audition or pass muster with any corporate committee. It seemed too good to be true. As he recalls, "First I agonized and then I jumped at it."

Almost immediately he regretted the decision. He learned quickly what happens when a network takes a pleasant local show and makes it national. "They gave me writers, cue cards—everything I hate. Even worse, the show was taped. I hated taped show." The half-hour daily show premiered on November 30, 1981 without a permanent co-host, but soon added Mary Hart as Regis's vis-a-vis. Her chores ranged from stomping through grapes barefooted, interviewing athlete Jim Palmer in only his jockey shorts, and being nagged "everyday to expose the most intimate details of my private life."

Variety panned the time-filler: "Philbin is back on the national scene, still giggling.... In the New York market, this innocuous fluff airs directly after the syndicated 'Donahue show—and the contrast was particularly deadly." Not accepting that offbeat Philbin was the program's best asset, the network kept trying to tone down the host's feistiness. The show died as of April 9, 1982, a victim of network tampering and for the failure of a lot of NBC affiliates to carry the program, having been burned by the David Letterman fiasco. Ironically, the departed program won an Emmy as Outstanding (Daytime) Variety Series.

NO THREAT TO ARNOLD

Regis bounced back later in 1982 with "Regis Philbin's Health Styles" on the Cable Health Network (presently called Lifetime Cable). Focusing on a mix of cooking, fitness and health, the program underwent many name changes during its several years on the air through 1987. Meanwhile, Regis who had the knack for making lasting industry friendships, was rescued by John Severino, the former general manager of Los Angeles's KABC-TV in the 1970s. He was now president of the ABC-TV network and asked Philbin to host the ninety-minute daily "The Morning Show."

To do so required Regis moving back to New York City, which he and his family did. Joy Philbin would recall of her irrepressible, joyfully unsophisticated spouse: "I'll never forget the first spring day when Regis took a lawn chair and a magazine out to the center island on Park Avenue and stretched out. He couldn't understand why the girls and I were so horrified that someone we knew might recognize him."

"The Morning Show" was taped at TV facilities just seven blocks from where Philbin had been born. Cyndy Garvey returned as Regis's TV teammate from 1983 to 1984, followed by Ann Abernathy. Ann, having just moved to Manhattan from Oklahoma City, was astounded her first day on the program to discover that Philbin was not there when they began taping. In her words: "It wasn't until the second segment that he walked in—dripping wet in his slicker and galoshes, carrying an umbrella with his picture on it! He had just raced through Central Park, on foot, to get there!"

With "lets try anything" Regis and his home-spun philosophy and humor at the helm, the show moved up in the ratings, becoming the #1 New York City morning program and winning several local Emmys. With the Big Apple as inspiration, Regis found lots of things about which to complain. As he explains, "I think aggravation is a great source of humor. More people can relate to it. More people want to hear you're aggravated than you have a comfortable life.... And living in New York, it doesn't matter how much money you make, you're still going to be aggravated. It comes easily in New York. To live in this city is to be irked."

After Ann left the show and Regis's wife Joy had been co-hosting for a time, Kathie Lee Gifford joined Philbin as his talkathon collaborator. Their salt-and-pepper personalities had just the right mix of vinegar and honey to create genuine chemistry. Kathie Lee was soon signed as permanent co-host, with Joy occasionally filling in (but rarely able to get a chance to say anything due to her motor-mouth spouse). As of September 5, 1988, "The Morning Show" became "Live with Regis & Kathie Lee." It was now being distributed nationally by Buena Vista. Before signing the deal with the syndicator, Regis gruffly told his future bosses, "Look, you guys want to syndicate the show, we'd love it, but don't change anything. I don't want to change that opening. Just put it up on the [satellite] bird and let it go."

With "Live with Regis & Kathie Lee" syndicated nationally, now the entire country had access to what had previously been a New York area delight. *Newsday* rated it "the coffee klatsch of morning shows." As one loyal viewer described the addictive show: "it's kind of like watching a fire on the street—you stop for a minute, are drawn into watching it, and before you know it, you're late for work."

People magazine offered, "He may seem like a game show host with no prizes.... Sure he's pleasant and charming but don't hold that against him. He's also witty, if harmlessly so. He can insult guests and get away with it. He can talk about mundane frustrations in his own life...and not put us back to sleep." The ratings continued to zoom upward and Regis (as well as Kathie Lee) were entrenched as national celebrities. Philbin's belated success confirmed the astrologer's prediction made almost two decades earlier on the swansong episode of "The Joey Bishop Show."

Despite or because of his celebrity status, Regis more freely indulged his bent for performing in clubs. He had established a twice-yearly tradition of performing at the Club Bene in New Jersey. Then, he began branching out, playing at Hershey Park in Pennsylvania and elsewhere. In 1989, he and Kathie Lee did a stage show together as headliners at Trump Plaza in Atlantic City. Their act consisted of part improv, part stand-up comedy, part vocalizing. They would continue to appear as a club duo in later years.

ROLLING ALONG

Regis also expanded into the arena of commercial endorsements. In the early 1990s he joined in partnership with the ballet world's Mikhail Baryshnikov and others to open a Manhattan restaurant. In 1991 Regis and Kathie Lee co-hosted "The Miss America Beauty Pageant" and repeated their chore in the fall of 1992. For many of their eighteen million view-

ers-fans they had become America's new sweethearts and were now seen on over 210 stations coast-to-coast.

However, unlike such talk show hosts as Oprah Winfrey, Regis, so far, has no profit participation in the syndication property. He does lead the good life, now having a suburban Connecticut home, not that far from co-host Kathie Lee. In his "spare" time, Regis makes guest appearances on other TV shows, including a late 1992 appearance on "Jeopardy" as a celebrity contestant. The high ratings for that quiz show episode led to speculation that one day Philbin might host his own new TV game show.

Although Regis Philbin had clearly arrived in the show business world, he retains his quirky casualness. When a media reporter wants to interview him, he might find himself suddenly on "Live with Regis & Kathie Lee" conducting an impromptu questioning session with Philbin. Determined to perfect his keyboard skills, Regis takes daily piano lessons on the set, right after taping the show. He still remains a big sports enthusiast, especially of football and particularly of the Notre Dame squad.

As to his rocky road to success, Philbin insists, "I wouldn't recommend it to anyone. It's been a long, hard, up-and-down trail. It really has. I wish I could have made it a hit the first time I did it. Thing is, always I've had local shows, I made a success out of them." He also acknowledges another sensitive point, "I was always the punching bag of the press, but just to be on top now makes you forget all that." When asked to weigh his degree of fame, he says, "Do I consider myself a star, like a big movie star or a Johnny Carson or somebody like that? No, no, I really don't. I wouldn't know how to accept that kind of feeling." Although obviously pleased with his current lofty genre standing, Regis cannot quite believe he has finally made it. "You keep looking over your shoulder for the next calamity to happen."

TV & CABLE SERIES:
The Regis Philbin Show (San Diego local, 1961-1964)
The Regis Philbin Show (Syndicated, 1964-1965)
The Regis Philbin Show (Los Angeles local, 1966)
The Joey Bishop Show (ABC, 1967-1969)
Philbin's People (Los Angeles local, 1969-1970)
Tempo (Los Angeles local, 1970-1972)
Regis Philbin's Saturday Night in St. Louis (St. Louis local, 1972-1975)
A.M. Los Angeles (Los Angeles local, 1975-1981)
Neighbors (ABC, 1975-1976)
Almost Anything Goes (ABC, 1976)
The Regis Philbin Show (NBC, 1981-1982)
Regis Philbin's Health Styles [Regis Philbin's Lifestyles/The Regis Philbin Show]
     (Cable Health/Lifetime, 1982-1987)
The Morning Show (New York City local, 1983-1988)
Live with Regis & Kathie Lee (Syndicated, 1988-)

FEATURE FILMS:
Everything You Always Wanted to Know About Sex, But Were Afraid to Ask (1972)
Sextette (1978)
The Man Who Loved Women (1983)

Chapter 19
SALLY JESSY RAPHAEL

Each of today's female TV talk show hosts has very distinctive oncamera characteristics. e.g.: Joan Rivers (flippant), Oprah Winfrey (salt of the earth), Jenny Jones (buoyant), Whoopi Goldberg (soft-spoken), Jane Whitney (refined). If any quality best represents Sally Jessy Raphael, it is concern. Her chatter show philosophy is, "I'm trying to reach one person. There isn't a crowd out there. There's just one other human being and we're trying to figure out life together."

A consummate professional, Raphael is a patient listener. Through pointed and sometimes unexpected questions, she coaxes platform guests and studio audiences to be responsive in their most thoughtful manner. Even when Sally Jessy showcases exploitive topics to gain crucial rating points, there is a leavening of common sense to her presentation. Despite the hysteria some of these explosive segments cause among the panel and studio audience, she remains an unflappable moderator.

Like Larry King, Sally Jessy's talk show beginnings were in radio, a medium in which, for many years, she performed daily (in addition to her TV program). As she explains of her media passion: "Radio makes me feel wanted and needed.... When I'm on the air giving advice, I have a gut identification with my audience and they with me."

In analyzing herself, Sally Jessy insists, "I'm a gambler at heart, a chronic, incurable risk taker." That she is! She is also "a study in persistence." In her professional career, she was fired eighteen times and quit three times before making a success of herself. The always candid Raphael says: "I've lost a little bitterness. In the '60s, I was angry at a system that didn't have [many] women on the air. Now I've mellowed.... I was mad until I earned over $25,000 a year. But no one told me it would take so many years to get anywhere at all." Now earning over $2 million yearly in a profession she adores, Sally Jessy is proof positive of her life theory: "big dreams are wonderful...dreaming stretches you to strive to be the very best you can."

SOLID SUPPORT

Just as Raphael's career has been a traumatic roller coaster ride, so has her personal life. After a failed first marriage, she found contentment with husband No. 2. Over their decades together, many of them existing gypsy style from hand to mouth, it was he who was her primary support system. ("Whenever, I'm feeling down," says Sally Jessy, "he makes me go back into the battle.") Together, they have raised a brood of children (two from her first marriage, two from his prior marriage, one adopted and three unofficial foster kids). They also have shared and survived back-to-back tragedies in 1992. Their adopted son nearly died in an auto accident (lingering for days in a coma) and, just weeks later, one of her daughters expired from an accidental drug overdose.

Rallying back from these calamities, Sally Jessy confirms, "You learn more from ten days of agony than from ten years of content[ment]."

The most noticeable outward difference between the Sally Jessy of the 1960s and that of the 1990s is her choice of professional wardrobe. In her apprentice years, 5'2" Raphael's favored practical slacks and sensible shoes. Today, she is a model of trendy femininity with her haute couture designer fashions and modish short blond curls. Then there is the matter of her over-sized eye glasses with their trademark red frames.

A season or so ago, she conducted a 900 number phone-in campaign so viewers could help her select new spectacles. However, the new frames remained inescapably bright red. Why? Long ago, Raphael decided, "Those glasses were *me*. They were my little rebellion against tradition, a visual message that hinted at the fiery sparks of drama in my inner personality."

One of two children (there was a brother Steve), she was born on February 25, 1943 (some sources say earlier) in Easton, Pennsylvania. Her dapper father (whom she called "Pop-Up") was a real estate broker who dabbled in rum exporting, etc. Her mother was a professional painter. Sally Jessy spent her childhood in affluent Scarsdale, New York with summers in Pennsylvania and long family trips to Puerto Rico where her dad had financial interests.

Freely admitting that "I have no wrong-side-of-the-tracks stories," she had a pampered youth, filled with ballet, piano and voice lessons and constant trips to the theatre and concerts. She recalls, "I was privileged and I knew it. My father was very much a dreamer who told me I would never have to work and my mother thought that whatever I did was fabulous, even if I coughed."

HER DREAM WOULD COME TRUE

As an adolescent, Sally Jessy fantasized about someday having a show business career, especially in radio. Her idols were Arthur Godfrey and Jean Shepherd. At age twelve, she attended acting camp at the MacArthur Summer Theatre in Vermont. Philip Burton, the adoptive father of actor Richard Burton was in charge and youngish Richard was frequently there that summer. When she was thirteen, the family was residing in White Plains, New York and she made her radio debut on WFAS-AM in White Plains hosting "The Junior High News." On Saturdays, she took dramas classes in Manhattan at the prestigious Neighborhood Playhouse. The next summer she apprenticed at the Westport Playhouse in Connecticut and, besides painting scenery there, performed on stage with Geraldine Page in "The Empress."

After graduating high school, she went to the Carnegie-Mellon University in Pittsburgh to study acting. She discovered quickly that she was NOT a good Method actor and that she hated the discipline of dormitory life. Then her instructors insisted she narrow her professional interest to either acting or directing. Rather than make a choice, she left the University. Instead, she enrolled in the new department of broadcasting started by Columbia University and NBC. Classes were held at 30 Rockefeller Plaza at the network's headquarters. Eventually, she received a B.F.A. degree from Columbia University, as a broadcasting major.

During her mid-teens, her father suffered a series of debilitating heart attacks which generated huge medical bills. As a result, the family had to move from their comfortable home to an inexpensive Riverdale apartment. Her father had two extremely expensive operations which seemingly only accelerated his physical decline. The family was soon deeply in debt.

They moved frequently, changing their surname and background often to cover their bad credit. The adjustment was difficult on everyone, especially Sally Jessy. Years later, she would reflect: "I think when you've had nice things, it's very hard not to have them.... some of the drive I have probably comes from trying to regain some of those things." A few years later, her father died in a Veteran's Administration Hospital. By that time, Sally Jessy had escaped the painful scene through marriage. Her brother Steve, then in the Air Force, tended their father during his final years.

THREE IS A CHARM

By the early 1960s, Sally Jessy was living full-time in San Juan, married to Andrew Vladimir, whom she would describe later as "preppy...a nerd." He was in the advertising business, earning $4,000 annually. She was the mother of two daughters (Allison, Andrea) and had already embarked on her dream career—in radio. By now, she had adopted her professional name of Sally Jessy Raphael, the surname being her mother's maiden name. As she would explain, in Puerto Rico "everyone has three names. If you don't have three names, they think you're strange."

Her radio career did not begin glamorously, as she earned only $2 a day. One station she worked at was "owned by a housewife and her husband. The husband went out and sold advertising, and she ran the station. I broadcast from her front porch. When she didn't like my show, she'd part the kitchen curtains and wag her fingers at me over the dishes." But what excited Sally Jessy at this and other small stations who employed her, was that she got to do everything from news to the weather to field reporting. At station WHOA, which broadcast from over a garage, she was also a jack of all trades.

In 1964, Raphael asked herself, "Did I really want the power in my life to be in someone else's hands? The answer was no, and I determined from that moment on that I needed to live more on my own terms." As such, she and Vladimir divorced. Soon thereafter, she met Karl Soderlund, a former member of the U.S. Air Force, who was the divorced father of two. He had wound up in Puerto Rico where he managed a radio station. He hired Sally Jessy to work on the air for him. Soon, she became a popular local personality with her radio program on WKYN.

Sally Jessy, her two children and Karl began sharing quarters together (they would marry later). The household not only encompassed her two daughters, but soon included a twelve-year old newspaper boy, Robbie, who become one of their unofficial foster children. (Neither Sally Jessy nor Karl could ever say no to a person in need, especially a youngster.) By now, Sally Jessy's mother, Dede, had relocated to San Juan and Raphael bought her an art gallery. (To increase her income, Dede used to paint canvases under aliases and then showcase these fictitious artists at her gallery.) Another of Sally Jessy's investments was partial ownership in a perfume factory.

ADIOS

Always energetic and with many interests (including horse track betting), Sally Jessy was among those patrons instrumental in starting a volunteer public library in San Juan. As an enthusiastic friend of homeless animals, she became associated with New York-based writer Cleveland Amory, a frequent visitor to Puerto Rico and a devotee of humanity to animals.

Life seemed to be going well for Sally Jessy. However, one day, the owner of WKYN had an impulse to switch over all broadcasting to the Spanish language. Although she spoke Spanish well, Sally Jessy was fired from the radio station and her popular talk show was suddenly over. To make ends meet, she found temporary work as an Associated Press wire service reporter. Among her assignments was one traveling to Port-Au-Prince in Haiti to interview President Francois "Papa Doc" Duvalier. The interview ended abruptly because he would not speak English, but insisted on conversing in French, which Raphael did not know fluently.

With Soderlund as her agent, Sally Jessy and her flock migrated to Miami where she obtained a job at radio station WIOD ("Wonderful Isle of Dreams"). For $275 weekly (which included Karl's services as well), she hosted an all-night program (1 AM to 6 AM). Utilizing a call-out format, she relied on phone directories from all over the country to target her calls.

A recurring routine on the program was her attempts to reach Fidel Castro in Cuba. The show developed a loyal following, with one of its celebrity listeners being insomniac Miami resident, Jackie Gleason. To save on living expenses, the family became caretakers (at $220 monthly) for a four-acre estate on Biscayne Bay. To furnish the empty thirteen-bedroom (decaying) mansion, they relied on the Goodwill Thrift Shop. After a year, the Miami period ended when the WIOD management refused to grant Sally Jessy a raise.

Thereafter, Sally Jessy, Karl, Allison and Andrea (along with a poodle and cat) set out in their beat-up car looking for work. As they traveled from city to city, the group frequently had to sleep in the auto and dine on a diet of crackers flavored with ketchup. Despite the hardships of this hand-to-mouth existence, Andrea would recall years later: "It was always a party. Sometimes I craved a little stability...but I most remember the magic she created. She and my stepfather just seemed to make things happen." The family's destination was New York City, but there were no offers there for Raphael's services.

Next, Karl negotiated a contract for Sally Jessy to work at a Hartford, Connecticut radio station. The salary was a whopping $20,000 yearly (nearly double her Miami salary) for hosting only a two-hour noontime show. They set up residence in an unfurnished place in Glastonbury, Connecticut, using sleeping bags and eating by sitting on the floor.

TOO GOOD TO BE TRUE

The "good" times ended after a brief twelve weeks. Not only had the novice station owner misjudged the temper of the region (he attempted a liberal programming policy in a very conservative town), but the salary offered Sally Jessy was unrealistically high. At holiday time, she was fired. After New Year's, the discouraged group returned to Puerto Rico. By this point, the frequently fired Sally Jessy and Karl had developed a routine to salvage their self-esteem. They permitted themselves no more than three days of reveling in self-pity, then they would get practical and look for new employers.

Back in San Juan, Sally Jessy found no work. Eventually, Karl devised a novel method to get his wife employment. Before approaching a Ft. Lauderdale radio station about her hosting a noontime celebrity interview show, they visited local businesses. Thus they were able to drum up advertisers before the program was even suggested to management. The gimmick worked and she was hired. They moved into a rented house in Coconut Grove. Also in this period, Raphael hosted an interview/disc jockey show on a Miami rock music station.

Her luck improved when, during the 1969-1970 season, she found additional employment. The new assignment was hosting "A.M. Miami," a ninety-minute local TV show. She and producer Rita Eklund coordinated the entire show. The work included arranging all aspects of the guest lineup, which sometimes encompassed 20-25 visitors per program. Always hustling to make ends meet, Raphael, in this phase, had a frantic daily schedule. She did her morning TV show and then rushed to Ft. Lauderdale for her noontime radio interview program. Later, she returned to Miami in time to handle her late evening chores at the rock radio station.

This merry-go-round led to some amusing situations. One day, actor Eddie Albert was in Miami as part of a whirlwind tour to promote his latest film. His press agent jockeyed him from interview to interview, with the movie star benumbed from jet lag and the hectic pace. In the course of one day, Sally Jessy interviewed Albert on each of her three programs, with Albert trying to figure out why this woman looked so familiar. As a lark, after he answered questions on her late night radio show, she rushed to the hotel where he was scheduled to dine. Grabbing a napkin and an order book, she pretended to be his waitress. She told the star, "In show business, Eddie, you do what you have to do."

A GROWING FAMILY
Now settled in Miami, Sally Jessy's mother moved to an apartment nearby to her daughter. By now, young Robbie had rejoined his foster parents. Because Sally Jessy never wanted to get pregnant by Karl (because it would take away time from work), they extended their family in 1972 by adopting an infant baby. The boy, Jason, soon became known as J.J.

With Raphael's faltering luck, there followed a string of tragedies. Sally Jessy's mother was raped and the trauma eventually led to her suffering a stroke. As a result, Dede had to be moved to a nursing home. Then on Thanksgiving day, 1974, Raphael was fired from her TV forum. Management had decided to make "A.M. Miami" more of a public service program, and Sally Jessy was out. Meanwhile, while on a job searching expedition, the family almost had a fatal car accident in Charleston, South Carolina.

Forced by economics to leave Dede in a run-down Miami nursing home, Sally Jessy, Karl and their brood relocated to New York City. Once again, she hoped to make a connection with a major radio station. Soderlund found employment at the Ford Modeling Agency, where he developed a new broadcasting division. Living on an extremely tight budget in their modest Upper East Side apartment, the family often survived on food stamps. To keep her sanity until she found work, Raphael used shopping as therapy. To keep her "hobby" economical, she made a passion of collecting low-priced eggbeaters.

In 1975, Raphael obtained part-time work at Manhattan's WINS radio station. She was hired as overnight anchor on the all news program. She did this for several months. Next, she moved over to prestigious WMCA radio, first as an occasional fill-in for talk show host Barry Gray. In 1976, just as she was about to move to Pittsburgh to work at KDKA, Ruth Meyer, WMCA's station manager, hired her to work full-time at that radio station.

SHE DOES IT ALL
Among her chores during the next five years, Sally Jessy co-hosted a morning talk program with Barry Farber. As fill-in work, she appeared on New York City's Channel 11 as replacement for anchorwoman Pat Harper on the 10 PM news. However, these eight months at WPIX-TV were among Raphael's worst in the business, as the station tried to alter her image drastically.

While enjoying her WMCA stand and coping with WPIX management demands, Sally Jessy brought her ailing mother north. Dede was placed in the best facilities Raphael could afford: a seedy local nursing home. Later, Dede developed ovarian cancer, was operated on, declined further and spent her final months at a "wonderful" Catholic nursing home a few blocks from her daughter's apartment.

Dede died in the summer of 1978. Years later, Sally Jessy acknowledged that she still felt guilty over her "lax" attitude toward her mother in those final months. At that time, through a combination of fear, frustration and exhaustion, she dealt with the highly emotional daughter-parent situation by adopting a policy of polite avoidance.

Complicating life even further, in 1976, Karl opened a restaurant (The Wine Press) on First Avenue on the Upper East Side. For more than four years, he struggled to make the operation succeed, using his wife's broadcasting income to cover some of their mounting debts. Neither Karl nor Sally Jessy were experienced enough to make the establishment survive and the business closed, finally, in 1981. By then, Soderlund owed a tremendous amount of back taxes, a problem that would haunt the couple for years to come.

FIRED ONCE AGAIN

At the height of Karl's Wine Press problems in early 1981, Sally Jessy was let go from WMCA. One media columnist of the day explained it: "Sally has not kept up with the times." This firing was the start of a year-and-a-half slump for Raphael. She made the rounds of stations and placed ads in the trade papers. Nothing happened. Then a NBC executive whom Raphael had met while she was helping out at The Wine Press gave her a network entree. No sooner had Sally Jessy arranged an appointment with the contact than he left the corporation. Her resume was turned over to another contact, but he too left NBC. Finally, a third entree, Maurice Tunick, proved helpful. He was the producer of Talknet, the fledgling talk radio syndication arm of NBC, which packaged assorted genre shows. He told her she could audition for a hosting job by doing an hour's test at WRC, a NBC-owned station in Washington, D.C.

Rushing to D.C. on that July 4, 1982 weekend, Sally was scheduled to go on the air at 1 PM. Since it was a holiday, no one expected the test would have much impact either way on listeners. Although the program's forte was politics, Sally Jessy took a chance at doing what she did best: talking about everyday events and problems. On the air, Raphael, a wonderful raconteur, told a story about children fulfilling their mothers' dreams. When she finished, she asked listeners "How do you feel about that?" In Raphael's words, "The phones haven't stopped ringing." Sally Jessy was hired for a hosting job because, said Maurice Tunick, "there was no other choice to be made. She's the good neighbor we always wished we had next door."

Beginning in the fall of 1982, Raphael began her Talknet stint, broadcasting from a studio on the 8th floor of 30 Rockefeller Plaza. When she went on air from the 11 PM-2 AM time slot, there were only twenty stations signed up for the program. Within the next years, that number rose to 300 and her national audience reached over a million listeners. During the course of a typical program, callers phoned in from all parts of the country and from all walks of life (including that Wisconsin dairy farmer Sally Jessy helped to find a bride).

Raphael would talk, without any up-front preparation, to about 25-30 individuals per show. (Said Raphael at the time: "I treat more people in a night than a psychologist treats in a whole life.") Sally Jessy estimated that about 75% of her calls dealt with matters of romance, made either by lonely people wanting to meet a mate or persons involved in unsatisfactory marriages or relationships. As Raphael described it: "We deal with teenage sexuality. We deal with unwanted pregnancies. We deal with what to do when you're broke and out of work and we deal with depression, low self-esteem, feeling low, increasing one's romantic potential...." Because Raphael had overcome so many problems in her own life, she displayed a noticeable empathy and optimism on the air, which endeared her to her listeners.

IMPORTANT LISTENERS

Two listeners to her talk radio program in 1983 were TV talk show host Phil Donahue and his actress wife, Marlo Thomas. They were vacationing in Mexico, but heard Raphael's show via its Albuquerque outlet. When Donahue returned to New York City, he spoke to his TV syndicator, Metromedia, about Sally Jessy. This, in turn, led Phil Donahue's producer Burt Dubrow to put Raphael on "Braun and Company," his Metromedia-distributed TV interview show based in Cincinnati. After her first visit, she was invited back not because she was such a sparkling interviewee, but because she enjoyed a large following from her radio chores. Next, she was asked to guest host the show for a week.

As a result of this television exposure, Walter Bartlett, Metromedia's CEO, offered her own half-hour local program to emanate from St. Louis. "In Touch with Sally Jessy Raphael" began telecasting on October 17, 1983. It was taped at St. Louis's KSDK-TV. Viewers, at first, were underwhelmed by this latest entrant to the TV talk show arena. She was abrasive, too fat, wore pants, etc. Under the guidance of her syndicator, she learned "I had to come across as warm, comfortable, and feminine, the kind of friend you'd like to chat with over coffee."

From the start, Sally Jessy realized that women were her primary audience, and she focused her choice of guests and themes to this entire target. One of the first visitors on her TV format was "Stephie," who had been a caller on Raphael's radio program. Stephie, then 29, had been raped at age fifteen, and discussed candidly the trauma and lengthy recovery period required thereafter. Within six months of Raphael's TV show debut, her increasingly popular program was being syndicated nationally.

From 1983 to 1987, Sally Jessy commuted from Manhattan to St. Louis. She still had her nightly radio program which she did three evenings live from New York and two nights live from Missouri. As always had been true, the Raphael-Soderlund household was fluid, altering constantly with new replacements. For example, in 1983, 25-year-old Catherine Owens, a family friend of Sally Jessy's ex-husband, came from Ireland to New York for a visit. She remained with Sally Jessy and Karl for three years; when she moved out, her sister Sarah moved in. This casual hospitality did not seem strange to the family; it was their particular way of life.

IT PAYS THE BILLS

Between her TV and radio shows, commuting, and being a wife-parent, Sally Jessy found time to write *Finding Love: A Tactical Guide for Men and Women* (1984). She prepared this book over a eight-month period "based on my experience. I had things I wanted to say and I also wanted the money."

The year 1986 marked Sally Jessy's thirtieth anniversary in broadcasting (going back to her junior high days). She said, "In the 30 years, they got good five years ago. When you can pay your credit cards, it's good. It's been five years since we could pay our rent, eat and pay off American Express at the same time." She also admitted, "Television is probably the most important thing to me right now. On every level it's a fight and a challenge, and I like a good fight...there's never been a woman talk show host who hasn't been something else first." As to succeeding in the high-profile medium, she acknowledged, "It's a stretch, but I'm working at it."

A big change occurred in 1987. NBC's Talknet network had been sold, with Sally Jessy moving over (in January 1988) to ABC radio for her nightly three-hour call-in program. Meanwhile, in June 1987, Metromedia relocated her syndicated TV show to WTNH-TV in New Haven, Connecticut to make it easier on their New York City-based star. Early segments at the Connecticut studio featured Raphael interviewing nudists, skating with roller derby queens (the Bay City Bombers), combatting the Girls of Glow (female wrestlers) and hitting the street of the Big Apple with Times Square prostitutes. Such exploitive programming gave Raphael a high profile within the industry and with viewers. In 1989, "Sally Jessy Raphael" not only expanded to an hour time slot, but moved yet again, this time to Unitel Studios in Manhattan.

In 1987, with her growing success and solvency, Sally Jessy and Karl purchased a bed-and-breakfast business in rural Pennsylvania. Their choice was the historic Isaac Stover House, a Bucks County inn situated near the Delaware River. By then, the family had their Manhattan apartment as well as a country house in Montrose, New York. Situated in northern Westchester County near Peekskill, they called their home Hare Hollow, and it contained the usual Sally Jessy menagerie of household pets.

HER FIRST EMMY

After decades in the TV industry, Raphael earned her first Emmy in the 1988-1989 season, winning in the Daytime Division as Outstanding Talk/Service Host. She beat out the competition which included Phil Donahue, Oprah Winfrey, Regis Philbin and Kathie Lee Gifford, as well as Lifetime Cable's Linda Dano and Nancy Glass of "Attitudes." (The following season, Sally Jessy would lose the Emmy for hosting, but her top-rated program would win the Best Talk/Service Program trophy.)

Not long before her Emmy win, Raphael had been asked to compare herself to her rivals. As she viewed it: "I see Phil as a political animal, caring about the country, secretly wanting to run for the United State Senate. Geraldo is the investigative reporter, opening vaults and things. Oprah is darned good—a single black woman and coming from that experience. I'm a married lady with children. My constituency is the Midwest—God, country, Mother, and apple pie."

Just as Sally Jessy had done a bit of TV acting (appearing on the series "The Equalizer") in the late 1980s, so she entered the new decade in a different medium. Her autobiography, *Unconventional Success*, written with Pam Proctor, was published in 1990. While her 1991 phone-in campaign for advice on changing her famed eyeglasses was highly promoted, she kept her cosmetic surgery (to tone up her facial look) on a low key. When not working, her favorite hobbies included collecting Japanese dolls and satisfying her wanderlust. To accommodate the latter, she would often embark on long-distance trips with family friends.

As her fans well know, on a personal basis, 1992 was an unkind year for vivacious Sally Jessy. On January 11, 1992, her nineteen-year-old son, J.J., was in a near fatal car crash in New York's Putnam County. His vehicle served out of control and smashed into a tree. As a result, he suffered a crushed chest, fractured skull, facial cuts, as well as broken arms and legs. Sally Jessy and Karl were at their Manhattan apartment when the police contacted them about the accident. During the ten days J.J. was in a coma, Sally Jessy kept a bedside vigil at the hospital. After he regained consciousness, he underwent several difficult operations to rebuild his crushed body. The process included inserting steel plates in his face and metal rods in his legs.

TRAGEDY STRIKES

On February 2, 1992, Jason was still recovering, when an exhausted Sally Jessy and Karl were awakened at 5 AM by their longtime producer/friend, Burt Dubrow. He told them that their daughter, Allison, was dead. It seemed that on February 1, Allison, 33,

Sally Jessy Raphael interviewing actress Gloria Lorin on "Sally Jessy Raphael."

and her boyfriend, a 45-year-old computer engineer, went to stay at her mother's private residence behind the Isaac Stover Inn in Bucks County, Pennsylvania. During the night, the boyfriend woke and realized Allison wasn't breathing. On the bedside table was a bottle of rum and painkilling pills she used for a recurrent back problem. He called the paramedics at 3:23 AM. Seven minutes later, they arrived. After trying to revive her for a half-hour, she was rushed to Doylestown Hospital where she was pronounced dead.

Initially, there was much speculation whether 5'10", 190 pound Allison had committed suicide. Having trained as a gourmet chef, she had worked at several top restaurants, until a bad back caused her to quit and to return to living with her parents at the time of her death. She was known to have a long history of depression, alcoholism and massive weight gains. However, after the autopsy, the coroner ruled that the death "was a tragic accident." Per the official report, Allison was judged to have died "from respiratory arrest," caused by an inadvertent mixture of drink, (over the counter and prescription) medication, and from the results of being a chronic heavy smoker.

Allison's funeral service was held on February 4, 1992 at Manhattan's Riverside Memorial Chapel. Among the more than 200 who attended were Phil Donahue, Joan Rivers and Geraldo Rivera. Additionally, Sally Jessy and Karl held a special private service in the hospital where Jason was recuperating, so he could attend this family tribute for Allison. After her daughter's death, Sally Jessy went into seclusion with her family. She resumed taping her talk program as of February 17, 1992. At the end of that program, she told viewers, "I'd like to take these last couple of minutes of the show to share with you my memories of Allie." She showed a montage of photos of Allison and herself.

GOOD RATINGS

Having endured such double pain, life returned to "normal" for Sally Jessy. However, at the end of May 1992, Raphael hosted an emotion-packed TV outing. At the end of the hour, J.J. walked out on stage. In the studio audience were the doctors, nurses, ambulance workers, et al. who had all contributed to saving her son's life. A tearful Raphael told them: "I owe all of you a big apology. I've taken every opportunity over the years to knock the medical profession [especially in regard to her father's heart treatment and surgery]. Someone once told me that you don't like doctors until you need one. Boy, were they right. You saved my son's life and for that I'll be eternally grateful."

Anyone who thought the media circus was over, was wrong. In June 1992, the press reported growing friction between Sally Jessy and her mending son. She wanted J.J. to enroll at a summer program at a New England school. She said she would pay for the education, allow him to keep his car, credit cards and to live rent free. He refused the offer. In a mood of "tough love" against his regime of sleeping all day and partying all night, she made him leave home.

A month later, he was in another car accident, this one caused by a woman failing to stop at an intersection stop sign. This time, J.J. was uninjured. (Ironically, the crack-up occurred about four miles from the site of his earlier car crash.) A few months later, Jason was back with his family, now having agreed to attend college. However, that did not happen as he had to undergo additional surgery due to gangrene in his legs.

Thereafter, he moved into his own apartment in New York City and began working as a shoe store salesman. Meanwhile, Michelle Kramer, 20, one of the two passengers in Jason's car that fateful January 1992 day, had filed a multi-million dollar law suit against J.J. and Sally Jessy. The plaintiff alleged that, as a result of the young man's careless driving, she had been injured critically. (She claimed that due to the crash, she had suffered several broken bones, hospitalization, memory loss, etc.)

BOUNCING BACK

Bad luck continued to haunt Sally Jessy in the fall of 1992. A favored uncle passed away. She had painful liposuction surgery to tone up her midriff area, as well as new cosmetic surgery to her face to redefine the cosmetic changes she had had done to her face earlier in the year (which for a time had left her face stiff and somewhat lopsided). While Raphael and her husband were on a three-week European vacation, thieves stole $130,000 in jewelry from her hotel room.

By year's end, resilient Sally Jessy, was back to her normal pace, performing twenty hours weekly between her TV and radio schedule. As always, she was her infectiously blunt and honest self, intent on being "the common man...the common woman." She says she has no intention of slowing down the pace. She remains level-headed about her belated success, which she acknowledges is not on the same plateau as that of later-arriving Oprah Winfrey. As to Raphael's fame, Sally Jessy accepts that it "is just a moment in time. Every path that goes up also goes down. If you don't have a hobby or close family and friends, then you are pretty sad."

TV & CABLE SERIES:
A.M. Miami (Miami local, 1969-1974)
In Touch with Sally Jessy Raphael [Sally Jessy Raphael] (St. Louis local, 1983-1986)
Sally Jessy Raphael (Syndicated, 1986-)

Chapter 20
GERALDO RIVERA

"I've come to the conclusion that for any writer to write a positive story about me now, it would be an act of such tremendous personal courage that I can't expect it. Bashing me is trendy...."
—Geraldo Rivera

"I will never do the prudent things, when I think the right thing is different.... I keep a high profile because I refuse to change my basic approach to life. I refuse to be like others because I don't see what they are doing as being necessarily better than what I do."
—Geraldo Rivera

Of all of today's TV talk show hosts (including bombastic newcomer Howard Stern), five foot, eleven inch, 160-pound Geraldo Rivera is the most controversial. Little in his professional or personal life has ever been done simply or quietly. (Even his mixed ethnic background—he is half-Hispanic, half-Jewish—has caused contention for and from Rivera.) He thrives on being aggressive, brash and super tenacious, and is never happier than when stirring up a major storm.

Whether it be a righteous expose of a decrepit state mental institution or jumping into a free-for-all with skinheads, Rivera the warrior is always eager to take on the challenge. Sometimes he is praised for his efforts. On other occasions he is denounced as the childish, egotistical king of "Trash TV." Whatever the case, he unfailingly emerges from the headlined situation as its center of attention.

If you asked Geraldo, he would classify himself as a seasoned, idealistic exponent of advocacy journalism, with a high allergy to social injustice. According to some critics, such a title is debatable. Highly-regarded news analyst David Brinkley said once, "I never thought of Geraldo Rivera as a reporter." And Tom Shales (*Washington Post*) has labeled him "The Jerry Lewis of journalism" who is "Pugnacious, argumentative, given to fantasies of martyrdom." On the other hand, genre peer Phil Donahue contends, "He's a good reporter and I'm proud to compete with him." Former co-worker Barbara Walters has championed Rivera: "He is one of those people who really cares, and it shows. There is no one quite like Geraldo, and I mean that in the best possible way." Another "20/20" associate, Hugh Downs, observed, "He is easily outraged by injustice and it's a measure of the man that he gets more outraged about injustice against somebody else than against himself."

A REAL CASANOVA
In another mark of the man, Geraldo is definitely the most sexually charismatic of present-day TV journalists/emcees/hosts. *TV Guide* agreed that "Walking down the street with Geraldo is like walking down the street with Elvis." He has that self-centered magnetism and rugged good looks which

have propelled his career for decades. He has long thrived on being the Casanova of the Airwaves, projecting the same macho charm that made Errol Flynn, another womanizer, such a favorite with female viewers.

For many years, being the king of the boudoir and adding a few more notches to his belt seemed to be one of his major reasons for existence. The fact that, at any given moment, he might have been married or involved in a "committed" relationship, never seemed to bother hedonistic Rivera. (In recent years, since his latest marriage, and especially since becoming a father again in 1992, he has worked to put that image/lifestyle behind him.)

Above all, Geraldo Rivera is an opportunistic survivor. Like a chameleon, he has shed many skins, including his excessive male chauvinism, as he has matured and times have changed. Being a born ringmaster of TV news circuses, he has a native sense of what will keep him in the limelight and stir up the ratings, no matter how tactless the approach or how gauche the results. Without a doubt, Geraldo Rivera, the news follower, will be a newsmaker for years to come.

He was born on July 3, 1943 at Beth Israel Medical Center in New York City, the son of Allen Cruz Rivera and Lillian (Friedman) Rivera. (The Riveras already had one child, Irene, and later there would be another daughter, Sharon, and a son, Craig.) Even at birth, Geraldo was causing controversy. His mother, whose forebears were East European Jews, had insisted that the birth certificate read "Gerald Miguel Riviera." She wanted to de-emphasize her son's Hispanic ethnic background so he could avoid being a victim of prejudice. Similarly, before she agreed to marry Cruz Rivera, a native of San Juan, Puerto Rico, she had made him add "Allen" to his first name. Years later, the adult Geraldo would reflect, "If you add them together, I'm actually a one man majority.... [But being Puerto Rican and Jewish] are two distinctive identities and it was very difficult for me as a kid to handle them both. So I guess I compromised by being one or the other at various times in my life."

THE EARLY YEARS

The Riveras were a hard-working blue collar family. Cruz, at one period or another was a taxi driver, dishwasher and diner counterman. At the time of Gerald's birth, he worked for a defense plant in the cafeteria kitchen. Lilly was employed sometimes as a waitress. During the boy's first seven years, the family lived in Williamsburg, a poor neighborhood of Brooklyn. In 1950, they moved to West Babylon on Long Island. Until the age of eight, Gerald was a bedwetter, was underweight, had allergies and was asthmatic. As a part-time job, he sold and delivered the *Long Island Press*. When he was eleven, his brother Craig was born. Soon thereafter, Cruz's nephew, Wilfredo, came from Puerto Rico to live with the Riv(i)eras.

For his thirteenth birthday, Lilly insisted that Gerald have a Bar Mitzvah. Not long after "becoming a man," Gerald experienced first hand anti-Semitism when a group of local neo-Nazis rallied outside the small local temple and verbally insulted the Jews inside. It was also during this time that Mrs. Rivera discovered that her husband was having a long-term affair with a cafeteria co-worker. For a spell, she and her children moved to Brooklyn, but eventually reconciled with her errant spouse. For his sixteenth summer, Gerald visited his paternal grandparents in San Juan, and for the first time, developed a strong sense of his Puerto Rican heritage.

By the time Gerald entered West Babylon High School, he had matured into a tough kid, which allowed him, later, to be co-captain of the football team. He also gravitated away from the mild-mannered Corner Boys (which mostly just "hung out") to joining the Valve Grinders, a car club. As such, he got involved in stealing hub cabs, which lead to taking tires and then escalated to borrowing the cars themselves. However, he soon got caught, which cured him of this habit. He made his local TV debut ("Herb Shelton's TV Dance Party") as an upperclassman, and admitted: "I had a craving for the ladies, even in high school. My basic goal was to keep one steady and one on the side, a strategy I would follow well into adulthood."

Since the principal at West Babylon High had been a naval officer during World War II, he encouraged Gerald to attend New York State Maritime College at Fort Schuyler. After taking remedial courses in English and math at a Brooklyn community college, Riv(i)era was accepted at the military institution. While there, he was forced to be (and soon thrived on being) very disciplined both in the classroom and on the athletic field.

A WILDCAT

Gerald quit the Maritime College after his sophomore year, repelled by the regimen and by the torments of an upper classman. As a lark, he and a pal drove cross country and enrolled at the University of Arizona in Tucson. With a free summer before classes began, they proceeded on to Los Angeles where Riv(i)era worked in a clothing store. That September his friend remained in California, while Gerald went back to Tucson.

Painfully sensitive about his mixed background, Gerald tried several approaches while on campus to ingratiate himself with his fellow students. At one point, he let classmates believe he was the son of a prosperous restaurateur of Spanish descent. At another juncture, he tried to be the super WASP. ("Here I was, this little hood from New York with the Brooklyn Spanish-American accent. I wanted to be like them, to belong. So I said my name was Jerry Rivers and I did everything I could to please them. But they never accepted me.") Eventually, unable to mingle in fraternity circles, he took up with the mostly Mexican teammates from his soccer team. He smoked a lot of marijuana during these campus years and, for cash, would take exams for others.

During his senior year (1964-1965) at the University, Gerald met Linda Coblentz, a transfer student from North Carolina. By then, he and a pal, Vic Furio, had made an imaginative pact. So as not to be drafted for Vietnam duty, they would each marry, and then go to work as vacuum/Fuller Brush sales agents in Africa. A week before Gerald was to marry Linda, his buddy joined the Marines. Nevertheless, on August 20, 1965 Riv(i)era and Linda married in Scottsdale, Arizona, where her parents lived. The newlyweds moved to California, living in a motel in Huntington Beach, while Gerald went back to work at the clothing shop. Tiring of this, the couple decided to try New York City. In route to the East Coast, Mr. Coblentz suggested that his son-in-law go to law school.

By the start of 1966, Riv(i)era had been accepted at Brooklyn Law School for that fall, and the couple was living in Manhattan's East Village. That summer he worked at a South Bronx department store in the ladies' cottons department. After completing his first year at law school successfully, he won an internship in the Manhattan District Attorney's office, working for Frank Hogan. Meanwhile, Linda was taking art classes and waitressing. During his second law school year, he had to help the family business.

TOUGH TIMES

Cruz now owned a 24-hour diner in Long Island that was failing. After attending classes all day, Gerald would work at the restaurant at night as a short-order cook, with Linda filling in as a waitress. Despite everyone's efforts, the diner closed and Cruz declared bankruptcy. Gerald maneuvered to save the family's Long Island house, but, thereafter, his father was a shadow of his former self.

It was in early 1968, that Gerald and Linda broke up their marriage. By that summer, he had his first bachelor pad and found a job working as legal assistant for the Harlem Assertion of Rights. By now, he was known as Geraldo Rivera. He had grown a moustache which, he says, "has become both a professional trademark and a personal symbol of my ethnic rebirth." He also joined New York's Puerto Rican Bar Association. After graduating from law school (19th out of a class of 330), he was accepted to a federally funded program which trained/sponsored lawyers to advocate for the poor. Already militantly pro-minority, Rivera helped to start the Black and Brown Lawyers Caucus to equalize pay for black/white recruits to this program.

Geraldo was assigned to the Community Action for Legal Services (CALS), working from their lower Manhattan office. Meanwhile, he bought for next to nothing a small tenement building on Avenue C. As an outraged champion of victims of discrimination, Rivera was among those of the Black and Brown Caucus who descended on the Office of Economic Opportunity in Washington, D.C. in November of 1969. For his efforts, as well as many others of the group, he was arrested. Also that fall, he became involved with the Young Lords, mainland-born Puerto Rican activists, becoming their chief attorney.

In 1970, when his CALS internship ended, Geraldo had already developed high visibility as an activist. His reputation led to a meeting between Rivera and Al Primo, news director at WABC-TV, New York City's Channel 7. Primo needed a Puerto Rican to complement his ethnically diverse news team. Geraldo had been earning $200 a week for CALS; Primo promised him $300 weekly to start, and to raise it $50 per year for the next five years.

HEARD BUT NOT SEEN

To prepare for his new career, Geraldo took courses at Columbia Journalism School. During this period, he ended a relationship with a divorced woman attorney who had a legal abortion. Then he began dating a black woman, a fellow journalist at Columbia. (She would depart for a Chicago posting and, two years later, would die in a plane crash.)

It was in September 1970, that Geraldo did his first story for Channel 7. He covered the losing candidate in the state race for nomination for Attorney General. The news story went on the air, but was edited so Rivera was not seen. Soon thereafter, he developed a method in interviewing that became his trademark. He had to interview a group of truant kids. Rather than be the typical standoffish, objective TV journalist, he used a hands-on approach, casually sitting on the tenement steps with them. In October 1970, he accepted a non-salaried post on the Board of Corrections, but had to resign shortly thereafter, as there was a conflict of interest with his newscasting chores. Geraldo's resignation letter exposing the bad conditions of local jails was printed in the *New York Times*.

Within a few months of becoming an instant journalist, Geraldo had gained a unique reputation as a popular street reporter. Meanwhile, he had earned the enmity of several co-workers, who thought it self-serving for Rivera to adopt the posture of the shaggy-haired, jeans-clad broadcaster. (He was a far cry from the usual media journalist, with the trademark blow-dried hair and the *de rigeur* raincoat.)

Rivera's sudden reputation as an "opportunistic" newshound arose from a February 1971 assignment. He arrived at the Greenwich Hotel to cover a fashion show. He and his camera crew appeared just as a man was about to jump from the roof of the hotel. Soon after the mishap, the victim's twin brother rushed out of the building and blurted out the whole story to Geraldo. This sensational news account was aired and it led Rivera to demand the station renegotiate his salary. Before long, Rivera, the self-styled ghetto reporter "was out to change the world." One of his TV news crusade was a three-part feature, "Drug Crisis in East Harlem," which later formed the basis for a half-hour special. As his journalistic fame increased, his salary likewise increased to $800 weekly, and, by the fall of 1971, was up to a $50,000 a year.

OUT OF THE ORDINARY

Not all of Geraldo's reporting focused on the downtrodden. When John Shubeck left the station's culture beat in 1971, Geraldo inherited the spot. Usually this was considered a fluff assignment, but Rivera tried something different (for the time). His first celebrity interview was with singer Engelbert Humperdinck. Rather than use a studio or hotel room for the chat, Rivera walked with Engelbert along city streets for the conversation. For his spotlight on singer Johnny Mathis he set up a baskeball hoop in a room at the Waldorf-Astoria Hotel and filmed his interview as they played one-on-one basketball. Now hobnobbing with celebrities and high society, Rivera met Edith (Edie) Vonnegut, daughter of famed novelist Kurt Vonnegut, at a cocktail party. She was about 22, he was almost 28. Within a day, the couple were living together. That December, he and Edie married at Kurt's house in Barnstable, Massachusetts.

Reviewing this period of his life, Rivera would assess, "There has never been a time—then or since—when I was more original or creative. I was constantly probing, constantly experimenting...." He and his wife lived in a duplex apartment on the top two floors of his East Village brownstone. It was on January 1972 that the (in)famous Willowbrook story first broke. A radical doctor friend of Geraldo's called to inform him that a social worker had been fired from the Willowbrook State School on Staten Island. She had been let go from this institution for the mentally retarded for her encouragement of parents with children there to organize in order to improve conditions.

Rivera leaped into action, staging a commando raid with his camera team, to gain sensational footage of the deplorable conditions at the school. His actions resulted in several TV news pieces on this sprawling hell house facility. The adverse publicity thus generated caused Governor Nelson Rockefeller to restore $20 million to the Department of Hygiene's slashed budget. Meanwhile, crusader Rivera had gained national attention. He made his first appearance on network TV, a guest on Dick Cavett's late night talk show. This outing led to Geraldo supervising a half-hour prime time special on Willowbrook.

The Willowbrook expose created an amazing snowball effect. Random House advanced Geraldo $15,000 to write *Willowbrook: A Report on How It Is and Why It Doesn't Have to Be That Way* (1972). He helped to set up the One-to-One Foundation, a charity to lobby for, and help, the mentally retarded. In his new celebrity posture, Geraldo became friendly with Marian Javitz, a former actress, and then currently the wife of Jacob Javitz, the United States Senator from New York. Rivera claims they began a hush-hush affair which lasted until 1985.

LOOKING FOR A CAUSE

As a member of Channel 7's "Eyewitness News" team, Rivera created several hard-hitting TV reports ("Migrants: Dirt Cheap," "The Littlest Junkie"), enhancing his reputation as an advocacy journalist. With his new media stature, he was earning $750-$1,250 per appearance on the lecture circuit. Jumping from cause to cause, he became a supporter of George McGovern in his presidential bid against Richard Nixon.

In October 1972, Geraldo was to appear at a fundraising rally at the Palace Theatre on McGovern's behalf. The station (and the ABC network) told him his appearance would be a conflict of interest. He was suspended, but, not letting the matter rest, he debated the problem on air with the ABC Network News President. Thereafter, he was off the air for three weeks. More damaging to him, the incident established Rivera as an outsider in the network news division. Nevertheless, his agent renegotiated his yearly "Eyewitness News" contract to $350,000.

Increasingly, Rivera was becoming more and more the odd man out. Because he could not get onto network news, he and his agent worked to promote Geraldo through the network's Entertainment division. As part of this drive, he did a highly-rated personality profile on local news with Muhammad Ali. He went to the boxer's training camp in the mountains of Pennsylvania where he was filmed in the ring with Ali.

Determined to prove himself a creditable field journalist, he jumped when ABC News assigned him to go to Chile to the city of Santiago where a coup was underway. (He spoke Spanish and could assist veteran newsman Charles Murphy.) When Rivera interviewed General Ugarte after his bloody victory, the journalist was extremely bullying and arrogant, intent, so he says, on forcing the interviewee's cards. However, by the time this news feature aired, it went by almost unnoticed, since world attention had turned to the Yom Kippur Wars in which some Arab nations were allied against Israel.

ALWAYS AN OUTSIDER

Geraldo and his camera crew flew to Tel Aviv. During his three-week stay there, Geraldo stepped on many toes, but returned with outstanding footage. Nevertheless, all his work there backfired when several fellow journalists accused him of grandstanding. They even insisted he had faked a particular Arab attack so Geraldo could be taped bravely covering the events.

With his wife, Geraldo wrote a children's book, *Miguel Robles: So Far* (1973). However, he and Edie were not getting along well together. In his 1991 autobiography, he would claim that among his many affairs at this time was one with singer/comedian Bette Midler (she disclaimed his version of the circumstances).

Rivera had formed Maravilla (Spanish for "miracle") Productions in 1973 and, for $65,000, produced a pilot of a hip late night magazine show. The "Good Night America" pilot aired on July 30, 1973 and got a thirteen week commitment beginning in early 1974. *Variety* acknowledged the "enormous potential" of his "soft spoken affability and hard-nosed docu[mentary] content" and cited his "awareness concerning the interests, motivations, value standards and language of...'the rock generation.'"

As of April 4, 1974, Rivera's "Good Night America" became an every-other-Thursday run that lasted three years. On the second show, he smoked a marijuana joint during the ninety-minute program. This was a first, but it was censored before the episode was aired. As he traveled around the country filing segments for his high-profile late night offering, he spent less and less time on local news.

ANOTHER ONE BITES THE DUST

By now jet-setting Geraldo's marriage to Edie was in name only, and his extra-marital dating accelerated. (He and "Pie" would eventually divorce in 1975.) By mid-year, he was doing a 2-3 minute daily network radio commentary, but before the end of the year he had lost this outlet. When ABC-TV's "Good Morning America" went on the air in competition to NBC's "Today Show" Geraldo was one of the inaugural reporters on the show. His appearance there led WABC-TV to give Rivera an ultimatum to drop out of "Good Morning America" or lose "Eyewitness News." He chose the former which provided a $500,000 annual salary.

As a swinging bachelor, Rivera moved to digs on Central Park West. When not dating the occasional secretary girlfriend, he was seeing Francine LeFrak, the blonde daughter of a billionaire real estate developer. He and Francine became engaged. Nevertheless, he was soon involved with two married women, one a news reporter based in Latin America, the second Sheri Braverman, the wife of a TV producer associated with "Good Night America." In between his complex bedding schedule, he chalked up 200,000 miles of travel in 1976 for his TV work. In the fall of 1976, Geraldo relocated to the west coast to avoid Francine and to pursue Sheri, who by then was separated from her spouse. Together, they rented a beach house near Malibu and, on December 31, 1976, they were married by a rabbi.

Before long, Sheri, who had been employed at Capitol Records for ten years, began running Geraldo's business life, easing out his prior agent. But scarcely had the couple wed, than Geraldo began cheating on his wife. His typical behavior led to their almost divorcing three weeks after they were married. Says Geraldo, "From that moment, she honed her vigilance to an art form." By June 1977 "Good Night America" had left the air. Rivera protested the cancellation so loudly that he was removed from "Good Morning America."

However, Geraldo was out of work for even less than a day. Roone Arledge, the new president of ABC News, contracted him to do special assignments for the network "Evening News." These TV pieces were often biased and impassioned (such as the one on David Berkowitz, Son of Sam) or sensational (e.g., his coverage of Elvis Presley's death in August 1977). With his income assured, Rivera and his wife, bought a $250,000 house on 3 acres in the foothills of Los Angeles's Santa Monica mountains. (This was in addition to the Central Park West apartment which he purchased.) One of the Riveras's neighbors was Barbra Streisand whose then live-in boyfriend was Jon Peters. Peters, an ex-hairstylist turned show business entrepreneur, became good friends with Rivera. It was he who engineered Geraldo's $750,000 yearly contract as chief reporter for "20/20."

BRIGHT YELLOW

"20/20" debuted on June 6, 1978. Geraldo's first story ("Rabbit Kill") was downright sensational: the use of live jack rabbits as bait to train greyhounds for racing at dog tracks. It was an audience-grabber. Later investigative reports from Geraldo focused on Agent Orange, the political situation in Laos, and pharmacies' gouging of customers. It was during this time that Rivera insists he had a brief relationship with Margaret Trudeau, the estranged wife of the Canadian Prime Minister, Pierre Trudeau. She denis any involvement with him.

Geraldo also claims that he pursued a liaison with Liza Minnelli that remained unconsummated because she always backed off at the last minute. Despite his wobbly marriage, on July 2, 1979, Sheri gave birth to their son, Gabriel. Rivera, in his autobiography, relates that after becoming a father, he had a final orgy (with luscious twins) and then entered into a year of being a responsive family man.

In February 1980, Geraldo did a story on "Arson for Profit" for "20/20" that won an Emmy, followed by exposes on a soy-based infant formula, and on the production of faulty aluminum wiring. By this point, Sheri had become his full-time business manager. In the spring of 1980, Ted Turner offered Rivera $500,000 a year to join the fledging Cable News Network (CNN), with company stock as part of the deal. Geraldo declined, when ABC raised his annual salary to $1 million. Even with his affluent status on "20/20," Geraldo remained irreverent. It was not unlike him to appear for a telecast, well-dressed from the waist up, and, unseen by home viewers, wearing gym shorts and sneakers.

As the cock of the walk in mid-1980, Rivera developed an extramarital relationship with C. C. Dyer. A broadcast journalism major from New York University, she was thirteen years his junior and a production assistant on his "20/20" staff. Sheri left New York for California, taking Gabriel with her. As a result, Geraldo became a bi-coastal lover as he sought to maintain both relationships. However, he and Sheri finally divorced in 1984.

ANYTHING FOR RATINGS

One week on "20/20," Rivera might be interviewing Barbra Streisand on the set of YENTL in England; the next doing a follow-up trip to war-torn Lebanon. In later series installments, attention-grabbing Rivera would run with the bulls in Pamplona and would interview New York City subway vigilante, Bernhard Goetz. In 1985, Geraldo claims he had renewed (via a handshake) his "20/20" contract for three years and $3 million.

However, whatever arrangement had been made fell apart in October 1985 when he publicly criticized Arledge Roone for having censored Sylvia Chase's "20/20" piece on John F. Kennedy's and Robert Kennedy's romantic ties with Marilyn Monroe (and her subsequent death). To bolster their cause, Roone *et al* cited other recent indiscretions by Geraldo, including his $200 contribution to a candidate running for mayor on Cape Cod. More damaging was the revelation that Geraldo's staff member/girlfriend C. C. Dyer had allegedly dispatched an ABC messenger to pick up an ounce of marijuana from an acquaintance at CNN to give to a friend.

As a result of the brouhaha, C.C. Dyer resigned and returned home to Buzzards Bay on Cape Cod. Rivera, himself on the verge of being dismissed from the network show, recollects going out in public with long-time friend Marion Javitz. When she discovered he was doing this to legitimize himself, she ended their association and told him to stick by C.C. Eventually, Geraldo resigned from the network and received a cash settlement.

His last "20/20" appearance was on Thanksgiving eve of 1985. His network news farewell included: "I've always been sort of a square peg trying to squeeze into the round hole of network news. Maybe I'll do what my buddy Hugh Downs did when he was my age and went sailing off after the sunset. Eventually, he came back. So will I."

THE INFAMOUS VAULT

At liberty, he attempted to get a job on CBS's "60 Minutes" but was turned down. With a nearly million dollar overhead for his lavish lifestyle, as well as alimony/child support and caring for his parents, Rivera was desperate. He wrote an episode on speculation for "Miami Vice," which was rejected. He did occasional fill in substitute hosting for CNN's "Larry King Live." That cable network now offered him $200,000 annually to do a morning talk show. He rejected it, hoping for a better deal.

Finally, with no options left, he signed for $50,000 as a replacement for Robert Stack to host a two-hour syndicated special on "The Mystery of Al Capone's Vault." For anyone else, that April 27, 1986 assignment would have been just another job; for some it would have been a tremendous career embarrassment (especially when the taped live telecast revealed nothing of consequence in the vault). But not for Rivera, who traded heavily on his "name" to engineer tremendous publicity for the outing. It caused the show to capture a strong 34.2 national rating.

The success of that broadcast led to several offers from syndicators, including the Tribune Syndicate who agreed to pay him well for several future specials: "American Vice: The Doping of a Nation" (1986), "Innocence Lost: The Erosion of American Childhood" (1987), "The Sons Of Scarface: The New Mafia" (1987). He also became a regular contributor for "Entertainment Tonight." When he did "Murder: Live from Death Row" (1988), *People* magazine rated it "the single most disgusting and abhorrent event in television." On a personal level, after long avoiding a permanent commitment to C.C., the couple finally married in July 1987 and they honeymooned in Sicily. In the fall of 1987, Geraldo's father died of heart trouble, with his widowed mother thereafter residing permanently in Sarasota, Florida.

In 1986, Rivera had taped a pilot for a daily talk show, similar to the format of Phil Donahue's and Oprah Winfrey's. The show sold and bowed in the fall of 1987. In true Geraldo fashion, his show soon developed a reputation for being highly controversial (some said trashy), exploitive and frequently prurient. However, the tastelessness created its own brand of interest. His most memorable show would, of course, be the confrontation between white supremacists and black activist Roy Innis.

Rivera got in the middle and came away with a broken nose. He proudly displayed his bandaged proboscis for days thereafter. Nothing was too sacred or innocuous for Rivera's TV forum, including a visit to a topless donut shop and Bad Girls Week. By 1990, finally heeding his critics, a chastised Rivera said that some of his shows' themes were too much and that "I'm embarrassing myself." He should have remembered that when he agreed to appear, as himself, in the tawdry feature film THE BONFIRES OF THE VANITIES.

OVEREXPOSED

By 1991, Geraldo and C.C. had been living in Monmouth County, New Jersey for two years. They had purchased an old Victorian house (called Rough Point) by the Neversiak River. That year, his "Geraldo" became the first regularly scheduled American TV program to be broadcast in Russia. That fall his nationally syndicated primetime show, "Now It Can Be Told," went on the air, packaged by his Investigative News Group company.

His brother Craig was a reporter on the short-lived series, which failed to live up to such TV rivals as "Inside Edition" or "A Current Affair." Far more sensational was Rivera's latest published book, his autobiography entitled *Exposing Myself.* Several unhappy subjects of the best-selling tome insisted that the author had "an overactive imagination." *TV Guide* labeled the volume "Geraldo's Latest Low Blow." Profits from the successful publication went to charity.

Geraldo Rivera on location for "Geraldo."

If people thought his memoirs were tacky, so were Rivera's TV show topics during the crucial sweeps weeks of late 1991: Cannibalistic Serial Killers, Women Who Love Mass Murderers, Rat Pack Sex, etc. One of his more spectacular participation stunts occurred on the February 1992 show during which Geraldo subjected himself to liposuction on stage, with some of the removed fatty tissue used to smooth out his facial wrinkles.

There was wry humor to Rivera taking the role of a talk show host and author who is murdered for his lifestyle excesses on the TV movie: PERRY MASON: THE CASE OF THE RECKLESS ROMEO (May 5, 1992). However, it seemed *deja vu* when Geraldo got in a new scuffle with sixty neo-Nazis in August 1992. He had flown to Janesville, Wisconsin to cover a summit of "hate groups" for his TV show. When one of the racists called Rivera names and kicked him in the left leg, it set the explosive talk show host off, and he got into a fight with the heckler.

The end result was his being handcuffed and arrested, along with his victim/assailant. His staff who, naturally, taped the entire encounter, bailed him out. Later, all charges were dropped. The headlined-event became a focal point of his fall TV season, with the host insisting, "I did nothing I regret. I'm a man with pride and dignity and I'm not ashamed about standing up to bullies. And I gave better than I got—by far." To celebrate his 1,000th episode on the air (September 21, 1992), Geraldo hosted a "They Said It Couldn't Be Done!" party aboard a yacht birthed in the East River. The celebrity turnout included most of his Manhattan-based genre show rivals. By now, Geraldo's TV show was syndicated in 199 markets.

ON A DIFFERENT LEVEL

On November 7, 1992, C.C. gave birth to their daughter, Isabella Holmes Rivera, at a Manhattan hospital. What made this event so noteworthy was the fact that on his TV program, as well as others, the Riveras had discussed their long-time efforts (including her several operations and test-tube procedures) to become parents. "Coincidentally," the same night he became a proud father again, Geraldo could be seen playing himself on two TV sitcoms ("Empty Nest" and "Nurses").

When asked these days how he feels about the caliber of his TV show, Rivera reacted, "A lot of critics simply seem to forget what I am. What I do isn't 'Nightline.' It's a program that runs at four in the afternoon with an audience that's two-third women. So I'm criticized on the Ted Koppel scale, but I exist in a Phil Donahue world." As to his future, Geraldo, fifty-ish, says, "I have never had a life plan. I never thought I would be on TV in the first place. Life is full of random chances, kind of like a day at Coney Island."

TV & CABLE SERIES:
Nightly News [Eyewitness News] (New York City local, 1970-1975)
Good Night America (ABC, 1973-1977)
Good Morning America (ABC, 1975-1977)
20/20 (ABC, 1978-1985)
Geraldo (Geraldo Live] (Syndicated, 1987-)
Now It Can Be Told (Syndicated, 1991-1992)

FEATURE FILMS:
The Bonfires of the Vanities (1990)
Perry Mason: The Case of the Reckless Romeo (NBC, 1992) [TV movie]

Chapter 21
JOAN RIVERS

Dishing is what Joan Rivers does best. As "Queen of the Barbed One-Liners," she is one of the brashest insult comediennes in the profession. Because of her chosen work, she equates laughs with money in the bank. Nothing is too insulting and she has willingly broken taboos on many subjects. Nor is anything too intimate (her life or the audience's) for the sharp-tongued, 5'3" blonde to dissect. She has made her fortune with faultfinding self-assessments. However, when she discovers a celebrity target full of foibles and flaws (e.g., Queen Elizabeth, Elizabeth Taylor or Madonna), that individual better watch out. acid-tongued Joan River is both tenacious and an expert harpooner.

Known as "The Mouth," Rivers is a living exponent of her trademarked expression "Can we talk?" It was only a matter of time before this non-stop gabber would turn her addiction to chatter to the talk show forum. Since the late 1960s, she has hosted several such TV programs, honing her

Joan Rivers promoting her comedy album "What Becomes a Semi Legend Most"

skills as she learned on the job. When asked what makes her different from other such practitioners, she says, "I think my humor. Even at its most serious, the humor comes through. It is lighter and more entertaining than the others. I think that sets us apart."

In her decades in show business, Joan Rivers has not confined herself to standup comedy. She has authored best-selling books and scripted TV movies and theatrical films. She has starred on both Broadway and TV, directed her own feature picture, and made several comedy albums. More recently, she has turned to a new arena: hosting a cable network shopping program.

As a multi-talented entertainer, Rivers admits that her love and compulsion for the industry began way back. "Since my earliest memories, my dream has been to make a living doing that one thing—performing on a stage—which made me feel I belonged, made me feel adored and, paradoxically, safe." According to Joan, "show business is a tar baby. If you touch it, you can't let go. When I started out, if an audience would laugh at me one night, I would chase that high for another three months." Regarding her professional determination and will power, she observes, "They say you need three things in show business: talent, luck and drive. And luckily, I have the drive. I'm one of those people who just has to go on."

TWO FACES OF JOAN

In the spotlight, Joan is a gutsy, riveting personality. Out of the limelight, it is a far different situation. She confesses, "On stage it's easy. I just go into another person—the mouthy neighbor who says everything that one thinks. The problem comes when people expect that other woman to show up at a dinner party and in walks quiet me." There is also the matter of her hyper-vanity. Over the years, she has transformed herself from 1950s chubby and a bit dumpy to 1990s petite and chic.

She may be concerned about her age (shaving off a few years), forever reshaping her body and face (admitting publicly to several cosmetic surgery operations) and addicted to shopping for the latest fashions (you should see her lavish wardrobe closets!). However, her primary fetish is her weight. Joan claims, "My whole life is fat! I've worried about fat since I was eleven. Five pounds can make the difference between whether I'm happy or sad that day."

One of Rivers's best assets is her ability to survive. She stuck it out through a long, unrewarding apprenticeship, which included a suicide attempt in a moment of depression. That is par for such a chancy profession. However, having reached a degree of acclaim, she suffered several career setbacks that would have discouraged most other people. But she kept on. Then in the mid-1980s, at the height of her popularity, she underwent two humiliating ordeals.

Long assumed to be a heir apparent to Johnny Carson when he left "The Tonight Show," she found it was still a man's world. Carson and the NBC network favored a male successor. Their decision led to her leaving her fill-in chores on "The Tonight Show." When she did, long-time mentor Carson, turned his back on her and the industry chill was freezing. She bounced back, or so she thought, hosting her own competing late night talk. She was on the air for less than a season before Fox Broadcasting dismissed her. Her bosses at the struggling new network made it quite apparent that she had been fired.

Joan somehow coped with those high-voltage embarrassments. Then, soon afterwards, her long-time husband, Edgar Rosenberg, committed suicide. His death heightened the tensions between Rivers and her only child, Melissa. This conflict led to a well-publicized parting of the ways between widowed mother and teen-aged daughter. With the abandonment cycle now complete, industry insiders insisted the former Joan Molinsky of Brooklyn was down and out. Not so. She bounced back both professionally and personally.

HIGH EXPECTATIONS

Joan Alexandra Molinsky was born in Brooklyn, New York on June 8, 1933. She was the younger of two daughters (the older was Barbara) born to Meyer Molinsky and his wife, Beatrice (Grushman) Molinsky. Beatrice and her sister had fled Russia with their mother, Hannah, in 1917 and settled in New York City. Hannah became a midwife and took in boarders, while the two daughters sweated at sewing machines in a blouse factory. Hannah's husband remained in Russia, but her two sons, Alex and Sacha soon came to the United States.

Alex became a dentist and moved the family to a big apartment on Riverside Drive. In 1928, Beatrice met Meyer Molinsky, also a Russian Jewish refugee. He was then a poor young man just out of medical school. After a three-week courtship they married and settled in Brooklyn. Having known elegance back in Russia, Beatrice had high expectations of her spouse. However, he was far less aggressive than his ambitious wife. He was content to be a general practitioner treating the poor, while she demanded much more.

Early in life, Joan became aware of the household friction between her mother and father. (Both her parents reacted to their tremendous fear of poverty in far different ways: Meyer was a penny-pincher, Beatrice craved luxuries and fancy residential addresses to prove to one and all that she was not a failure.) It was from Meyer that his younger daughter learned her sense of humor, taking delight, even as a toddler, in mimicking his patients. Beatrice insisted the family budget be stretched to allow Barbara, and later Joan, to attend the Brooklyn Ethical Culture School rather than go to a public facility. The determined Mrs. Molinsky also saw to it that Joan, like her sister, took elocution, piano and violin lessons. This was all in preparation for a life in the upper classes.

When Joan was ten, Mrs. Molinsky marched down to her husband's medical office, and without informing him, raised his fee schedule. A battle ensued. When Joan and her sister returned home that day, their mother had vanished. She left a note, "Be good and I love you both. I'll come and get you when I can." Meyer's stern mother, Manye, moved in to run the household. A week later, Beatrice reappeared—defeated. Joan claims that then and there she determined to be a career woman who did not have to depend on anyone.

SORTING IT OUT

When Joan was eleven, she sent a photograph of herself to Metro-Goldwyn-Mayer, but never had a response from the Hollywood studio. About age twelve, when she went to summer camp in Vermont, she began calling herself J. Sondra Meredith, thinking that would make her more ritzy. In the seventh grade, she switched to the less progressive and more basic Adelphia Academy. However, she carried her emotional baggage with her to the new school in Brooklyn. She was tremendously upset at being chunky (with big hips) and developed into a first-class nerd who founded the school newspaper.

To escape being such a loner and outsider, Joan joined the school drama club and took acting classes. She dreamed of becoming a movie star. At fifteen, she saw Ray Bolger in the Broadway musical "Where's Charley" and became convinced that she wanted a show business career. Next, she entered a *Photoplay* magazine acting contest to "Discover the Stars of Tomorrow." She was one of ten local finalists and came in second, winning a year's subscription to the magazine.

In her mid-teens, Joan took classes twice weekly for a year at the Edith Bector School of the Theater on Riverside Drive. It was through the Bector School that she learned that Universal Pictures needed extras for a new Jack Carson picture, MR. UNIVERSE (1951) shooting partially on location in New York City. Joan got a part as a walk-on, being paid $15.56 a day.

By the time Joan graduated high school, the battling Molinskys had relocated to more prestigious Larchmont, where they now owned their own home. Somewhat brainwashed by her mother's social ambitions, Joan abandoned temporarily her plans to become an actress. Instead, she enrolled at Connecticut College for Women (where her sister was attending). On campus, Joan discovered she was of two minds. Part of her was conservative and materialistic like her mother, part of her was down to earth like her father. But neither Joan liked pretending, as her mother had taught her, to be really rich and well-bred. After her second year there, she transferred to Barnard College, which allowed her to live at home. She became an English literature major, studied anthropology and took acting courses. At school, she appeared in productions of "Juno and the Paycock" and "Mourning Becomes Electra."

INTO FASHION

Having graduated Phi Beta Kappa from Barnard in 1954, she was accepted by the Westport County Playhouse to join their summer apprentice staff. However, with pressure from home and her own insecurities (about her weight, her looks, her talent) she backed out. Instead, she joined the executive training program at Lord and Taylor's Department Store in Manhattan. (Earlier in her teens, she had had summer jobs at Wanamaker's Department Store, realizing "that money was a way out of the prison for all of us.") In 1955, when she was 22, Joan was hired away by the Bond Stores to be a fashion coordinator, at a very respectable $150 weekly salary.

Her first adult romance was with David Fitelson, the son of a theatrical attorney, who was working for the Theatre Guild. However, her relationship was far more serious with Jimmy Sanger, the son of the merchandise manager at Bond's. Although still entranced with David, she persuaded herself (with others' help) that she really cared for Sanger. They married in 1957, but she discovered quickly that he was very stubborn. ("Our marriage license turned out to be a learner's permit," she would quip.) After six months, the marriage was annulled.

Finally determined to do what she wanted, Joan began her show business career. Her angered parents cut her off financially. Having attended typing/stenography school, She took occasional temporary jobs to support herself. Her sister Barbara, who had become an attorney, helped out. After months of making fruitless rounds of casting offices, an actor pal introduced her to a director casting an off-off-off Broadway showcase of "Seawood."

In the drama, performed in the attic above the director's apartment, Joan appeared as a lesbian. The object of her affection on stage was another young Brooklyn-born performer named Barbra Streisand. This assignment was followed by little seen revivals of "Bernardine" and "See the Jaguar." Socially, she began dating Nick Clemente, an ex-Marine who wanted to be an actor.

PEPPER JANUARY

By the late 1950s, Joan had concluded that becoming a comedian might be easier than winning a Broadway role. She auditioned for Jack Rollins, who specialized in managing comedians, such as Woody Allen. However, he told her she was NOT ready. Eventually, she found work through a different agent who proved to be very seedy. Billed as Pepper January she began her career in Boston at a strip joint, emceeing a show filled with exotic dancers. However, she got fired after only one night. A brief booking in Springfield, Massachusetts followed. After that, her ten-per-center gave up on her, demanding the return of all rights to the act name ("Pepper January, Comedy with Spice").

To survive financially, Joan became a temporary fashion coordinator for Claire Mallison and Associates, a Manhattan company who were photographers' reps and ran a photo studio. Meanwhile, she kept auditioning for managers and agents. One of these try-outs was for a casting agent named Tony Rivers. Joan decided to adopt the surname of this American Indian and she became Joan Rivers.

There followed a brief stint as a magician's assistant in Canada. Then Joan met and became friendly with Treva Silverman, an aspiring comedy writer. With Treva's boyfriend at the piano and Joan singing, the team performed in a revue (written by Silverman) in the Catskills. Occasionally, there would be minor club jobs, but the joints were generally tawdry and, most frequently, Joan was fired.

In a moment of reconciliation with his rebellious daughter. Dr. Molinsky negotiated for Joan a booking at his country club in New Rochelle. For a time, Joan alternated between living at home, and then moving out. Sometimes, accompanied by her boyfriend Nick, she would employ a series of ruses to obtain free lodging at various Manhattan hotels.

SMALL STEPS

By 1960, Joan had formed a truce with her parents and was back at home. She was on Broadway briefly in a revue showcase, "Talent '60." After that, she had minor club engagements which ranged from performing at Cherry Grove in Fire Island to a gig at a Catholic church in Queens. She managed an appearance on Jack Paar's TV talk show. Although she thought she had done a good job, the mercurial Paar did not like her.

Next, Rivers joined "Broadway USA," a USO show which toured Korea, Japan and several Pacific Islands. The following year, she was back on Broadway in the brief-running revue, "Talent '61." Joan hoped things were improving when her agent maneuvered her into an audition as replacement to Anna Marie Alberghetti in "Carnival," a Broadway musical. After she croaked "Just in Time," director Gower Champion shouted out: "Hold it! Why are you here? And, what's more important, why am I here?"

Finally, after months of trying, Joan was allowed to perform on talent night at the chic Bon Soir Club in Greenwich Village. As a result, the management hired her as the opening act for a summer revue. A physician she met through her family, told her to look up his brother, an agent at the William Morris firm. This, in turn, led to her being hired for the Second City, a Chicago-based improvisational troupe.

She arrived in the Windy City in mid-September 1961. The tightly-knit cast at Second City included Avery Schreiber, Hamilton Camp, Tony Holland and Del Close. It took quite a while for Joan the outsider, inexperienced in extemporaneous comedy, to be accepted by the troupe. Nevertheless, as her self-confidence flourished, she "came to believe, totally—for the first time in my life—that my personal, private sense of humor, my view of the world, could make smart adults laugh." For a while in Chicago, she dated Dick Schaal, a late arrival to the Second City cast. (He later married actress Valerie Harper.) From her Second City experiences, Joan learned "to short-circuit thought and hitch impulses directly to [my] tongue."

LIBERATED COMEDY

Returning to New York, Joan had made peace again with her parents and was living with them in Larchmont. Hoping for a break-through, Rivers made the round of Greenwich Village clubs and began performing at the Showplace. By the winter of 1962, she had become liberated as a

Joan Rivers of the early 1970s.

comedian, gaining inspiration from nonconformist comedian Lenny Bruce. Following Bruce's lead, she "began freeing my mouth, letting things pop out of it, letting it bring a bit of surprise and shock into the act." She found "Performing my act was my therapy. When I verbalized my unhappiness, made it funny, and everybody laughed, I had a soothing space of relief." In November of that year, she rejoined, for a short time, the Second City troupe who were now performing in New York City.

On a personal basis, Joan had reconciled with her old love, David Fitelson, but then had broken with him for good. Then, she became engaged to a budding lyricist, not knowing that he was gay. In August 1963, she joined a show touring European non-commissioned officers' clubs. Later in the year, she teamed with Jim Connell and Jake Holmes in an act entitled Jim, Jake & Joan. After the trio headlined at the Bitter End in mid-1964, Rivers realized that she only could be happy performing alone.

However, by this point, Joan, now over thirty, unmarried and slightly used up, thought herself a loser. Despite her down mood, she was hired to perform for a week at the Duplex in the Village. One of those who caught her act was high-powered Roy Silver who managed such top-flight comedians as Bill Cosby. With Silver's encouragement and insight, Joan dropped her routine of one-liners and consciously constructed a unified stand-up comedy act, frequently featuring herself as a flat-chested desperate debutante.

In late 1964, Joan, who was gaining an industry reputation for being clever with lines, was hired to write for Phyllis Diller's TV sitcom. Even though that job soon fell through. she was hired in early 1965 for Allen Funt's CBS-TV program, "Candid Camera." Rather than construct sketches for him as she did for "The Ed Sullivan Show", and others, she found herself being used on camera as the girl who baited unsuspecting passersby for the comedy vignettes.

During this period, Rivers had attempted several times to be booked as a comedian on "The Tonight Show." She finally made it to the prestigious showcase on February 17, 1965. It was everything she had dreamed about: "It was like telling...[a joke] to your father—and your father is leaning way back and laughing, and you know he is going to laugh at the next one...." Buoyed by her successful outing, she quit "Candid Camera."

JOAN AND EDGAR

In this buoyant period (June 1965), she met Edgar Rosenberg. He was a forty-year-old German refugee who had come to New York in 1948. He had moved from being a bookstore clerk to working at an ad agency. Then he joined NBC as a production supervisor and coordinator. At the time of his meeting Joan, he was producing a series of movies for and about the United Nations. Joan, then living in a tiny apartment over the Stage Deli in Manhattan, had been approached to rewrite a script that Rosenberg intended for Peter Sellers.

She agreed to go on a writing trek to Jamaica. Sellers never showed up for the conference, nor did the assigned collaborating author. After several days alone with Edgar, the script was abandoned but a romance blossomed. Three days after returning to New York City, Joan and Edgar were married by a judge in a Bronx courthouse on July 15, 1965. Always putting career first, she performed two shows that night at the Bitter End. Thereafter, the Rosenbergs resided in his fancy East Side apartment.

With Edgar as her booster and agent/manager (replacing Roy Silver), Joan's career expanded. She performed in major clubs throughout the United States to increasing acclaim. She appeared on the TV shows of Mike Douglas, Ed Sullivan and Merv Griffin and made her first comedy album ("Joan Rivers Presents Mr. Phyllis and Other Funny Stories"). In addition, she did a dramatic cameo in the Burt Lancaster movie, THE SWIMMER (1968), playing a slutty girl with a heart of gold.

On January 20, 1968, Melissa Warburg Rosenberg was born. The occasion prompted a slew of new self-deprecating jokes by Rivers, such as "When I had my baby, I screamed and screamed. And that was just during conception." With Edgar as executive producer, Joan starred in September 1968 in a syndicated daily half-hour TV program, "That Show Starring Joan Rivers." *Variety* judged it "lively" and praised the "crass, aggressive comedy talents" of its star.

A NEW QUEEN EMERGES

The series lasted for 260 segments. By the time it vanished in 1969, she was a regular guest host on "The Tonight Show." She began her Las Vegas career by being the opening act for Charles Aznavour at the Flamingo Hotel. In New York City, she worked frequently at the Downstairs at the Upstairs in the late 1960s and early 1970s, with Barry Manilow sometimes as her opening act. She toured in the comedy "Luv," with Mickey Rooney and Dom DeLuise. By now, the Rosenbergs were living in a plush Fifth Avenue apartment. She was fast becoming the Queen of Put-Down Humor.

With Edgar and former agent Lester Colodny, Joan wrote a comedy about urban frustrations and women's lib in which she starred. The show toured in 1971 and opened on Broadway as "Fun City" on January 3, 1972. The play folded after nine performances. It was a traumatic event for the Rosenbergs who had put so much energy, time and money into the project. To change their luck, they moved to Hollywood.

Idealistic Edgar sought to become an independent film producer, but after six months gave up his office. Meanwhile, Joan continued to perform on "The Tonight Show, appeared frequently on TV's "The Hollywood Squares," was an opening act in Las Vegas, and tried out new material at a small Beverly Hills showcase, Ye Little Club. She and Edgar wrote a pilot for a projected Florence Henderson TV show, but that evaporated as did the production of their drafted film script for ROXY HAUL. As a solo writer, Rivers had more success with a TV movie she authored. THE GIRL MOST LIKELY TO.... (1973) starred Stockard Channing, and was an extension of Rivers's own real-life fantasy of killing everyone who ever had been mean to her.

While struggling professionally, the Rosenbergs were coping with a shaky marriage. They separated twice in 1973, with Joan telling the press: "We're still together in business, and we want to do this with taste and discretion.... I mean, I'm not going on the 'Johnny Carson Show' and make jokes about it!" The couple reconciled and, as part of the peace pact, they purchased a twelve-room home in swank Bel Air.

The $325,000 status symbol house had been acquired largely to assuage Edgar's bruised ego. However, it was Joan who had to go on road tours, take any sort of TV guest shots, etc. to meet the family's now $8,000 weekly expenses. For three years she wrote a three-times weekly column for the *Chicago Tribune* syndicate. Another source of income was her book, *Having a Baby Can Be a Scream* (1974). It sold over 1.5 million copies in hardcover, another 2.5 million in paperback, with the book being updated in 1984.

THE WRITING CAREER

In 1976, Joan's mother died, and the next year Rivers became a filmmaker by co-writing, directing and finding backing for RABBIT TEST, an offbeat comedy starring Billy Crystal. (She and her daughter, Melissa, had bits in the film.) The picture was released in February 1978 and bombed. The next month, the hour-long TV series she conceived and wrote bowed on CBS. "Husbands, Wives & Lovers" focused on five couples in contemporary Southern California. Not lasting long, it went off the air on June 30, 1978. She then co-wrote an early draft of the Bette Midler film, THE ROSE (1979). Joan, who had already begun a regimen of plastic surgery to improve on mother nature, was taking pot shots in her comedy act at chunky Elizabeth Taylor, dowdy Queen Elizabeth II, swaggering Mick Jagger, haughty Nancy Reagan, and, of course, her own "declining" looks.

In 1981, witty, caustic, masochistic Joan began touring the U.S. with "squeaky-clean" comedian David Brenner. While they never became pals off stage, their act on stage was very successful and, in 1982, they were booked into the Riviera Hotel in Las Vegas. Ironically, in 1983, it was Rivers who beat out Brenner to host nine weeks a year on "The Tonight Show" for $250,000. Also that year, she had a well-received one-night engagement at Carnegie Hall and found herself on the cover of *People* magazine in April.

She did TV commercials and her own line of acerbic comic greeting cards. Her latest comedy album, "What Becomes a Semi-Legend Most?" earned gold record sales and was nominated for a Grammy Award. In August 1983, she was named permanent guest host of "The Tonight Show Starring Carson." (Joan claims it was Bill Cosby who phoned Fred De Cordova, the show's executive producer, to suggest that position.)

As Johnny's fill-in, Rivers has said, "I never did well with the old-time stars.... their brains had been studio-washed; they were always so careful." It was in this period she began her famed teasing of actress Joan Collins and a catty rivalry with Victoria Principal regarding her engagement to the younger Andy Gibbs, a singer. Whenever, Rivers attempted to break tradition on "The Tonight Show" by booking avant-garde comedians (Arsenio Hall, Pee Wee Herman, Howie Mandell) or new wave talent, she met with resistance from traditionalist De Cordova.

MORE PROJECTS

It was in 1984 that Joan and Edgar went to London (where he had lived previously) and she appeared as a solo guest on "Audience With...." on London Weekend-TV. This led to the BBC network signing Joan for a series of six one-hour specials ("Joan Rivers: Can We Talk?") which would be taped in 1985 and aired in April 1986. She also authored *The Life and Hard Times of*

Heidi Abromowitz (1984), a fictitious account about her imaginary trampy friend. It became a best-seller and led to a 1985 Showtime-Cable special "Joan Rivers and Friends Salute Heidi Abromowitz."

In December 1984, Edgar was 59 and his physician feared that the professionally frustrated man was about to explode from hypertension. After a heated fight with daughter Melissa who did not want to go away to college, he had a massive heart attack. He was rushed to UCLA Medical Center where he remained in a coma for two weeks, during which time his heart stopped twice. After six weeks he came home.

Then began his pervasive depression, in which he alternated between being a frightened youngster and an assertive, rebellious adult. On two occasions, when his wife and daughter opposed his wishes, he checked into a hospital. According to Joan, "we began living by unspoken rules. All of us were careful not to upset him and cause another heart attack...." During this period, for the first time since her marriage, she took real charge of her own life.

In 1985, Joan, who had become active in several charitable causes (including AIDS research and relief for the homeless), found herself performing on the road a good deal without Edgar in tow. She realized suddenly that she was having fun and that was because she was away from her husband. As she continued her chores on "The Tonight Show," she kept asking the powers to be whether she would be Carson's replacement when and if he retired. She received no answer. However, in mid-1985 when Carson signed a new two-year contract with NBC, she was given only a one-year extension. She thought this peculiar since their pacts were usually for the same time frame.

JOCKEYING FOR POSITION

After seven years and three rewrites, Joan's autobiography, *Enter Laughing*, written with Richard Meryman, was published in 1986. It rose to #4 on the *New York Times'* best sellers list. Melissa was now a freshman at the University of Pennsylvania in Philadelphia, and Edgar had a new project. He had followed mogul Rupert Murdoch's purchase of 20th Century-Fox Pictures and his plan to launch a fourth TV network. Rosenberg thought this might be an ideal alternative showcase for Joan if "The Tonight Show" post evaporated.

Then, Rivers obtained a smuggled copy of NBC's ten choices to replace Johnny Carson when he left the air. She was not on it. With prompting from Barry Diller, CEO at the new Fox network, she negotiated a letter of understanding with Fox. Under the terms of the letter, she would receive $5 million a year for three years to host a new late night talk show.

April 25, 1986 was the last Johnny Carson-hosted "The Tonight Show" on which Joan performed. The week of May 2, 1986 proved to be her final week of regular hosting on the program. On May 5, news of the next day's press conference (to announce her Fox pact) leaked out. According to Rivers, after learning of the faux paux she attempted to phone Carson, but he refused to accept her call. The situation became a media circus. Johnny told the Associated Press, "I think she was less than smart and didn't show much style."

Joan responded that the situation, "Upset me so much. I can't tell you. I started to cry...[it] hurts, hurts, hurts.... I wanted it to end nicely—I'm a lady, my mother brought me up right. I knew I owed him a call." As of May 6, she was fired and Garry Shandling took over her hosting duties, soon to be in tandem with Jay Leno as Carson's fill-in. As the ruckus accelerated, Rivers moaned: "I've become a tabloid tootsie." She insisted: "There's NO fight. All I did was defend myself against statements that NBC put out. Never him. Never him."

A FAILED ATTEMPT

In preparing for her showcase talk show, Joan attempted to woo co-workers from "The Tonight Show" to join her staff. Her efforts failed. Edgar and Barry Diller engaged in daily battles of wills to make everything "identical to the Carson show," and Joan was not able to realize that her husband had grown far too unreasonable in his demands. To tone up for her series, she had additional cosmetic surgery. Finally, on October 9, 1986, "The Late Show with Joan Rivers" bowed—live from Los Angeles. Clint Holmes was her announcer/sidekick, with bandleader Mark Hudson and "The Party Boys and the Tramp" as his musicians.

Joan's opening remarks included: "I have a whole monologue...which I won't do tonight.... I am just—it's been five months and so much has been said and so much has been written.... I'm just...so happy to be here." Her debut guests included Elton John (who performed "The Bitch Is Back"), Cher, David Lee Roth and Pee Wee Herman. The reviews for the opening shows were not promising. Thomas Shales (*Washington Post*) suggested: "Maybe Rivers should spend less time at the beauty parlor and more time with her writers." Fred Rothenberg (*New York Post*) judged: "Joan Rivers finally got her own talk show. The next step is to make it funny."

Before long, it became a booking war between Joan's and Carson's rival shows. She called in favors from friends, and lured Nell Carter, Lily Tomlin, Michelle Phillips, Lucille Ball, et al. on her program. Industry insiders noted that Rivers, now afraid of antagonizing her guest roster, was displaying "more gush than guts." Almost from the start, she and Barry Diller lost the ability to communicate with one another, the situation worsened by Edgar's petty, insistent demands. In the midst of the pressure, Rosenberg checked into the hospital, convinced he was having a stroke. By this point, Edgar and Joan were a couple in name only.

Meanwhile, her show staff began falling apart. Some of Joan's on-the-air targets (i.e. Victoria Principal on purpose, Jane Russell by accident) threatened and/or planned law suits against the sharp-mouthed host. By the end of 1986, Rivers's ratings had leveled off at 3.0, not up to the 4.0 level promised the sponsors by Fox. At the end of February 1987, she was told the contract of her producer, Bruce McKay, would not be renewed when it expired in a few weeks. She realized the end was at hand.

When she took a week's vacation to Paris with daughter Melissa in March 1987, she wanted Arsenio Hall to be the guest host. Fox refused. Before the month was out she had lost artistic control of the program. She was fired as of May 15, 1987. At the end of her final show, she told viewers "It's nobody's fault." (That same evening on "The Tonight Show," a triumphant Carson, in talking about much-mocked TV evangelists Jim and Tammy Bakker said to the audience: "Don't worry about Tammy Bakker. She just got an offer from Fox Broadcasting.... I've been saving that one for a long time.")

TOUGH TIMES

Some days after her TV talk show debacle, Joan was fulfilling a club engagement at Caesar's Palace in Las Vegas. She told ringsiders: "You are looking at a woman who has finally been able to make Johnny Carson happy." But what would have made Rivers happy, would have been an invitation to come back onto "The Tonight Show," as Carson had done with other one-time rivals (David Brenner, Dick Cavett, Alan Thicke and Merv Griffin). Joan settled her Fox contract for over $2 million. However, it was a bittersweet finale, especially after the network brought in Arsenio Hall to host her former show and he proved to be a sizeable hit.

In August 1987, Joan went to England to appear on British TV with Barry Humphries of Dame Edna Evereage fame. Rivers was too upset by recent events to be any good. Afterwards, she and Edgar, who had accompanied her, went to Ireland. By then, he was a total hypochondriac. On the flight home, she told him again that if he did not obtain psychiatric care, she would separate permanently from him.

He insisted that, after he completed a business trip to Pennsylvania, he would comply. On Wednesday, August 12, he was in Philadelphia and he and Joan (on the west coast) spoke. He stated he would be back in California on Friday and would check into a hospital. He also announced "I'm so depressed, I'm going to kill myself." Thinking this was yet another one of his many bids for attention, she retorted: "Don't do it till Friday, because Thursday I'm having liposuction." He laughed.

On August 14, 1987, Edgar was found dead in his Philadelphia hotel room. He had consumed bottles of Valium and Librium which he swallowed with several miniature bottles of scotch and brandy from the room's courtesy bar. He left a note stating: "I cannot see myself lying more weeks in hospitals. I'm tired. I ache mentally and physically. I've had it."

Rosenberg was methodical to the end. Before committing suicide, he taped separate messages for Joan, Melissa and for his good friend Tom Pileggi. He placed the tapes in individual hotel envelopes, along with a separate sheaf of business papers and instructions placed in an envelope addressed to "Joan Rosenberg." He also left tips for the hotel's maids, luggage boy, and the dining room's maitre 'd.

Joan and Melissa were at their Los Angeles home when they received the bad news. After the autopsy, Edgar's body was cremated and a funeral service was held at the Wilshire Boulevard Temple in Los Angeles. On the tape left for Joan, Rosenberg said: "I cannot bear to be a fifth wheel. I know this is not your fault. I had the heart attack, and I'm a changed person. But believe me, when I fought [in the industry], I fought for you.... If somebody had not been the bastard, you might have been cut up like salami."

LIFE SAVERS

During this horrendous period, Joan credits two women with saving her sanity. One was actress Mariette Hartley, whose father had killed himself and who was a part of a network of suicide survivors. Another was Iris Bolton, whose twenty-year old son had committed suicide and who ran a support group for suicide survivors at her family counseling center (The Link) in Atlanta. Another salvation for Joan was her Yorkshire terrier dog, Spike.

By the fall of 1987, Rivers's career and personal life were a mess. Since her Fox firing, her nightclub bookings had decreased dramatically. The only TV work she could scrape together was on "The Hollywood Squares," but no longer as a focal guest figure. She and Melissa were at loggerheads with one another, and both were visiting psychiatrists regularly.

Needing a total change of scenery, Joan sold her Bel Air home. With the funds, she purchased a relatively modest beachside residence and a Manhattan coop apartment just off Fifth Avenue. In December 1987 she toured the club circuit in Australia and then was back in New York for Christmas to have a reunion of sorts with Melissa.

In 1988, Joan began dating a humorous man named Bernard Goldberg. That ended when he thought her career was an impediment to their relationship. Her salary was now a fraction of what it had been before the Fox firing. That March she learned that Lincoln Center was planning a new repertory company. She called to submit her resume and this, in turn, led to her replacing the replacement of Linda Lavin as the mother in Neil Simon's "Broadway Bound." She joined the cast of this comedy on June 21, 1988 and proved that she could be a resourceful actress. She remained with the play till it closed at the end of that September. Meanwhile, that August, she also did standup comedy at Michael's Pub.

ANOTHER CHANCE

During her run in "Broadway Bound," the Tribune Corporation, who syndicated Geraldo Rivera's TV talk show, asked Rivers to host her own Manhattan-based daytime syndicated talk program. Her new series, "The Joan Rivers Show," bowed on September 5, 1989. Michele Greppi (*New York Post*) reported: "the two years that have not been kind to her have been kind to her. The trademark edginess has been tempered with an appealing vulnerability."

With her new showcase a respectable hit, Joan's life began falling into place again. Melissa graduated from college that year and she and Joan came to a new understanding, woman to woman. On several occasions, Rivers was spotted as Malcolm Forbes's date. She and writing partner Tom Perew wrote the baby dialogue and jokes for the mega hit, LOOK WHO'S TALKING (1989). On June 28, 1990, in New York, Rivers won an Emmy. beating such daytime host competition as Oprah Winfrey, Phil Donahue and Sally Jessy Raphael.

In accepting the award, Joan said: "It's so sad that he's not here because it was my husband, Edgar Rosenberg, who always said you can turn things around. And except for one terrible moment in a hotel room in Philadelphia, when he forgot that, this is really for him because he was with me from the beginning."

In 1990, very modish in her chic attire, Joan continued to dish the gossip on "The Joan Rivers Show." She also made a guest appearance in the CBS-TV movie, HOW TO MURDER A MILLIONAIRE. Her follow-up autobiography (*Still Talking*), also written with Richard Meryman, was published in 1991 and proved to be a substantial hit. When Johnny Carson went off the air in May 1992, Joan featured a tribute to him on her talk show. However, Carson refused to permit Joan to use a "Tonight Show" clip for her salute.

At this time, she was still residing in her Manhattan duplex, with her dog Spike and a staff of two. Socially, she was escorted about town by several eligible older men. Now approaching sixty, she underwent additional plastic surgery to freshen her image.

STILL MOVING FORWARD

October 1992 was a key month for the show business veteran. She began her new USA Cable network series, "Joan Rivers' Gossip! Gossip! Gossip," a half-hour weekly show with international news and using two to three gossip columnists on each program. (One of those columnists reporting tidbits was daughter Melissa.) Rivers and Donald Trump had cameos in the NBC-TV miniseries, "Lady Boss" (October 11-12, 1992) and, according to *TV Guide*, made "everyone else look good." On the next evening, she was the star of "Joan Rivers and Her Funny Friends," a charity benefit presented at New York Town Hall.

She also had a Showtime Cable special ("Joan Rivers: Abroad in London") airing. Having merchandised a successful jewelry line and a new line of sportswear on the QVC home shopping cable network, she hosted a hour special on QVC ("Joan Rivers' Classic Collection Fashion"). This led to future QVC outings as well as to a live TV special on Los Angeles' Channel 5 in December 1992. The latter was devoted to hawking Christmas items which viewers could purchase via an 800 number.

Joan, now at work on yet another book, has no plans to slacken her pace. She enthuses: "I would do everything [regarding filmmaking]. Everything.... I always love to have a lot of projects....." She also intends to remain based in the Big Apple: "I love living in New York. I just truly am very happy that you can make a living where you want to be." As to her social life, she quips facetiously: "at my age, I don't really go out anymore. It's not nice." Of her lengthy professional life, she reflects, "nothing has ever come easily for me. My whole career has been just hard, hurting little steps." She also observes of the realities of show business: "I've yet to meet one person who got to the top with generosity."

TV & CABLE SERIES:
That Show Starring Joan Rivers Show (Syndicated, 1968-69)
The Tonight Show Starring Johnny Carson (NBC, 1983-1986)
The Late Show Starring Joan Rivers (Fox, 1986-1987)
The Joan Rivers Show (Syndicated, 1989-)
Joan Rivers' Gossip, Gossip, Gossip (USA, 1992-)
Joan Rivers Classics Collection Fashion (QVC, 1992-)

FEATURE FILMS:
Mr. Universe (1951) [extra]
The Swimmer (1968)
Rabbit Test (1978) [also co-producer, director, script]
Uncle Scam (1981)
The Muppets Take Manhattan (1984)
Spaceballs (1987) [voice only]
How to Murder a Millionaire (CBS, 1990) [TV movie]
Lady Boss (NBC, 1992) [TV miniseries]

Joan Rivers as a comedy guest on "Super Dave" the 1988 cable series starring Super Dave Osborne.

Chapter 22
RUTH WESTHEIMER

Some call her simply "Doctor Ruth," others refer to her as "Grandma Freud." Detractors label her as that "smurfish sex therapist." Some insist her "warm giggle sounds like a gerbil in heat" or that "She looks more like a retired jockey than an expert in psychosexual therapy." Impressionists have a field day imitating "Doktor Vooth" with her broad Germanic accent and highly infectious (tee-hee) laugh. Actually, Westheimer is a forthright, enthusiastic type of person who makes even super cool David Letterman nervous on the air. Automobile mogul Lee Iacocca once said (with more than a healthy grain of truth), that if he ever ran for U.S. president, he would take Dr. Ruth as his running mate, reasoning, "I would tell everybody what to do and she would tell them how."

By any name, diminutive (4'7") Dr. Ruth Westheimer is a phenomenon. Not since Alfred Kinsey and Masters and Johnson has any one person in the American media become so synonymous with the subject of sex therapy. She has made a joyful crusade of instructing the world to wear condoms, not to worry if we prematurely "ejaculate" and, most of all, to "have good, safe sex."

However, there is far more to the amazing life story of Dr. Ruth. This remarkable woman narrowly escaped the Nazi holocaust, became an Israeli freedom fighter and, in the early 1950s, arrived in the United States "with absolutely nothing." She admits proudly, "I've worked hard to get where I am, but—if you'll excuse the cliche—what's happened to me could only have happened in America."

She was born Karola Ruth Siegel on June 4, 1928 in Wiesenfeld, Germany, the village where her mother Irma Hanauer had grown up. Irma, the daughter of a cattle dealer, had come to Frankfurt in 1927 to be a helper in the Siegel household and soon became involved romantically with the family's only child, Julius. She became pregnant and the couple married. After Karola was born, she and her mother remained in Wiesenfeld, with Julius visiting on weekends. After the baby's first year, Karola and Irma moved to Frankfurt where Julius wholesaled notion goods for a living.

THE EARLY YEARS WERE GOOD

Karola, who was quite short like her parents, had a comfortable upper middle class early childhood. She shared her parents' apartment with Julius's widowed mother, Selma. Ruth recalls that this Orthodox Jewish household was a strange mix: her mother was very tightlipped and her grandmother was quite domineering. From her beloved, hard-working father, she gained her joy and love of learning.

Her first years were rather idyllic, even when she began the first grade at the Samson Raphael Hirsch School for Girls where classmates often made fun of her because of her height. (For a long time, she was not even tall enough to ride a bicycle, the principal mode of transportation for the family.) By this time, the Nazi party had risen to power in Germany, and very quickly the undercurrent of anti-Semitism had exploded into a national hatred.

By 1938, even the patriotic Siegels had accepted the fact that they were no longer safe in Germany. That fall the local synagogue was burned and classes stopped at Karola's school. Then, Julius was taken away by the Gestapo for a six-week period and just as suddenly released. The Siegels now intended to flee, but the aged Selma refused to leave her homeland. In desperation, it was agreed that Karola should leave the country. She was to be part of the Kinder transport, in which a selected group of German Jewish children were being relocated to neutral Switzerland where they would be cared for through the support of Swiss Jewish charity.

On January 5, 1939, ten-year-old Karola joined other Jewish youths being shepherded out of Germany. The Siegels wanted to believe that this separation would only last a few months. They reasoned that, perhaps by then, the anti-Semitic wave would have evaporated and Karola could come back. Or another

Dr. Ruth Westheimer in the mid-1980s.

option, they thought, was for the entire family to emigrate to Palestine. As fate had it, that day at the Frankfurt railroad station was the last time Karola ever saw any member of her family.

Karola and the others went by train to Heiden, a Swiss village about fifty miles from Zurich. During the next six years, this was to be her home. The German refugees, not well treated by their Swiss hosts, lived in a barn turned into a dorm. (After three years, Karola and some of the others would move into the old wooden main house.) When not in school, the newcomers had a long list of daily chores, which included house cleaning and caring for the younger refugees as well as being at the beck and call of the Swiss shelterers.

LUCKY TO BE ALIVE

During her years there, Karola and the others learned NEVER to complain. They were admonished constantly that they were lucky to be alive. Besides, each six months they had to go to the local police station to renew their permits, and there was always the possibility, as they were reminded continuously, that they could be shipped back to Germany.

At first, Karola and her family were able to write back and forth. To cheer up their child, the Siegels's letters remained optimistic; to keep up her own spirits and not seem ungrateful, Karola made her correspondence deceptively upbeat. By now, Jews were not permitted to travel out of Germany, so there was no question of the Siegels visiting their daughter. The last letter Karola received from her family was dated September 14, 1941. In September 1942, there was a brief note from her maternal grandparents in Wiesenfeld saying that the parents and grandmother were safe in Poland. After that she heard nothing. (Years later she would learn that after her parents and grandmother had been deported to a ghetto in Lodz, Poland, they had been shipped to a concentration camp where they died.)

During her Swiss years, the young Ruth kept a daily diary, wanting to retain each memory. She forced herself to believe that one day she could share these experiences with her reunited family. This hope was shared by all the refugees. Not only did they live in a vacuum in Switzerland, but the youngsters were in great denial about their families' fate. As such, they created a peculiarly "ordinary" existence, filled with much the same hopes, concerns and joys of any adolescent. The only problem was the tremendous underlying emotional strain of covering their ongoing trauma.

During this Swiss period, Karola was always studying, hungry for knowledge. She learned to speak French. She had romantic feeling for Max, a boy at the camp, then came Walter, who was also short like her. Their relationship broke off eventually. In April 1943, Karola's schooling ended (for a long thereafter). She had no relatives to pay for high school classes and besides, it was felt, it was not important for a female to be well educated.

COPING WITH THE TRUTH

By 1944, Ruth, still in denial, was writing in her diary, "Every day I am less sure that I will ever see my parents again." A few months later she entered the thought, "I would so much like to relive the days with my parents. I did not know what my parents meant to me." During these years, she was full of ambitions. She dreamed first of becoming a doctor, but then more realistically thought of becoming a kindergarten teacher. Like many, she hoped to go to Palestine with her family after the war.

June 4, 1945 was Karola's seventeenth birthday, which she spent at the Swiss shelter. By now she had a degree in domestic science. She had been accepted at a Swiss kindergarten teachers' academy with classes to start in October. However, with the ending of World War II in Europe, all plans were changed. She had to decline the schooling offer. By now, the Red Cross was publishing a weekly list of people who had survived the concentration camps, and the Swiss made all the youths gather to read these postings. On one level, Karola accepted the reality that her family was dead, but on another plane she told herself, "you, a tiny little grain of sand among all that horror, you are so occupied with yourself. Stop making such a to-do about yourself." As her salvation, she developed a dogged determination to look on the bright side of any situation.

By July of 1945 the German refugees knew they could not remain in Switzerland indefinitely. At least, they had the goal of making their way to Palestine to join in the Zionist cause. Karola was among the migrants who went by train to France and then by British ship to Palestine. She arrived in Haifa, where she was taken to a refugee camp. Karola's uncle (her mother's brother, Lothar) who had gone to Palestine before the war, came to find Ruth at the camp and they had a brief reunion.

Next, she went to live on a kibbutz not far from Haifa, working eight hours a day (picking olives and tomatoes, doing housework in the kitchen, cleaning toilets). At night she slept on a straw-filled mattress, crowded in a tent with three others. Once again, she was subjected to being a second class citizen, this time by Polish Jews who had come to Palestine before the war. During this transition period, Karola was recovering psychologically from past horrors. She wrote in her diary, "Everything is dead, gray and empty. I don't live; I only vegetate." However, she took hold of herself emotionally. She dropped her Germanic first name and substituted her middle name, Ruth. She abandoned her Orthodox Judaism for Zionism.

BITING OFF MORE THAN SHE COULD CHEW

By the fall of 1946, Ruth had transferred to another kibbutz, one which boasted a kindergarten teacher seminary. She planned to earn her tuition for the three-year course by working in the kitchen there for an additional three years. While in this servitude she began educating herself as well as learning Hebrew. After a time, she realized that she could not go through with this extended six-year plan.

Eventually, she found an opportunity through distant relatives in Jerusalem who introduced her to influential friends. They, in turn, got Ruth accepted at a Jerusalem kindergarten seminary. Thus, she left the Yagur kibbutz in February 1947. Until school started, she worked in Jerusalem, first as a baby-sitter and maid and then as a waitress. On June 4, 1947, her nineteenth birthday, she made her final diary entry: "I know that I need so much love.... I will achieve my goal!"

Ruth was at the teachers' seminary, living in a residence for young women, when the British and the United Nations announced plans to divide Palestine into a Jewish and an Arab state, with a small internationally administered zone around Jerusalem. This decision led to the outbreak of guerilla warfare between Jews and Arabs. Already a zealous Zionist, Ruth joined the Haganah, the Jewish underground army.

Her training included learning to take apart and put together machine guns, and she was taught how to shoot and use hand grenades. Because she was so short, she was used frequently as a messenger. On May 18, 1948, the British High Commissioner for Palestine left and David Ben-Gurion proclaimed the independence of the state of Israel. That day, the Arab armies invaded Israel. On June 4, 1948, her twentieth birthday, Ruth was injured by the shrapnel from an Arab bomb, with her legs, especially her feet, being severely damaged. The wounds required a lengthy convalescence. (Ruth would quip later that she was happy to have remained intact, "Otherwise I might have been even shorter.") By late January 1949 the final armistice was signed and, in the spring of 1949, Ruth completed her teachers' studies.

By this point, Ruth had met the Rumanian-born David, three years her senior. He was a soldier, short like her. Coming from a well-to-do family, he was well-educated and wanted to be a doctor. When he proposed marriage, she accepted and they wed in Jerusalem in November 1949. (She would admit later, "I married the first man who asked me.") Because there were no medical schools yet in Israel, once David was out of the army, he went to Paris for his studies.

In early 1951, Ruth followed him to France. While David studied, Ruth found work as director of a kindergarten for Jewish children. To earn additional money, she began teaching Hebrew to French Jewish children, and for two summers worked at a youth camp on the French coast. She also began a one-year course at the Sorbonne so she could complete her high school credentials. That accomplished, she entered the Institute of Psychology at the Sorbonne, working toward a license.

SEPARATE WAYS

In the summer of 1954, Ruth and David returned to Israel. In September she returned alone to Paris. Her husband had decided to remain behind to obtain his master's degree in Middle Eastern studies, having abandoned medicine. Unable to survive the strains of their adult student life, the couple had decided to divorce. Once in Paris she obtained the decree through the mails.

In the 1950s the West German government was making restitution to individuals who had suffered from Nazi war crimes and had not yet finished their education. A check for $1,500 finally reached Ruth in Paris. On an impulse, she decided not to complete her Sorbonne stud-

Dr. Ruth Westheimer in 1992.

ies. Instead, she convinced her French boyfriend, Dan, to join her on a trip to the United States. Once in New York, Ruth read an ad in a German Jewish newspaper offering a scholarship for a master's degree in sociology at the New School for Social Research. The requirement was that the recipient be a Nazi victim.

On a whim, Ruth applied and was awarded the funding. She and Dan took a room in Washington Heights, not too far from the George Washington Bridge. To supplement her income and because she did not yet know English well enough, she took a job as a housemaid. Then she found employment at the French Embassy placing exhibits, hanging pictures, sweeping, etc. After gaining the equivalent of a B.A. degree, she began studying for her master's in psychology.

When she got pregnant, she and Dan married, and, in 1957, she gave birth to Miriam. After years of marriage with Dan, Ruth realized that her second marriage was a failure: "Intellectually, it was just not tenable. I had always to think, what can I talk to him about next?" The couple separated and she went to Tijuana, Mexico for a divorce. In 1959, after failing her oral exams twice, she finally obtained her M.A. in sociology, writing her thesis on the experience of 100 German Jewish children who spent World War II in Switzerland.

TALL AND SHORT OF IT

It was while skiing in the Catskill with a 6' tall boyfriend, that she met 5'5" Manfred (Fred) Westheimer. This German Jewish refugee was one year older than Ruth. He had served in the U.S. Army during World War II, then studied engineering and was now chief engineer for a Manhattan consulting film. He also was living in Washington Heights. They married on December 10, 1961 and, in 1963, she gave birth to their son Joel.

By now, Ruth had a part-time job as a researcher dealing with patient care at the School of Public Health and Administrative Medicine at Columbia University. During this time she encountered psychotherapist Arnold Bernstein and began treatment with him. (It was Bernstein who confronted the emotionally-blocked Ruth with the reality that she was indeed an orphan. Once she accepted this fact, he worked with her to cope with her troubled childhood.)

In 1965, Ruth became an American citizen. (She would not abandon Israel, for she would teach there nine years in a row and would send both her children to Zionist summer camps there.) When funding for her Columbia University project ran out, she found work with Planned Parenthood as a research associate. A week into the new job, her boss quit and she took her place.

As the new director, her project was taking contraception/abortion histories of 2,000 women in Harlem, using a staff of 24 minority women. This year-long assignment taught her the value for both contraception and legalized abortion. By 1970, through additional night classes, she obtained her Ph.D in Education. That July she herself required an abortion because her baby was not developing properly. During the surgery, which had just become legal in New York, she underwent a partial hysterectomy.

POLITICAL SAVVY

The early 1970s found her teaching at Lehman College in the Bronx, her subject being the Psychological Foundation of Education. Because she understood the politics of her profession, she soon moved up to becoming an associate professor. By now, she had developed a speciality, instructing (would-be) educators on how to teach sex education. Westheimer claims that her life changed in 1974 when she attended a lecture given by Dr. Helen Singer Kaplan, the U.S's most renowned sex therapist. Thereafter, she attended Kaplan's classes at Cornell Medical School in New York City, which led to her receiving a certificate as a psychosexual therapist from Cornell. She soon opened her own office on Manhattan's East 79th Street.

Ruth had never forgotten her past, but now was able to deal with it rationally. In fact, she told her harrowing story to Alfred Hasler, a famous Swiss journalist. He turned their ten days of interviews into a fourteen-part newspaper narrative. That, in turn, was published as *Die Geschichte der Karola Siegel* [The Story of Karola Siegel] in 1976. (Earlier, Ruth had tracked down her Swiss classmates and they held an emotionally-charged reunion in Israel.)

In the budget crunch of 1976-77, Ruth was laid off from Lehman College and began teaching a course in human sexuality at Brooklyn College, taking a cut in pay and a drop in position to assistant professor. A year or so later, she was fired for reasons she chooses not to reveal. She appealed the decision to the union, and spent $5,000 of her own money defending her cause. When she lost the case, she was broken-hearted. As she recalls, "It made me feel as I did when I got kicked out of Germany. Angry, helpless, rejected. As it turns out, it was my big break."

Between her new teaching chores at assorted local colleges and her private practice, Ruth made it a policy to always volunteer to give lectures—no matter where and despite the low or non-existent pay. In early 1980, Dr Ruth agreed to speak to the community affairs managers of radio stations in the tri-state area on the need for sex education. The conference was held at the St. Moritz Hotel in Manhattan. One of those attending was Betty Elam of WYNY, a local FM station owned by NBC. Impressed by Ruth, Elam asked Westheimer to be a guest on a forthcoming Sunday morning public affairs program.

That airing was well received, which prompted WYNY-FM to offer Westheimer her own weekly Sunday midnight show. The fifteen-minute program, "Sexually Speaking," debuted in May 1980. From the very start of her broadcasting career, Westheimer was immediately explicit "because it is my strong feeling that in talking about sexual matters you should not use euphemisms or mince words." At the end of the show she would ask listeners to send in letters; she received a whole stack of them. For her efforts she received $25 per program, a losing proposition because of garage parking, eating out, etc. As a publicity stunt, the station offered listeners a "Sex on Sunday" t-shirt. WYNY-FM received over 3,500 requests!

A STAR IS BORN

Not only listeners were delighted with the vivacious, explicit, heavily-accented Dr. Westheimer, but so were the critics. *Newsweek* magazine applauded her "effervescent blend of candor, humor and common-sense practicality." The show soon moved to Sunday at ten PM and was expanded to an hour-long session. As a new feature on the extended program, she got to answer listeners' questions, always cautioning callers that she was NOT a medical doctor and would NOT do therapy on the air.

What she would do would attempt to educate and give general advice. (She would frequently end her active with "You're going to be fine. You betcha.") Her nickname of "Dr. Ruth" occurred when a young female caller could not pronounce her last name and called her "Dr. Ruth." By the end of 1981, with the *New York Times'* publication of a feature article ("A Voice of Sexual Literacy") on Westheimer, her success was assured. She was to the 1980s and pop culture what Dr. Joyce Brothers had been to an earlier generation. Dr. Ruth was continuing the trend of such media therapists as Los Angeles-based Dr. Toni Grant, but adding her own refreshing twists to the subject.

Branching out into other media, Dr. Ruth was a guest on assorted radio and TV shows including Ted Koppel's "Nightline" and "Late Night with David Letterman." She began writing *Dr. Ruth's Guide to Good Sex with Harvey Gardner* which was published in 1983 and later would be translated into three languages. Now an increasingly hot commercial commodity, she contracted with Metro-Goldwyn-Mayer Pictures to do STARRY NIGHT WITH SPRINKLES, a movie which would deal with Dr. Ruth (playing herself) and the interweaving lives of listeners who call her show for advice. The film plans were aborted, but Westheimer would make a few features, generally playing herself. (Ironically her scenes for the French-made ONE WOMAN OR TWO, 1987, were shot in the same Sorbonne classrooms where she had studied in the early 1950s.)

As the media blitz over Dr. Ruth continued, her recognition quotient accelerated. By now, "Sexually Speaking" had reached the point where, typically, there were over 4,000 call-ins on her program (which were pre-screened by producer Susan Brown before a listener went live with Dr. Ruth). It was estimated that Westheimer's weekly outing, in which she was a full partner with NBC, had over 250,000 listeners, making it the Big Apple's most popular show in its particular time slot.

ONION RINGS AND RUTH

As of September 2, 1984, the program was syndicated nationally and was expanded to two hours. With her nationwide popularity, Dr. Ruth began popping up more often on network talk shows, including Johnny Carson's "The Tonight Show" and David Letterman's "Late Night." Her most repeated anecdote of kinky sex was the one about the young man who called her on radio to discuss his girlfriend who liked to toss onion rings on his erect penis. Thereafter, whenever she was on Letterman's series, before a station break, a picture of a plate of onion rings would flash into view.

With all her national exposure, it was natural for Dr. Ruth to be offered her own TV program. Former network chief Fred Silverman induced her to do an ABC-TV pilot for a TV talk show, but the sample entry was too lavish and received no buyers. She next went to Channel 5 in New York City for a local show (at $1,000 weekly) which had a thirteen-week run. The station wanted to renew the entry, but the parent company in Boston vetoed the notion.

Meanwhile, on August 27, 1984 she began "Good Sex with Dr. Ruth Westheimer" on the Lifetime Cable Network. Larry Angelo, without an accent, was her co-host. On the half-hour show, which aired nightly, Ruth used actors to reenact case histories. The show featured a segment entitled "Ask Dr. Ruth" in which passersby on the street (Manhattan's Sixth Avenue) had an opportunity to pose questions to Westheimer via video tape. On Wednesday and Thursday evenings, the show was an hour long and devoted to phone-in calls. Later in the program's run, celebrity guests would pose their own questions. *Variety* found the host "bouncy, cheerful." It judged that the new entry was "about a subject most people find of interest, and it's done with a cheerful determination to be entertaining."

Before long Dr. Ruth's popularity had swept the country. Besides her radio and TV chores, she began authoring a syndicated advice column. Soon, there would be a "Terrific Sex" home video and a "Good Sex" board game. She did commercials (for condoms, typewriters, a soft drink, department stores, and chocolate mousse). She appeared on "Hollywood Squares" and went to China with "Lifestyles of the Rich and Famous."

RUTH THE WRITER

An embarrassing situation occurred with the publication of her new book, *A Young People's Guide to Sexual Information* (1985). Because of a typo, there was misinformation about the rhythm method of birth control and the "safe" (the text meant "unsafe") time to have sexual intercourse. The book had to be recalled and reprinted, leading a chagrined Westheimer to admit, "Even big shot people like myself make mistakes."

Her third book, *Dr. Ruth's Guide for Married Lovers* appeared in 1986. In June of that year, her daughter Miriam married. (After college, Miriam had lived on a kibbutz in Israel and then joined the army there before meeting her husband-to-be and returning to the U.S.) Westheimer's dramatic autobiography (*All in a Lifetime*), written with Ben Yagoda, was published in 1987. She dedicated the book to her parents and grandparents, explaining, "The set of values, the joie de vivre, and the positive outlook they instilled in me live on in my life and the new family I have created to carry on their traditions."

While her Lifetime Cable show went off the air in 1986, in January 1987, she was back on the air with "Ask Dr. Ruth," a syndicated version of the same format, only watered down for general TV audiences. Larry Angelo again co-hosted and sitcom star Nell Carter was her first celebrity guest. However, this diluted adaptation of "Dr. Ruth" was not terribly exciting fare and after thirteen weeks was dropped.

She returned to Lifetime Cable with "The All New Dr. Ruth Show" (1988-1990) and later hosted a TV program directed at teens, "What's Up, Dr. Ruth?" In 1988, she won an ACE Award, the cable industry's version of an Emmy. She authored *Sex and Morality: Who Is Teaching Our Sex Standards?* (1988) with Lou Lieberman, and the duo later wrote *Dr. Ruth's Guide to Erotic and Sensuous Pleasures* (1991).

STAYING IN THE LIGHT

Pushing into the 1990s, Dr. Ruth, whose son had graduated from Princeton University and had begun his own independent life, continued lecturing (at a very hefty fee) and had her own radio show, "You're On the Air with Dr. Ruth." She frequently wrote newspaper and magazine articles including her regular *Redbook* column. Her subjects, of course were always human sexuality and sexual expression (e.g., "What's So Good about Sex after 30-Plenty," "Dr Ruth Asks: Are You Having Fun Together?").

When not preoccupied with her professional interests, she found time for hobbies, including skiing and her doll collection. On weekends, she escaped to the family's country home in Peekskill, New York. Most of all she enjoyed bargain-hunting (she is famous for loving free-bee gifts and samples) and dining out. In the fall of 1992, she popped up everywhere on TV: on a soap opera ("One Life To Live"), a dramatic series ("Melrose Place"), on a special ("Phil Donahue's 25th Anniversary Show") and in commercials.

Always eager to reach new viewers, Westheimer made a guest appearance as herself on the TV time travel series, "Quantum Leap" in January 1993, in a segment in which Sam (Scott Bakula) leaps into Dr. Ruth's body! Meanwhile, in August 1992, she had begun her latest TV series, "Dr. Ruth's Never Too Late," an original, half-hour daily cable program geared to mature viewers. Once again, it featured celebrity guests (such as Phyllis Diller, Hugh O'Brian, Rue McClanahan), as well as experts in assorted fields, and dealt with a wide range of topical issues. The show is videotaped in New York City.

Now a grandmother (her daughter has a son, Ari), Dr. Ruth remains the eternally bubbly optimist, exhorting viewers, "So you're worried about money, jobs and the prospect of losing them. Remember, sex is free-and pleasurable! Just remember to 'use p-r-r-r-otection!'" Despite her reputation for frankness, she is not a believer in destroying a sex relationship by revealing too much of one's private fantasies. Her recipe to one and all is "Have good sex!"

TV & CABLE SERIES:

Dr. Ruth Westheimer
    (New York City local, 1984)
Good Sex! with Dr. Ruth Westheimer (Lifetime, 1984-1986)
Ask Dr. Ruth
    (Syndicated, 1987-1988)
The All New Dr. Ruth Show
    (Lifetime, 1988-1990)
What's Up, Dr. Ruth?
    (Syndicated, 1990)
Dr. Ruth's Never Too Late
    (Nostalgia, 1992-)

FEATURE FILMS:

Electric Dreams (1984)
One Woman or Two (1987)
Forever Lulu (1987)

U.S. Representative Pat Schroeder (D-CO), Mary Alice Williams (NBC News) and Sharon Pratt Kelly (Mayor of Washington, D.C.) pose with Ruth Westheimer, star of "Dr. Ruth's Never Too Late" cable talk show.

Chapter 23
OPRAH WINFREY

She must be doing something right. As the queen bee of her own television empire, Oprah Winfrey currently grosses well over $60 million annually. TV journalist Maria Shriver, who first met Winfrey professionally more than a decade ago, says: "On TV, Oprah's gift is her interest in so many things—and she asks the questions people really want to know. She has no inhibitions. She doesn't worry about her image or her credibility. She just asks from her gut." The *Washington Post* calls Oprah "the lovable mouth of the midway...the zaftig gab queen...every woman's friend, the kind of brassy neighbor who barges into your house and immediately goes to the refrigerator for a little Cheese Whiz and bacon dip. And you love her for it."

How does frank-talking Oprah stack up against other female talk show hosts? Walter Goodman (*New York Times*) analyzes, "Ms. Winfrey comes on as more serious than Ms. [Joan] Rivers yet more streetwise than Ms. [Sally Jessy] Raphael. An energetic performer, she makes busy use of her audience, moving nonstop through the aisles and slipping now and then into a just-folks dialect. Often the audience stars."

Oprah Winfrey of the early 1980s.

Winfrey has a simpler explanation of her successful TV show personality: "All I'm doing is being myself. Whether I'm talking to Vietnam vets or Dudley Moore—whatever the subject—I think I have a natural curiosity and a sensitivity to people that makes it easy."

On "The Oprah Winfrey Show," as with her competition, typical episode themes range from "Feuding Friends" to "How Do You Know When a Woman Is Orgasming?" (Sometimes the show will feature a negative subject because, says its host, "It's a dangerous development in society and people should know about it.") What makes Winfrey's handling of such overused talk program fare so special? She reasons: "We go for the gut. We go for the absolute gut. My theory is that everybody is the same. I want the same thing that people in Spokane want: to be loved.... So we try to pick subjects that everybody can relate to, and do it in such a way that every single person who's watching can listen to us and say, "Yeah, that's it. I know exactly what you're talking about.'"

HEART ON HER SLEEVE

Intriguingly, Oprah is unafraid of being very human and self-revealing on air. She may break down in tears as guests discuss having been sexually abused as a child (as she was). Or, Winfrey may come forth with her own bad memories of being raped when the subject arises on her program. When strolling through the studio audience, it is not unusual for her to hug one of them, or to lean on a guest's shoulder. Then, there are the occasions when she puts her foot in her mouth in front of millions of viewers.

Once, her program featured a handicapped guest who had no hands. Not thinking, Winfrey blurted out to the visitor that she guessed it would be tough to put on a dress with twenty buttons. The feisty panelist responded: "Yes, it would probably be something like you putting on panty hose." Sometimes, Winfrey's probing can throw an interviewee off base. For example, years back, Oscar winner Sally Field was visiting on camera and sassy Oprah popped out about Field's then boyfriend, movie star Burt Reynolds, "Does Burt sleep with his toupee on or off?" The flustered (and a bit perturbed) Field could only mumble: "I...beg...your pardon...."

In another area, Oprah Winfrey is a pathfinder. She is the first black woman to host a major TV talk show geared for a predominantly white national audience. In her own way, she has done as much as "Today Show" anchor Bryant Gumbel in breaking down racial roadblocks. As she said in the mid-1980s when her Chicago-based show was migrating from the local level to national syndication, "television managers are beginning to understand it's not skin color that people look at on TV. If you're good, you can transcend racial barriers."

That is not to say that she is blind to her very visible heritage. Winfrey, who categorizes black women into fudge brownies, gingerbread and vanilla creams, terms herself fudge. She explains: "You will never see me on TV and say, 'Gee I wonder if she's mixed?'" She is also extremely aware of her position as an ethnic role model. Once, she had the Grand Dragon of the Ku Klux Klan on her program. It prompted her to confess later: "It was as if the burden of every black person was on my back."

THE WEIGHT OF IT ALL

Ironically, there is another facet of Oprah which has humanized her to millions of viewers: her weight! Roseanne Arnold to one side, not since singer Kate Smith or actresses Elizabeth Taylor and Delta Burke, has any show business personality been subjected to so much scrutiny about her poundage. At 5'6'" the pug-nosed Winfrey weighs from 180 to 190 pounds, sometimes ballooning up higher. As her viewers well know, she would start diets, go off them, and start again. In such periods, it has been difficult for her to retain her equanimity.

Whenever she dines out publicly, everyone from the maitre d' to diners across the room crane their necks to observe what the celebrity is being served, how much she is consuming and what she allows herself for dessert. This syndrome only intensified after her 1988 crash diet which saw her dramatically shed 67 pounds, and then, later, gain it all back. Coming to terms with this eating problem is one of the hardest challenges of Oprah's life.

Oprah Gail Winfrey was born out of wedlock on January 29, 1954 in Kosciusko, Mississippi. Her mother was Vernita Lee, a domestic, and her father was Vernon Winfrey, a barber. Originally, the future TV celebrity was to have been named Orpah, after Ruth's sister-in-law in the Bible. However, the midwife transposed two letters in her first name on the birth certificate.

Before she was a year old, Oprah was sent to live with her maternal grandmother, Hattie Mae Lee, on a farm seventy miles northeast of Jackson, Mississippi. The nearest neighbor was a blind man up the road. Oprah recalls of this period: "It was lonely. I had one corncob doll. I rode a pig bareback and spent most of my time reading Bible stories to the barnyard animals."

TOUGH LOVE

A bright and curious child, Oprah had few intellectual outlets. She was also a mischievous tyke, which led her strict grandmother to reprimand her with a switch. Winfrey the adult says, "Sure, Grandma whipped me, she sure did. But she taught me about life, and I loved her so." It was from outgoing Hattie that Winfrey developed her gregarious nature. One of Oprah's great desires was to have "Shirley Temple movie-star curls. All the little white girls had bouncy hair." (Winfrey had to settle for her hair being braided into seventeen plaits by her grandma.) She also wanted a movie star's nose. Once, she tried to shape one by sleeping with a clothespin on her nose "to get it to grow up instead of out."

In 1959, at age six, Oprah received her first pair of shoes. She also went to live with her mother in Milwaukee. At the time, Vernita was working as a cleaning woman and was on welfare. She and her young daughter lived in a three-room flat in a housing project, along with Oprah's younger half-sister, Patricia, and a younger half-brother, Jeffrey. Little Oprah claims she played with cockroaches, giving them names and feeding them bread crumbs. (Her half-sister denies this oft-told cockroach incident.)

At school, when six white children were about to beat her up, first-grader Oprah told them about Jesus of Nazareth and what happened to the people who tried to stone him. Thereafter, the kids called her "The Preacher" and left her alone. A quick learner, Winfrey skipped the second grade. Even in these formative years, she was developing goals. When she watched Sidney Poitier accept his Academy Award for LILIES OF THE FIELD (1963) she told herself, "I'm going to be there."

When she was ten years old, Oprah was molested by a cousin. "Nobody was home, and he raped me. And then he bought me an ice-cream cone and brought me to the zoo as payment for not telling anybody. I didn't know what was happening." All that year (the fifth grade) she had stomach aches, convinced she was pregnant. "I would excuse myself to go to the bathroom so I could have the baby there and not tell anyone. I didn't tell a soul till I was 22."

Subsequently she was abused sexually by a boyfriend of her mother and by a friend of her cousin. These traumatic experiences, says Oprah "made me a sexually promiscuous teenager." When her mother was frequently out, Winfrey would bring men to her home where her bedroom walls were plastered with magazine photos of pretty white girls.

TROUBLED TEEN

At thirteen, the scholastically advanced adolescent was bussed into an all white neighborhood for her schooling. She became the darling of the liberal set. "It was the first time I realized I was poor. And after seeing how the other half lived, I started having some real problems. I guess you could call me *troubled*—to put it mildly."

That year, Oprah had saved up to buy a dog. However, her mother threatened to give it away because he soiled the floor. Rebelling, Oprah ran away herself. At school, Winfrey thought her butterfly-framed eyeglasses were unfashionable and begged her mother for new ones. When her parent would not (or could not) oblige, Oprah stole money from her mother's purse. Then she staged a phony robbery and smashed her old glasses. To give her flimsy story credibility she pretended to have amnesia, but she did not fool her mother.

A few months after the eyeglasses episode, Oprah spotted Aretha Franklin getting out of a taxi. Winfrey walked up to the famed soul singer and concocted a tale of how she was abandoned and needed $100 to get back to Ohio. With the booty from Franklin, Oprah immediately marched over to the Sheraton Hotel where she registered. She ordered room service for three days until the money ran out.

Later, she sought refuge at a church whose minister sent her home. By now, Vernita wanted to put her daughter in a state detention home for delinquent girls. However, there was a long waiting list. Instead, Oprah was sent to Nashville to live with her father and his wife, Zelma. Unknown to the family, Oprah was pregnant. Her baby boy was born prematurely, but died soon after birth. Winfrey regards this event as "the most emotional, confusing and traumatic of my young life."

MUCH NEEDED STRUCTURE

By now, 1967, Vernon was not only a barber, but a member of the Nashville city council. He was a stern man but accepted Oprah into his household with welcoming arms. For the first time in a long while, the teenager had a structured life and felt loved. Winfrey says, "He's a very focused, disciplined person and wise. I was a very good student in Milwaukee, but I wasn't rewarded for it there. Whereas in my father's house that's all I did." A strict man, Mr. Winfrey made her learn five new words daily and would march her to the library each week for extra studying.

She excelled at East Nashville High School. She was elected to student council president with the slogan, "Vote for the Grand Ole Oprah." She also won an Elks Club oratory contest. The prize money provided for full tuition at Tennessee State University in Nashville. She also attended a White House Conference on Youth in Washington D.C. The confirmed overachiever would reflect: "It never occurred to me in the midst of poverty that I wasn't as good as anyone else. I always knew I'd do well."

In 1970, sixteen-year-old Winfrey, who previously had been a baby sitter, had her first real summer job. For $150 weekly she did telephone sales for the Kirby Vacuum Cleaner Company. In 1971, she got a job as a news reporter at the local Nashville (black) radio station, WVOL. She had gone there initially to collect a watch prize from the "Miss Fire Prevention" contest the station had sponsored. A worker there asked if she'd like to hear herself on tape. After listening to her well-modulated speaking voice, he summoned the station's news director. He, in turn, hired her on the spot to read newscasts over the air.

By the fall of 1971, Oprah had entered Tennessee State University, majoring in speech and drama. (Her father was not in favor of this career choice, reasoning: "I'm not sending you to school to become an actress."). The next March she won the Miss Black Nashville and Miss Black Tennessee contests, which gave her an entree into the Miss Black America pageant where she emerged a runner-up. With such publicity, the college student was offered a job at WTVF-TV, the local CBS network affiliate.

The nineteen-year-old accepted the position, but with reservations: "No way did I deserve the job. I was a classic token." With encouragement from one of her instructors, she used her position as an evening news co-anchor to advantage. ("I was one happy token.") Because of her TV work, Winfrey was now earning $15,000, but still remained very much under her father's supervision.

JUST BEING HUMAN

When not emulating her role model, Barbara Walters, Oprah had to cope with her ethnic allegiance: "No one's asked me about my psychological health at that time. Frankly, I felt that most of the kids hated and resented me. They were into black power and anger. I was not. I guess that was because I was struggling just to be a human being." She also was having disastrous relationships with men. Whenever she trusted someone, he abused her one way or another.

By 1976, Oprah had completed her University course work, although she was a few credits short of earning her diploma. (She would be awarded an honorary degree in 1987.) She was anxious to be on her own and, therefore, accepted work at Baltimore's WJZ-TV to be co-anchor and reporter on the six o'clock news. The desk assignments she could handle. However, trudging into the field was difficult, especially when she had to maintain her objectivity at the scene of a tragedy. ("I can only be myself, so it's very hard for me to all of a sudden become 'Ms. Broadcast Journalist' and not feel things.")

Also, she was experiencing problems at the station in positioning her professional image. An ad campaign which asked "What's an Oprah?" failed. In additiona, there was no chemistry between she and co-anchor Jerry Turner. Station executives altered her name to Cindy Winfrey and promoted her as being of Hispanic background. Concerning this denigrating period, Oprah recalls, "I was told my hair was too thick, my eyes too wide apart, my nose too broad, my chin too big and my hair a frizzy disaster. They tried to make me look Puerto Rican. A New York beauty salon put some miracle ingredient on my hair that made me bald. I looked like Kojak. I was humiliated."

During the time she lost her hair, she could not find a wig to fit properly. She wore a scarf over her head and cried constantly. She was comforted by Lloyd Kramer, a Jewish man she was then dating. "He stuck with me through the whole demoralizing experience. That man was the most fun romance I ever had."

Oprah also turned to food during this humiliating period, and the once svelte young woman blossomed to 190 pounds. In 1977, the TV station demoted her to her local lead-in announcer for the network feed of "Good Morning America." She demonstrated her tenacity and kept on her job. Eventually, her employers switched her to handling an unpromising morning program, "Baltimore Is Talking." Her co-host on this talk show was Richard Sheer. Thrilled to be out of the news arena, she enthused, "This is what I was born to do. *This* is really breathing." She would remain with the show for seven years. During this phase, in 1978, she participated in Baltimore's Black Theatre Festival, appearing in a production of "The History of Black Women Through Drama and Song."

BAD, BOLD MOVES

On a personal level, Winfrey had become involved with a married man, a lengthy relationship which ended badly. (She even contemplated suicide at one point.) Thinking back, she says, "If I start to talk about it, I'll weep on the floor. But I tell you, I will *never* travel that road again. The next time somebody tells me he's no good for me, I'm gonna believe him."

In 1983, Debbie DiMaio, the producer of "Baltimore Is Talking," was networking for a new job. She sent a program tape to WLS-TV in Chicago. Not only was she hired to rekindle a dying local program, "A.M. Chicago," but station manager Dennis Swanson was intrigued by the footage he had seen of Oprah. Swanson hired Oprah to take over the talk show. DiMaio concedes, "It was a bold move to hire a black female to host a talk show in a city so racially polarized." During the four months before Oprah could move to the Windy City, she plotted out the shape of her new assignment. Wondering if she was up to the task, she began overeating again, a crutch against failure.

When Oprah's talk forum debuted in January 1984, Phil Donahue was king of the hill with his Chicago-based nationally syndicated gab show. He had been Mr. Chicago for several years with his top-rated, controversial showcase. Winfrey changed all that—fast. Within four weeks, "A.M. Chicago" was on a par with Donahue's offering; after three months she shot ahead of her rival in the ratings. Undoubtedly, part of Oprah's appeal was her newness in the Chicago market. However, she attracted viewers for just being her own impressive self. On air, she would take her shoes off, admitting "Oww, my feet hurt," or complain about her nose being too broad. Then, there was the May 16, 1984 program on which she admitted to the world that she knew she was fat. (On that particular outing she talked about the recent evening when she had ransacked the refrigerator for a snack. She had to settle for heating frozen hot dog buns in the microwave, covering them with maple syrup and then ravenously devouring them.)

There was another reason why Oprah succeeded so "suddenly." As she analyzed her fresh success, "Part of the reason I've been able to do so well in Chicago is that for the first time in my career, I am alone. Up until now, I've always been paired with somebody else. The thing about working with a co-anchor or a co-host is that it can be stifling, like a bad marriage. somebody always got to surrender to the other person. And usually, the person doing the surrendering was me. But I knew that I would just bide my time and get good at this—so good that moving to the next place would be easy. That's why I feel very good about where I am right now. I feel I've earned the right to be here." In comparing herself to Donahue she noted, "he's more intellectual in his approach. I appeal to the heart and relate to my audiences."

NATIONAL ACCLAIM

Winfrey began getting national recognition, with *People* magazine lauding her as "a mind as quick as any in television..." Since the Chicago area had responded so favorably to her half-hour format, the station expanded the proceedings to an hour under the new title "The Oprah Winfrey Show." Meanwhile, her newly overshadowed competitor had "coincidentally" left town. Ostensibly to have more time with his actress wife Marlo Thomas, Phil Donahue relocated himself and his talk program to New York City. (Upon departing, he wished Winfrey well, but not in his time spot.) As to her own social life, Oprah told the local media, "Mr. Right is on the way, walking from Africa."

While Oprah was undergoing her TV metamorphosis, musician and film composer Quincy Jones happened to stop over in Chicago. While relaxing in his hotel room, he turned on "The Oprah Winfrey Show." He was so impressed by her presence he rushed to tell filmmaker Steven Spielberg about his find. Spielberg was then casting for the movie of Alice Walker's novel, *The Color Purple* (1982). Oprah had always enjoyed acting but not enough to go through a long apprenticeship (waiting tables or whatever). She was thrilled to be offered the part of Sophia.

In the course of the picture her role required her to age from the independent young wife to a disfigured older woman now under the thumbs of demanding whites. Ironically, Winfrey, who had been suffering through another of her crash diets, had to gain thirty or more pounds for her screen character. However, it was worth it. Not only was THE COLOR PURPLE (1985) a box-office winner, but it received eleven Oscar nominations, including one for Winfrey as Best Supporting Actress. (She also received a Golden Globe nomination as well as sterling notices. *Chicago Tribune* film critic Gene Siskel cited her as "Shockingly good.")

On several levels, THE COLOR PURPLE was a great learning experience. Winfrey confesses, "I went through the whole film thinking Steven Spielberg hated my guts. At the premiere, he said to me, 'I realized how terrified you were, and that that was working for you. That's why I never gave you any reassurance.' I wanted to break down and weep because all that time I thought, 'He does like me.'" Of her mentor, Quincy Jones, Oprah reflected, "I truly learned how to love as a result of this man. It's the first time I came to terms with: 'Yes, I love this man, and it has nothing to do with wanting to go to bed with him or be romantically involved. I unconditionally love him.'"

OPRAH SPELLED BACKWARDS

In August of 1986, the fast-rising Oprah formed Harpo Productions, geared to production of feature films, TV movies and music videos. That same month, *Playgirl* magazine listed Winfrey as one of America's ten most admired women. On September 8, 1986 "The Oprah Winfrey Show" went into national syndication. Its distributor, King World Productions, estimated that by 1988-1989, the show should be generating revenue of $150 million or more, and that its star would receive 25% of such earnings. Now known as "the wild woman of morning TV," she was humble enough to acknowledge Donahue's pathfinding efforts. "He established the fact that women were interested in more than mascara. He set the standards."

Having signed a five-year contract with King World, Oprah soon moved into a $850,000 seven-room condo apartment. Her new home was on the 57th floor of an exclusive Michigan Avenue high-rise with a magnificent view of Lake Michigan and the Chicago skyline. The condo had been owned previously by tycoon Evangeline Goueltas. Winfrey retained some of the gaudy excesses: i.e. a marble bathroom with gold-plated swan faucets, a wine cellar, and a chandelier in the closet. (The next year, she would purchase a 160-acre Indiana farm.) Although she now boasted a chauffeur-driven Mercedes limousine and had a lavish wardrobe, she sought to balance her perspective. She worked at local soup kitchens on holidays, served as Big Sister to the young and needy, and supplied worthy applicants with tuition to the Chicago Academy for the Arts.

There were other changes in her life. She had undergone a spiritual reevaluation. "It's not being born again. It's an evolution, a realization of how life works—meaning that God is the center of the universe. Once you understand that, it's all really very simple." She had also met 6'6" Stedman Graham of North Carolina. He was a former basketball player, who would become the executive director of Athletes Against Drugs. A part-time model, he later became a public relations executive. She claims that it was not until two years after meeting Stedman (who had a teenage daughter from a prior relationship) that she agreed to go out with him. Having been a doormat in so many prior relationships, Winfrey had developed a creed: "I will never give up my power to another person."

THE NEW MEDIA DARLING

In 1987, Oprah exclaimed, "I feel I'm ripening, coming into my own. It's an exciting time, an exciting age." She also earned about $11 million that year from her TV show, speaking engagements and movie deals. (She had played another character role in NATIVE SON, 1986, and did a cameo as herself in Billy Crystal's THROW MAMA FROM THE TRAIN, 1987.) As an increasingly popular TV talk show hostess, she had become a media darling. Don Merrill (*TV Guide*) praised her: "Beneath a homey personality that invites confidences, there is a confident, talented journalist digging for truth." That season both she and her program won Emmys in the daytime categories.

Not only was Winfrey constantly in the limelight, but so were her family members. Her father was interviewed frequently and, on one occasion, said, "Oprah's offered me all these gifts, but I don't need anything except maybe a better TV at the [barber] shop so I can watch her show." He also added, "The best thing about Oprah's being famous is to let young folks know she came from a poor family." The TV celebrity acknowledged that she had bought her mother a house and a new wardrobe, but stated her parent made her feel "there are dues to pay."

Additionally, Oprah reflected, "This doesn't solve all those years of my feeling unloved, but my mother did the most she could."

Within 1988, Oprah received the Broadcaster of the Year Award from the International Radio and TV Society. To prepare for an upcoming TV movie, THE WOMEN OF BREWSTER PLACE (1989), Oprah underwent a much-promoted liquid diet. She lost 67 pounds and shed her trademark camouflage wardrobe for form-fitting designer jeans, etc. (To demonstrate the amount of her loss, she dragged a cart filled with 67 pounds of animal fat onto the TV stage set.)

She continued to be a notable philanthropist with charitable donations and fundraising efforts, including her $1 million check to the all-black Morehouse College in Atlanta. She donated her $100,000 fee from Revlon cosmetic commercials to a fund for inner city schools. *Ebony* magazine honored her with its Dramatic Arts Awards. Always the entrepreneur, she became a (limited) partner in Chicago's The Eccentric Restaurant.

The two-part ABC-TV movie, THE WOMEN OF BREWSTER PLACE (March 19-20, 1989), based on Gloria Naylor's novel, dealt with seven black women struggling in a black ghetto. Oprah was Mattie Michael, determined to improve her life. The four-hour telefilm did well in the ratings, and co-producer Winfrey was praised as a performer. Her flourishing TV talk show continued to win Emmy Awards. On December 9, 1989, at the annual NAACP Image Awards, she received four Hall of Fame Awards (for acting, entertaining, producing and journalism.) That same month, her half-brother, Jeffrey, died of AIDS.

BIG TIME BABY

Now seen on 213 TV stations nationwide, Oprah was continuing to beat her closest daytime rival, Phil Donahue, in viewership. (She had a 9.8 rating, while he, on 226 stations, was averaging a 6.6 rating.) Her distribution had expanded to Canada, England, the Netherlands and even to Poland. Already the part-owner of three TV stations, she acquired a 88,000-square-foot Chicago sound stage facility which she planned to use for film and TV moviemaking. The renovations cost $30 million. Meanwhile, her talk show made history as the first syndicated talk program to rank #1 in all three key women's demographic markets.

Between the grind of "The Oprah Winfrey Show," the star found time to shoot segments at her new Harpo Productions facilities for "Brewster Place." In this half-hour spin-off series, she repeated her role of the determined Mattie. The show debuted on ABC-TV on May 1, 1990. However, it never found a sufficiently large audience and was cancelled after four of its eleven already taped segments had aired. It was one of Oprah's few professional failures.

That fall, ABC-TV created a bizarre special, entitled "America's All-Star Tribute to Oprah Winfrey." The hour-long show, taped at the Bob Hope Cultural Center in Palm Desert, California, aired on September 18. Such diverse personalities as Bob Hope, Whoopi Goldberg and First Lady Barbara Bush (via tape) offered praise, as the subject sat in her box seat gamely displaying a variety of appropriate responses. Summing up the event, *Variety* decided, "this shameless hour of celebrity nonsense and insipid clips didn't do her any credit." The next month, Winfrey was among the array of name figures who appeared in the documentary, LISTEN UP: THE LIVES OF QUINCY JONES (1990).

As her industry fame and power increased, Oprah played a bit with the format of her popular show, occasionally using a round-table forum format, called "Conversations with Oprah." She also pursued other types of entertainment products, ranging from "After School Specials" ("The Less Than Perfect Daughter," 1991) to prime-time telefilms (OVEREXPOSED, 1992) to theatrical short subjects.

REDEEMING VALUES

Typically, there was an overriding educational theme to her ventures, often exploring mistreatment experienced by females and children. One of her more remarkable efforts was "Scared Silent: Exposing and Ending Child Abuse" an hour-long documentary which aired on September 4, 1982. It was telecast simultaneously on three networks (CBS, NBC and PBS) and was later seen on ABC. In this very personal project, she was among those who discussed being such a victim. She stated on air: "I was, and am, severely damaged by the experience. All the years that I convinced myself I was healed, I wasn't. I still carried the shame and I unconsciously blamed myself for those men's acts." Dedicated to eradicating child abuse, Winfrey helped to write the Child Protection Act and has testifed before the Senate Judiciary Committee and other groups on the subject.

In May 1992, Oprah tried the Barbara Walters interview route with an ABC-TV network special: "Oprah: Behind The Scenes" on which she interviewed Meryl Streep, Dustin Hoffman and Goldie Hawn. She repeated the bland format with her second "Behind The Scenes" (November 4, 1992) on which her subjects included Richard Gere and Jodie Foster. Two days later, she was among Phil Donahue's peers who paid tribute to the talk show veteran on his televised "25th Anniversary Special."

Since becoming a national institution, Oprah's fans are not only well versed in their favorite's latest weigh-ins, but are attuned fully to the newest twists in the on-again and off-again relationship between Winfred and Stedman Graham. (She says of him, "Stead is my rock. The first man I have ever known who truly wants me to be the very best I can be.")

At one point, the newsmaking couple had been scheduled to marry in early 1989. That fell through and they re-set the wedding date for Christmas of 1990. That too was readjusted, after their summer 1991 hideaway vacation to the Caribbean, to September 1991. But wedding bells never chimed. On each occasion, reportedly, she was the one to back out, fearful of the commitment. Then the nuptials were announced for June 1992, a date which came and went. As she explained, "there was a time in my life when I needed marriage to validate myself, But now, I'm very content with what my relationship gives me."

HERE COMES THE BRIDE

In October of 1992, at her Indiana farmhouse, Stedman again proposed marriage—this time she accepted. On November 6, 1992, while a guest on WFSB-TV in Hartford, Connecticut where best friend Gayle King Bumpus was interviewing her, Oprah surprised viewers with a special scoop. She announced that she, 38, and Stedman, 41 were engaged officially. The couple were now targeting June 1993 for their much-delayed Chicago church ceremony. Relying on her new diet guru, Winfrey hoped to shed a great deal of excess weight (she had mushroomed to over 200 pounds) before the marriage. As to having a child, she has said: "Sometimes I think, yes...and other times I must admit having a child is not a deep yearning. Maybe I'm afraid."

Today, Oprah Winfrey is worth about $250 million. With $1.4 million of those funds she purchased a house in Telluride, Colorado in March 1992, and for another $3 million acquired 80 surrounding acres. (She likes to ski and snowmobile). She plans to build a new home there in the next few years and convert the existing log and stone home into a guest house.

She allows that she is "sick, sick, sick, sick, sick" of all the attention focused on her figure and her food intake. "We all make it an issue—I'm as guilty of that as anybody. I would like to reach a point where it is not an issue with me. I wish that I'd kept the weight off, but I do *not* feel like a failure. I feel like someone who has a weight problem." On another level, she says: "I don't believe in failure. It is not failure if you enjoyed the process. Does failure mean 'Brewster

Place' didn't work?... I learned from my mistakes on 'Brewster Place.'" Regarding ambition, she concedes: "I have a lot of things to prove to myself. One is that I can live my life fearlessly. but I don't have anything to prove to the world. My work isn't about that. I just want to do things that mean something to me."

Oprah admits that she doesn't watch much TV, rather she pays "attention to life. Actually, the reason I don't watch is because I'm such a mimic." On the subject of talk shows, she has said: "The problem with most talk shows...[especially local ones] is that everybody's pretending to be a talk show host.... Well, you really can't afford to do anything but be yourself, after all. Even if people don't like the subject or are not particularly interested in the subject, if you just always remain yourself or are able to tap into whatever it is about yourself that you can allow to be seen on camera, it works so much better." She also observes, "It's interesting to me that I'm called a 'talk-show host' because I understand in my heart that there is something deeper, stronger, and more important going on with the people who are affected by the show.... People have become far smarter about TV than they were."

As to the future: "At this moment, I'm doing exactly what I'm supposed to be doing....and I don't necessarily believe this is the top. But I don't want to get lazy, either. I don't want to be lulled by the voices of the world telling me something is it and buy into that.... At the same time, I am a woman in process. I'm just trying like everybody else."

TV & CABLE SERIES:
Baltimore Is Talking [People Are Talking] (Baltimore local, 1978-1983)
A.M. Chicago (Chicago local, 1984-1985)
The Oprah Winfrey Show (Chicago local, 1985-1986)
The Oprah Winfrey Show (Syndicated, 1986-)
Brewster Place (ABC, 1990)

FEATURE FILMS:
The Color Purple (1985)
Native Son (1986)
Throw Momma from the Train (1987)
The Women of Brewster Place (1989) [TV movie]
Listen Up: The Lives of Quincy Jones (1990)

The pre- and post-diet Oprah Winfrey on "The Oprah Winfrey Show" in 1989.

MAKING A QUANTUM LEAP
Scott Nance

Everything you ever wanted to know about "Quantum Leap" is in this exciting new book! Learn how the series was created, how each story is filmed, and meet stars Scott Bakula, Dean Stockwell, and the writers and directors behind the hit.

$14.95.....160 Pages
ISBN # 1-55698-312-3

THE UNOFFICIAL TALE OF BEAUTY AND THE BEAST
Revised 2nd Edition   Edward Gross

THE UNOFFICIAL TALE OF BEAUTY AND THE BEAST is the ultimate "bible" to the series, providing in-depth interviews with story editor-producer Howard Gordon, Directors Paul Lynch, Alan Cooke and Richard Franklin; a look at the creation of the series and an incredibly detailed episode guide. This revised second edition adds an interview with Ron Perlman, who has captured the hearts of millions via his portrayal of the noble lion-man, Vincent and an interview with actor Tony Jay, best known as Underworld villian, Paracelsus.

$14.95.....164 Pages
ISBN # 1-55698-261-5

COUCH POTATO INC.   5715 N. Balsam Rd   Las Vegas, NV 89130   (702)658-2090

Use Your Credit Card 24 HRS — Order toll Free From: **(800)444-2524** Ext 67

THE COMPLETE LOST IN SPACE
John Peel

DANGER. . . DANGER. . . DANGER!

Don't miss this book!

The complete guide to every single episode of LOST IN SPACE including profiles of every cast member and character

The most exhaustive book ever written about LOST IN SPACE.

$19.95.....220 Pages
ISBN # 1-55698-145-7

THE DOCTOR WHO ENCYCLOPEDIA:
THE BAKERS YEARS
John Peel

This volume contains references for *all* the characters who appeared during the Baker years, and then examines all if the monsters that have come up against the good doctor in a special section. Want to know who the Trakenites are? Or where the Synge hails from? The answers are all here. THE DOCTOR WHO ENCYCLOPEDIA: THE BAKER YEARS is the perfect companion piece to John Peel's THE TREK ENCYCLOPEDIA

$19.95.....171 Pages
ISBN # 1-55698-160-0

FORTY YEARS AT NIGHT: THE TONIGHT SHOW STORY
Scott Nance

The Tonight Show began as a local variety show in the early 1950's and eventually established itself as a piece of American Culture. This entertaining book chronicles the show's 40 year history and gives behind the scenes views through the eyes of Ed McMahon, Doc Severson, executive producer Fred de Cordova, as well as many of the stars who have appeared throughout the years.

$14.95......150 Pages
ISBN# 1-55698-308-5

EXPOSING NORTHERN EXPOSURE
Scott Nance

Complete with interviews and episode guide, this book tells the story of the Emmy Award winning television series "Northern Exposure." You get a behind-the-scenes look of the shows creation, and profiles of all the actors and creative talents who bring the show to life.

$14.95......160 Pages
ISBN 1-55698-324-7

THE L.A. LAWBOOK
Edward Gross

* "L.A. Law" is the winner of two Emmy Awards, including Best Drama

This illustrated companion provides viewers with a welcome roadmap through the ongoing subplots and character interactions in this unique television show over the past five years.

Edward Gross is the author of many books on the entertainment industry. He lives in East Meadows, NY.

$14.95......160 Pages
ISBN # 1-55698-295-X

ORDER FORM

_____ Trek Crew Book $9.95
_____ Best Of Enterprise Incidents $9.95
_____ Trek Fans Handbook $9.95
_____ Trek: The Next Generation $14.95
_____ The Man Who Created Star Trek: $12.95
_____ 25th Anniversary Trek Tribute $14.95
_____ History Of Trek $14.95
_____ The Man Between The Ears $14.95
_____ Trek: The Making Of The Movies $14.95
_____ Trek: The Lost Years $12.95
_____ Trek: The Unauthorized Next Generation $14.95
_____ New Trek Encyclopedia $19.95
_____ Making A Quantum Leap $14.95
_____ The Unofficial Tale Of Beauty And The Beast $14.95
_____ Complete Lost In Space $19.95
_____ ..doctor Who Encyclopedia: Baker $19.95
_____ Lost In Space Tribute Book $14.95
_____ Lost In Space With Irwin Allen $14.95
_____ Doctor Who: Baker Years $19.95
_____ Doctor Who: Pertwee Years $19.95
_____ Batmania Ii $14.95
_____ The Green Hornet $14.95 _____ Special Edition $16.95

_____ Number Six: The Prisoner Book $14.95
_____ Gerry Anderson: Supermarionation $17.95
_____ Addams Family Revealed $14.95
_____ Bloodsucker: Vampires At The Movies $14.95
_____ Dark Shadows Tribute $14.95
_____ Monsterland Fear Book $14.95
_____ The Films Of Elvis $14.95
_____ The Woody Allen Encyclopedia $14.95
_____ Paul Mccartney: 20 Years On His Own $9.95
_____ Yesterday: My Life With The Beatles $14.95
_____ Fab Films Of The Beatles $14.95
_____ 40 Years At Night: The Tonight Show $14.95
_____ Exposing Northern Exposure $14.95
_____ The La Lawbook $14.95
_____ Cheers: Where Everybody Knows Your Name $14.95
_____ SNL! The World Of Saturday Night Live $14.95
_____ The Rockford Phile $14.95
_____ Encyclopedia Of Cartoon Superstars $14.95
_____ How To Create Animation $14.95
_____ How To Draw Art For Comic Books $14.95
_____ King And Barker:an Illustrated Guide $14.95
_____ King And Barker: An Illustrated Guide II $14.95

100% Satisfaction Guaranteed.

We value your support. You will receive a full refund as long as the copy of the book you are not happy with is received back by us in reasonable condition. No questions asked, except we would like to know how we failed you. Refunds and credits are given as soon as we receive back the item you do not want.

NAME:_____

STREET:_____

CITY:_____

STATE:_____

ZIP:_____

TOTAL:_____ SHIPPING_____

SEND TO: Couch Potato, Inc. 5715 N. Balsam Rd., Las Vegas, NV 89130

BORING, BUT NECESSARY ORDERING INFORMATION

Payment:

Use our new 800 # and pay with your credit card or send check or money order directly to our address. All payments must be made in U.S. funds and please do not send cash.

Shipping:

We offer several methods of shipment. Sometimes a book can be delayed if we are temporarily out of stock. You should note whether you prefer us to ship the book as soon as available, send you a merchandise credit good for other goodies, or send your money back immediately.

Normal Post Office: $3.75 for the first book and $1.50 for each additional book. These orders are filled as quickly as possible. Shipments normally take 5 to 10 days, but allow up to 12 weeks for delivery.

Special UPS 2 Day Blue Label Service or Priority Mail: Special service is available for desperate Couch Potatoes. These books are shipped within 24 hours of when we receive the order and normally take 2 to 3 three days to get to you. The cost is $10.00 for the first book and $4.00 each additional book .

Overnight Rush Service: $20.00 for the first book and $10.00 each additional book.

U.s. Priority Mail: $6.00 for the first book and $3.00.each additional book.

Canada And Mexico: $5.00 for the first book and $3.00 each additional book.

Foreign: $6.00 for the first book and $3.00 each additional book.

Please list alternatives when available and please state if you would like a refund or for us to backorder an item if it is not in stock.